CONFLICTED IDENTITIES AND MULTIPLE MASCULINITIES

MEN IN THE MEDIEVAL WEST

GARLAND MEDIEVAL CASEBOOKS
VOLUME 25
GARLAND REFERENCE LIBRARY OF THE HUMANITIES
VOLUME 2078

GARLAND MEDIEVAL CASEBOOKS

CHRISTOPHER KLEINHENZ AND MARCIA COLISH, *Series Editors*

SEX IN THE MIDDLE AGES
A Book of Essays
edited by Joyce E. Salisbury

MARGERY KEMPE
A Book of Essays
edited by Sandra J. McEntire

THE MEDIEVAL WORLD OF NATURE
A Book of Essays
edited by Joyce E. Salisbury

THE CHESTER MYSTERY CYCLE
A Casebook
edited by Kevin J. Harty

MEDIEVAL NUMEROLOGY
A Book of Essays
edited by Robert L. Surles

MANUSCRIPT SOURCES OF
MEDIEVAL MEDICINE
A Book of Essays
edited by Margaret R. Schleissner

SAINT AUGUSTINE THE BISHOP
A Book of Essays
edited by Fannie LeMoine and
Christopher Kleinhenz

MEDIEVAL CHRISTIAN
PERCEPTIONS OF ISLAM
A Book of Essays
edited by John Victor Tolan

SOVEREIGN LADY
*Essays on Women
in Middle English Literature*
Edited by Muriel Whitaker

FOOD IN THE MIDDLE AGES
A Book of Essays
edited by Melitta Weiss Adamson

ANIMALS IN THE MIDDLE AGES
A Book of Essays
edited by Nona C. Flores

SANCTITY AND MOTHERHOOD
*Essays on Holy Mothers
in the Middle Ages*
edited by Annecke B. Mulder-Bakker

MEDIEVAL FAMILY ROLES
A Book of Essays
edited by Cathy Jorgensen Itnyre

THE MABINOGI
A Book of Essays
edited by C.W. Sullivan III

THE PILGRIMAGE TO COMPOSTELA
IN THE MIDDLE AGES
A Book of Essays
edited by Maryjane Dunn and
Linda Kay Davidson

MEDIEVAL LITURGY
A Book of Essays
edited by Lizette Larson-Miller

MEDIEVAL PURITY AND PIETY
*Essays on Medieval Clerical Celibacy
and Religious Reform*
edited by Michael Frassetto

HILDEGARD OF BINGEN
A Book of Essays
edited by Maud Burnett McInerney

JULIAN OF NORWICH
A Book of Essays
edited by Sandra J. McEntire

THE MARK OF THE BEAST
*The Medieval Bestiary
in Art, Life, and Literature*
edited by Debra Hassig

CONFLICTED IDENTITIES AND
MULTIPLE MASCULINITIES
Men in the Medieval West
edited by Jacqueline Murray

CONFLICTED IDENTITIES AND MULTIPLE MASCULINITIES

MEN IN THE MEDIEVAL WEST

EDITED BY
JACQUELINE MURRAY

GARLAND PUBLISHING, INC.
NEW YORK AND LONDON
1999

Published in 1999 by
Garland Publishing Inc.
A Member of the Taylor & Francis Group
19 Union Square West
New York, NY 10003

10   9   8   7   6   5   4   3   2   1

**Library of Congress Cataloging-in-Publication Data is available from the
Library of Congress.**

Printed on acid-free, 250-year-life paper

Contents

Acknowledgments

There is perhaps no more collaborative form of scholarship than a collection of essays. The process of blending the individual insights of many scholars into a work of coherence is at once its own challenge and its own reward. I have been particularly fortunate to have had the most learned and cooperative of colleagues to work with in the preparation of this volume. I must thank them all for making this editorial experience a pleasure.

A number of people helped with the preparation of this volume at various stages. In particular, I would like to thank Joyce Salisbury for her inspiration, Leslie Howsam for her unfailing generousity, Laura Gardner for her technical expertise, Marion Corkett for her sharp eye and, especially, Susan Riggs for her patience and wisdom. Sheila Campbell came to the rescue when the world of computers took on a peculiarly Kafkaesque quality. To her we are all indebted.

Jacqueline Murray

Introduction

JACQUELINE MURRAY

The past decade has witnessed a remarkable proliferation of studies, both scholarly and popular, of men and masculinities. Indeed, for a research area that could have been dismissed as little more than a regressive and reactionary response to women's studies and feminist studies, the study of men is proving to be remarkably rich and resilient. It is a research area that is emerging from the excesses of the angst-ridden, drum-beating male equivalent of early seventies feminist-consciousness-raising groups to generate some important insights into the nature of masculinity and femininity, of men and women, in societies past and present. Yet, for all this intellectual respectability, the study of medieval men, in their historical and cultural subjectivity, remains unusual, even innovative and, occasionally, controversial and contested.

In 1987 Harry Brod made a plea for what he called men's studies.[1] Brod addressed head-on the feminist objections that men were already the subject of virtually all research, by insisting that what was needed were qualitatively different kinds of studies about men, studies firmly rooted in earlier feminist scholarship, informed by the kind of critical perspectives that had done so much to shape women's studies. Despite the earnest eloquence of Brod's *apologia,* resistence to the new men's studies continues. Seven years later, in the Preface to the first essay collection devoted exclusively to masculinity in the Middle Ages (tellingly entitled, "Why Men?"), Thelma Fenster retraced much of the same ground, making many of the same arguments as had Brod, but for an audience of medievalists.[2] Fenster identified the scholarly approaches that render women invisible as the very same ones that obscure and hide men *as men.* Gender, she reminded us, is not the sole preserve of women. Then, as now, gender was relational: to understand medieval society we need to study medieval women *and medieval men.*

However compelling Fenster's argument, and however popular and influential *Medieval Masculinities,* resistence to the study of men and masculinities endures. For many medievalists, gender continues to be perceived as the domain of women. Just as, too frequently, women rather than men are perceived to "have gender," so, too, gender studies continue to be conflated and confused with women's studies. Yet, gender is only meaningful in relational terms. Men and women must be studied not so much in opposition to each other, as in relation to each other. The mutual influence and interdependence that characterize the social relations between the sexes, characterize how concepts of man and woman, masculine and feminine emerge in a given time and place. In order to arrive at richer, deeper, fuller, more complex, more meaningful understandings of medieval society, then, we must reinsert men into the picture, men *qua* men, men in their historical and cultural specificity.

Part of this process means giving to medieval men something of the same kind of attention that scholars have lavished on medieval women for the past twenty-five or so years. This process is still in its infancy. *Medieval Masculinities* (1994) remains a widely influential and foundational collection that has done much to stimulate research in a multitude of areas. Its essays cross time, space and discipline, moving from *Beowulf* to bachelors and medicine to mendicants. More recently, *Becoming Male in the Middle Ages* (1997)[3] has brought together essays that are equally as wide-ranging, many of which reflect the new research directions of the contemporary academy. For example, questions of sex, sexuality and embodiment figure prominently, as do the approaches of literary theory.[4]

The present volume takes as its starting point the complexities and interplay of the multiple and competing masculinities found in medieval society. Eschewing the idea of a fixed or hegemonic masculinity, the essays reflect the view that "[t]he many different images and behaviors contained in the notion of masculinity are not always coherent: they may be competing, contradictory and mutually undermining."[5] For medieval society, in particular, this diversity is well illustrated given its various ideological fonts (Roman, Germanic, Christian), the spatial and temporal distances included in "the Middle Ages" and the multiplicity of social institutions that could shape and influence men's experience. In the Middle Ages, competing and contradictory messages about what it meant to be a man circulated, creating individual crises and social confusion among some men, and security and complacency among others. While the ideologies of masculinity might be contested and fraught, depending on variables of time and space, social position and individual experience, they also reinforced social order, could provide a sense of security and a knowledge of one's place in the world. This is where we see most clearly the relationship between masculinities and patriarchy, for masculinities reflect patriarchy back on itself. Masculinities naturalize and normalize patriarchy and patriarchy imbues masculinities with the power and privilege that underscore male experience and identity through so much of human history.

There are a number of themes and aspects of medieval masculinities that the twelve essays included here bring to the fore. The multiplicity of coexisting and competing visions of masculinity are immediately apparent. The most obvious distinctions are between secular and religious values but, as Jo Ann McNamara and Vern Bullough demonstrate, the medical and scientific theories of antiquity also continued to exert an influence on how medieval theorists understood gender. The strains of the ecclesiastical vision of celibacy, as a means of freeing men from human ties to allow them to pursue God and salvation, are apparent in the essays by Megan McLaughlin, Brian McGuire and Jacqueline Murray. Psychological and emotional stress and social alienation could render religious men bitter, confused and alienated.

Equally apparent, however, are the difficult expectations placed on men by secular society. The remnants of warrior values endured long and exacted a harsh toll on medieval men. Andrew Taylor shows how the demands of physical prowess and bravery required men to deny their individual real emotions. Similarly, Jenny Jochens reveals how homosocial society could require the suppression of homosocial desire. The hierarchical nature of secular society could also strain men's sense of self, given masculinity's basis in power relations. Thus, Rachel Dressler, Susan Mosher Stuard and Ruth Mazo Karras all examine how masculine identities were constructed, consciously and unconsciously, in oppositional terms. In the secular world honor, too, figured large in a masculine sense of self, although it might mean different things for different groups. A king's honor could be linked to his queen's behavior according to John Parsons. Andrew Taylor shows how a knight's honor was directly related to his conduct in battle, while Rachel Dressler shows how knights might enhance their honor through the appropriation of symbols.

Power and its exercise was intimately linked to masculine performance and male roles. Shannon McSheffrey and Susan Mosher Stuard examine how power and responsibility were an essential aspect of having achieved full manhood. Self-control was important, as well. Karras exposes how a university education socialized adolescents into civilized and self-controlled men, while McSheffrey argues that *seniores* who did not exercise self-control could lose social standing and honor.

If masculinity is relational, then how men interacted with others influenced their sense of masculine identity and their place in the world. Stuard and McSheffrey discuss the social and familial relations of civic leaders, whose ability to govern their families and households was part of their ability to govern society. This is similar to the king's need to govern his wife, that Parsons discusses. Yet, what of those without paternal authority? Megan McLaughlin examines how spiritual fatherhood might have compensated for those excluded from biological paternity. McGuire similarly examines how an older brother might try to exercise patriarchal authority over younger brothers and sisters, not always successfully.

Desire, emotional and sexual, was also a source of tension for medieval men. The celibate man was supposed to suppress his desires to the point he felt nothing. This struggle against the body could lead to rather twisted visions of human and sexual relations, be it the emotional alienation of Gerson that McGuire discusses, or the psychosexual visions of Hugh of Lincoln that Murray examines. Jochens' study of a Norse love triangle similarly shows the emotional anxiety occasioned by desire, especially when it did not fit into socially sanctioned categories. While Bullough's reflections on Chaucer's Pardoner suggest a more sophisticated and complex understanding of gender and desire than is often acknowledged for medieval society, both his essay and Murray's highlight the central importance of the male genitalia in definitions of masculinity.

However tense medieval men's relationships with women might have been, it was male/male relationships that figured most prominently in a man's life. Male bonding occurred at every point in life, whether it was through university initiation rituals (Karras), over the battle stories told at court (Taylor), or in the shared theological discussions of the cloisters and schools (McLaughlin, McGuire). Men judged themselves against each other, whether it was knight vis-à-vis magnate (Dressler), warrior against warrior (Taylor), brother with brother (McGuire), or merchant bankers with their clients (Stuard).

Despite this diversity, the essays contained in this volume together underscore the manner in which cultural and social order require shared assumptions. These assumptions do not have to be consistent or necessarily agree with each other; they simply need to be generally recognized and accepted. Thus, celibacy and its antithesis, sexual prowess, might seem mutually incompatible but they nevertheless coexisted and both were essential features of medieval society. The point is, societies tend to overlook the logical inconsistencies that leap to the fore when scholars try to analyze their value systems systematically. We demand too much of the past if we expect smooth consistency. Individuals and societies are more complicated than that and appear to have an infinite ability to accommodate the inconsistent. Indeed, when we examine the very theoretical underpinnings of medieval ideas about gender, it is exposed as a tissue of inconsistencies; ones with which we must grapple but ones we are unlikely to reconcile any more than did medieval society. This point is underscored by the volume's opening essay.

Jo Ann McNamara's reflections on the medieval gender system illustrate the inherently relational nature of the understanding of men and women, as well as how the ideology of masculinity was deployed in the service of patriarchy. McNamara traces the enduring influence of the two contradictory notions of gender developed by the Greeks—the theories of the alterity and of the continuum of male and female—and examines how Christianity incorporated and accommodated these notions. Shifts in family structure and social and religious organization resulted in the modification and transformation of the relative merit placed on men and women and the characteristics traditionally associated with each sex. In particular, the privileging of chastity, for both women and men, proved a challenge to the traditional hierarchy of the sexes and of gendered virtues. McNamara carefully traces the changing values from late Roman society through to the cloistering of female religious in the eighth century, demonstrating how the theories of gender continuum and gender alterity alternately served to enhance, and then reduce, women's social and moral position vis-à-vis men. At the same time, men were deprived of, and then provided with, access to those feminine characteristics, including chastity, that enhanced their access to holiness. McNamara concludes that the Christian gender system that evolved over the early medieval centuries continued to rest on contradictory premises which were never adequately resolved.

While chastity may play an inordinate role in the gender hierarchy of Christianity, it is the family which is the fundamental social institution in most times and places. How, then, do celibate men fit into the structure of an institution based on marriage and procreation—two activities from which they are excluded by definition? Megan McLaughlin investigates how, deprived of biological fatherhood, medieval clerics, nevertheless constructed roles for themselves as spiritual fathers, capable of begetting and raising "children in the faith." Using the letters of the eleventh-century reformer, Peter Damian, McLaughlin examines how he constructed an understanding of both secular and spiritual paternity that was complex, ambiguous and unstable. While spiritual fatherhood was linked to pastoral care, nevertheless, it exhibited many of the qualities associated with secular, biological fatherhood. Deploying Judith Butler's performative theory of gender to great effect, McLaughlin shows how paternal identities needed to be continuously recreated. Startling, too, is the conjunction of paternity and violence, a conjunction that McLaughlin suggests may be part of the process by which men establish and maintain their male identities.

Brian McGuire, too, takes as his subject the emotional life of a celibate man: the fourteenth-century French cleric, Jean Gerson. McGuire uses Gerson's letters to examine the enduring nature of his ties with his natal family and the emotional aridity that characterized so much of the rest of Gerson's life. Preoccupied with the need to save his own soul, Gerson tried to cut himself off from his peers, yet his ties with his brothers indicate an enduring bond of affection and a sense of responsibility. Ironically, Gerson felt abandoned by his brothers' entry into monastic life. For Gerson, the bonds of human affectivity were transient, not enduring beyond this life. Ultimately, one was left alone on the road to salvation.

The kind of emotional alienation exemplified by Gerson was certainly one of the results of a religious value system that minimized human contact or construed it as dangerous. Yet, this value system, based as it was on clerical celibacy, was one of the most influential. The prevailing moral code, the value system that the church sought to disseminate throughout society and project onto the population as a whole, was one that denigrated sexual relations and privileged chastity. But the body/soul dualism that underlay so much of Christian moral theology contained many of its own stresses and strains. For Peter Damian, celibacy may have been a refuge from unsatisfactory, even hurtful, human interrelationships; for Jean Gerson it may have been a refuge from emotion and affectivity. For other men, celibate life was more difficult, not only because it required the suppression of the body but also because it was accompanied by social ambiguity. While notions of spiritual fatherhood or relationships with one's natal family might have addressed some of these problems, the physical and psychological stresses remained. Not surprisingly, much of this stress was located in the male body.

Phyllis Chesler has suggested that having a penis is what makes all men like one another and unlike women.[6] The male genitals, then, are inextricably linked to a man's sense of self and his masculine identity. But what did this mean for the medieval man who was celibate? As Jo Ann McNamara has asked: "Can one be a man without deploying the most obvious biological attributes of manhood?"[7] Was the need for this signifier of masculinity so sharp in medieval society that it can explain the Church's prohibition of self-castration? Can this explain the seeming absurdity of the Church insisting that a man have functioning genitals, while at the same time forbidding that they be used as they were intended by nature? Jacqueline Murray examines some of the problems associated with the imperative to celibacy that confronted medieval clerics who lived in the world and interacted with both men and women. The difficulty with which the genitals were controlled led some men to celebrate their absence, despite ecclesiastical prohibitions against castration. Thus, Peter Abelard viewed his violent castration as a relief from his body and its uncontrollable lust. Hugh of Lincoln sought the same kind of relief in the psychological forum, experiencing a mystical castration that freed him, too, from his body. Ironically, though, while both men ultimately embraced celibacy through the rejection of their male bodies, they continued to seek the company of women, those sources of sexual temptation that proved so difficult for the celibate to resist. Both also maintained their masculine identity despite the real or fictive mutilation of their physical marker of masculine superiority.

These perspectives on celibate men point to the multiple ambiguities and conflicts associated with masculine identity. Was someone a "man" if he did not fulfill the role of father? Was someone a man if he did not fulfill the male sexual role? Vern Bullough's essay reminds us that sex and gender difference also had a physiological dimension, based on the balance of the humors. Men were believed to be warm and dry, women cold and wet. The humors were linked to other sex characteristics such as a man's ability to produce semen, a key factor for assessing virility. But this reliance on the balance of the humors to distinguish male from female—the same continuum that McNamara discusses—also opened the possibility of gender ambiguity and confusion based not on external factors, such as the presence or absence of genitalia, or social factors, such as the possession of paternal authority, but on the internal balance between warm and cold, dry and wet. Bullough uses this medical perspective to address one of the problems that has both fascinated and vexed medievalists for years: the conundrum posed by Chaucer's Pardoner. In the end, Bullough concludes that in the Pardoner Chaucer may have created an aberrant character, but one that was, nevertheless, recognized as part of the social community because he was part of the gender continuum. Bullough suggests that Chaucer's own ambiguous perspective may, in fact, be more sophisticated than our modern attempts to categorize the Pardoner as this or as that.

Ambiguity of sex and gender might have been considered to upset the established natural and social order, and perhaps even to threaten clearly demarcated masculinity but ambiguity was as prevalent in medieval values and society as it is in any complex culture. Jenny Jochens reveals how medieval men could struggle against formal compulsory heterosexuality in a society that really did not recognize homoaffectivity or homoeroticism but which was profoundly homosocial. Jochens examines the Norse sagas that treat of a complicated love/hate relationship between two poets, one older, one younger, and a woman. Through a close reading of the texts, Jochens reveals a complicated set of emotional, and possibly physical, relationships between the two men and the woman they both love. Certainly, the heterosexual desire of the two men cannot be doubted. More complicated, however, are the relations between them, relations that may have been characterized by desire, yet were also constructed in specific ways by social constraints that did not tolerate homosexual acts and did not admit homoaffective desire, obscuring both behind the tradition of libel. Yet, the complicated relationships revealed in the poets' writings suggest a depth of feeling and an emotional ambiguity that may appear startling in the warrior society of the Norse sagas. Ironically, while neither man dared to acknowledge the passive role, both could envision themselves as the active partner in homosexual acts.

The role of envisioning or constructing one's own identity or masculine reality is widespread. Ultimately, it is that process of trying on, discarding or retaining attributes, whether consciously or unconsciously, that constructs the meaning of masculinity in a given time or place. After all, all identities are constructed against an Other, all identities are relational. This is as true of the relative position of masculine identities between men as it is between men and women. The complex and profound process of constructing a specific masculine identity, in opposition to other masculine identities, is illustrated in Rachel Dressler's examination of thirteenth- and fourteenth-century English tomb effigies. The ide-

alized masculinity portrayed in knightly effigies speaks to the social tensions between different groups of men–the magnates with whom the
knights identified and the clerics from whom they sought differentiation.
The corporeal muscularity and martial iconography of the effigies stood
in sharp contrast to the feminized bodies of clerical effigies. Similarly,
the knights' effigies allowed for a self-representation that laid fictitious
claim to parity with the highest nobility. These effigies reveal both social
tension between men and how one group sought to construct a specific
masculine identity through physical robustness and martial prowess.

If masculinity holds within it the implication of superiority, for
knights this was as much an issue of class as it was of gender. The knight
aped his social superiors in order "to be a man" just as he distanced himself from the feminized clergy. Indeed, the strains of masculinity, and the
constraints it placed upon men, would appear to have been particularly
difficult for the fighters in medieval society. Andrew Taylor's examination of French court culture complements Dressler's observations about
the construction of virile masculine identity. Just as effigies allowed
knights to appropriate the identity and the masculinity they sought, so
the literature of the court constructed and reinforced the masculine values
of the knights as a social group. Literature, and even more so conversation and oral recitation, constructed and reinforced the kind of behavior
and feelings that were deemed acceptable for a manly knight and a
knightly man. Through stories told and retold in endless and ongoing
conversations, what it meant to be a man was defined and men were
socialized into those values. Thus, bravery in battle was promoted and
encouraged and inculcated; fear was denied. Yet, Taylor finds fissures in
this discourse of bravery, fissures that show even the bravest warrior
might also have experienced fear in battle. The tyranny of masculinity,
however, suppressed even the possibility of recognizing, much less artic-
ulating, that fear.

The ideology of masculinity promoted a certain patriarchal view of
culture and the social order. Through the complex process of socializing
men, the shared assumptions and values, and the shared fictions, so
essential to cultural cohesion and social order, were inculcated. Cracks
and fissures were suppressed and ignored by common consent. Definitions of masculinity moved between social groups, were appropriated,
shared and modified. So it is that Ruth Karras examines the appropriation of knightly visions of masculinity by late-fifteenth-century German
university students. The process by which these students, far removed from
the battlefield, were socialized shows something of the transforming and

transformative power of masculine socialization. Rites of passage were one means by which a boy became a man and a man was received into the group. The experience of a university education could be as much part of the process of creating masculine identity as were the battlefield and court. In this case, though, it was the masculine ideal of a man of letters whose education carried with it the wisdom and moderation that were the characteristics of a "civilized" man.

The notion of the civilized and wise man, as opposed to the strong, brave and passionate warrior, was a masculine identity particularly appropriate to the urbanized context of the later Middle Ages. It is the urban *seniores*, the wise but firm patriarchs ruling over families, businesses and cities, who are the subjects of Susan Mosher Stuard's essay. Focusing on the upper echelons of fifteenth-century Venetian and Florentine society, Stuard examines how civic leaders, those bankers who dominated international finance, carefully constructed themselves as the peers of their clients, Europe's royalty. Through the careful control of luxury consumption, by means of sumptuary legislation aimed not at the lower orders but rather at the women and young men of their own rank, the *sapientes* reserved for themselves the highest status fashions and guaranteed their desirability, by ensuring they would not be devalued through association with women or youth. Stuard thus reveals how the masculine values of the Italian urban elites were as patriarchal, hierarchical and restrictive as those of northern warrior society, although their articulation was profoundly different from the overt masculine physicality of the warrior.

One of the central features of masculinity is the exercise of power and authority over women, younger men and men of lower status. Thus, patriarchal authority figures largely in how masculinity was constructed and how it operated in society. Shannon McSheffrey examines the exercise of authority and its relation to masculine identity in fifteenth-century London. Using the records of ecclesiastical courts, McSheffrey reveals that respectable masculinity included not only exercising control and influence on others but also governing oneself and preserving one's own reputation. A man had a duty to supervise those in his neighborhood and those under his control, preserving sexual propriety and social order. But a man also had to observe these behavioral norms himself, in order to maintain his position as a respectable patriarch. Thus, duty and responsibility were concomitant with masculine authority.

The manner in which duty and responsibility could influence and define gender was perhaps nowhere as central as in the role and image of the king. At this highest level of society, the expectations and imperatives to manliness, masculine prowess and bravery, patriarchal authority, sapiential wisdom and good governance all intersected. The king had much invested in his appropriation and performance of masculine identities. Yet, as John Parsons shows, the king's image was also vulnerable to many influences and potential detractions. In particular, how the queen acted, and how her relationship with the king was publicly presented, had the potential to enhance or diminish the king's image. He, more than other men, had more to lose through accusations of uxoriousness or threats to his honor but because of his position, criticisms had to remain indirect. Parsons examines various examples of how the portrayal of a queen indirectly constructed the public image of the king. The queen could be used to uphold the social order and enhance the king's honor, or, conversely, to criticize a king and highlight his weaknesses. Here, again, the relational nature of gender is underscored.

As this overview makes clear, all of the essays gathered here, while based on the reading of texts, nevertheless, seek to push beyond text and into society. While the focus is very much on ideas about men, the essays also show the beginnings of the process of examining individual men and tracing how ideas of masculinity actually functioned within society. Together the essays serve as a call to medievalists to continue the examination of the intersection of the competing and contradictory masculinities that uneasily coexisted in medieval society. Certainly, the effects of such contradictions were dramatic and can be found in every corner of society. By examining the conflicted identities and multiple masculinities of medieval men, there is no question that we will come to a more sophisticated understanding not only of gender relations, but also of the social, political, religious, economic, cultural and institutional history of the Middle Ages.

NOTES

1. Harry Brod, "The Case for Men's Studies," in *The Making of Masculinities. The New Men's Studies,* ed. Harry Brod (Boston: Allen & Unwin, 1987), 39–62.

2. Thelma Fenster, "Preface: Why Men?" in *Medieval Masculinities. Regarding Men in the Middle Ages,* ed. Clare A. Lees (Minneapolis: University of Minnesota Press, 1994), ix-xiii.

3. *Becoming Male in the Middle Ages,* ed. Jeffrey Jerome Cohen and Bonnie Wheeler (New York: Garland, 1997).

4. Another collection of essays has also recently been promised: *Masculinity in Medieval Europe,* ed. Dawn Hadley (Harlow, Eng.: Longman, forthcoming 1998).

5. Andrea Cornwall and Nancy Lindisfarne, "Dislocating Masculinity. Gender, Power and Anthropology," in *Dislocating Masculinity. Comparative Ethnographies,* ed. Andrea Cornwall and Nancy Lindisfarne (London: Routledge, 1994), 12; and Nigel Edley and Margaret Wetherell, "Masculinity, Power and Identity," in *Understanding Masculinities. Social Relations and Cultural Arenas,* ed. Máirtín Mac an Ghaill (Buckingham, Eng.: Open University Press, 1996), 106.

6. Phyllis Chesler, *About Men* (New York: Simon and Schuster, 1978), 211.

7. Jo Ann McNamara, "The *Herrenfrage:* The Restructuring of the Gender System, 1050–1150," in *Medieval Masculinities,* 5.

An Unresolved Syllogism
The Search for a Christian Gender System

JO ANN McNAMARA

The "facts of life," rooted in the too, too solid flesh, seem to subject human society to an immutable tyranny of genes, blood and sex. Like all tyrannies, however, the biological regime is subject to internecine strife.Our understanding of the physical body itself relies on the culturally manipulated training of scientists.[1] Sexual similarities and differences appear and disappear in historical context. The gender system requires strong institutional support to resolve the tensions between them. The Bible suggests that God himself set the puzzle. Gen. 1:27–28 tells us that God created man in his own image, male and female, and gave them dominion. A short page later, Gen. 2:21–22 floats the familiar tale of Eve's creation from Adam's rib to be his helper. The Greeks started with "nature" as the base of all human relationships. Grounding human society on sexual relationships, they produced two contradictory premises: (1) all human beings share the same characteristics on a continuum of varying degrees; and (2) humanity is divided into males and females with different and complementary functions. They failed to resolve the syllogism but they produced a workable social compromise that hid the stubborn gap between the continuum and alterity models.

Until the time of Christ, the single-gender continuum justified the class and racial prejudices of the Greeks. In *The Republic*, Plato reduced the differences between women and men to procreative functions and advocated equal education and training for everyone according to rank. Thus, the "best" women and men could be paired to produce the "best" children.[2] Aristotle even rooted procreative differences in the defective manliness of women.[3] Both authors muted sexual differences to make

1

gender support a social hierarchy that reduced lower-class Greek males and foreigners of both sexes to "natural" inferiority to highborn Greek men and women. Virtue (manliness) meant authority, freedom and self-control, the legacy of wellborn and disciplined parents whose daughters also were superior to ordinary men. Massage, diet, exercise and education completed their maturation into virtuous adults and their modification established the superiority of men over women.[4] Plato recognized that females educated as strenuously as males would qualify as guardians in his ideal Republic and expected them to hold offices there.

On a more mundane level, the social threat of this logic was blunted by barring women from education for civic life. Men were thus obliged to seek suitable companions and competitors only among themselves. Upper-class men disciplined themselves in every public act to maintain their masculinity. The sexual act itself was framed as an act of domination. Even homosexual relationships reflected the hierarchy of old over young, master over slave, masculine authority over feminine yielding.[5] Lower-class males were downgraded to effeminacy by their sedentary labors, their subordinate status and their fluid characters.

Neither the Greeks nor the Romans questioned the potential of some women for superior masculinity on this continuum. Marriage was vital to their social security. It deprived young women under paternal or conjugal control of maturation into independent and active individuals, assuring their subordination in society at large. Simultaneously, it gave husbands the experience they needed to gain adult authority as they trained them as domestic surrogates. Within the household, wives exercised their lesser masculinity by wielding authority over effeminate slaves who generally took over the task of nursing and raising the children.[6] Even Aristotle conceded that marriage was a constitutional relationship (as opposed to the master/slave relationship or the "royal" relationship of fathers and sons). The Romans underlined the effeminacy of lower-class men by withholding legal recognition from their unions.[7] Nevertheless, freedmen and even slaves emulated their social superiors by treating women of their own class as wives.[8] By the first century, these unions gained broader recognition and paternal dignity democratized even as it lost public authority to the imperial government. The early Christian Fathers were more than satisfied with the Roman family as model for their developing church. Paul recommended marriage to men over the uncertain path of celibacy. As one early apologist boasted, Christians differed ethically from pagans only in their fidelity to their marriage vows and their commitment to raising their children rather than exposing them.[9]

According to Genesis, God cursed women with desire for their husbands which produced their subordination.[10] Paul used conjugal authority as the model for Christ's relationship to the church. A bishop demonstrated fitness to govern in the time-honored fashion, by passing the test of domestic authority as husband to one wife. Male and female elders (presbyters) shared the guidance of the "household of faith" as married partners governed secular households. The evolution of the presbyterate "naturally" allotted public sacerdotal roles to men and denied them to their wives. Accordingly, the authors of the Pastoral letters expected women to yield naturally to a subordination that fully justified their exclusion from leadership positions. The Pauline vision of the Christian hierarchy was totally compatible with the traditional single-gender system as long as Christian women were contained within the traditional family structure.

But Christianity was young, vulnerable to the profound social changes under way in the first century. Christian men mostly sprang from the lower classes where the gender hierarchy was not so strongly supported. Moreover, the Christian God arrogated ultimate paternal authority to himself and encouraged men and women alike to approach him as children. The resulting Christian image of universal siblinghood was perfectly in tune with the imperial world in which it was formulated. The Roman conquest of the Mediterranean destabilized the social arrangements of conquered peoples and the collapse of the Roman Republic destroyed the homosocial arena where patrician men reaped the rewards of their self-discipline. Beginning with Augustus, the emperors monopolized paternal powers and responsibilities. In Aristotelian terms, they transformed the "constitutional" relationships of patrician men with one another into the "royal" relationship of a father over his sons. The empire became a universal household wherein the father/ emperor delegated power to his empress and even to slaves of the imperial household over their immature children.

Disempowered men responded with childlike self-indulgence.[11] Augustus and his successors failed to hold them to the burdens of marriage and paternity. Without their collaboration, the traditional checks on female manliness dissolved, while unsupported men let themselves sink into passive effeminacy. Logically, "nature" should have guaranteed that within marriage the vast majority of women would bow to the superior virtues of men. In fact, in that relatively equal arena, many men found, to their shame, that their wives flouted their authority with impunity. Social critics demonized sex-crazed, power-hungry viragos scrambling up the gender continuum as men surrendered their money, their potency and even their lives.[12] Of course, numerous legal and social restraints continued to block ambitious women but within marriage a henpecked husband had very little support. Pagans and Christians began to construct a new morality of marriage based on mutual self-discipline and shared interests. Plutarch and Paul both formulated an ideal of spiritual and intellectual comradeship within marriage.

But even comrades are not equals. The principle of the continuum still held the possibility open that women might command the leading role. Christian logic was especially inescapable. Women, in noticeable numbers, embraced the new religion, irrefutably demonstrating their superiority over their pagan husbands.[13] Christian apologists learned to glory in the paradox of the manly Christian woman but only her martyrdom could resolve the contradiction between her conjugal and religious duties. Logically, the believing wife should have been given precedence over the unbelieving husband and, by extension, the morally superior wife over the inferior husband within the family of the faith. Socially and politically, this was just the sort of radicalism that Christian apologists were trying to moderate in the gospel preachings.

Over several centuries, theorists groped their way through the linguistically confusing concept of feminine virtue.[14] Gradually the alterity principle strengthened and a separate feminine gender evolved. The self-control that certified masculinity was subtly rewritten as feminine self-abnegation. Self-subordination to the authority of a husband unworthy of her respect became an act of feminine heroism. An image of womanhood coalesced around the qualities of patience, mercy and charity, demanding discipline and cultivation equally with the manly virtues of courage, justice and fortitude. Marriage framed a gender system that united complementary virtues. Alterity reinforced the dependence of meek women upon forceful men and articulated the power of womanly gentleness to moderate manly rigor. The royal couple acted out this tension in the ceremonies of the Christian empire and the barbarian kingdoms that succeeded it.[15] Manliness regained its classical claim to the exercise of worldly power but womanliness prevailed on a new Christian moral continuum.

Feminine virtue logically inspired the concept of masculine vice. Between 350 and 450, wealthy patrician women patronized and inspired a peculiarly vocal minority of gifted men as their logothetes. They melded the manly virtue of self-control with the womanly virtue of chastity, granting the moral high ground to women who submitted dutifully to their husbands' demands.[16] The yielding woman competed with the aggressive man for the authority bestowed on those who could command their passions. The sober husband of the Stoic vision, who performed as teacher, supporter and guide of helpless, unstable womanhood, became a victim of his own disordered hormones. Criticizing even the licit sexual encounters that led to procreation, Ambrose, Gerontius, Jerome and others painted loathsome pictures of the grossness and sexual brutality of men. They decried women's humiliation in the marriage market and praised her modesty in shrinking from male attention. They sympathized with the housewife diverted from spiritual contemplation by the maddening distractions of housekeeping. They lingered over the pain and terror of childbirth which sacrificed the health and even the lives of women to masculine lust. Jerome came close to heresy in his denunciations of marriage and his passionate advocacy of the perpetual virginity of Jesus' mother.[17]

Thus, on the continuum that still dominated the public world, women become more manly in their self-controlled submission to the marital duty. The complementary relationship still produced competition. Male potency required sexual expression but female potency grew as men yielded to the sexual attractions of women. As sexual desire was gradually gendered male, men conceded power to women over their fragile continence. Palladius offered a prime *exemplum* to women who feared to expose men to their powerful attractions, in the story of Alexandra, who immured herself in a tomb, which he heard from Melania the Elder.[18] The suffering of Monica, his abused mother, made Augustine keenly aware of the power of passion over the male psyche. Thus, alterity justified the subordination of women but did not ensure their inferiority. And it required men to engage in a struggle with their own passions that they might not win. On the other hand, women redefined their own traditional virtue of chastity. The virgin or widow, in firm control of her physical and emotional integrity, challenged the power structure that rested on sexual potency.

In their initial organization of the churches, Paul and his immediate followers did not adjust the old gender system for the unmarried women who were so palpably present among the followers of Christ. But other sources clearly indicate that, from apostolic times, women themselves integrated the ideal of virginity into the fabric of Christian social teaching. Anonymous apocryphal literature equated conversion with sexual renunciation and often placed women first in embracing the means of salvation. It glorified girls who defied the authority of parents to give them in marriage and wives who refused the legitimate sexual claims of their husbands. It elevated the call to win souls for Christ above the command to be fruitful and multiply. The heroism of "virile" virgin martyrs inspired patristic writers to rebuke irresolute, effeminate men for their backwardness.[19] A Christian vision of progress charted human moral evolution from promiscuity through marriage to virginity and moved women from base inferiority to equality to moral superiority.[20] A new, feminine continuum transcended the old masculine system. Virgins led the march to heaven, followed by chaste widows, and then by chaste wives. On earth, their moral superiority did not entitle them to temporal authority, nor did they claim that it did. Instead, their very distance from worldly entanglements proclaimed their purity, their integrity, their progress from the discredited ancient city to the new Jerusalem.

Clerical as well as secular men continued to prove their capacity to govern others by governing their wives. The sexual act proved their authority but robbed them of the virgin's self-command. The conundrum is well illustrated in the story of Pinian, a young aristocrat, manfully embarking on his traditional duties. His young wife, Melania, begged to keep her virginity but yielded dutifully to his sober authority and agreed to bear him two children to perpetuate their respective lineages. This display of masculine virtue turned into an act of tyranny when his wife forced him to watch her sufferings in childbirth. She became a martyr to his worldly interests which crumbled to ash when the two children died. Pinian's masculine authority eventually earned him a distinguished episcopate. His wife became a saint. Freed from conjugal slavery, she shed her worldly possessions and the corruptions of power, preferring the monastic life as the better part.[21] Manliness had to be wholly reconsidered in the light of the new continuum. Purity was fundamentally incompatible with the engaged mastery that defined classical manhood. Having reduced masculine potency to a species of vice, it challenged men to seek an acceptable access to womanly virtue. Many men fled to the desert, seeking an extension of the old continuum from the natural to the supernatural. They abandoned the mastery of others and connected selfmastery with subordination to God alone.[22] In solitude, they looked for an expression of potency without domination, ascesis with only one's own self for competition. The superhuman dimensions of the enterprise reconciled them to the idea that the grace of God could equally empower women. Brothers and sisters alike could strive for transcendent selfmastery in the solitary spaces.

The monastic system did not pretend to eliminate sex. Triumph over temptation and mastery of lust remained central to the quest for virtue. The prudent John Cassian urged his monks to avoid women just as they would shun food while striving for control of gluttony. Virgins anxiously locked themselves away from men who might otherwise be unable to refrain from raping them. Monastic practice did, however, abandon gender or attempted to join ascetic males and females in an elite third gender that superceded the old hierarchy altogether. Monks and nuns dressed in similar costumes concealing their physical characteristics. The whole scheme of monastic life emphasized such purity and integrity that cults formed around fictional women who proved the extraordinary discipline of the monks by living unsuspected among them until death revealed all things.[23] Men who overcame their manly weaknesses equaled women who never surrendered their manly strength. Satisfying and fruitful syneisactic alliances formed between friends, relatives or even couples who renounced their sexual claims. The third gender exalted itself above the sexually active whom they associated with other worldly forms of excess and corruption.[24]

The existence of this chaste elite, however, only aggravated the contradiction between the gender continuum ranking women as virgins, widows and wives and the ecclesial ranking of married men as bishops, priests and laity. Monks, who equated sexual temptation with the temptation to go back to the world, scorned the priesthood.[25] They, rather pointedly, lived almost without benefit of the sacraments. Benedict's Rule discouraged communities from admitting priests because their pride and self-importance made them poor material for the regular life.[26] By implication, nuns who used the same rule were equally superior to the ordained clergy in religious life. But they were not exposed to the same temptation that beset their brothers. Lay people repeatedly bypassed the logical difficulties of reconciling the two hierarchies and forced reluctant monks to accept episcopal office. Sex and power, hopelessly intertwined, awaited them there. Clergy working in the world had to maintain their manhood and their chastity simultaneously. John Chrysostom complained that one of the burdens of the priesthood was ministry to women who, loose or chaste, exuded charms that a poor feeble male could barely withstand.[27] From Augustine through Pope Gregory, displaced monks treated their priesthood as a stain on their purity. Martin of Tours maintained that the episcopate drained him of much of his miraculous power.[28]

The new virtue of monasticism had transcended gender but back in the world monks again became simple men who had to deal with women they could neither dominate sexually nor ignore behind claustral walls. Virgins and chaste widows did not usually seek the desert but played an active role in urban church life. They distributed food, clothing and money to the poor, visited the sick, cleaned and decorated clerical domiciles and churches and took part in processions and other ceremonies. As deacons and canonesses, a title that occasionally flickers in the early eastern sources, they intruded tentatively into the ecclesial hierarchy.[29] Many of them were wealthy or at least modestly self-supporting. Gregory I had two aunts among the *ancillae dei,* consecrated women, virgins or widows who lived in their own homes.[30] Some shared houses with other consecrated women or even men. Others, who were less economically secure, lived in clerical households as housekeepers, helpers or servants.[31] In most cases, those women could count on the chaperonage of a clerical wife but not if the priest were celibate or the bishop a monk. More than one anxious bishop was dismayed by the syneisactic fashions of the fourth and fifth centuries which brought men and women together under one roof, renouncing sex and collaborating in a life of religious service. Chrysostom, in particular, advanced the proposition that sexual temptation was irresistible in propinquity.[32]

Classical biology was full of traps for individuals who resisted the demands of nature. Sexual self-control turned women into men, not just metaphorically. Normally recessed female testicles might descend if a woman persisted in playing a manly role. A man exposed too long to the contagion of femininity might find his penis withdrawn into his body.[33] Pope Gregory I described the transformation of Galla, a widow whose chastity raised her body heat to manly temperature, causing her to grow a beard.[34] The man who cooled his ardor too effectively risked effeminacy. Though he praised his sanctity, Gregory of Tours, found more than a hint of effeminacy in the virgin Gallus, whose sweet singing voice survived the normally destructive effects of puberty.[35] Men who suppressed their natural heat and learned to be indifferent to feminine lures lost their natural authority. Bishop John Chrysostom denounced syneisactic men who lived amidst female trappings and devoted themselves to the care of female companions, comparing them to toothless lions.[36] Martin of Tours tried to separate even clerical couples who had taken vows of chastity on the grounds that women did not belong on a battlefield.[37] This was the course taken by Bishop Faro of Meaux, who could only keep his vow of abstinence because his resolute wife left his house and refused to return.

In opposing syneisactism, Chrysostom rejected the argument from alterity that necessitated the cooperation of women and men in separate spheres. But his denial, carried to its logical conclusion, would undermine the barriers that kept manly women from rising in the ecclesial hierarchy. Clerical marriage remained the arena where men tested their virtue and developed their authority. Like Paul, Gregory I reminded married men that God provided the conjugal bed as a lawful refuge from the perils of lust.[38] With this safeguard, he could praise the presbyter of Nursia who loved *suam presbyteram* as a sister but avoided her as an enemy for fear of temptation.[39] Temptation came to anchor masculine chastity, guaranteeing virility while fortifying self-control. In their fantasies, anxious prelates associated syneisactism with men's foolish endeavors to test their powers of endurance. Basil of Caesarea threatened to depose a seventy-year-old bishop suspected of sharing a bed (chastely) with a consecrated virgin.[40] Irish tradition maintained that their earliest fathers had survived similar dramatic tests.[41]

These bizarre contests robbed women of agency. Their sexual power became passive and almost unconscious while men's triumph over their own weaknesses guaranteed their masculinity. Indeed, women were practically displaced by the devil as the agent of temptation. Gregory I wrote of the saintly bishop of Fulda whom demons almost ensnared into an intimate relationship with his consecrated virgin housekeeper.[42] The woman remained oblivious and chaste, curiously lacking in virtue because of her passivity. When Gregory came to eulogize his hero, Benedict of Nursia, he depicted him rolling in a bed of nettles to rid himself of a phantom woman he recalled from his youth.[43] With perhaps exaggerated dismay, the Christian fathers bemoaned their own lapses among the fleshpots. Men began their struggle for self-denial where women ended. Like Pinian, they proved their manhood by losing their virginity and subordinating women. Then they struggled to limit their sexual appetites and finally to overcome them. Men who actively resisted seduction transformed their vulnerability into virile ascendancy.

Gendered chastity deprived feminine self-control of its heroic qualities by emphasizing women's physical revulsion from sex. In the popular topos of the transvestite virgin, the manly woman was driven to the desert as monks returned to grapple with the world. From persecuted virgins to reformed prostitutes, virile women never had to struggle with diabolic studs tempting them back to the fleshpots. Women mutilated themselves to repel men but no Scholastica tormented her own naked body to rid herself of sexual memories. Neither virgins nor widows sought, as did Augustine, to delay the embrace of chastity. The struggle restored men to their superior place on a single-gender continuum.

Chastity achieved within marriage restored their right to authority over women. Many contemporaries of Melania and Pinian turned their own homes into small monasteries, seeking inspiration from one another to protect them from the corruptions of the world.[44] Sixth-century Gallic councils repeatedly tried to initiate the married clergy into the third gender by legislating abstention from conjugal relations.

The imposition of sexual abstinence on clerical couples depended on their mutual capacity for self-control. Fears of pollution, deeply rooted in Christianity's Jewish history, prompted commands for priests to withdraw from their wives in preparation for sacred rituals.[45] Paul had expressed reservations about the compatibility of conjugal relations and sacramental rites. Athanasius urged priests to be celibate if possible but certainly abstinent when celebrating the eucharist.[46] The Council of Elvira embedded the requirement in canon law.[47] A letter attributed to Gregory I maintained that a priest who enjoyed his conjugal rights risked soiling those whom he was bound to cleanse.[48] Spiritual marriage not only assured the purity of priests but provided purified partners qualified for some share in their sacred activities. Thus, it undermined the alterity that precluded the sacramental activities of women. In the sixth and seventh centuries, clerical wives joined celibate virgins in housekeeping chores that extended into the sacred precincts of the altar. They took up church design and at least one bishop's wife took over supervision of the building works for the cathedral. They ranged from baking the eucharistic bread, handling altar vessels and lighting candles to liturgical services like ringing bells and distributing communion. In 511, three bishops complained of priests traveling with women who assisted them in celebrating mass and distributing communion to peasants in Breton villages.[49] Consecrated women encroached closely on sacramental preserves by anointing the sick with blessed oil.[50]

The powerful class structure of the age did not support a strong system of alterity. The prevailing "royal" pattern, coupled with the pressures of high male mortality among the warrior aristocracy, demanded that birth and conjugal families alike frequently deploy women in manly roles. Wives, daughters, mothers and sisters led armies, directed governments, commanded wealth and patronage.[51] Aristocratic family interest also loomed large over church administration. Secular patrons of both sexes controlled ecclesiastical offices and often reduced ordination to a casual formality or simply delegated sacramental services to a chaplain. Church office was often simply an extension of a secular career and reflected the same gender relationships. Gregory of Tours was proud of the clerical caste system from which he sprang but he prescribed conjugal continence as a qualification for episcopal couples governing their dioceses.[52] Gallic councils attempted to clarify the distinction between consecrated women and ordained men. They required female deacons to be unmarried and gradually forbade any ordination to women, letting the office die. But they set clerical wives apart by special acts of consecration which extended even into widowhood, when priests' wives had distinct costumes and responsibilities in return for their vow never to remarry.[53] These "deaconesses, priestesses and bishopesses" were, as a matter of course, regulated as members of the clergy though they held no discernible office.[54]

Spiritual marriage turned clerical homes into a species of small monastery, not noticeably different from small establishments of hermits and *ancillae*. By the seventh century, these modest communities blended with the great monasteries founded to evangelize the European wilderness. Single-sex communities, paired communities and even mixed communities alike depended on clerical services for the confection of the Eucharist but recognized few other priestly prerogatives. The ordained clergy were but a dependent minority subject, even in religious matters, to the jurisdiction of lay abbots and abbesses. Far from resisting, Merovingian bishops aggressively recruited wealthy women and established them in authority over the clergy, monks and nuns in their establishments.[55] Abbesses, bearing the shepherd's crook, gave blessings, distributed preconsecrated wafers to their congregations and heard nonsacramental confessions. Out on the missionary frontiers, they exercised many of the administrative powers of bishops.[56] This network of powerful monasteries, acting as surrogate episcopal centers, was spread primarily by Irish monks, reflecting the system that had adapted church governance in their own rural homeland. They brought it directly to Scotland and northern England, while continental monks may have contributed to the inspiration of the monk-pope Gregory I, who sent a Benedictine community to begin the evangelization of the south.

Augustine of Canterbury, who structured the newly converted English church into a series of monastic chapters supporting episcopal centers, may have been inspired by his namesake, Augustine of Hippo, who is said to have imposed the common life on his own cathedral clergy. The so-called Augustinian rule began to circulate a century later.[57] Though English cathedral chapters continued to observe the Benedictine Rule, the Augustinian tradition may have conveyed the notion of canons and canonesses to them. There is no evidence that the English studied his regulations for the associated community of women headed by his sister. Nevertheless, future bishoprics like Ely and Chester began as monasteries for women who were replaced by men at an unknown date.[58] When they were founded in the seventh century, the logic of the third gender tended toward the continuum and the erasure of differences rooted in sex. The power and prestige of a woman like Hilda of Whitby was clearly equal to her contemporaries in the episcopate.

Hilda and the other great abbesses of late-seventh-century England resemble the women who appear as "canonesses" in the constitutions passed by the Council of Aachen in the early ninth century. They are described as "prelates" over communities of sanctimonials and seem to be commensurate with lay abbots, outside the confines of the Benedictine Rule. The bishops at Aachen admonished them not to act as lords but as shepherds sharing the communal life with the virgins rather than gadding about in vanity and luxury outside the convent.[59] The title "canoness" first appears in the west in an English penitential ascribed to Bede (d. 735) or to Archbishop Egbert of York (732–66), with no indication of its meaning.[60] Presumably, the women had some connection to the cathedral chapters. They could have been the *ancillae dei,* whom we have seen elsewhere, who had adopted a title, possibly introduced from the east by the Greek Archbishop of Canterbury, Theodore of Tarsus, in the mid-seventh century. Or they could have been the wives of canons, linked with virgins and nuns in the *Penitential* by reason of their sexual abstinence. Their duties also remain a mystery but Theodore of Tarsus restricted women's liturgical activity to reading the lessons and ministering to the *confessio* of the holy altar.[61] His stated purpose was to bar their infringement on functions reserved for ordained men.

What seems to be clear in all of this is that a situation had developed in the English church that stirred the sexual anxieties of the male clergy. Neither the single-sex continuum of the third gender nor the alterity inherent in marriage had sufficed to maintain their liturgical monopoly. This difficulty was probably aggravated by the growing dominance of monasticism with its tendency to erase gender distinctions over the clergy. Gregory I, at the beginning of the seventh century, and Bede, at the end, expressed their concerns with ritual purity, citing the prophet Isaiah that holy vessels must be kept clean for the lord's service. Literally, this meant those cloths, dishes and cups routinely washed by the women attached to the church. Bede warned against profaning them with common usage. Theodore of Tarsus specifically prohibited women from handling altar vessels and offerings and from standing among the priests.[62] The Archbishop went so far as to prohibit menstruating women and women after childbirth from entering church or receiving the sacraments.[63] The link thus established from Leviticus, between female bodily functions and impurity, justified the exclusion even of consecrated women from the altar.

It is hard to know how much influence these prescriptions had on actual practice in the English church. But some protest may have encouraged Bede to create the appearance of a preemptive strike by injecting a letter attributed to Gregory I into the early chapters of his history.[64] The letter argued that women's natural functions were part of God's creation and, therefore, the process of purging physiological impurity could not be considered a moral fault disqualifying women from the reception of the sacraments. However, menstruation did represent impurity, balanced by men's regular emissions of seed in response to nocturnal illusions. Following Cassian's analysis, Gregory (or Bede) took it for granted that no healthy man could repress his emissions altogether but he expected priests to minimize them through control of their appetites in general and particularly to control their impure thoughts prior to celebrating the sacraments. If they failed, however, they could repair the situation with a thorough cleansing. In effect, pollution was gendered along the familiar continuum of self-control. The passive involuntary character of menstruation enhanced the rigorous control men exercised over their own purgations.[65] The fault of a man who consented or provoked an emission was serious but reparable. A menstruating woman was blameless but she had no control over her courses.

Gregory I also provided a figurative reading of Isaiah in his *Pastoral Rule,* demanding purity in a prelate as a holy vessel in himself.[66] Similarly, Bede typed the priest as a vessel of the lord who risked pollution by using his consecrated mouth and hands in offensive ways.[67] Men were vessels for the grace of God which they poured out in the sacraments. Implicitly, as their opposite numbers, women became vessels containing impurity, not only their own noxious fluids which drained out monthly, but the impurities of men who did not practice monastic self-control. The sexual authority that secular priests exerted over their wives thus represented complex dangers that had to be confronted with the utmost care. Cassian urged his monks to purify themselves as vessels of the Holy Spirit by avoiding unregulated contact with women.[68] Whether or not they willed it so, women became the devil's instruments to break the discipline of men but also, when properly controlled, to regulate their purification.

Bede and his contemporaries injected a new erotic consciousness into the sensibility of the third gender.[69] In the eighth century, reformers resigned themselves to the thesis that the libidinous desires of men and the heedless fragility of women were insuperable barriers to syneisactic cooperation. Thus, Bede turned a cold eye upon the easy relations of the nuns of Coldingham with monks attached to their community and ascribed a destructive fire to the vengeance of God on their frivolous ways. His distaste points toward the strict segregation between monastic men and women that the late-eighth-century biographer of Saint Leoba projected backward on her home convent of Wimbourne.[70] Though it is unlikely that such strict cloistering was practiced when Leoba went out to join Boniface's mission to Germany, it was certainly the ideal for the Carolingian age to come. In the early eighth century, small communities dotted the landscape, often made up of members of a single family who had simply decided to convert their whole menage. Bede urged bishop Egbert of York to confiscate some of the "innumerable places . . . allowed the name of monasteries . . . where chastity was ignored by men devoted to loose living and fornication . . . and do not even abstain from virgins consecrated to God."[71] He hoped he would use the land to establish new bishoprics. This may have been the fate of Ely and Chester and others. Only a decade after Bede's death, England undertook a program of "reforms" that moved monks toward clericization. The Synod of Cloveshoe (747) assumed the centrality of the Eucharist in monastic spirituality and tied the purity of monks to their readiness to perform the sacrament.[72]

In the same period, the English missionary, Boniface, complained at length to Pope Zachariah on the conditions he found in the continental church. Zachariah responded by urging the newly anointed Frankish king, Pippin, to take action against bigamous and fornicating clergy, lay people usurping ecclesiastical offices and ministries and general lack of discipline.[73] Pippin responded by commissioning Boniface to undertake comprehensive reforms of the Frankish church in a series of councils.[74] Boniface attempted to restore the priestly hierarchy and to enforce the rules regulating conjugal restraint among married priests. Between 742 and 747, he took steps to impose the Benedictine Rule, with its provisions for stability and mild claustration, on all houses of both sexes.[75] In 789, Charlemagne, perhaps motivated by the same sentiments that informed Bede's letter to Egbert, ordered bishops to combine smaller houses into unified large congregations. These smaller houses were probably women's communities which in this period often became monkeries in the transition. Women and men were still treated as monastic equals but their tendency to group together against the sexually active laity and clergy was inhibited by the growing disbelief in their capacity for innocence.

Forced segregation began to replace voluntary compliance as warrant for the clergy's innocence. The Frankish church began to look at the communal tradition of Augustine and Hilary of Poitiers. In 754, Chrodegang of Metz, who succeeded Boniface as head of the Frankish episcopate, organized his cathedral clergy into chapters of canons.[76] This effort to secure a celibate, or at least segregated, clergy was even suggested for the parish level, but never applied there.[77] In Charlemagne's reign, the canonical rule was applied even to many venerable old monasteries like St Martin of Tours and St. Denis.[78] This early attempt at monasticizing the secular clergy segregated them, at least at night, from the lay people of their communities and, perhaps most importantly, from the *matricularii,* women, consecrated or otherwise, who filled so many of the cathedral spaces. It also would have effectively separated them from their wives.[79] Chrodegang's rule was paired with the rule for monks at the Council of Ver.[80] Charlemagne favored the canonical over the monastic rule, perhaps because its provision for private property reduced the expense of supporting the community. Nevertheless, the emperor issued numerous capitularies regulating monks in accordance with the Benedictine Rule.[81] He sent to Monte Cassino for a copy with which he intended to replace the diversity of rules in Frankland. He sponsored the early work of the reformer Benedict of Aniane, who produced a "reformed" interpretation of the Benedictine Rule, emphasizing stability and obedience, but depriving the communities of much of their original autonomy.

Benedict of Aniane did not emulate Boniface in his effort to submit women to the Benedictine Rule, which many nunneries already used in modified forms. The Synod of Aachen devised a capitulary of sixty-nine chapters for all monasteries to be instituted and respected by royal officials. The monastery of Cornelimunster was designated as a *schola monachorum:* two monks from every monastery would be sent there to be trained in the practice of the new rules. No similar training ground was suggested for women and only five out of fifty-three female institutions joined his reform.[82] Two works by Benedict of Aniane praising and defending the virtues of the Benedictine Rule were widely circulated among the monasteries. In his appendix, he attached a Concordance addressed to women, combining Athanasius's address to virgins and the Rule of Caesarius of Arles with Benedict, subtly underlining the point that the rules were not the same for both sexes.[83] Ninth-century hagiography strongly propagandized the Benedictine Rule as beyond the strength of all but the most exceptional women. Ardo, Benedict of Aniane's biographer, says he was familiar with all the virgins and widows in the vicinity of his first monastery and generous with alms for them.[84] But he did not try to organize them into a community.

The third gender had given men access to the array of Christian virtues previously characterized as feminine. Benedict of Aniane initiated a slow process of reintegrating the celibate chaste back into the original continuum, with women again reduced to their "natural" effeminacy. Given a much broader mandate by Louis the Pious, Benedict paired the rule with a comprehensive rule for canons at the Synod of Aachen in 816, imposing quasi-monastic principles of modified claustration, regular offices, common sleeping and meals and absolute obedience upon the cathedral clergy. In an even more comprehensive mode, he virtually invented a whole new order of women, the *sanctimoniales canonicae*.[85] Though this group must originally have been conceived as a community made up of the ill-defined women (including canons' wives) found around any cathedral, the rule was soon adopted by many of the older great autonomous women's monasteries in preference to the Benedictine Rule, though the reasons for the change remain mysterious.

The rule of Aachen made frequent mention of the frailer nature of women which required greater confinement and care. The implication is not that they are physically weaker but mentally. They must be watched with men because they might give themselves up to chatting and other light behavior. It refrains from the suggestion that the men might make advances but only that the women might not be strong. Similarly, they are in danger of such indecent behavior as dressing and talking vainly, especially when incited by their maids.[86] Thus, it seems, women do the tempting but are not particularly tempted themselves except by other women. Thus, they are controlled by external discipline in contrast to the men addressed by Cassian and others, who must contain their own minds.

The Carolingian process of separating male from female monastics was definitively reinforced by a clericizing of the male monasteries. Despite the Rule's emphatic distrust for monastic priests, the "reformers" tended to ordain as many monks as possible. Toward the end of the eighth century, the monks of Monte Cassino began to commemorate the dead daily with a Mass in preference to their traditional, nonsacramental, offices.[87] Monastic priests spent much of the day trying to satisfy the growing demand for private masses.[88] This downgraded the liturgical activity of women who had to employ male priests to say the masses commissioned in nunneries. Charlemagne stipulated that the benediction following compline, an act customarily performed by an abbess for her flock, be given by a priest.[89] The very presence of women in the places sacrosanct to men became a species of blasphemy. His biographer counts among Benedict of Aniane's miracles the rescue of married women, who entered an empty oratory used by monks following their flocks. The women knelt in the stalls usually occupied by the brothers and became imprisoned there by a supernatural power, tormented with jerks and twists until rescued by the monks sought out by their terrified husbands.[90] Despite repeated prohibitions by the emperors, councils and popes, women continued to play diverse liturgical roles even in cathedral churches through the tenth century.[91] But against this, the Cluniac network, which took up Aniane's work, tended to define purity by the absence of women and Cluny set the agenda for the hierarchy that emerged in the eleventh century.

By defining a womanless institutional space, chaste celibacy allowed men to enhance the feminine characteristics that gave them access to saintliness. Women are removed from the field of struggle, to rely passively on their bridegroom in castimony.[92] Men confronted the enemy, lust, embodied as a woman and driven from the field. In the end, the Christian gender system continued to rest on contradictory premises. It succeeded only in reproducing the single-gender system that worked so well socially as long as women were safely excluded from it. In the thirteenth century, Aquinas returned to the Aristotelian continuum to justify the exclusion of women from the clergy by reason of their subordination. But, concealed and cloistered, virile women remained potentially superior on the continuum or in command of their own virtues in a system of alterity. The syllogism was never resolved and its unsteady foundation continues to undermine the gender structures built upon it.

NOTES

1. Thomas Laqueur, *Making Sex: Body and Gender from the Greeks to Freud* (Cambridge.: Harvard University Press, 1990).

2. Plato, *The Republic,* ed. Lewis Campbell and Benjamin Jowett (New York: Garland, 1987), 3.B.5.

3. Aristotle, *Politics,* trans. H. Rackham (1932; reprint, London: Heinemann, 1967), 1.1260a.

4. This line of argument has been fully developed by Michel Foucault, *The Care of the Self, History of Sexuality,* vol. 3, trans. Robert Hurley (New York: Vintage Books, 1988). More recently, the same principles have been applied to the understanding of the body in the Pauline scriptures by Dale B. Martin, *The Corinthian Body* (New Haven: Yale University Press, 1995).

5. K.J. Dover (*Greek Homosexuality* [New York: Vintage Books, 1978]) first established the point. A more up-to-date gender analysis may be found in Jonathan Walters, "No More Than a Boy: The Shifting Construction of Masculinity from Ancient Greece to the Middle Ages," *Gender and History* 5 (1993): 20–33.

6. Xenophon, *Oeconomicus* 8.17–19, trans. Sarah Pomeroy (Oxford: Oxford University Press, 1994), 153.

7. Susan M. Treggiari, *Roman Marriage:* Justi Coniuges *From the Time of Cicero to the Time of Ulpian* (New York: Oxford University Press, 1991), 44 ff.

8. Keith R. Bradley, "Child Care at Rome: the Role of Men," in *Discovering the Roman Family: Studies in Roman Social History* (New York: Oxford University Press, 1990), 37–75.

9. Mathetes, "Letter to Diognetus," 5, in *AnteNicene Fathers,* vol. 1, ed. A. Cleveland Coxe (Grand Rapids, Mich.: Eerdmans, 1975), 26–27.

10. Gen. 3:16.

11. Foucault laid out the loss of masculine prerogatives that turned upper-class men toward bachelorhood on the one hand and more "companionate" marriages on the other, though he excluded the agency of women from the discourse on marriage that ensued.

12. In an article called "Gendering Virtue"[to be published in Sarah B. Pomeroy, ed., *Plutarch* (New York: Oxford University Press, 1998)] I have tried to underline the impact on women's increased presence in Roman society.

13. Justin Martyr, *The Second Apology for the Christians,* 2, in *Writings of Justin Martyr,* trans. Thomas B. Falls, The Fathers of the Church, 6 (New York: Christian Heritage, 1948), 120.

14. See Clement of Alexandria's plea that men emulate the peace-making instincts of women in preference to praising Amazons as equal in warlike virtues to men. *Stromata,* 4.8, in *AnteNicene Fathers,* vol. 2, ed. Alexander Roberts and James Donaldson (Grand Rapids, Mich.: Eerdmans, 1975), 419–20.

15. Kenneth Holum, *Theodosian Empresses: Women and Imperial Dominion in Late Antiquity* (Berkeley: University of California Press, 1982) saw this ceremonially acted out in the imperial rituals of the Theodosian house. I have extended the idea into the early Middle Ages in "Imitatio Helenae: Sainthood as an Attribute of Queenship in the Early Middle Ages," in *Saints: Studies in Hagiography,* ed. Sandro Sticca (Binghamton: CMERS/SUNY, 1996), 51–80.

16. I have expanded this thesis in "Muffled Voices: The Lives of Consecrated Women in the Fourth Century," in John A. Nichols and Lillian T. Shank, eds., *Distant Echoes: Medieval Religious Women I* (Kalamazoo, Mich.: Cistercian Publications, 1984), 11–29.

17. Jerome, *Against Jovinian,* in *Nicene and Post-Nicene Fathers,* 6, ed. and trans. W.H. Fremantle (Grand Rapids, Mich.: Eerdmans, 1979), 346; and Jerome, *Against Helvidius on the Perpetual Virginity of the Blessed Mary,* Ibid., 334.

18. Palladius, *Lausiac History,* 45, ed. and trans., Robert T. Meyer, Ancient Christian Writers, 34 (Westminster, Md.: Newman Press, 1965), 122.

19. For multiple examples, see Jo Ann McNamara, "Sexual Equality and the Cult of Virginity in Early Christian Thought," *Feminist Studies* 3 (1976): 145–58.

20. Methodius, *The Symposium: A Treatise on Chastity,* trans. Herbert Musurillo, Ancient Christian Writers, 27 (Westminster, Md.: Newman Press, 1958).

21. Gerontius, *The Life of Melania the Younger,* trans. Elizabeth A. Clark (Lewiston, N.Y.: Edwin Mellen, 1988).

22. Thus, Peter Brown sees early monasticism as virtually a womanless movement, *The Body and Society: Men, Women and Sexual Renunciation in Early Christianity* (New York: Columbia University Press, 1988).

23. Vern L. Bullough has surveyed the history of female saints disguised as monks in "Transvestism in the Middle Ages," in Vern L. Bullough and James A. Brundage, *Sexual Practices and the Medieval Church* (Buffalo, N.Y.: Prometheus Books, 1982), 43–54. The biographies of Eugenia, Pelagia and others are available in *Patrologia Latina, 73.*

24. See my article "Chastity as a Third Gender in the Work of Gregory of Tours," forthcoming in Kathleen Mitchell and Ian Wood, eds., *The World of Gregory of Tours* (Leyden: Brill).

25. This is typical of Antony and Pachomius. See David Brakke on Athanasius's treatment of both, *Athanasius and the Politics of Asceticism* (Oxford: Clarendon Press, 1995).

26. *The Rule of Saint Benedict,* c. 60, ed. A.C. Meisel and M.L. de Mastro (New York: Image Books, 1975).

27. John Chrysostom, *Sur le sacerdoce,* 6.8, trans. Marie Malingray, *Sources Chrétiennes,* 272 (Paris: Cerf, 1980), 331–35. For commentary, see J.N.D. Kelly, *Golden Mouth: The Story of John Chrysostom, Ascetic, Preacher, Bishop* (Ithaca, N.Y.: Cornell University Press, 1995), 84.

28. Sulpicius Severus, *Dialogue 1, Postumianus* 2.4, in F.R. Hoare, *The Western Fathers* (New York: Harper Torchbooks, 1965), 106.

20   *Conflicted Identities and Multiple Masculinities*

29. Adolf Kalsbach, *Die altkirchliche Einrichtung der Diakonissen bis zu ihrem Erlöschen* (Freiburg i. Br.: Romische Quartalschrift für christl. Altertumskunde und Kirchengeschichte 22, 1926), 27.

30. J. Siegwart, *Die Chorherren und Chorfrauen-Gemeinschaften in der deutschsprachigen Schweiz vom 6 Jahrhundert bis 1160; mit einem Überblich über die deutsche Kanonikerreform des 10 und 11 Jh.* (Freiburg: Studia Friburgensia, 1962), 47.

31. Council of Tours, 567, c. 14, *Concilia Galliae,* ed. C. de Clercq, *Corpus Christianorum series latinorum,* 148A, (Turnholt: Brepols, n.d.), 191.

32. See especially John Chrysostom, *Les Cohabitations suspect; Comment observer la virginité,* ed. and trans. Jean Dumortier, Nouvelle Collection de Textes et Documents (Paris: Société Guillaume Budé, 1955).

33. Laqueur, *Making Sex,* 125–26: stories and didactic pieces warning of spontaneous sex changes, particularly concerning athletic and heated women who sprout penises "by rupturing the ligaments" which enclose genitalia.

34. Gregory I, *Dialogues,* 4.14, trans. O.J. Zimmerman (New York: Fathers of the Church, 1959), 205–06.

35. Gregory of Tours, *Liber Vitae Patrum,* 6.2, ed. Bruno Krusch, *Monumenta Germaniae Historica Scriptorum Rerum Merovingicarum* 1, 2.

36. Chrysostom, *Les Cohabitations suspect,* 11.

37. Sulpicius Severus, *Postumianus,* 2.11.

38. Gregory I, *Pastoral Rule,* 3.27, ed. Floribert Rommeland, trans. Charles Morel, *Sources Chrétiennes,* 382 (Paris: Cerf, 1992), 447–57. He rejected the idea of forcing married men to give up their conjugal rights, though, somewhat inconsistently, he advised that unordained men who could not do so voluntarily should not be advanced to the priesthood.

39. *Dialogues,* 4.11.

40. *Letter 55,* in *Letters of Basil of Caesaria,* trans. Agnes C. Way, Fathers of the Church, 13 (New York: Christian Heritage,1951), 144–45.

41. Louis Gougaud, *Christianity in Celtic Lands* (Dublin: Four Courts Press, 1992), 88.

42. *Dialogues,* 3, 7.

43. *Dialogues,* Book 2.

44. I surveyed this question in "Chaste Marriage and Clerical Celibacy," in Bullough and Brundage, *Sexual Practices and the Medieval Church,* 22–33. It has been far more thoroughly treated in Dyan Elliott, *Spiritual Marriage: Sexual Abstinence in Medieval Wedlock* (Princeton: Princeton University Press, 1993).

45. John E. Lynch, "Marriage and Celibacy of the Clergy: the Discipline of the Western Church: a Historico-Canonical Synopsis," *The Jurist* 32 (1972): 20.

46. Brakke, *Athanasius,* 184,

47. Canon 33, in Samuel Laeuchli, *Power and Sexuality: the Emergence of Canon Law at the Synod of Elvira* (Philadelphia: Temple University Press, 1972), 130.

48. Bede, *A History of the English Church and People,* 1.27, trans. Leo Sherley-Price (Baltimore: Penguin Books, 1968), 79–81.

49. *"Litterae trium episcoporum Gallicorum anno 511 scriptae,"* in *Monumenta de viduis, diaconnissis, virginibusque tractantia,* ed. J. Mayer (Bonne: Florilegium patristicum, 1938), 46–47.

50. The biography of St. Genovefa implies that the consecration of the oil itself was reserved for priests but when the saint ran out and a priest was not available, God obligingly increased her supply. *Life of Genovefa* 51, in *Sainted Women of the Dark Ages,* ed. and trans. Jo Ann McNamara and John E. Halborg, with Gordon Whatley (Durham, N.C.: Duke University Press, 1992), 35–36.

51. Evidence for these habits among the European peoples is widespread. For example, see Carol J. Clover, "Regardless of Sex: Men, Women and Power in Early Northern Europe," *Speculum* 68 (1993): 364–88 for Scandinavia; Karl Leyser, "The German Aristocracy from the Ninth to the Early Twelfth Century: a Historical and Cultural Sketch," *Past and Present* 41 (1968): 25–53 for Germany.

52. McNamara, "Chastity as a Third Gender."

53. For citations of numerous councils using the feminized forms of clerical address, see Lynch, "Marriage and Celibacy," 30 ff. Considering the church's prohibition on divorce, it is probable that ordination to the diaconate was not uncommonly used as a device for securing a practical annulment of some marriages and may explain the case of Queen Radegund. Fortunatus, *Life of Radegund* 12, in McNamara and Halborg, *Sainted Women,* 94.

54. Suzanne F. Wemple (*Women in Frankish Society* [Philadelphia: University of Pennsylvania Press, 1981], 138) is the only scholar to date to have combed through these conciliar collections for these glimpses of women's liturgical activities. In 394, bishops of the Council of Nimes denied that there were women serving as deaconesses in their churches but in 441 the council of Orange renewed the prohibition against their ordination or service in priestly functions demanding that women already so ordained must bow their heads for priestly benediction like ordinary people. Epaon (517) and Orléans (533) prohibited the consecration of widows "called deaconesses," restricting them to a benediction as penitents. Orleans (533) both punished married deaconesses who resumed the enjoyment of "their foul union," and resolved "because of the fragility of the female sex," to refuse the diaconate to any other women.

55. See particularly the lives of Burgundofara, Sadalberga and Austreberta in McNamara and Halborg, *Sainted Women.*

56. See the evidence collected by Joan Morris, *Against Nature and God: the History of Women with Clerical Ordination and the Jurisdiction of Bishops* (London: Mowbrays, 1973).

57. The shadowy history of the Augustinian tradition is traced by Adolar Zumkeller, *Augustine's Rule* (Villanova, Pa.: Augustinian Press, 1987).

58. I have discussed this mystery in more detail in *Sisters in Arms: Catholic Nuns Through Two Millennia* (Cambridge: Harvard University Press, 1996).

59. c. 7, *Monumenta Germaniae Historica, Concilia,* vol. 1, ed. F. Maasen (Hannover: Hahnoche Buchhandlung, 1984).

60. John T. McNeill and Helena M. Gamer (*Medieval Handbooks of Penance: a Translation of the Principal* Libri Poenitentiales *and Selections from Related Documents* [New York: Columbia University Press, 1938], 223) believe the author of this penitential and that of Egbert are the same. The preface mentions canonesses in a group with virgins, nuns and persons of other degrees within the church.

61. Ibid, Theodore's *Penitential,* 2.7. The *confessio* was the place relics were normally deposited.

62. Ibid., *Penitential,* c. 7.

63. Ibid, *Penitential,* c. 14.17 and 18.

64. *Ecclesiastical History* I.27. No copy of the letter has been found in Rome and no supportive references in other literature confirm Bede's attribution.

65. Cassian, *Institutions Cénobitiques,* 6.7, and 20, ed. and trans., J.C. Guy, *Sources Chrétiennes,* 109 (Paris: Cerf, 1965). Cassian believed that a determined monk could limit the inescapable pollution of nocturnal dreams to every three months or so to drain off noxious fluids.

66. *Pastoral Rule,* 2.2.

67. *Letter to Egbert,* in *Bede,* ed. James Campbell (New York: Washington Square Press, 1968), 317- 31.

68. *Institutions,* 6.15. This vessel image is also found for women repeatedly.

69. This is Stephanie Hollis's general thesis. In *Anglo-Saxon Women and the Church: Sharing a Common Fate* (Woodbridge, Eng.: Boydell, 1992), she traces the development of this deleterious alterity in the major pieces of seventh- and eighth-century Anglo Saxon literature. In particular, on 121, Bede is her villain.

70. Rupert of Fulda, *Life of Leoba,* in *The Anglo-Saxon Missionaries in Germany,* by C.H. Talbot (New York: Sheed and Ward, 1954), 205–26.

71. *Letter to Egbert,* 323–25.

72. c. 22, A.W. Haddan, and William Stubbs, *Councils and Synods with Other Documents Relating to the English Church to 870* (Oxford: Oxford University Press, 1964).

73. The entire correspondence is reproduced in *Letters of Saint Boniface,* ed. and trans. E. Emerton (New York: Columbia University Press, 1940).

74. The record of these reforms is published in *Monumenta Germaniae Historica, Leges,* vol. 2, pt. 1, ed. A Boretius and V. Krause (Hannover, 1890).

75. Wemple (*Women in Frankish Society,* 166) surveys the impact of this work on women.

76. Eugen Ewig, "The Papacy's Alienation," in *The Church in the Age of Feudalism,* by Friedrich Kempf et al. (New York: Crossroads Press, 1982), 19.

77. Ibid. cites "Capit. 23, 23: Presbyteri cleros quos secum habent solliciter praevideant ut canonice vivant," which he interprets as an extension to rural priests and their assistants. N. 23, this follows a provision imposing the canonical life on canons. Capit. 120, provides for scholars living in the priest's house. Capit. 22.59, and 19.5, provide for degradation if the priest fails to live canonically.

78. *Concilia aevi karolini, Monumenta Germaniae Historica, Concilia,* vol. 2, ed. A. Wermgenhoff (Hannover, 1893–1906), 685 ff.

79. Siegwart, *Die Chorherren,* 46.

80. E. Amann and A. Dumas, "L'église au pouvoir des laïques (888–1057)" in *Histoire de l'église* 7, eds. A. Fliche and V. Martin (Paris: Bloud and Gay, 1948), 83.

81. Ibid., 259.

82. Wemple (*Women in Frankish Society,* 167–68) notes a subsequent aggressive attack on nuns wearing men's attire, possibly to prevent their repeating the histories of the transvestite saints which were still in popular circulation.

83. *Patrologia Latina,* 103, contains the rules Benedict of Aniane used to compile the *Codex Regularum.* Part 1 concerns the eastern fathers; part 2, the western fathers; part 3, women.

84. Ardo, *Life of Benedict of Aniane* 19, in *Soldiers of Christ,* ed. Thomas F.X. Noble and Thomas Head (University Park: Pennsylvania State Press, 1995), 232.

85. It is generally agreed that canonesses did not exist before this time as a regulated group, *Consuetudines monasticas,* ed. D.B. Albers (Monte Casino, 1900–1912), 2, 79. E. Lesne, "Les ordonnances de Louis le Pieux," *Revue d'histoire de l'église de France* 6 (1920): 161–75; 321–38; 449–93, also discusses the opposition.

86. Aachen, c.21, the maids are blamed for inciting the nuns. The same for Cloveshoe, c. 20.

87. Frederick S. Paxton, *The Creation of a Ritual Process in Early Medieval Europe* (Ithaca, N.Y.: Cornell University Press, 1990), 134.

88. *Monumenta Germaniae Historica, Capitularia,* 1.347–48. Berlière, U., *L'ascèse benedictine des origines au XIIe siècle* (Maredsous: Editions de Mared-

sous, 1927), 156. The demand accompanied the process of excluding laity from participation in the Mass and transforming it into a private ceremony carried on by the priest, Josef Jungmann, *The Mass of the Roman Rite: Its Origins and Development (Missarum Sollemnia),* trans. F.A. Brunner, 2 vols. (New York: Benziger, 1951–1955), 305–306.

89. *Admonitio generalis,* 76 (*Monumenta Germaniae Historica, Capitularia,* vol., 1.60, 789) ordered abbesses to cease blessing male members of their congregations by laying hands and making the sign of the cross on their heads; they could not veil nuns. Nuns were forbidden to approach the altar, touch the sacred vessels, and help distribute the Eucharist. Clerics were to remove altar linens and hand them over to women at the rail for washing. Women should not go near the altar, 44. Communion should not be distributed.

90. Ardo, *Life of Benedict of Aniane,* 26.

91. Episcopal letter to Louis, 829. Women not to ring bells, light candles, Conc. 2, 210; capit. 1, 364. Wemple, (*Women in Frankish Society,* 146) cites Bishop Hatto of Reichenau's portrait of the fourth-century Verena who carried the wine to the altar daily. Ca. 861, Bishop Prudentius of Troyes mourned the death of Maura, a local virgin living in her father's house, who made vestments and linens, kept the draperies clean and maintained the lamps in the church. In 868 the Council of Worms even revived the female diaconate for women over forty. Atto of Vercelli (ca 940) noted that deaconesses had once baptized and held ecclesiastical office though in his own time it was an abbatial office, apparently held by lay abbesses or resident patrons.

92. The word was apparently a neologism which Benedict or one of his scribes inserted into the Rule for Canonesses emphasizing the alignment of religious women with secular married women rather than with either the secular or regular clergy.

Secular and Spiritual Fatherhood in the Eleventh Century

MEGAN McLAUGHLIN

Around the year 1060, the Italian reformer Peter Damian wrote a letter to Duke Godfrey of Tuscany, in which he recounted a story he had heard about one of Godfrey's predecessors. According to Peter, Margrave Obertus of Tuscany had angered the emperor and been forced into exile, leaving his wife behind. A number of years later, he returned to find that she had borne a son in his absence. Obertus asserted that the child was not his and accused his wife of infidelity; she denied the charge, and eventually the case was settled through an ordeal. A crowd of bishops, abbots and priests assembled in a great hall, while Obertus sat among them without anything to distinguish him from the other men present. As the clerics wept and prayed, the boy was set loose in the hall, with the understanding that if he went up to Obertus—whom he had never seen— he would clear his mother of the charge of infidelity. Needless to say, this is precisely what happened:

> the boy promptly went up to him, and took hold of him as if attracted by one whom he knew very well. It was thus that he freed his mother of suspicion as he went to his father at the inspiration of God. And so, a mother's shame was swept away, a son was granted to his father, and the unaccustomed love of both parents for one another was restored by their child. All who were present, overwhelmed by such a miracle, cel-ebrated with the joy they had hoped for, and happily gave proper thanks to God whose work it was.[1]

Did this poignant little story with its ultimate happy ending have a special appeal for the man who reported it? Peter Damian's own childhood was not a happy one. Both his parents died when he was still a baby, and he was left in the care of one of his brothers and his wife, who treated the little boy badly.[2] Lester Little has argued that this early trauma left Peter searching—like Obertus's son—for a father to call his own. Little goes on to suggest that he eventually found his surrogate father in Romuald, the saintly hermit who sparked and shaped the monastic revival in eleventh-century Italy.[3] Peter, of course, became a hermit himself. His earliest surviving work is a life of Romuald, and the figure of the hermit recurs at frequent intervals in his writings. But Romuald may not have completely satisfied Peter's yearning for the father he never knew. Throughout his career, first as a hermit, then as a monastic reformer, and eventually as a cardinal bishop and campaigner against the problems of simony and nicolaitism in the secular church, Peter continued to write about fathers and fatherhood. His letters and sermons thus provide a treasure trove of paternal references, drawn partially from the Bible, but derived also from his personal experiences as a man living in the eleventh century.

How are we to account for Peter's preoccupation with figures like Obertus and Romuald? Is Little correct in thinking that the reformer's personal history created a kind of "father fixation," which simply played itself out in his writings? Or did broader changes in society and culture create an audience which found his references to paternity especially compelling and which may have encouraged him to return repeatedly to the theme of fatherhood? Over twenty-five years ago, Jo Ann McNamara and Suzanne Wemple first argued that the eleventh and early twelfth centuries were a period of restructuring in the western European gender system.[4] They suggested that this restructuring was caused by the interaction of various social and economic changes, and was precipitated by the Gregorian reform movement, with its urgent call for clerical celibacy. In a recent article, McNamara has developed this thesis further, arguing that the process of restructuring began with a "masculine identity crisis," which she dubs the *Herrenfrage*.[5] As celibate men came to monopolize many of the most important positions, not only in the Church, but also in the educational establishment (and, one might add, in government bureaucracies), the very nature of masculinity came increasingly into question. Could celibates, deprived of "objects for the sexual demonstrations that proved their right to call themselves men,"[6] really be considered men at all? And if such celibates claimed authority over non-celibate men, as the clergy increasingly did over the laity in this period, what did that say about the masculinity of the latter? The central question for McNamara, however, is what effects this crisis of manhood had upon women, and especially upon celibate women, many of whom had enjoyed relative freedom from male domination during the early Middle Ages. The *Herrenfrage,* in her view, gave rise to the *Frauenfrage,* that crisis of male control over women which many authors have observed beginning in the twelfth century.[7] Thus she argues that gender anxiety contributed to men's growing misogyny and even to outright violence against those women who deviated in any way from the pattern of female submission being newly reinscribed after 1150.

One may disagree with the exact formulation or with various details of McNamara's thesis, but the notion that there was a "crisis of masculinity" during the period from 1050 to 1150 is certainly a plausible one. It seems obvious that many eleventh-century clerics must have struggled to create and maintain their identity as males, given the new expectations being imposed on them in this period. The most basic problem was this: if clerics obeyed the laws of the church—as a growing number of them chose or were compelled to do in this period—they would be expected to eschew precisely those practices (violence, the pursuit of wealth and—above all—sex) that eleventh-century society defined as "manly." Certainly, as celibates, they should have been cut off from the culturally powerful and emotionally very resonant masculine role of father. But paradoxically, many medieval clerics did still aspire to fatherhood. While they obviously could not have biological children so long as they maintained their celibate status, they were able to construct an identity for themselves as spiritual fathers, as men who begot and raised "children in the faith." In this essay, I will examine one such cleric's efforts to create a paternal identity for himself and for other men in the same situation. I have chosen to focus on Peter Damian because of the great wealth of material to be found in his letters and sermons.[8] The question remains, however: can Peter's depiction of fatherhood be considered evidence for a crisis of masculinity in the eleventh and early twelfth centuries, or does it simply reflect the peculiarities of his psychological makeup, rooted in his childhood trauma? Only a more detailed study of other writers from the period will answer this in satisfactory way.[9] What we can say at this point is that Peter's portrayal of paternity—both secular and spiritual—as complex, ambiguous and, ultimately, unstable is at least consistent with what one might expect to find in a period of gender crisis.

Fundamental questions received widely varied answers in Peter's writings. For example: was fatherhood really a desirable state for a

Christian, or was it better to avoid having children at all? In a letter on chastity, Peter described a common motivation for having children:

> Many of those who are in bondage to the delights of carnal pleasure long to perpetuate their own memory through their posterity. This they pursue through every waking moment, since they are sure that they will not be wholly dead in this world if they continue their name in a fruitfully surviving progeny.[10]

However, in Peter's view, chastity was a much better means to this end:

> But much more eminently and happily do celibates achieve this objective toward which those who bear children strive with such burning ambition; and that, because they are always remembered by him who because of the condition of eternity is not restrained by the laws of time. On the word of God, a name better than that of sons or daughters is promised to eunuchs [Isa. 56: 4–5], because without any threat of oblivion they deserve to have their name remembered forever, something that generations of children succeed in achieving only for a brief time.[11]

The key phrase from Isaiah, "a name better than that of sons or daughters," was based, of course, on the assumption that having children was good. Nevertheless, in this passage Peter suggested that not having them was even better, and this is the assumption behind many of his other writings on chastity.

Certainly, members of the secular clergy were to follow the dictates of church law and avoid having children. Otherwise they would be subject to the wrath of God, as is clear from Peter's account of a tenth-century bishop, Alberic of Marsica. Alberic swore to the Emperor Otto that he was celibate, even though he was in fact living with a concubine. When Otto visited Marsica, Alberic disguised his lover as a nun, but took her back into his bed after the emperor had left. Together they had a son, whom Alberic eventually made bishop of Marsica in his place. The sinful father continued to yearn for high office and schemed to put out the eyes of the abbot of Monte Cassino and become abbot in his stead. But on the very day that the rightful abbot lost his sight at the hands of Alberic's henchmen, Alberic himself suddenly died. His son, that "apostle of Anti-Christ," also suffered constant troubles and eventually died at the hands of his own men. "It is obviously right," Peter noted, "that such a death should happen to them who panted after the highest ecclesiastical dignity against the will of God, and it is likewise right that the sweet life which they imagined in their minds should lead to bitterness, and prosperity which falsely smiled upon them should lead to calamity."[12] Biological fatherhood and care for the prosperity of one's children in the flesh were not appropriate for bishops and other secular clerics.

However, in a letter to Bishop Cunibert of Turin written in 1064, Peter took the apparently paradoxical position that a celibate bishop should also be fertile. Urging Cunibert to prevent the clergy of his diocese from marrying, Peter warned the bishop that otherwise his own chastity would be sterile. Citing Lev. 22: 24 ("You shall not offer to the Lord any animal whose testicles are crushed or bruised or cut or missing"), he continues:

> But if God so hates sterility in the brute beasts which are offered to him through the ministry of priests, how much more does he disdain it in the priests who offer sacrifice to him? Surely just as offspring in the flesh are required of [the beasts], so priests should propagate holiness in others. Only then will your chastity be approved in the divine gaze, if it is extended by propagation among your clerics.[13]

This is the position that Peter takes in most of his letters—urging members of the clergy to avoid "sterility" and pursue spiritual fatherhood—while of course avoiding secular paternity through chastity.[14]

But how was an eleventh-century cleric to go about this? From a biological point of view, becoming a father is a fairly straightforward business. However, we should bear in mind that from society's perspective, paternity was not always so clear. The slow progress of pregnancy, which so clearly identified a mother by her swelling uterus, might actually occlude the identity of the father in the eyes of the world. Especially if there had been a separation between the parents around the time of conception, questions might be raised about who had fathered a child—as in the story of Obertus. Sometimes only a miracle could settle a question of disputed paternity. Oddly enough, spiritual fatherhood could—at least in this regard—be much less ambiguous, since it often depended not on the mysterious processes occurring within the female body, but on more open activities. For Peter, it was clear that the public celebration of the sacraments by priest or bishop turned the celebrant into a spiritual father. The role was most closely associated with the sacrament of baptism. As Peter, writing on behalf of Pope Nicholas II, pointed out to his fellow bishops:

since you are the husband, the spouse of your church, symbolized by
the ring of your betrothal and the staff of your mandate, all who are
reborn in her by the sacrament of baptism must be ascribed to you as
your children.[15]

Not only those whom a bishop had personally baptized became his spiritual children, but all those baptized within his diocese. Peter also associated fatherhood with the sacrament of penance. In another letter he
wrote:

it is the common expression to call [someone who has confessed to and
received penance from a priest] a son by penance just as we also say
son by baptism . . . he is properly called a son who receives penance,
and a father who administers it.[16]

A man who performed the sacraments and held ecclesiastical office
might be able to "bear children" in the faith, yet if he led an immoral life
those children would be illegitimate. The true "wife" of a bishop, according to Peter, was virtue:

Therefore, a bishop must beware of marrying a soiled or meretricious
wife, but should always display the integrity of a chaste and pure manner of living. From such a life he will be able to beget legitimate children, not bastards, as he endeavors, with God's grace, to produce the
noble fruit of good works. And so it behooves a bishop to marry a
priestly wife from whom he might procreate offspring who will reflect
their father's character. Thus it was properly stated in Scripture, "He
shall not mingle the descendants of his father's kin with the lowborn of
his tribe" [Lev. 21:15]. Now a bishop joins the descendants of his
father's kin with the lowborn of his tribe, when by his mean way of life
he hardly differs from the crowd . . . But that a bishop might beget offspring worthy of its noble lineage, he must not abandon the path trod-
den by his forefathers, namely that of holy bishops who preceded him,
lest by his ignoble life he dishonor that outstanding ancestry and lose
the privilege of the episcopal office in which he had functioned
unworthily.[17]

This passage is somewhat obscure, but the implication seems clear
enough: an immoral bishop will people his diocese with immoral clerics
and layfolks. Such "children" will be bastards who (as Peter points out in

another letter) will bring dishonor to the good name and nobility of the spiritual family of which the bishop is the head.[18] In the eleventh century, then, spiritual "fertility" was linked with pastoral care and ecclesiastical office, but these should be coupled with purity of life to ensure "high quality" offspring.

Among Peter's beloved monks and hermits, spiritual procreation did not always require sacramental function or ecclesiastical office, but could simply be linked with personal holiness, which made a man spiritually potent and thus able to beget sons in the faith. Officially recognized saints were often described as fathers by those who imitated their virtues, but the members of a religious community could also serve as father figures to their fellow monks or hermits. In several letters, Peter describes an exchange he had with one of his own teachers, the holy hermit Dominic Loricatus. Among Dominic's many spiritual gifts was that of weeping over his sins—a gift which Peter greatly desired for himself.[19] He reports:

> I would often reproach him [that is, Dominic] over the lack of tears caused by my dryness, saying, "Alas, my father, these tears of yours do not bear fruit, since they cannot beget tears in others when they ask. For I would surely wish that since you are a father to me, your tears should also beget my tears."[20]

In this passage, the ambiguity of paternal identity is particularly evident. Note Peter's frustration over this instance of "sterility" in a man he had chosen as a spiritual father. Apparently, he had hoped that the powerful, if intangible, bond between them would produce direct spiritual "fruit." (One might also note his ambivalent attitude toward Dominic, whom he appears to blame for his own spiritual failings even as he expresses affection and respect for him.)

Once entered into—either through the celebration of the sacraments or through holy example—the role of spiritual father entailed many of the same obligations as that of a secular father. Most obviously, the paterfamilias was expected to discipline his offspring, and might be subject to public criticism if he failed to do so. Peter noted examples from his own day of secular fathers who demanded and received obedience from their sons; spiritual fathers were expected to do the same. Writing to his secretary, Ariprandus, about the importance of discipline within the monastic community, Peter contrasts the behavior of true fathers with that of stepfathers, who spoil the children entrusted to them:

> Now stepfathers spoil their stepchildren, but fathers very often use hard blows on their own offspring. The former spare those whom they hate, but the latter instruct and punish those whom they love. Consequently it is written, "A father who spares the rod hates his own son, but one who loves him keeps him in order." [Prov. 13:24][21]

Yet, if stern discipline was the most salient obligation of the secular or spiritual father, it could be carried too far. Peter considered excessive cruelty inappropriate for a true father. Writing to Cadalus of Parma, the antipope during the years 1061–64, Peter accuses him of causing the deaths of many people in Rome: ". . . you claim the Romans as your children; but you have decided to put them to the sword, not like a father, but rather like a cruel stepfather."[22] Step-fathers represented the hatred that led to both extremes, whether of neglect or of cruelty. Loving fathers corrected their children appropriately.

How was discipline to be maintained? In the case of both secular and spiritual fathers, physical punishment in the form of beatings or imprisonment might be employed. However, there were also legal sanctions to back up a father's authority over his children. When a monk from another monastery criticized the disciplinary practice of flagellation and refused to accept his abbot's orders, Peter Damian reminded him of the penalties for disobedience:

> just as an actual father may disinherit a rebellious son, so may a spiritual father in a display of strict justice expel a disobedient subject from the Church. Hence the Apostle says, "We had earthly fathers and paid due respect to them; should we not submit even more readily to our spiritual father, and so attain life?" [Heb. 12: 9]. And just a bit before that he said, "Can anyone be a son, who is not disciplined by his father? But if you escape the discipline in which all sons share, you must be bastards and no true sons." [Heb. 12:7–8] . . . Wherefore, dear brother, put a stop to vilifying and abusing your father.[23]

Other references in Peter's writings suggest that disinheritance (or at least the threat of disinheritance) really was used by eleventh-century fathers to encourage obedience in their children.[24] Excommunication was the logical equivalent for clerics who eschewed private property. Just as earthly fathers could prevent their disobedient children from enjoying their share in the family property, so spiritual fathers had the power to keep rebellious sons from their inheritance in heaven.

Sometimes, though, fathers actually had to abdicate their position of authority in order to assert it. For only by becoming obedient themselves could they inculcate the virtue of obedience in their offspring. In a particularly rich and beautiful passage from a sermon on St. Apollinaris of Ravenna, Peter presented a series of father figures, linked by this theme of obedience in the face of dreadful demands.[25] At the center of the passage is the figure of Abraham, called by God to sacrifice his only son Isaac : "Take your son, Isaac, whom you love, and offer him to me as a burnt offering" [Gen. 22: 2]. Peter explains that "it would have sufficed the Lord to have said 'Take your son,' but He added, 'Isaac, whom you love,' so that by drawing back to the father's ears his love for his son, it would be proven how much the love of God dwelled in his heart." Peter's reading lays bare the logic of the scripture: Abraham's feelings as father must be lacerated if he is to prove his love of God.[26] By choosing the path of obedience in the face of such torment, Abraham the father actually becomes the son who is sacrificed. As Peter points out, he "immolates himself on the altar of his heart."

But just as God's words to Abraham make clear exactly what obedience will entail, so do St. Peter's words to Apollinaris, when he sends him off to martyrdom in Ravenna. Apollinaris is plainly told that torture and certain death await him, but he makes no excuses—his obedience is like Abraham's in its exquisite anguish. For Peter Damian, this pattern of pain reveals the beauty of the divine plan:

> For we who learned the first fault of disobedience, badly instructed by Adam, were instructed in the first virtue of obedience by this blessed martyr. And just as [Adam] taught his carnal offspring the first disobedience (among other germs of vice), not by speaking, but by lying, so [Apollinaris] first instructed his spiritual sons in obedience (among other examples of virtue) not by speaking, but by acting.[27]

In Abraham and Apollinaris, the stern and commanding figure of the father as disciplinarian dissolves into something simultaneously softer and stronger.

Peter recognized that fatherly love could lead to tenderness as well as sternness. While affection and nurturing love were often associated with the role of mother in his writings, as in those of other monastic thinkers, they could also be seen as aspects of paternity.[28] The image of God's love for the souls of the faithful, for example, was modeled after the physical love of biological fathers. Thus, when a noble couple lost their infant son, Peter comforted them with the thought that God was now the baby's parent: "He has gathered him into his own arms, kissed him like a loving father, and as his own son took him with joy into his own eternally restful bedchamber."[29]The expectation that fathers would openly display their love for their offspring, derived from the example of secular fathers and of God the Father, applied to spiritual ones as well. In the letter about the importance of monastic discipline mentioned earlier, Peter describes his secretary, Ariprandus, as his "dear son," and sends him "the fondness of paternal love."[30] In another letter, he thanks Archbishop Henry of Ravenna for his "kindly and paternal affection."[31] Recommending a certain "brother Henry" to Bishop Ubertus of Sarsina, Peter urged Ubertus to "keep him with you as your dearest son. Show him the love of a tender father, since you will never regret the public praise he will always bestow on you wherever he may go."[32]

Sometimes, though, fathers failed in their disciplinary obligations because of their excessive or wrongly directed love for their children. The biblical father most often mentioned in Peter's letters is Eli, who suffered a terrible fate because he "honored his sons above the Lord" [1 Sam. 2–4]. Eli appears in at least sixteen letters, written over a period of some twenty years.[33] No other father from the Bible (with the exception of God himself) appears nearly as often. Peter clearly associated Eli's role as high priest with that of bishop in his own time. Most of his references to Eli come in letters composed after 1057, when Peter was made cardinal bishop of Ostia; most of them also occur in letters addressed to bishops or in which episcopal obligations are discussed. Sometimes, indeed, the association is explicit: writing to Pope Nicholas II in 1061, for example, Peter compared the high priest's two sons with incontinent bishops, and Eli himself with their metropolitan.[34] Presumably, then, we can read in Peter's preoccupation with the figure of Eli his own anxieties about the episcopal/paternal role—in particular, the difficulties of balancing love with authority, honor for one's spiritual sons with honor for God. For what is interesting about the story of Eli is that he did not simply ignore his sons' sacrilegious behavior. His fault was that he remonstrated mildly with them, instead of firmly correcting their sin. Yet, God's anger for this fault was great and his retribution severe. The Philistines slew the wicked sons in battle and seized the Ark of the Covenant from the Israelites. And when Eli heard the news of this disaster, he fell from his seat, broke his neck and died. There was a lesson here for bishops who failed to correct the clergy under their jurisdiction— especially for bishops who treated incontinent priests too mildly. "What did it profit Eli," Peter wrote in 1064 to Bishop Cunibert of Turin, "that he himself did not fall into lust, since he corrected his fornicating sons with paternal tenderness, but not with priestly austerity?"[35]

Displays of affection were considered appropriate for fathers, but certainly not at the expense of discipline. Moreover, the extension of affection into anything more erotically charged was extremely culpable. Given his personal abhorrence of sexuality, as well as his prominent role in the campaign against nicolaitism, it is hardly surprising to find Peter applying the incest taboo to spiritual fathers as well as secular ones.[36] However, the violence of the language he uses in condemning sexual relationships between spiritual fathers and their children is striking, and reminds us that spiritual incest was considered a serious sin in this period.[37] Peter insisted, first of all, that bishops and other clerics avoid sex with the women under their jurisdiction:

> Clearly, if a father incestuously seduces his daughter, he will be promptly excommunicated, forbidden communion and either sent to prison or exiled. How much worse, therefore, should be your degradation, since you had no fear of perishing with your daughter, not indeed in the flesh, which would be bad enough, but rather with your spiritual daughter? . . . if you commit incest with your spiritual daughter, how in good conscience do you dare perform the mystery of the Lord's body?[38]

In his notorious attack on homosexuality among clerics, the *Liber Gomorrhianus,* Peter applied the same rule to sex between spiritual fathers and their sons:

> What an unheard of crime! What a vile deed, deserving a flood of bitter tears! If they who approve of these evil-doers deserve to die, what condign punishment can be imagined for those who commit these absolutely damnable acts with their spiritual sons?[39]

Peter considered this form of incest far more abhorrent than the same act with a spiritual daughter:

> Who will make a mistress of a cleric, or a woman of a man? Who, by his lust, will consign a son whom he has spiritually begotten for God to slavery under the iron law of satanic tyranny? . . . the same sentence is rightly inflicted on him who assaults his own daughter, or who by sac-

rilegious intercourse abuses his spiritual daughter, and on him also
who in his foul lust defiles a cleric whom he has ordained. Perhaps we
should distinguish here the quality of both crimes: in the two prior
cases, even though he practices incest, he is sinning naturally, because
he sinned with a woman; in the latter case, by his shameful action with
a cleric he commits a sacrilege on a son, is guilty of the crime of incest
on a man, and violates the law of nature [*naturae iura dissoluit*].[40]

For Peter Damian, homosexual incest clearly violates the law of nature,
while heterosexual incest—however heinous a sin—does not. Nevertheless, the penalty in both cases is the same, which seems to undercut the
distinction he has just made and to confuse his condemnation of these
practices.

It has been the goal of recent feminist theory to "denaturalize" the
institutions of heterosexuality and sexual hierarchy, to bring into question their origins and functions and to propose alternatives to the
assumption that gender and sexual behavior follow automatically from
biology. In her influential book, *Gender Trouble,* Judith Butler has written that "Gender ought not to be construed as a stable identity or locus
of agency from which various acts follow; rather, gender is an identity
tenuously constituted in time, instituted in an exterior space through a
stylized repetition of acts."[41] She argues that gender is performative—
created through the very "bodily gestures, movements, and styles" that
are so often thought to be expressive of some inherent, natural identity. I
introduce Butler here because it seems to me that her performative theory of gender gives us a useful way to think about masculinity—and
more precisely, about fatherhood—in the eleventh century. Peter
Damian's allusions to secular fathers show them as continuously obliged
to create paternal identities for themselves, for fear of familial disorder,
social stigma and even divine wrath if they failed. Even more evident in
his writings, however, is the remarkable spectacle of celibate clerics
"performing" fatherhood in ways that echoed—even if they avoided
reproducing—the "gestures, movements, and styles" of secular fathers.
We see them generating children through the celebration of the sacraments, imposing discipline on spiritual sons and daughters, expressing
(appropriately limited) affection toward those offspring. Peter's writings
can be seen as not only records, but actual instances of gendering performances, for through the written word, this hermit, a man who was often
isolated from others, was nevertheless able to "tenuously constitute"
himself as their father.

Yet the evidence of those writings also points up the limitations of Butler's theory and, in particular, its failure to account for the social nature of gendered performances. Paternal behavior in and of itself is clearly insufficient to create and maintain paternal identity. The role of the father is not—as Butler seems to suggest—a one-man show, but rather part of the social drama of family life. To perform fatherhood, in other words, one must be joined on the stage by someone enacting the role of the child. This is most clearly illustrated by the case of the Marquis Obertus discussed at the beginning of this essay. His identity as father was not established by his own performance of the role—indeed, he refused to "go on" in the part by denying he was the father of the child born in his absence. Rather, it was his interaction with his son, who picked him out from among all the men assembled in the hall, which created the identity of father for him. In the same way, the identity of spiritual fathers might only be established through interaction with their spiritual offspring.

Peter wrote a long letter to an older hermit named Teuzo, scolding him for living in an urban setting and getting drawn into urban politics. He urges Teuzo—as a father might urge a son—to practice obedience and humility, and suggests that he should model himself after the hermits of Peter's own community (including Dominic Loricatus, Peter's own spiritual father). The tone is certainly that of a superior upbraiding a somewhat recalcitrant subordinate. However, at the conclusion of the letter, Peter unexpectedly turns Teuzo into the spiritual father, by casting himself in the role of obedient son:

> And now, my dear father and lord, I throw myself at your feet and with tears humbly beg your pardon. I ask that you kindly forgive what I have said, and that in the sweetness of your charity you will not reject one who has presumed to taunt you so boldly, so long, however, as what I said above is accepted as having your welfare at heart. I do not refuse in offering satisfaction to bare my back to your rod, and in the future to submit with reverence to the paternal demands of your holiness. I hope that this correction of mine will not fail to bear fruit for you, since to your way of thinking, so grave and mature, and certainly so holy, what a younger man has dared to say may perhaps taste bitter . . .[42]

It was not Teuzo's own behavior, but Peter's act of submission, that made the difference in the older man's identity.

In part because of the ambiguities inherent in the role of father, but even more because maintenance of that role depended on the behavior of others as well as the father, paternal identity was always tenuous and often unstable in Peter's writings. We have already seen how, in his sermon on St. Apollinaris, Peter turned the archetypical father figure of Abraham into the son who is being sacrificed through his act of obedience. In the *Life of St. Romuald,* we find the even more startling picture of a biological father becoming subordinated to his own son, who undertakes the role of spiritual father. The young saint had been very much under the thumb of a powerful and domineering parent—so much so that, when he sought conversion to the monastic life, the monks hesitated to accept him into their community for fear of angering his father.[43] Years later, however, when Romuald had become the head of the community, his father decided to convert and become a monk as well. However, he had trouble accepting the monastic discipline and ran away for a while. When he eventually returned, Romuald had him shackled and beaten like any other runaway monk.[44] Thus, we find a formerly obedient son—now playing the role of spiritual father—enforcing the obedience of his biological father—now playing the role of the son.

A related form of role reversal appears in a letter to Desiderius of Monte Cassino. Peter tells Desiderius how Abbot Aymard of Cluny[45] resigned his office to Mayeul, and retired to the infirmary of Cluny to live out his last days. One evening the old man asked for a piece of cheese, but the cellarer—who was busy with other things—rudely refused to give it to him, and complained that he couldn't deal with the demands of so many abbots. Aymard was scandalized, and the next morning asked his servant (for he was blind) to lead him to the chapter house. Once there, he addressed the new abbot as follows: "Brother Mayeul, I didn't place you over me so that you could persecute me or lord it over me like an owner over his slave. But I actually chose you so that you might show compassion *as a son to his father*" [emphasis mine]. "Are you my monk or not," he demanded, and Mayeul replied, "I am, and I never was more yours than I now profess myself to be." "If you are my monk," rejoined Aymard, "then give up your seat immediately and return to the place you used to have." Mayeul humbly did as he was told, and Aymard—as though resuming his former rank—took the abbot's place and ordered the haughty cellarer punished. When that was taken care of, Aymard stepped down again and ordered Mayeul to resume his place. For Peter, this story illustrated the monastic virtues of humility and obedience.[46] For us, however, it may illustrate both the reliance spiritual fathers had to place on their spiritual sons in order to establish paternal identity, and the wild swings that might occur in that identity.

Studies of masculine roles in medieval Europe have lagged far behind studies of feminine roles. Certainly, much less has been written on fatherhood than on motherhood in the Middle Ages.[47] It is true that some excellent research has been done on medieval interpretations of the male role in procreation.[48] And a number of scholarly works have been devoted to the image of God the Father in Christian theology.[49] But very little is known about the ordinary man's experience of fatherhood in the Middle Ages, let alone about what fatherhood may have meant to celibate priests and monks.[50] Peter Damian's letters and sermons provide us with a starting point for the study of fatherhood—both secular and spiritual—in the eleventh century. They reveal some of the images and ideas that an eleventh-century cleric associated with the paternal role: potency, stern authority, affectionate tenderness, the incest taboo. More significantly (for surely these images and ideas are not very surprising in themselves), Peter's writings reveal the complexities—the ambiguities and instability—that he saw *within* the paternal role. We have seen, for example, that men were expected to "make themselves eunuchs for the kingdom of heaven," while remaining fruitful, that they were to assert authority by modeling humility and obedience, that they were to be both stern and loving to their children, but not too much of either. Perhaps the most startling aspect of Peter Damian's depiction of fatherhood in the eleventh century is his willingness to accept the possibility that men will switch—sometimes very quickly indeed—between the roles of father and son. We moderns sometimes assume that premodern people must have seen gender as natural and unchanging, and that they had no notion that gender roles could be conditional or determined by context. But Peter seems well aware of how unstable the role of father could be.

A final point: it is striking how often Peter associates various forms of violence with paternity. Some references to beatings, and even to imprisonment and disinheritance are only to be expected, of course, given his assumption that a father's primary duty was to discipline his offspring. But what is significant is how regularly paternity is *asserted* through violence or the threat of violence in Peter's writings. Teuzo, Romuald and Aymard are actually established as spiritual fathers through emotional and physical violence, when their sons are humbled and beaten. Obertus is identified as a biological father through the legalized violence of the ordeal. Not only the children, but the fathers themselves suffer in Peter's world. Thus, when Alberic of Marsica undertakes the role of father in defiance of the laws of the Church, his punishment is death. And in order to instruct their children in the duty of obedience, Abraham must sacrifice what he loves best, while Apollinaris must submit to martyrdom.

Can this recurring conjunction of violence and fatherhood be explained solely through Peter's own early experience of death and grief? Or does it perhaps suggest that something should be added to the thesis that the *Herrenfrage* led to the *Frauenfrage?* McNamara has argued convincingly that the crisis of masculinity in the central Middle Ages led to increased misogyny and violence against women. But were women the only ones to suffer from the restructuring of gender roles in this period? I would suggest that men's struggle to create and maintain their identities as men inevitably involves doing violence to other men, and even to their own nature, as well as to women. It may well be this dynamic which we see at work in the writings of Peter Damian.

NOTES

1. Peter Damian, Letter 68 (1059–1063), ed. Kurt Reindel, *Die Briefe des Petrus Damiani,* 4 vols. (Munich: Monumenta Germaniae Historica, 1983–1993), 2: 294–95; trans. Owen J. Blum, *The Letters of Peter Damian,* The Fathers of the Church, Mediaeval Continuation, vol. 3 (Washington, D.C.: Catholic University of America Press, 1989-), 84. I have used Blum's translation for letters 1–90. All other translations are my own.

2. John of Lodi, *Vita beati Petri Damiani,* 1 (*Patrologia Latina,* 144: 115–16).

3. Lester K. Little, "The Personal Development of Peter Damian," in William C. Jordan, Bruce McNab and Teofilo F. Ruiz, eds., *Order and Innovation in the Middle Ages: Essays in Honor of Joseph R. Strayer* (Princeton: Princeton University Press, 1976), 328–29. Nira Gradowicz-Pancer has recently suggested that the search for an adequate father led many early medieval saints to convert: "Papa, maman, l'abbé et moi: Conversio morum et pathologie familiale d'après les sources hagiographiques du haut Moyen Age," *Le Moyen Age* 102 (1996): 7–25.

4. Jo Ann McNamara and Suzanne Wemple, "The Power of Women through the Family in Medieval Europe, 500–1100," *Feminist Studies* 1 (1973): 126–41; revised and reprinted in Mary S. Hartman and Lois Banner, eds., *Clio's Consciousness Raised: New Perspectives in the History of Women* (New York: Harper and Row, 1974); reprinted in Mary Erler and Maryanne Kowaleski, eds., *Women and Power in the Middle Ages* (Athens: University of Georgia Press, 1988).

5. Jo Ann McNamara, "The *Herrenfrage:* The Restructuring of the Gender System, 1050–1150," in Clare A. Lees, ed., *Medieval Masculinities: Regarding Men in the Middle Ages* (Minneapolis: University of Minnesota Press, 1994), 3–29.

6. McNamara, "The Herrenfrage," 5.

7. Herbert Grundmann, *Religious Movements in the Middle Ages,* trans. Steven Rowan (Notre Dame: University of Notre Dame Press, 1995); Gottfried Koch, *Frauenfrage und Ketzertum im Mittelalter* (Berlin: Akademie-Verlag, 1962); Brenda Bolton, "*Vitae Matrum:* A Further Aspect of the *Frauenfrage,*" in Derek Baker, ed., *Medieval Women* (Oxford: Blackwell, 1978), 253–74.

8. My findings are in keeping with what Peter Stearns has said about western fatherhood in general, that it was "Janus-faced, and . . . hard to capture in a single formula": Peter N. Stearns, "Fatherhood in Historical Perspective: The Role of Social Change," in Frederick W. Bozett and Shirley M.H. Hanson, eds., *Fatherhood and Families in Cultural Context* (New York: Springer, 1991), 34.

9. I am currently engaged in writing such a detailed study.

10. Peter Damian, Letter 31 (1049); Reindel 1: 324; Blum 2: 47–48.

11. Ibid.

12. Peter Damian, Letter 157 (1069 or 1071); Reindel 4: 82–83.

13. Peter Damian, Letter 112 (1064); Reindel 3: 260–61.

14. This attitude was modeled by St. Romuald, who strove to avoid sterility and to bear "spiritual fruit": see Peter Damian, *Vita beati Romualdi,* 35, 37, 43, ed. Giovanni Tabacco, *Fonti per la storia d'Italia,* 94 (Rome: Istituto storico italiano per il medio evo, 1957), 74, 78, 85.

15. Peter Damian, Letter 61 (1059); Reindel 2: 214–15; Blum 3: 10.

16. Peter Damian, Letter 31 (1049); Reindel 1: 299; Blum 2: 19.

17. Peter Damian, Letter 59 (after 1058); Reindel 2: 197–99; Blum 2: 398–99.

18. Peter Damian, Letter 47 (before 1057); Reindel 2: 49; Blum 2: 258–59.

19. On the significance of tears, see Owen J. Blum, *St. Peter Damian: His Teaching on the Spiritual Life* (Washington, D.C.: Catholic University of America Press,1947), 79–80.

20. Peter Damian, Letter 44 (1055–1057); Reindel 2: 25; Blum 2: 235.

21. Peter Damian, Letter 54 (1057–1058); Reindel 2: 141–42; Blum 2: 346–47.

22. Peter Damian, Letter 89 (1062); Reindel 2: 538; Blum 3: 333.

23. Peter Damian, Letter 56 (1058); Reindel 2: 161; Blum 2: 368.

24. For example, the father of St. Romuald, who pushed his reluctant son into warfare: Peter Damian, *Vita beati Romualdi,* 1, ed. Tabacco, 14–15.

25. *Sancti Petri Damiani Sermones,* 32, ed. Giovanni Lucchesi (Turnhout: Brepols,1983), 190–92.

26. On Abraham as a father figure, see Jérôme Baschet, "Medieval Abraham: Between Fleshly Patriarch and Divine Father," *Modern Language Notes* 108 (1993): 738–58.

27. *Sancti Petri Damiani Sermones,* 32, ed. Lucchesi, 191.

28. On the association of nurturing with motherhood in spiritual writings, see Caroline Walker Bynum, "Jesus as Mother and Abbot as Mother: Some Themes in Twelfth-Century Cistercian Writing," in *Jesus as Mother: Studies in the Spirituality of the High Middle Ages* (Berkeley and Los Angeles: University of California Press, 1982), 110–69.

29. Peter Damian, Letter 15 (after 1045); Reindel 1: 151; Blum 1: 141.

30. Peter Damian, Letter 54 (1057–1058); Reindel 2: 139; Blum 2: 344.

31. Peter Damian, Letter 58 (1058); Reindel 2: 191; Blum 2: 390.

32. Peter Damian, Letter 32 (1049–1054); Reindel 1: 331; Blum 2: 54–55.

33. Peter Damian, Letters 31 (1049), 40 (1052), 47 (before 1057), 61 (1059), 67 (1059–1063), 89 (1062), 95 (1063), 97 (1063), 111 (1064), 112 (1064), 117 (after 1064), 120 (1065/66), 132 (1065–1071), 142 (1066), 162 (1069), 174 (undated).

34. Peter Damian, Letter 61 (1059); Reindel 2: 213; Blum 3: 9.

35. Peter Damian, Letter 112 (1064); Reindel 3: 285. In this passage, Peter refers Cunibert to his earlier letter to Pope Nicholas (see last note).

36. On his personal attitude, see Little, "Personal Development of Peter Damian," 332–34; on his teachings concerning celibacy, see especially Jean de Chasteigner, "Le célibat sacerdotal dans les écrits de saint Pierre Damien," *Doctor Communis* 24 (1971): 169–83, 261–77.

37. Joseph H. Lynch, *Godparents and Kinship in Early Medieval Europe* (Princeton: Princeton University Press, 1986), 219–81. Lynch focuses on "incest" between members of the laity related through baptismal sponsorship; however, the attitude toward "incest" between clerical fathers and their spiritual children seems to have been similar.

38. Peter Damian, Letter 61 (1059); Reindel 2: 214–15; Blum 3: 10–11.

39. Peter Damian, Letter 31 (1049); Reindel 1: 294–95; Blum 2: 15–16.

40. Ibid.

41. Judith Butler, *Gender Trouble: Feminism and the Subversion of Identity* (New York: Routledge, 1990), 140.

42. Peter Damian, Letter 44 (1055–57); Reindel 2: 33; Blum 2: 242.

43. Peter Damian, *Vita beati Romualdi,* 1–2, ed. Tabacco, 14–15, 18.

44. Peter Damian, *Vita beati Romualdi,* 12–13, ed. Tabacco, 33–37.

45. Peter refers to Aymard as "Markward."

46. Peter Damian, Letter 106 (1064); Reindel 3: 182–83.

47. Recent works in English on motherhood include Clarissa Atkinson, *The Oldest Vocation: Christian Motherhood in the Middle Ages* (Ithaca, N.Y.:

Cornell University Press, 1991); Anneke B. Mulder-Baker, ed., *Sanctity and Motherhood: Essays on Holy Mothers in the Middle Ages* (New York: Garland, 1995); John Carmi Parsons and Bonnie Wheeler, eds., *Medieval Mothering* (New York: Garland, 1996); Lisa M. Bitel, "Reproduction and Production in Early Ireland," in Samuel K. Cohn Jr. and Steven A. Epstein, eds., *Portraits of Medieval and Renaissance Living: Essays in Memory of David Herlihy* (Ann Arbor: University of Michigan Press, 1997), 71–89; Anne Rudloff Stanton, "From Eve to Bathsheba and Beyond: Motherhood in the Queen Mary Psalter," in Lesley Smith and Jane H.M. Taylor, eds., *Women and the Book: Assessing the Visual Evidence* (Toronto: University of Toronto Press, 1997), 172–89.

48. See especially Jane Fair Bestor, "Ideas about Procreation and Their Influence on Ancient and Medieval Views of Kinship," in David I. Kertzer and Richard P. Saller, eds., *The Family in Italy from Antiquity to the Present* (New Haven: Yale University Press, 1991), 150–67; Joan Cadden, *Meanings of Sex Difference in the Middle Ages: Medicine, Science and Culture* (Cambridge: Cambridge University Press, 1993).

49. *God as Father?* ed. Johannes-Baptist Metz and Edward Schillebeeckx, Concilium, 143 (New York: Seabury Press, 1981); Peter Widdicombe, *The Fatherhood of God from Origen to Athanasius* (Oxford: Clarendon,1994).

50. Brent D. Shaw, "The Family in Late Antiquity: The Experience of Augustine," *Past and Present* 115 (May, 1987): 3–51, includes an excellent discussion of the social practice of fatherhood, but for a rather early period. On fatherhood in the Middle Ages, in addition to the works cited earlier, see M.A. Claussen, "Fathers of Power and Mothers of Authority: Dhuoda and the *Liber manualis*," *French Historical Studies* 19 (1996): 785–90.

Jean Gerson and Traumas of Masculine Affectivity and Sexuality

BRIAN PATRICK McGUIRE

Jean Gerson (1363–1429) is one of a small number of late medieval people who tells us a great deal about himself.[1] In the course of his career as theologian and chancellor at the University of Paris,[2] Gerson drew on his own life experience in order to provide sermons and treatises of advice for the good Christian. When he wrote in French, as he often did, he was careful to couch his advice in general terms so that he did not become too suggestive to his readers about sexual matters. But when he wrote in Latin, Gerson could be direct and specific about his concerns and drop hints that he was drawing from his own experience.

In what follows here, I will provide a portrait of Gerson as a deeply intellectual and spiritual medieval Christian cleric who dedicated a great part of his life to providing guidelines for sexual behavior. At the same time I will use some of his letters to indicate how Gerson expressed his affective needs by transferring his emotions to members of his biological family, especially his two brothers. I am aware at every step of the way that it is methodologically dubious for the historian to penetrate the psyches of people who have been dead for centuries. I do not intend to conjure up a form of resurrected psychohistory. My goal is to make use of Gerson's own words and definitions in order to define the perimeters of his emotional and sexual life. I will keep to statements where Gerson is direct and obvious about his purposes and where he directly or indirectly was referring to himself. The result will be my own construction of Gerson, one that is different from any portrait of the man that has been made in the last century.[3]

Gerson's own point of view and personal dilemmas are important for the medieval historian because his position at Paris and his tireless writings and diplomatic efforts made him into a spokesperson of medieval Christendom. Gerson spent a lifetime trying to cope with the intellectual, spiritual, institutional and emotional challenges of late medieval Christianity. What he called the reformation of the Church was a major concern for Gerson. Much of its restructuring was to take place through a heightening of standards among the clergy. Priests were to learn more Latin, study more theology and give better sermons. At the same time they were to take more seriously their duties as pastors of souls, especially in the confessional. Gerson's technique for confession, as we shall see, perhaps best exemplifies his desire, even obsession, to get down to the specifics of sexual behavior in order to cleanse the individual soul and purify the Church.

GROWING UP AND REGRETTING SUCCESS

Jean Gerson was born on 14 December 1363 as the first of twelve children, of whom ten survived early childhood.[4] His father, Arnoul le Charlier, lived in the hamlet of Gerson, not far from Reims, either as a tenant farmer on lands belonging to the abbey of Saint Rémi or as a craftsman. His mother, Elisabeth la Chardenière, may have come from a less modest background, but the family can be considered as belonging to the upper layer of the country people who made up the overwhelming majority of the medieval population.

The next son, also called Jean, grew up to become a monk at the great Benedictine abbey of Saint Rémi. Another son, Peter, died in childhood. The two youngest boys, Nicolas (b. 1382) and Jean (b. 1384), became monks in the Celestine Order founded by Pope Celestine V, the controversial pope of 1294 who had resigned, willingly or not, after five months. For the sake of clarity, since three sons were called Jean, I will refer to them as Jean Gerson, Jean the Benedictine, and Jean the Celestine.

I have dedicated another study to Gerson's sisters and his relationship with them.[5] It is sufficient here to summarize my findings and point out that Gerson maintained contact with his sisters for years after he became chancellor at the University of Paris in 1395. He considered himself to be their spiritual guardian and sent them several treatises containing advice. He encouraged them to remain at the family home, even after the death of the parents, and to live a pious life based on religious observances and manual labor.

Gerson's attempt to guide his sisters sprang from a desire that they live in a way that their oldest brother thought would bring them to eternal salvation. But Gerson's plans for his sisters also reflect a sense of the family's limited economic resources. As he once wrote to his sisters, he and his brothers who had entered the religious life were not interested in taking any of the family patrimony.[6] What remained after the death of the mother in 1401 and the father in 1404 was, in Gerson's mind, sufficient for the surviving sisters, provided they did not marry.

Marriage, with the economic requirement of a dowry, would have weakened the fragile and modest arrangement that the sisters apparently established in their parents' old age. At the same time, however, Gerson had negative expectations from marriage in terms of the way husbands treat wives. He provided a portrait of married life that exceeds, in its negative characteristics, anything written by Church Fathers such as Jerome and Ambrose, who had recommended virginity.[7] For the sake of economic stability, as well as for the salvation of their souls, the sisters were encouraged to stick together and not to give way to the delusions and dilemmas of married life.

The young Gerson and his parents seem not to have even considered the possibility of marriage for him. At the age of fourteen, in 1377, he went to Paris to do the arts course. Later, in 1401, Gerson wrote to his brother Nicolas that he, as the oldest son, never had the possibility of choosing a career in the way the younger sons did:

> God showed great mercy to you, since you had no relatives or friends who wanted you to become something great in the world and so would have been opposed to your intention [to become a monk]. It is, and always has been, quite different for me, as well as for countless other people who read in the book of experience that one's enemies are the members of one's own household (Matt.10:36). In order that we can take care of their children, they want us never to be children.[8]

Gerson here revealed an ambiguity about family bonds that was to follow him for much of his life. On the one hand, he felt a sense of loyalty to the members of his family, to care for them and make it possible for them to live good Christian lives, with their material needs cared for. On the other hand, he felt that this obligation prevented him from becoming the person he might have been: he had to find a career that would enable him, he implies, to provide for his biological family instead of his own spiritual needs.

This conflict between family and individual concerns could be summarized in the warning Gerson cited from the Gospel of Matthew against family or household entanglements. Gerson wanted to be loyal to his siblings, but he felt that they held him back and bogged him down, both in his personal development and perhaps even in terms of his eternal salvation.

Gerson's sense of being limited by his modest background and obligations to his younger sisters and brothers was not a figment of his imagination. The family was not well off, and Gerson, as the oldest son, was clearly expected to do well at Paris and get a good prebend that would provide social position and income to benefit the family. Again, however, Gerson felt ambivalent about advancing family interests through his own success in the Church. In early 1400, he wrote to his colleagues at Paris from a self-imposed exile at Bruges. Here he had gone in order to be a parish priest and to escape from the moral dilemmas of Paris academic life. He defended his decision to abandon a lucrative career that might have helped his brothers and sisters. It was more important for him to save his own soul from shipwreck:

> What if someone should object about the provision [of offices] for my brothers and the honor of my friends? I concede that this carnal consideration could in the end overcome me, especially when my parents in the flesh who live in the country cannot take care of such matters. Indeed towards my brothers and sisters themselves I by no means act without masculine courage nor do I lack concern for the younger ones who could climb to the heights. But in the face of imminent and total shipwreck one can only stay afloat if even the dearest, the most necessary goods are willingly cast overboard.[9]

Gerson took by the horns a dilemma that plagued his life: concern for family needs and for his own salvation. He insisted that he did want to use his own resources in order to see that his family members could advance (assumedly by making it possible for the brothers to come to the University of Paris). But Gerson had come to feel that his obligations at Paris had weighed him down to the point where he could no longer keep his soul afloat. The storm of moral conflicts had become too overwhelming, and now he had to cast aside every bit of excess baggage. This included his bonds with his brothers, whom he could have helped by staying in Paris instead of retreating to Bruges.

The image of shipwreck was one that Gerson used more than once in order to convey his situation. In a much earlier letter, perhaps from 1382,

Gerson, as a needy student at Paris, pleaded with a benefactor, possibly the theologian Pierre d'Ailly, for economic support in order to avoid a shipwreck in his career and life. Piling classical images on top of each other and displaying his knowledge of rhetoric, Gerson told his benefactor that he could not continue his studies unless he received more financial aid. Gerson enumerated the great friendships of classical antiquity and asked that he be remembered in the network of friendship that had grown up around Pierre d'Ailly at the wealthy College of Navarre. Here Gerson had been admitted as what we would call a scholarship student, but his funds had run out.

Under the circumstances, Gerson insisted, it was impossible for him either to turn to his parents for money or to return home and give up his academic career. This would be a terrible blow for the family and make his parents the laughing stock of their community. As he wrote to his benefactor:

> I also hope that the holy and manifest poverty of my parents will draw you. They earn a meager existence in heat and sweat through their own manual labor. After God they have all their hope in you. Under the shadow of your wings they give me some basic help and nourishment. However modest it is, it is the greatest burden for them with regards to their social position, so that they now bear burdens beyond their abilities. I fear, may God forbid, that they will become a parable for the neighbors (cf. Ps. 68:12), a source of ridicule for strangers and a ribald refrain for base people.[10]

Gerson seems here to have been willing to use almost any argument to convince his benefactor that something had to be done. He was not just pleading on the basis of his parents' poverty. He was telling the recipient of the letter that the benefactor would also become an object of ridicule if the young Gerson had to leave Paris and go home:

> Perhaps the iniquitous will turn their contempt against you in murmuring their ridicule against my parents: "Ha! look at those whom a shady faith has deceived; an empty confidence has disappointed. They were leaning on a staff and thought it would hold up, but it gave way to them and they have fallen to the ground."[11]

A sense of near despair emerges from this letter in spite of its smooth literary polish. But Gerson apparently did get the support he needed. Pierre d'Ailly became his major ally, making it possible for Gerson to succeed him as chancellor of the university in 1395.

D'Ailly had stood for a reform program which aimed at getting rid of the abuses of former chancellor Blanchard, who was willing to let young aristocrats pass exams for a fee and to lower the standards of the faculty of theology.[12] But when Gerson, aged only thirty-two, took office, he found that it was still difficult to maintain moral and scholastic standards and to avoid favoritism on the basis of political power. In withdrawing to Bruges in 1400, he tried to solve once and for all the moral dilemma with which he had grown up: being the gifted boy whose brilliance impressed others but whose social background meant he needed powerful and rich allies. Gerson's reservations about the life he had led are clear in the first letter he wrote to his Paris colleagues:

> I am forced in material life almost to beg and to live in a downtrodden way, for the golden mean is not safe with bitter poverty, according to the requirements of one's position. Elsewhere I would be abundantly provided for and be able to provide for a household, but now it is necessary with great detriment to go without one and to live with grammar students and school boys.[13]

The income Gerson received from the chancellorship was so limited that he had to take in boarders in order to make ends meet. He found this situation humiliating, especially in a Paris where so much wealth was concentrated and available for churchmen who became the favorites and confessors of the nobility. This path had been open to Gerson in the late 1380s and early 1390s because he had become a popular preacher at court, but, as he himself acknowledged, he accepted the chancellorship in order to get away from the temptations of court life. But now he realized that he was as involved as ever with court matters.[14]

Gerson managed, in the course of 1400, to come to terms with these moral dilemmas and to reconcile himself to returning to Paris. He began to send eager letters to his colleagues at the College of Navarre with a plan for the moral and scholastic reform of the university. Some of the exhortations he sent to Paris concerned the need to limit the time allowed for chatting: "Nothing is more wasteful of that most precious thing, time, and nothing more of a hindrance to the perfection of those who study as conversations."[15] Gerson was not referring to what he called "base" talk but to everyday exchanges containing humor and news:

> I am deceived if anyone ever ascends onto the Lord's mountain and into the ark of contemplation unless he has come to terms with this empty talk. He has to become a person who refuses to listen and a mute

who does not open his mouth. And I glory in this one thing in the Lord, that the college made it possible that there were few opportunities for such confabulations. I rarely had a chance to talk and to experience leisure, since it was so rare that there was someone else with whom I could enjoy engaging in the exchange of words, for so great among us was the difference of background and studies.[16]

Here Gerson made use of his own personal experience as a kind of *exemplum* to be followed by other scholars. He had not wasted time on idle conversations at the College of Navarre because he was so different from his colleagues in terms of background and interests. Just beneath the surface of the text is the resentment of the boy from the other side of the tracks who made it into good society but did not forget how different he was. For Gerson, it was a *felix culpa,* a happy fault, that his nonaristo-cratic background kept him apart from most of the others at Navarre. The more his fellow students whiled away their time with rumors and jokes, the more he could hole up in his cubicle and swot over the Church Fathers.

Gerson's combination of pride in his own achievement and sense of inferiority to others is hardly surprising in the annals of academia, where the best students can be those who feel they have to be superachievers in order to overcome social or personal handicaps. The simultaneous dis-tance from human contacts and the desire to excel can lead such a bril-liant student into a lifetime pattern of competition with others and isolation from generous human contacts. Gerson's formula for success in the intellectual life meant that he distanced himself from members of his peer group. He concentrated his affectivity into a hierarchical system where only "talks with proven men . . . are profitable."[17] These were the men who knew what contemplation was like and what dangers it involved. Gerson was probably referring to men like Pierre d'Ailly, whom he saw as having achieved both academic success and spiritual integrity. Gerson would remain close to Pierre d'Ailly later in life and, as I will indicate below, came to treat him as a kind of father-friend. With members of his own generation at Paris, however, Gerson did not allow himself to look for affective bonds.

BEING SOFT ON AFFECTION: GERSON
AND HIS BROTHER NICOLAS

At some point after Gerson became chancellor at Paris in 1395, his younger brothers Nicolas and Jean (the later Celestine) came to live with him. We know that Gerson's family approved of the arrangement, for we have a remarkable letter from Gerson's mother, taken down by the younger daughter Poncete, encouraging the two boys to develop in the Christian life and to "make sure that the brother with whom you are living is always pleased with you, as he now is." Elisabeth la Chardenière added that if this did not happen and the youths lived badly, it would "almost kill" her.[18]

As Gerson confessed in his remarkable letter from Bruges in 1400, he felt responsible for the advancement of these brothers in the world, even though he at the same time felt guilty about using his position to see that they got preferment. Assumedly, the younger brothers were students at the faculty of arts. Gerson probably intended that they eventually advance to the faculty of theology, as he himself had done. From here they might land a lucrative post in the Church and secure their parents and sisters in a way that Gerson with his limited income as chancellor could not.

Nicolas and little Jean, however, were affected by the same currents of contemplative spirituality as their older brother. But, unlike Gerson, they followed their impulses and left academia in order to become Celestine monks. The first to do so was Nicolas, who made his profession on the feast of Saint Martin, 11 November 1401. This decision was a shock for Gerson, who had returned to Paris from Bruges earlier that same year. Gerson had probably assumed that he was going to resume the way of life he had known at Paris, with his two brothers as members of his household.

Three weeks after Nicolas had left to live as a Celestine monk, Gerson wrote him a letter which is remarkably open in describing his reactions after Nicolas had left for his monastery. Gerson started by confessing his own laxness of mind [*mollities animi*]. He realized that he was "still not wholly capable of loving heavenly things." This state of mind made him dependent on the presence of his younger brother:

> And so brother, after you had left and you were happily joined to that angelic society which exists in human bodies, and we were separated from the sight of each other, I indeed felt both on the road and at Paris a certain tenderness towards you in my heart, more than what I at other times had felt. Your absence then seemed to me more of a burden and my fate harsher than usual. I sighed for you as an ox that is separated from its mate. The trauma of separation from you was devouring me. It caused great pain and mangled my soul. Amid my thoughts and my

words about you, tears that were not asked for came to my eyes, and I was in pain.[19]

The reader of such a letter is well advised to be careful and to acknowledge that such statements were written by a celebrated theologian at Paris, who knew that everything he wrote was sooner or later eagerly read by an admiring public. Two decades earlier, Gerson, in his begging letter to his benefactor, had shown himself to be a master of style. Thus, I do not think we should take this letter at face value as a heartfelt cry of lost love from one brother to another. But in some manner, the letter does reflect Gerson's situation, for he was allowing himself to use his own feelings as a way of guiding others. As generations of monks and scholars before him, going back to Augustine and even Paul, Gerson drew on his own spiritual traumas in order to enlighten others and to warn them of the pitfalls awaiting them.

What seemingly starts as an admission of a sense of desolation and loneliness ends with a ringing assertion of the rightness of Nicolas's decision to enter the monastery. Gerson concluded the letter by warning Nicolas against allowing himself the same "treacherous softness" which he had experienced: "And so most beloved brother of my heart, do not waste away in your spirit if you by chance sense creeping into your soul that treacherous softness which I now described concerning myself."[20] The word "softness" is in Latin *mollities,* the same word Gerson uses to refer to the physical act of masturbation.[21] In indulging his own sentiments for Nicolas, Gerson accused himself of committing a kind of mental masturbation, locking into himself and choosing a state of wrongful affectivity.

In stating what was right for Nicolas, Gerson did not try to deny the nature of his own feelings. He was precise in describing the gap between what he should have felt and actually did feel:

> In the depths of my soul I was accusing myself of doing wrong. I also reproached myself for a foolish lack of nerve which grieved at your happy state, for I knew it would have been more correct to rejoice.
> . . . I struggled as reason illuminated by faith regularly struggles in the good Lord. This sense of reason strongly congratulated you on your status and sighed deeply at mine, nor was it fooled.[22]

Right reason would have to disregard the emotional response that had been Gerson's first reaction. In describing this conflict, however, Gerson provided concrete reasons why he was worried about his brother: "the vexation of the body . . . the abdication of sordid sensuality, the extension of fasts and vigils . . . the cold and heat."[23] He realized that Nicolas had entered into a harsh ascetic regime, and his concern was so grave that he composed a second letter, this time to Nicolas's superior. Here Gerson expressed his doubt whether the youth would be able to stand the ascetic practices: "Otherwise he will easily perish in his simplicity and fearfulness, or because of indiscrete fervor he will be dissolved in tears and other exercises of a religious observance which in itself is harsh."[24]

Was Gerson objectively correct that the Celestine vocation required almost more than a young man could bear? Or was Gerson using his own sorrow at losing his brother in order to question the Celestine way of life? So little is known about the Celestine Order in late medieval Europe that it is not easy to conclude that its ascetic practices were generally as extreme as Gerson indicated.[25] But there is no doubt that Nicolas chose the Celestines because they were respected for keeping to the spirit of their hermit founder and requiring many observances from their monks.

However one reads this letter, it is clear that Gerson was trying to come to terms with his own feelings for his brother. Gerson was shocked that Nicolas's departure had left him with so profound a sense of emptiness. He needed to get control of such an emotion. Combining his knowledge of what he should feel with his awareness of what he actually felt, Gerson composed a masterful piece of self-revelatory prose. Justifying himself by a desire to provide Nicolas with good advice and to protect his brother from too demanding an observance, Gerson conceded what he had felt. He denigrated himself for a kind of softness, *mollities,* and tried to fight it, but he still admitted that the sense of a deprived affectivity had hit him hard.

A TRIANGLE OF LOVE AND DISCIPLINE:
GERSON, NICOLAS AND JEAN

A few years later, Gerson's youngest brother, Jean, also left him to enter the Celestines. We do not know about Gerson's immediate reactions, but he did begin to write letters of advice to Jean. These are lost to us, but we do have a remarkable letter to Nicolas, dated to 1408, concerning the situation of the young Jean.[26] Gerson had been in Italy with Pierre d'Ailly in January that year, and on the way back to Paris, the two of them visited Nicolas, who now was at the Celestine house at Villeneuve near Avignon.

Jean was about to make his solemn profession at the monastery of

Limay, near Mantes, in the diocese of Rouen.[27] Gerson was worried that his little brother was demanding far too much of himself in his ascetic regime, and he had apparently warned him against some of his practices. From Gerson's letter to Nicolas, it is apparent that the latter had not approved of his older brother's involvement in Jean's profession. The letter deserves closer examination.

First, Gerson justified himself in writing to Nicolas: it had been agreed during his and Pierre d'Ailly's visit to Nicolas that Gerson could write him on his return to Paris concerning the situation of young Jean. Gerson defended himself here with a statement that is almost a classical tag on friendship but is extremely unusual for him, with his usual strictures about the dangers of wasting time on human contacts: "For the law of love is such that in speech or in writing, friends enjoy visiting each other, instructing each other, and consoling each other."[28]

But the claim of friendship is not sufficient. Gerson felt obliged to assert his own authority because of his age and learning. With this preface he began a long passage on how hard it is for people to be aware of their own "spiritual illness" [*aegritudinem animorum*]. They are like sick people who try to tell the doctor how to treat them. This is what has happened to Gerson. He, as a qualified spiritual doctor, was being ignored: "This is my situation, which began long ago and now continues: I am cast aside; I am told what to do" [*Res talis apud me pridem incepta continuatur: abjicior, doceor . . .*].[29]

This brief sentence indicates resentment that Gerson was not being listened to. It also shows, however, that Gerson, for a long time, had been involving himself in the spiritual direction of young Jean and felt that he had a right to direct Jean's life. Now that he was becoming a Celestine, Jean had extracted himself from the care of his older brother, something Gerson had a hard time accepting.

Did Jean become a Celestine because he needed to escape Gerson's all-embracing concern? Had the same been the case a few years earlier with Nicolas? The sources are inconclusive here, but Gerson's own letter shows how much of himself he invested with his brothers, as with his sisters, in exercising control over their lives and directing them toward what he believed to be best for them. One hardly needs to read between the lines to see that for both brothers, Gerson worried that the Celestine way of life would require too much of them. So far as he was concerned, it would have been better for them to remain with him in Paris.

Returning to the letter's text, we see how, after appealing to Nicolas to believe in the worth of his intentions for young Jean, Gerson came to the heart of the matter. Nicolas had apparently asked Gerson to stop writing Jean because the older brother's letters upset Jean and even gave him nightmares:

> But you perhaps will object, no, you certainly do object. You say these letters disturb our brother. They upset him. They deprive him of sleep and give rise to a plague of fantasies in him. So he should be left to himself and to God and given over to his own conscience. Why is it necessary to rummage through his secrets? Why is it necessary to speak through writings with someone who wants only peace and quiet?[30]

Gerson here was probably reproducing one of his conversations with Nicolas. Gerson did not deny that young Jean had been having "awful nightmares" [*Ecce jam accipio quod gravissimis torquetur insomniis*]. But, he insisted, such nightmares had not plagued him "while he was in the world" [*quam tamen in saeculo sibi contigisse non memini*]. In other words, while Jean was under Gerson's care in Paris, he had had no such problem! Without being specific, Gerson hinted that young Jean's miseries were due to his transference to the Celestines. The efforts of the monks to help Jean out of his troubles might well be worthless:

> O Christ who brings salvation, what is to happen to Jean when he is sick and old if such a torment comes over him while he is still young, vital and vigorous? No affliction can make him more dull of mind, slack in memory, unstable in the judgment of reason, and generally unfit for all things. Such a disturbance differs only a little from mania or madness. So what good will your attention and your community's prayers be able to do if he is transformed from a sane and bright person into a fool and a madman?[31]

While Gerson was convinced that Jean's condition was due to the strictness of community life, Nicolas apparently had claimed that it was Gerson's letters that had upset their brother: "Unwillingly he goes over them again and again, nor can any effort remove them from the house of memory" [*has volvit et revolvit invitus, nec a memoriae domo potest eas . . . seciudere*].[32]

    Gerson refused to concede that letters of advice could have such an effect. If Jean had been better balanced and able to endure the regime of fasting and vigils, such letters would not have had such an effect on him.

It was because he was already out of balance, weakened by an everyday life, that he could not endure, that he could not cope with Gerson's advice. Gerson was sure that Celestine requirements alone, in terms of maintaining wakefulness in long vigils, would have driven him mad.[33]

At the end of the letter, Gerson appealed to both charity and discretion, so that Nicolas would understand young Jean's needs. Gerson made it appear as if the brother with too much attachment to Jean was not he but Nicolas: "You will act mercifully if you act according to discretion. You will not be able to do so if any sensual attachment of your own hinders you from accepting advice given by others."[34] Gerson claimed that his advice was the best, and so Nicolas was bound to follow it. He denied that his intervention in the affairs of Celestine houses for the sake of his little brother was an indication of his own "sensual attachment." He acted as if he were a calm, impartial judge, worried that the poor youth was about to go mad and wanting to show Nicolas and his fellow Celestines that they were wrong about the cause of Jean's misery.

What one would do to have the original letters Gerson had sent to young Jean in order to see what it was that might have upset him! But without these sources, it is still possible to conclude that Gerson refused to let go of an attachment to his youngest brother. Thanks to the remark about how young Jean had been mentally healthy in Paris, Gerson indicated that he believed his brother had been better off before he had joined the Celestines. As when Nicolas had entered a few years before, Gerson worried that the Celestines were unreasonable in their demands in depriving the monks of sleep and food and leading them into a state where their brains "twist about in dizziness" [*hinc cerebri vertiginosa rotatio*].[35]

I do not question the genuineness of Gerson's concern for the welfare of his brothers. But I think that behind the good intentions, there was also a need for companionship and a bitterness at its loss. However much Gerson remained attached to his sisters and wrote them spiritual advice, he remained at a physical distance from them. After the death of his parents, Gerson's only close emotional bond remained with his two youngest brothers, who he felt let him down by leaving him for the monastic life.

Gerson's worries about Jean the Celestine seem to have proven groundless. We at least know that Jean remained a monk, and eventually became superior of the house at Lyon, where Gerson, himself, found refuge in November 1419, after his exile from Paris. It is Jean who collected Gerson's works after his brother's death and made sure that they were preserved for posterity.[36] Thus, it is probably Jean the Celestine we can thank for saving letters that have a personal element but which also reflect a perennial debate in Christianity on the value and degree of monastic asceticism.

Jean the Celestine may have kept these letters because of the general interest of the question, but he thereby made it possible to get a glimpse of the great theologian's affective life. Gerson revealed how much he needed his younger brothers and how they were unable to reciprocate these powerful feelings. Their stay in Paris convinced them that they had to form their own spiritual way of life and leave their brother behind.

This reading of Gerson's second letter to Nicolas reveals a triangle of affectivity in which Gerson's pursuit of Jean's loyalty may have pushed the latter into the arms of Nicolas, or at least into the monastic order to which Nicolas belonged. Gerson refused, however, to accept this choice as a fait accompli and questioned the vocation, especially when Jean began to have nightmares. Nicolas replied by telling Gerson that Jean's problems were his fault, a typical family response when one member expresses a commitment to another and a third is critical of what is happening. On the fringes of this triangle we have already noticed a fourth person, Pierre d'Ailly, who Gerson considered to be his ally in his criticism of young Jean's situation. Gerson took it for granted that he and Pierre understood each other. I will return at the end of this paper to Pierre d'Ailly. He may have been the one real friend that Gerson ever allowed himself and who did not come to distance himself from this powerful personality.

A LANDSCAPE OF SEXUAL TEMPTATION AND ACTIVITY

During the productive years after Gerson's return to Paris in 1400, he composed several works where questions of sexual behavior are prominent. Perhaps the most notorious of these is his short treatise on masturbation,[37] but Gerson also added reflections on sexuality in treatises where such matters could have easily been left out. Thus, in addressing the Cistercians on the feast of Saint Bernard, Gerson used the person and voice of Saint Bernard to warn his listeners against evil men who might tempt them into forbidden sexual acts:

> But above all else I warn you, good youth, and I repeat the point again
> and again in warning you: beware of the company of evil youths or of
> men of ill repute. You know how the worst conversations corrupt good

habits, and so all the more do touching and actions. O what habits! What crimes! No, I mean what deaths! O most heinous of crimes, for that association is to be feared in the worst form of contagion. Instead of the natural bond and institution by which it was fitting for us in mutual contact to be chaste and secure, this beastly corruption works on those whom the almighty God of nature will condemn if they do not come to their senses. God does so justly, for such people in the basest manner ruin those whom they ought to have saved and instructed, since they have been entrusted to them as youths of angelical purity.[38]

I have quoted the passage in full here because Gerson's language is so guarded that one needs to see several sentences together in order to grasp his meaning. He was apparently referring to clerical teachers who used their position in order to have sexual relations with some of their students. In recommending Bernard's "school of contrition and penance," Gerson revealed a fear that the university milieu at Paris was a home of pederasty.

There is no way to know if Gerson was objectively correct and if such sexual contacts were any more widespread at Paris in the early 1400s than they were in the academic milieu of the late twelfth century to which the Cistercian convert Alan of Lille reacted in his *The Plaint of Nature.*[39] What is of concern for us here, however, is that Gerson was worried about such matters. His Bernard encouraged the scholar-monks to triumph over their sexual temptations and so to avoid being plagued with them for the rest of their lives:

You must follow me; you must believe someone with experience. This brief struggle will bring the most wonderful fruit, unless you are over-whelmed and basely succumb. In that case you will be tortured by per-petual misery and the harshest lust. Even in old age, when you would think you will be safe from temptation, you will be condemned to forms of titillation.[40]

How did Gerson know enough about sexual temptation in old age in order to put such words into Bernard's mouth? Was he borrowing from some commonplace in the Fathers, or was he referring to what he heard in the confessional and may have felt in his own body?

At about the same time as he wrote his sermon on Bernard, in his *Practical Treatise on Mystical Theology* Gerson provided what might be an indication of his own interior situation. He was considering the "thoughts or affections and passions" that can come "from internal fantasy or the imagination":

> The reason can deal with them, or God from above can illuminate the mind or spirit with them. Similarly good angels can elicit them, or fallen angels can do so. Against such passions "we must struggle," much more than "against flesh and blood" (Eph. 6:12). Then our souls that have been purified and sanctified will sometimes have to bear the attacks of blasphemies and the most vile impurities, even in old age and in solitude. These temptations are of a type which are unknown to us so long as we live in the world among the average and more adolescent temptations of the flesh and the world [*quales ipsimet nesciebant dum in mundana conversatione inter medias temptationes carnis et mundi adolescentiores versabantur*].[41]

To what was Gerson here referring? In describing the practical requirements for the ascent of mind and soul to contemplation, he stopped for a moment to consider the reaction of the body. He saw the possibility that the person who concentrates on inner spiritual life, instead, can find the desire to blaspheme against God and to think about sexual acts. The intensity of movement toward one goal creates a reaction toward another. This process is unknown in those who "live in the world" and have banal temptations to masturbation, fornication and the like. The temptations Gerson here described have to do with what come in the older, experienced person who has learned self-discipline in terms of sexual behavior but still can stumble into a well of sexual desire.

Gerson, I think, was describing his own experience. The more he sought God and the angels through interiorization and meditation, the more he had to come to terms with the desires within himself. He knew well the *Lives of the Desert Fathers,* in which the temptation to interior fornication is very much discussed, and so this passage may well be a meditation on literary sources.[42] But Gerson's remark probably also sums up his situation as it was in 1402. Seeking mystical life as an addition and completion of his scholastic learning, Gerson at times was afraid he was going to lapse into a state of sexual obsession.

Gerson sought knowledge of God and of human beings, relevant for himself and for others in his care. In his brief treatise from this same period shortly after 1400, *The Art of Hearing Confessions,* I find the clearest manifestation of Gerson's concern with finding out about sexual behavior. Gerson was the recipient of a long line of confessional manuals that provided good advice on how to get the penitent to tell the confessor the full truth about his sins. In the main tradition of such advice, it was made clear that the confessor should not ask such specific questions, especially in sexual matters, that he might give his penitents inspiration to experimentation with sex. It would be better for a priest to remain discreet and not to open the door to a world of which his penitent was still unaware.[43]

Gerson refused to let this danger hinder the priest from asking penetrating questions:

> It sometimes happens, though it be quite rare with a conscientious and careful confessor, that a certain type of carnal sin or some vile circumstance is revealed, of which the sinner is not aware and of which he is not guilty. In this he will perhaps be scandalized or be taught in the future to do similar things. We do not accept that such a result is so much to be feared, as some experts claim, that a diligent investigation of sins therefore ought to be dropped.[44]

It was so important for Gerson to find out the truth of his penitents' actions that he preferred to risk giving them information they lacked about sexual activity. He was convinced that young men, and even boys, are usually quite aware of what they are doing: "We do not think they are to be asked as if they were ignorant" [*Nec inquirenda esse judicamus quasi nesciant*].[45]

In the literature of penance, the confessor was considered to be a doctor who had the right and obligation to cut out the infected matter of sin in order to save the patient.[46] For Gerson, this image meant that he had almost unlimited access to the deepest layers of his penitents' consciousness. If one believes that all forms of willful sexual activity outside of marriage are mortal sins and can lead the sinner into hell, then Gerson's procedure was reasonable. But it is important to note here that the procedure he recommended was more methodical and ruthless in its thoroughness than what was normally considered necessary in more traditional manuals for confessors:

> It is appropriate, as I have experienced, that children and male adolescents first be asked . . . about intimacy with male friends and servants, since they at first glance are less frightened, because such things are less unusual. Afterwards they can be asked about intimacy with women. First of all, if they at the age of five or six years ever lay in bed with

female servants, as is common for boys. If they are asked in conformity
with what was said above, there will certainly also be found repulsive
matters not only with servants but also with the more immediate
family.[47]

This passage is important in showing how Gerson saw sexual behavior.
He thought it often happened in bourgeois homes (where there would
have been maids) that boys had some kind of physical intimacy with
female servants. Moments of play could lead to touching and petting. At
the same time, it was usual for young boys to explore each other's bodies, to handle each other, and perhaps to masturbate together. Finally, it
was not inconceivable for Gerson that incest was present in some
families.

When such matters were revealed to the confessor, Gerson recommended that he maintain a neutral expression, "being quick and indirect"
and not to indicate disapproval. Slowly but surely the young man will be
encouraged to describe his present activities, especially in terms of relations with women. With women "the reverse order is to be followed in
making investigations."[48] First, the priest is to ask them if they have had
sexual relations with other women, and then later they are to be queried
about men or children. The question of incest, which young males might
have experienced without being aware of its gravity, was to be at the very
end of Gerson's list for female penitents.

Here, however, he revealed a great deal about himself and wrote, "I
do not have complete experience on this matter" [*sed experientiam
totalem non habeo*]. In other words, he had heard many more confessions from men than from women. In the male academic world of Paris,
he had concentrated on men and boys and felt he knew about their habits,
while women remained something of a mystery for him.

Elsewhere I have dealt at length with Gerson's willingness to "trick"
the penitent into revealing acts that he or she had not at all intended to
speak of in the confessional.[49] For Gerson, it was a question of getting
the penitent to describe in detail everything that had happened, even if
the narrative provoked the imagination of the priest and gave him an
erection![50]

It would be easy to dismiss Gerson's thoroughness as a vicarious
form of sexual indulgence or aural voyeurism. Gerson was himself aware
of the skepticism of his clerical readers, and he defended himself by
insisting that his method worked. He was capable of making penitents
reveal their deepest secrets and to bring them to absolution:

Perhaps someone might find fault with the boldness of a confessor who dares to reveal such matters, which scarcely can seem believable and can hardly be imagined, except by those who have experienced them and have been seduced or have otherwise been informed about them. Let each person think what he wants. I before God bear witness that I brought many persons to confession by such methods who admitted that they never, even at the moment of death, would say to anyone that they had done such things. But they praised God with all their hearts in giving thanks that they had revealed themselves in such a way.[51]

Gerson's penitents could have experienced the same kind of therapeutic relief that the patient today can feel with a psychologist or psychiatrist, when he or she enables the patient to formulate the content of a traumatic experience. Gerson knew how difficult and even dangerous it was to "descend into these abominations" and he insisted on the importance of "caution." But if "previous matters which have been confessed seem to lead to such a conclusion," then the priest should go ahead, unless he is "a shy and inexperienced surgeon, turning pale or unable to control himself in the face of such foul and terrible wounds."[52]

In order to make it easier for people to confess such sins, Gerson wanted the cases reserved for special confessors to be limited, so that ordinary people would be able to go to their parish priests, confess their sins and receive absolution. He viewed the sacrament of confession as a central means to provide salvation for as many as possible, and he warned that preaching in itself is insufficient [*praedicationes generales non sufficere satis puto*].[53] Such concerns earned him, later in the fifteenth century, the title of *doctor consolatorius,* consoling doctor.

Gerson's concentration with the technique and results of confession can be looked at in widely different ways. A generous Roman Catholic interpretation would emphasize his desire to reach out to everyone and make it possible, for as many as possible, to have access to a well-educated, insightful and understanding priest. A more skeptical historian might ask what personal needs were involved in Gerson's desire to get to the truth of human behavior and to make people reveal what they, themselves, might have forgotten or repressed.

I am inclined to accept the sincerity of Gerson's motives but to add that his need for the truth reflects something about his own affectivity. For Gerson, the process of making people admit to their sexual acts was so important that the Christian life, to a large extent, became a question of sexual behavior and control. The charge that the medieval clergy was more interested in sexual behavior than in love and concern for neighbor can fairly be made against Jean Gerson. In the formidable machinery of confession, which Gerson set up, the tender bonds of human affectivity easily disappear.

The intensity of Gerson's campaign to control sexual activity can also be seen in his *Treatise against the Romance of the Rose.* Here, he made use of the same allegorical language as the authors of the *Romance.* Instead of a court of love, he set up a heavenly court to condemn the teachings of the Fool of Love. Gerson used the person of Theological Eloquence to warn that the work corrupted the morals of young people:

> Human nature, especially in youth, is too prone to trip and slip and fall into the filth of every form of carnality. There is no need that you lead it there and push it down. What are more quickly caught up and burned in the fire of base pleasures than human hearts?[54]
>
> . . . Believe me, and not only me but also the Apostle Saint Paul (cf. 1 Cor. 15:33), and Seneca and experience, that bad words and writings corrupt good habits. In this way come sins without our feeling shame, and they remove every healthy bit of modesty which is in young people the principal safeguard of their good status in the face of all evils.[55]

Gerson concluded that all copies of the work should be burned, and he continued his campaign in letters to the men of letters who tried to defend the main author of the *Romance of the Rose,* Jean de Meun. In this heated debate, the feminist writer Christine de Pizan appealed to Gerson as an ally, but we can see from his lack of response how different his agenda was from hers. Christine was interested in the position of women, whom the *Romance* turned into sexual objects, while Gerson was caught up in protecting youth, especially of the male sex, from literature that might feed their imaginations.[56]

Pierre Col, the court humanist who defended the poem, warned Gerson that he did not know what he was writing about. The power of physical love would one day overcome Gerson, and he would fall madly in love! Gerson wrote back to Pierre Col that the God of love, and not false Cupid, would protect him.[57] Elsewhere, however, Gerson admitted that he, once at least, was on the verge of just such an experience. After getting to know a nun and having spiritual conversations with her, Gerson came to realize that he also was physically attracted to her. He managed to cut himself off from these feelings and concluded that all passion is a most dangerous companion for virtue, whether it is a matter of love or of religious zeal and correction of others [*Omnis quippe vehementia est ad virtutem periculosissima comes, ut ad dilectionem, ad zelum, ad correctionem et similes*].[58]

As in his literature on confession, Gerson was convinced that human beings deceive themselves about their actual interests, behavior and intentions. We hide from ourselves what we are and what we want. The job of the confessor is to extract these hidden and painful truths. The task of the pastor is to protect those in his care from sexually explicit art and literature. Most of all, the task of the individual Christian is to guard himself or herself from the delusion that affectivity can be completed in strong and saving bonds with any other human being.

A KIND OF FRIENDSHIP AND A HEAVENLY SOLITUDE

In about 1402 Jean Gerson wrote his former teacher and patron, Pierre d'Ailly, a covering letter accompanying a treatise *On the Spiritual Life of the Soul.* This relatively brief letter sums up the relationship between the two men that by this time had existed for at least two decades. Even when one subtracts an element of obligatory praise of the student for his former master, Gerson seems to have felt a genuine bond with d'Ailly:

> You then, the greater you are, the more, according to the wise man's counsel, you humble yourself in all things. But this humility should be less surprising for me, because you love and embrace my learning, limited as it is, of which you have been the nurturer, source and author until now . . . Through you and under you I have been decorated with this insignia of master. You also promoted me in the office of chancellor where I succeeded you, even though I was not of equal merit.[59]

Pierre d'Ailly was bishop of Cambrai at the time, and Gerson no longer needed his patronage. In recalling the debt of his youth, however, Gerson indicated that he and d'Ailly were in regular contact and maintained a close bond. This continuing connection can be seen in other letters, but the above text, with its expression of gratefulness without fawning or exaggerated praise, hints that Gerson looked upon d'Ailly as a kind of father-friend.

A few years later, in 1408 or 1411, it seems that the usual situation of father and son was reversed, and now it was Gerson who turned to d'Ailly to give him consolation. Gerson wrote that he was worried by d'Ailly's last two letters, which indicated "the anxiousness of your mind" [*anxietas animi tui*].[60] Gerson insisted that this sense of desolation was not necessarily bad:

> the beginning of salvation is the awareness that one is sick and suffering, for he who has lost feeling to evil does not feel such pain. It is therefore good that everything you see troubles you, in terms of what is temporal and mortal. Everywhere are emptiness, madness and falsity.

The solution to this sense of emptiness is not to reach out for another human being in the embrace of friendship. It is to withdraw into a necessary solitude. It is this which will give us rest and provide a foretaste of the joys of heaven, for Gerson sees heaven as a place not of community but of solitude:

> Is there not great solitude in heaven? Is it not a deserted place? Thus the Lord promises through the prophet: in you the deserts of the world will be remade (Isa. 58:12). In this desert the ninety-nine sheep have been left behind.[61]

Gerson here refashioned the parable of the lost sheep, in order to emphasize separation from the flock as a necessity to provide a basis for salvation. The shepherd, in rescuing the one sheep, does not go back to the others but takes the fortunate one with him to his desert of heaven!

This theology of heaven departed from a great tradition that had seen heaven in terms of the loved ones who would again find each other and rejoice in each other. We need only to think of Dante's vision in his *Divine Comedy,* where one saint after another welcomes the pilgrim to the highest circles of heaven. For Dante as for other medieval people, heaven meant the completion of human communities. For Gerson it meant getting away from them.

Gerson's bond with Pierre d'Ailly is the one relationship of his life to which he could commit himself without hesitation, guilt or regret. Here, alone, he allowed himself contact with another person for emotional fulfillment. Here, alone, unlike with his brothers, Gerson seems not to have been rejected. In this letter, Gerson reasserted and strengthened this bond, and yet at the same time he denied the permanence of such a friendship. It would not last beyond this life, for Gerson and Pierre d'Ailly could only look forward to a heavenly life in which they at last would find the solitude they needed.

Gerson did not rule out some kind of heavenly contact with the few others who made it that far. But he looked forward to isolation and insulation from the madness of this world and its people. Flee to your heavenly father, Gerson advised Pierre d'Ailly, his distressed spiritual father:

> We often act like big children in our adversities so that we wax angry in public affairs. We are indignant with ourselves or our neighbors and do not seek help. Nor do we flee, in looking to him who ought to save us from weakness of spirit and the tempest (Ps. 54:9), just as the child who has fallen should seek help not in himself but from the father or mother who looks after him.[62]

The solution to our troubles lies not in finding friends to aid us in our dilemmas but in finding the one father who can save us. Gerson counseled his father-friend to leave behind the troubles of the world and to isolate himself in prayer and contemplation.

This letter could be interpreted as a generous declaration of friendship and concern for the former teacher and guide. Beneath this level of involvement, however, is advice that the friend withdraw into himself and stop being involved. He has to put his trust in God and forget the world. He has to prepare himself for a heaven where he will be alone with God. In the end, the heavenly father reasserts himself and all other bonds disappear.

Gerson's remedy for himself, and for Pierre d'Ailly, can be called the way of solitary contemplation. After a lifetime of commitment to the Church, whose unity and purity it was so important for Gerson to preserve and protect, he looked forward to union with God in a vast desert of solitude. He would reach this state by concentrating his efforts on the love of God and, thus, implicitly, would distance himself from other people. Only then would he be able to achieve the wisdom he sought:

> Does anyone then wish to be and to be called truly wise? Let that person have both types of contemplation, both that of affectivity which gives taste, and that of intellect which provides the brightness of knowledge so that wisdom, meaning wise science, is formed. But if one must be lacking, then I think it would be better to share in the first rather than in the second type, as it is more desirable to have good and humble affectivity, devout towards God, rather than a cold intellect that is enlightened by study alone.[63]

Gerson emphasized the same need in his *Mountain of Contemplation,* written for his sisters and acknowledging their ability to follow the path of affective contemplation, when they were given the proper guidance. With them, as with his brothers and Pierre d'Ailly, he continued to be affectively involved. And yet, he would only go a certain distance with such involvements and looked forward to moving away from them to a solitary vision of God.

Gerson's encouragement to Pierre d'Ailly, that his friend trust totally in Jesus and let him take care of everything, reflects the same point of view to be found in the immensely popular *Imitation of Christ.* Jesus is our true friend, the only one who will take up our burden. As Gerson wrote to d'Ailly, once we have cast aside any belief that we can improve the world around us and put our faith in Christ, then "the burden will be made light for us, since we will place the whole load on the shoulders of his providence and goodness."[64]

There can be something attractive about this grand departure from a tradition going back to Jesus, Paul and Augustine of making communities of men and women that waited in common for the coming of the Holy Spirit. The relationship between the individual and God becomes all-embracing, a preview of what would happen during the Reformation. For Luther, also, the individual meets God in a desert of faith. The sense of salvation through faith alone replaced the whole cumbersome apparatus of late medieval church life.

Gerson wanted to simplify, to get beyond his own fears and to reach out for a totality whose existence he denied in the world. A lonely man in a world of highly educated men, he centered his affectivity on a sweet Jesus and an all-embracing Father. Only they, and not any human bonds, could lift Gerson out of his sense of impotence in the sexual filth and political morass of the world.

Gerson still believed in the Church and its community, even if his emotions and moral standards separated him from the people in the Church. From the point of view of a world that has moved past the promise of modernity, it is fair to conclude that Gerson, in his affectivity and sexuality, helped ready the way for the modern world of individualistic solutions, brilliant individual achievements and desperate alienation of human beings from one another. We live amid the wreckage of this brave but no longer new world, with its material achievements and spiritual desolation.

NOTES

1. Another person who communicates herself is Birgitta of Vadstena (Bridget of Sweden) (1303–1373), but it is difficult to use the contents of her visions in order to convey her human relationships. See my "Friendship in Birgitta of Vadstena: Tradition or Renewal?" in Alf Härdelin and Mereth Lindgren, *Heliga Birgitta—budskapet och förebilden* (Stockholm: Kung. Vitterhets Historie och Antikvitets Akademien, 1993).

For the chronology of Gerson's life, see Palemon Glorieux, "La vie et oeuvres de Gerson," *Archives d'histoire doctrinale et littéraire du moyen âge* 25–26 (1950–1951): 149–92. Glorieux edited Gerson's works: *Jean Gerson. Oeuvres Complètes* (Paris: Desclée, 1960–1973), 1–10. I will refer to Gerson's works as Gl, according to the Glorieux volume and page number.

Forthcoming in the Classics of Western Spirituality series is my introduction and translation of some of Gerson's spiritual writings: *Jean Gerson: Early Works* (New York: Paulist Press, 1998).

2. See Palemon Glorieux, "L'enseignement universitaire de Gerson," *Recherches de Théologie ancienne et médiévale* 23 (1956): 88–113.

3. The standard biography of Gerson remains that of James L. Connolly, *John Gerson. Reformer and Mystic* (Louvain: Librairie Universitaire, 1928). The Paris scholar Gilbert Ouy has spent a lifetime working on the texts of Gerson and has made many important contributions to our understanding of his life and writings. See, for example, his "Une lettre de jeunesse de Gerson," *Romania* 80 (1959): 461–72. Further Gerson studies by Gilbert Ouy are forthcoming.

4. The best study of Gerson's background remains Henri Jadart, *Jean Gerson. Recherches sur son origine, son village natal et sa famille* (Reims: Deligne et Renart, Libraires de l'Académie, 1881).

5. "Late Medieval Care and Control of Women: Jean Gerson and his Sisters," *Revue d'histoire ecclésiastique* 92 (1997): 5–37.

6. Ibid., 21.

7. Arguments contained in Gerson's *Discourse on the Excellence of Virginity*, which I have analyzed in "Late Medieval Care and Control."

8. Gl 2:47, from Letter 9. Here and in other passages from Gerson, I use my translation forthcoming in the Classics of Western Spirituality (note 1 above).

9. Gl 2:21, from Letter 2.

10. Gl 2:3, from Letter 1.

11. Ibid.

12. See Alan E. Bernstein, *Pierre d'Ailly and the Blanchard Affair. University and Chancellor of Paris at the Beginning of the Great Schism* (Leiden: E.J. Brill, 1978).

13. Gl 2:19, Letter 2.

14. As he wrote in the same Letter 2 to his colleagues (Gl 2:18): "Cogor rursus curiae fluctibus, etsi non semper, immergi, vel ingratus judicabor; a quibus ut emigrarem sola haec fuit occasio cancellariam postulandi . . ." For Gerson as a preacher, see Louis Mourin, *Jean Gerson. Prédicateur Français* (Brugge, Belgium: De Tempel, 1952).

15. Ibid.

16. Gl 2:35, Letter 5.

17. Ibid.: "Prosunt tamen, nec nego, probatorum virorum colloquia qui ascensum contemplationis et suae arduitatis discrimina suo labore suisque periculis experti sunt."

18. Gl 2:8, Letter b.

19. Gl 2:45, Letter 9.

20. Gl 2:47: "Quamobrem, frater dilectissime cordis mei, noli animo contabescere si forte persenseris irrepere in animam tuam mollitiem illam tibi insidiantem qualem de me nunc explicui."

21. Gl 8:71–75, *De confessione mollitiei*.

22. Gl 2:45, 46. Letter 9.

23. Ibid., 46.

24. Gl 2:48, Letter 10.

25. See the few references in the article "Célestins," *Dictionnaire d'histoire et de géographie ecclésiastiques* 12:102–104 (Paris: Desclée,1953).

26. This is Letter 23, in Gl 2:86–90.

27. See the information in Gl 1:122.

28. Gl 2:87: "Nam ea lex amoris est ut vel sermone vel scripto libenter se visitent, se instruant, se solentur amici."

29. Ibid.

30. Ibid., 88.

31. Ibid. Note the almost technical vocabulary of Gerson in describing mental disturbance: ". . . nam parum differt a mania vel furia talis turbatio."

32. Ibid.

33. Ibid., 89: "Scio de meipso quia si vigilare qualiter vigilant multi compellerer, parum vel nihil differrem ab insano . . ."

34. Ibid.: "Discrete vero id agere non poteris si propria et libidinosa quaedam te et tuos affectio sic te obsideat ut aliorum a te consilia non recipias . . ."

35. Ibid., 88.

36. See Gilbert Ouy, "Enquête sur les manuscripts autographes du chancelier Gerson et sur les copies faites par son frère le Célestin Jean Gerson," *Scriptorium* 16 (1962): 275–301, with the correction added in Danièle Calvot and Gilbert Ouy, *L'oeuvre de Gerson à Saint-Victor de Paris* (Paris: Éditions du Centre National de la Recherche Scientifique, 1990), 14, n. 19.

37. See my "Sexual Control and Spiritual Growth in the Late Middle Ages: The Case of Jean Gerson," in *Tradition and Ecstasy: The Agony of the Fourteenth Century,* ed. Nancy van Deusen (Ottawa: The Institute of Mediaeval Music, 1997),123–52, esp. 132–35.

38. Gl 5:329. See my "Gerson and Bernard: Languishing with Love," *Cîteaux. Commentarii Cistercienses* 46 (1995): 127–56, esp. 142–44.

39. Trans. and commentary by James J. Sheridan (Toronto: Pontifical Institute of Mediaeval Studies, 1980).

40. Gl 5:331: ". . . tu me sequere, tu experto crede. Brevis haec lucta fructum pacatissimum afferet nisi victus foede succumbas; alioquin jugi miseria torqueberis acerrimoque pruritu etiam in senio dum a malesuavibus damnabilibusque titillationibus, ab illecebris fovere sanareque te putabis."

41. *De mystica theologia. Tractatus secundus practicus* 8.12, in *Ioannis Carlerii de Gerson De mystica theologia,* ed. André Combes (Lugano: Thesaurus Mundi, 1958): 178–79.

42. As in the classic story of the brother in the desert who is tempted by lust and goes to an old man for comfort but is told, "Believe me, my son, if God permitted the thoughts with which my own mind is stung to be transferred to you, you would not endure them." *The Desert Fathers,* trans. Helen Waddell (Ann Arbor: University of Michigan Press, 1966), 77, from "The Sayings of the Fathers," Bk. 5.13, on fornication.

43. For references, see my "Education, Confession and Pious Fraud: Jean Gerson and a Late Medieval Change," *The American Benedictine Review* 47 (1996): 310–38, esp. 324–27.

44. *De arte audiendi confessiones,* 17a consideratio: Gl 8:14–15.

45. Ibid.

46. The image of the priest as the doctor who cures the wounds of the patient is enshrined in the important canon 21 of the Fourth Lateran Council of 1215 requiring annual confession and communion from all Christians. See *Conciliorum Oecumenicorum Decreta* (Basil: Herder, 1962), 221.

47. *De arte audiendi confessiones,* 19a consideratio: Gl 8:15.

48. Ibid.

49. McGuire, "Education, Confession and Pious Fraud," esp. 324–27.

50. *De cognitione castitatis* 9:63: "Potest autem hujusmodi casus diurnae pollutionis evenire circa eos qui de necessitate habent audire confessiones vel aliqua talia cogitare vel agere ad quae sequitur aliquando, renitentibus eis toto posse et sibi praecaventibus ab initio usque ad finem, talis passio foeditatis."

51. *De arte audiendi confessiones,* 20a consideratio: Gl 8:15.

52. Ibid., 21a consideratio, Gl 8:16.

53. Ibid. On this subject of reserved cases, see Thomas Tentler, *Sin and Confession on the Eve of the Reformation* (Princeton: Princeton University Press, 1977), 304–16.

54. Gl 7.1:305.

55. Gl 7.1.310.

56. The central texts in this discussion were conveniently brought together by Eric Hicks, *Le débat sur le Roman de la Rose. Edition critique, introduction, traductions, notes* (Paris: Editions Honoré Champion, 1977).

57. Gl 2:67, Letter 15: "Sane quod de theologis introducitur quos labi refers in amorem quandoque insanum, quemadmodum mihi ipsi comminaris, a quo malo me avertat non cupido falsus sed verus dilectionis Deus . . ."

58. *De distinctione verarum revelationum a falsis,* Gl 3:52.

59. Gl 2:63, Letter 14.

60. Gl 2:105, Letter 28.

61. Gl 2:105–6: "Numquid non magna solitudo coelum? numquid non est desertum? Hinc pollicetur Dominus per prophetam: aedificabuntur in te deserta saeculorum. In hoc deserto nonaginta novem oves relictae sunt."

62. Gl 2:106–07.

63. Gl 2:61, Letter 13.

64. Gl 2:107: "Hoc modo leve nobis fiet quia totum onus super humeros suae providentiae et benignitatis et misericordiae reponemus." It is not surprising that many nineteenth-century French writers considered Gerson to be the author of the *Imitation of Christ.*

Mystical Castration
Some Reflections on Peter Abelard, Hugh of Lincoln and Sexual Control

JACQUELINE MURRAY

One of the most enduring and troublesome questions that confronted the medieval clergy, especially those who lived in the world, deprived of the security of monastic walls, was how to maintain chastity in the face of constant temptation. In particular, after the suppression of clerical marriage in the eleventh century and the extension of celibacy to the secular clergy,[1] the question of how clerics were to restrain their sexual desire and yet be in the company of women, both in daily social interaction and as pastors and ministers, became urgent in the twelfth century. This was in part a result of the development of a bustling urban culture that embraced the nascent schools and lured more and more clerics from the monasteries into the world and contact with lay men and women. Furthermore, the gradual development and extension of sacramental confession and other aspects of the *cura animarum* meant that priests frequently found themselves ministering to female parishioners.[2]

Anxiety about clerical chastity was exacerbated for bishops, charged with the supervision of clerical morality, and for the individual cleric, faced with daily temptation as he interacted with the women who populated his world. Thus, while much of the discussion of clerical chastity emanated from the monastic environment, which was theoretically free from women,[3] nevertheless, it was the priests and scholars living in the world who actually faced the threat to chastity posed by women. To them, the idealistic admonitions or misogynistic diatribes of the cloister were cold comfort and, ultimately, even irrelevant.[4] This problem was intensified for the cleric who might actually have liked women and enjoyed their company. How was such a man to maintain social and/or spiritual interactions with women without fearing his own sexuality or risking his own chastity, while also avoiding the scandal that might ensue from his relationships with women?[5] The examples of two twelfth-century men, Peter Abelard and Hugh of Avalon, provide insights into this conundrum and the psychological lengths to which a man might go to justify his relationships with women and reconcile them with the prevailing standards of morality.

The problem of clerical chastity and contact with women had been recognized by the church very early on. Certainly, holy men were needed, even encouraged, to teach women, but nevertheless, a whiff of scandal could cloud such relationships. Origen, the great third-century teacher and theologian, found an infallible, if extreme, solution to the problem of teaching women while avoiding accusations of impropriety. According to Eusebius, Origen was motivated to castrate himself in order that he might teach Christian doctrine to both men and women without eliciting scandal.[6]

Origen's self-mutilation was based on a questionable interpretation of Jesus' metaphorical statement in Matt. 19:12: "For there are eunuchs who were born thus from their mother's womb; and there are eunuchs who are made by men; and there are eunuchs who castrate themselves on account of the kingdom of heaven."[7] With Origen, this metaphor came to refer both to the symbolic and the actual abandonment of the body and to the rejection of lust and sexual desire. It was also linked to questions of propriety and the ability of a man to teach women while still controlling his lust and avoiding situations that could lead either to intercourse or to public shame and scandal. The only way Origen could be certain to avoid accusations of immorality was to be physically incapable of such acts. Ironically, Eusebius characterized Origen's action as "proof of a mind youthful and immature" but also as evidence of his "self-mastery."[8]

Origen's example, however, was not one to be emulated and castration, as a voluntary means by which men could control their desire, was quickly condemned. The Council of Nicaea (325) proclaimed that a man who had been surgically castrated for medical reasons, such as testicular cancer, or violently mutilated by barbarians could remain a cleric. However, "if anyone in good health has castrated himself, if he is enrolled among the clergy he should be suspended, and in future no such man should be promoted. . . . This refers to those who are responsible for the condition and presume to castrate themselves."[9] Castration was not to be a substitue for self control in the ongoing struggle to tame the flesh.

While the Council of Nicaea put a damper on physical, voluntary self-mutilation, nevertheless, castration remained a useful metaphor for the quenching of desire and the taming of masculine flesh through ascetic practices. For example, Jerome (ca.325–419/20) observed that, "It is necessity that makes another a eunuch, my own choice makes me so."[10] It is, perhaps, no accident that Jerome was a great teacher of women and they were his devoted companions and supporters.[11] Even the more measured and reticent Augustine lamented in his *Confessions:* "I might have more carefully listened to these words and, thus made a eunuch for the kingdom of heaven's sake, I might have more happily awaited Thy embraces."[12] For Augustine, then, the metaphor of castration denoted the man who had subdued the desires of the flesh and was devoted to God.

Despite the extremity, illegality and moral condemnation of castration, it continued to have an inescapable lure, both metaphorically and literally, perhaps because it provided certainty in the face of unreliable and weak flesh, as well as incontrovertible evidence with which to silence accusations of impropriety. For example, in his *Dialogues,* Gregory the Great discussed the example of a devout man, Equitius, who was "much distressed as a young man by violent temptations of the flesh."[13] To control these desires he prayed fervently. Then, "One night while he was earnestly begging God for aid in this matter, he saw himself made a eunuch while an angel stood by."[14] Subsequently, Equitius no longer was troubled by the desires of the flesh. Moreover, we are also told that: "Relying on this virtue, which God had helped him to acquire, he took upon himself the guidance of communities of women just as he had done of monks."[15] Thus, Equitius, castrated by miraculous intervention, achieved the same ability to teach women without sexual danger or potential scandal as Origen had by his own hand. He did, however, warn his disciples "not to be too eager to follow his example, for they would be the cause of their own downfall in trying to do what God had not given them the power to do."[16] Men with whole genitals were at greater risk than those who had been castrated, whether physically or mystically.

These early examples of castrated masters, who were equally able to teach both men and women, were commonly known in the High Middle Ages. It is perhaps not surprising, then, to find that Peter Abelard, the great twelfth-century teacher of women, and himself the cause of great scandal, sought explicitly to place himself in the company of Origen. Indeed, while Abelard lamented the cruelty done to him, he also viewed his castration as a form of liberation, similar to that of Origen, but without the associated guilt, since he was an unwilling victim.[17]

Peter Abelard (1079–1142) is perhaps the most famous *castratus* in all of western history.[18] There are numerous studies which have sought to understand and interpret the significance of his castration to himself, to Heloise[19] and to their society. Furthermore, there is extensive discussion of the psychological, theological and symbolic meanings of this real, physical act of genital mutilation. Mary McLaughlin has argued that of all the causes of shame and guilt that Abelard experienced, from his condemnation at the Council of Soissons to his failure as Abbot of St. Gildas, it was the castration that "plunged him into the agonies of shame" because it "struck at the core of his physical identity."[20] This interpretation rests on the premise that physical integrity lay at the core of Abelard's identity as a man.

A more recent scholarly trend has been to examine Abelard as a teacher and intellectual. Although his castration might be understood to have weakened his claim to a fully masculine identity, a number of scholars have suggested that through his intellectual prowess, latinity and deployment of rhetoric, Abelard was able to overcome the social liabilities, popular ridicule and marginalization that we might expect to have accompanied his very public mutilation. Andrew Taylor has examined how Abelard's love of *disputatio* and his intellectual style were displays of aggressive masculinity not dissimilar to that found on the battlefield.[21] Martin Irvine has argued that after his castration, Abelard began a process of "remasculinization" that allowed him to retain a fully masculine position is spite of the feminized social position accorded to a eunuch. He concludes that: "For Abelard, the male body is only a shell for the masculine intellect, and the wholeness of one's mind and soul transcend the physical state of the body."[22] According to Bonnie Wheeler, Abelard was able to minimize the impact of his bodily castration by celebrating both his bodily sins with Heloise, that is, his sexual prowess, and his just punishment for this virile masculine behavior. Furthermore, by invoking Origen as the greatest Christian philosopher, and thereby linking his castration to his predecessor's genius and integrity, Abelard was able to enhance his own authority.[23]

Trying to determine the exact nature of Abelard's mutilation, and its physical consequences, has also occupied historians in recent years. Some authorities have suggested that both the penis and testicles were excised, leaving him without genitals and devoid of any means to fulfill sexual desire.[24] Yves Ferroul, however, has argued convincingly that only Abelard's testicles were removed.[25] Evidence to support this conclusion includes the general meaning of the Latin *genitalia,* to refer to the testi-

cles or scrotum, rather than the whole of the male sex organs.[26] The
somewhat later testimony of Jean de Meun who, in *The Romance of the
Rose,* stated explicitly that Abelard was deprived of his "testicles" also
supports this conclusion.[27]

The exact nature of Abelard's mutilation does have a significance
beyond prurient interest. Men who undergo postpubertal castration do
not necessarily lose their sex drive. Furthermore, they are also able to
experience erections and ejaculate a fluid that is produced by the prostate
and other glands.[28] As Yves Ferroul has argued, under the circumstances
"Abelard could have sustained a physically affective if not a fully sexual
relationship with Heloise," and so he could have elected to stay in the
world and in his marriage.[29] Why he did not has much to tell us about
how Abelard understood his sexual nature, both before and after he was
castrated by Fulbert's hit men.

As Abelard mulled over the events of his life, he came to see the
hand of God in his mutilation. His evaluation of his own castration
evolved from an act of punishment, to one of human vengeance, to a
divine punishment, until finally he saw it as an expression of divine grace
that elevated him above his own human imperfection.[30] If these stages of
understanding are examined it is possible to see how Abelard moved
away from a secular value system, that extolled manifestations of virility
and sexual prowess, to embrace clerical values that put a premium on
celibacy. In such a context, he then came to view his castration as a
viable, indeed, even reasonable, solution to the problem of the body and
sexual desire.

There is little sense of remorse or the privileging of celibacy in
Abelard's early descriptions of his seduction of and subsequent sexual
relationship with Heloise. Rather, Abelard presented himself as something of a "man about town." In his *Letter of Consolation* he observed
that he felt confident Heloise would not reject his advances because "at
that time I had youth and exceptional good looks as well as my great reputation to recommend me, and feared no rebuff from any woman I might
choose to honour with my love."[31] Abelard's memory placed him in the
role of the gallant lover whom women found irresistible.

Abelard reflected on his own sexuality in a remarkably frank and
self-conscious manner. He unabashedly and unashamedly recognized his
sexual attraction, admitting he was "all on fire with desire for this girl."[32]
Indeed, his metaphor of Heloise as "a tender lamb" brought to him, "a
ravening wolf," reinforced his own self-image as a man exercising an
appropriately aggressive virility. He wrote that: "In short, our desires left

no stage of love-making untried, and if love could devise something new, we welcomed it. We entered on each joy the more eagerly for our previous inexperience, and were the less easily sated."[33] Thus, Abelard acknowledged that he enjoyed the physical aspects of sexual intimacy, those physical acts so contrary to the life of the mind.

As Abelard described himself after his castration, there was still something of the secular ideology of masculine virility and sexual prowess in his language. He focused on his shame, how humiliated he felt and how his friends lamented his mutilation.[34] This secular view is even apparent in Abelard's rationalization that this punishment fit his crime, and in his lament that "a eunuch is such an abomination to the Lord that men made eunuchs by the amputation or mutilation of their members are forbidden to enter a church as if they were stinking and unclean."[35] Had he not been so thoroughly enmeshed in a genitally defined sense of masculinity, he might have remembered, instead, the Council of Nicaea's explicit exemption of involuntary *castrati* from such harsh evaluation.

Even Abelard's enemy, Fulk of Deuil, who wrote a biting "lament" after the castration, at the same time celebrated Abelard's sexual prowess and attractiveness to women. Through his sarcastic observation that now men need not fear that Abelard would seduce their wives or violate their marriage beds, and that he was now free to walk decently through a throng of married women, Fulk hinted at his adversary's physical attractiveness.[36]

While Abelard celebrated his own virility, as soon as his sexual activities began to be a source of difficulty, he placed himself in the position not of the virile lover, but rather that of the helpless victim of the desires of the flesh. He went to Fulbert, "accusing myself of the deceit love had made me commit," and asserted "I had done nothing unusual in the eyes of anyone who had known the power of love."[37] Perhaps most significantly, however, he subtly began to shift the responsibility for the seduction and affair onto Heloise, because "since the beginning of the human race women had brought the noblest men to ruin."[38] Abelard now placed himself in the role of the hapless, almost passive, victim of a woman's charms.

In his second letter to Heloise, Abelard portrayed himself as unable to resist his sexual desire. He reminded Heloise how his "uncontrollable desire" led them to behave "shamelessly" in the refectory at Argenteuil.[39] He referred to his "unbridled lust," the intensity of "the fires of lust" which bound him to Heloise,[40] and characterized their activities

prior to marriage as "fornication" and "wanton impurities."[41] Abelard
juxtaposed his own superiority and the strength of his desires with his
inability to resist the sexual lure of Heloise, saying: "Even when you
were unwilling, resisted to the utmost of your power and tried to dissuade me, as yours was the weaker nature I often forced you to consent
with threats or blows."[42] Thus, Abelard characterized his desires as irrational and irresistible, adopting the ecclesiastical model of reason's desperate attempts to tame the flesh. Even so, his assertion of his aggressive
sexual appropriation of Heloise may indicate the lingering attraction that
the secular ideals of virility continued to hold for him. He at once
escaped responsibility because sexual desire could not be controlled or
resisted, and yet he still remained the superior aggressive male actor who
was able to impose his desire on the weaker woman.

As Abelard began to reinterpret his sexual identity, he no longer
described himself in the language of sexual prowess and virility. Rather,
he began to identify with Origen, the teacher of women, whose physical
deficiencies placed him above reproach. Abelard almost sounded
relieved as he lashed out at those who would falsely accuse him, remind-
ing them that "my present condition removes suspicion of evil-doing so
completely."[43] He repeatedly invoked the necessity for a solution to his
uncontrollable lust. He characterized his mutilation as "that wound
which was wholly beneficial"[44] and had "cut me off from the slough of
filth in which I had been wholly immersed in mind as in body."[45] For
Abelard castration was more than a punishment or an expiation of his
sins; it was also a cleansing process. He explained: "Only thus could I
become more fit to approach the holy altars, now that no contagion of
carnal impurity would ever again call me from them."[46] He even linked
castration with salvation because henceforth he would not even be able
to defile his body. This rewriting of the meaning of his castration is
encapsulated in Abelard's rhetorical question: "when divine grace
cleansed rather than deprived me of those vile members . . . what else
did it do but remove a foul imperfection in order to preserve perfect
purity?"[47] Thus, for Abelard, castration became a positive act of divine
grace that freed him from the sexual demands of his body.

As Jean Leclercq so perceptively noted, Abelard's ultimate justification for his own castration was an act of aggression against his own
body.[48] This aggression was, as perverse as it may sound to modern ears,
a celebration of castration. For Abelard, as for his hero Origen, the solution to lust was castration. Origen arranged for a surgeon to effect his
release from the body and its sexual demands. While Abelard neither

asked for nor wanted to be castrated, nevertheless, he saw this as a legitimate means by which to overcome the sexual desires that he celebrated while embracing secular values and Heloise. He rewrote the meaning of his bodily desires not only by refocusing on his intellect, but also by shifting his allegiance from a secular ideology of masculinity, which celebrated sexual prowess, to an ideology of celibacy, as propounded by the Church. In choosing to sublimate his sexual desire and put aside his wife, Abelard chose the castration that had been forced upon him.

A similar positive evaluation of castration can be found some years later in the life of Hugh of Avalon (ca.1140–1200). At the age of eight Hugh accompanied his father into a monastic community and so had been reared in an atmosphere of asceticism.[49] He professed as a canon when he was fifteen and was ordained a deacon at nineteen. Hugh eventually entered the Carthusians and, in 1186, when he was forty-six, became bishop of Lincoln. He was renowned for his piety, integrity and effectiveness. In many ways, Hugh's life could not have been more different from that of Peter Abelard. Yet, Hugh, too, experienced great sexual temptations and struggles with his flesh and his solution was not dissimilar to that of Abelard.

As a newly ordained deacon Hugh was assigned to the parish of Saint-Maximin.[50] According to the *Metrical Life,* however, the young cleric had difficulty ministering to the women in his parish and became acutely aware of the temptations of the flesh. One woman, in particular, set out to seduce Hugh: "This particular young woman made an attempt upon the heart of Saint Hugh, bringing with her as it were conclusive arguments for passion."[51] The author uses this as an opportunity to indicate the depth of Hugh's chastity and his control of his flesh:

> As I say, this person sorely tempted Saint Hugh's mind . . . By these gestures she would have moved rocks, by these signs she would have moved adamant, yet Hugh was not moved either by signs or gestures. Neither her beautiful features nor her voluptuous dress nor the manifold signs of her favour could pierce him with the flame of enticement, but whatever she planned he either did not know or pretended not to know, and his manly strength was not unsinewed by desire nor softened by the feminine beguilement.[52]

Thus, the author presented Hugh as at once strong enough to withstand the woman's seduction, yet also so innocent that he did not fully appreciate the nature of her actions.

Clearly, however, Hugh was more vulnerable than the author wanted to admit. After the woman touched his arm, the author reports that Hugh was struck by shame and anger, recoiled from her and cut out the portion of his flesh that she had touched. He concluded that: "By this means mad passion was overcome, . . . Hugh rejoiced in his double triumph, and libido lay prostrate at the victor's feet."[53] The fact that Hugh reacted with both shame and anger indicates that, while he may previously have misconstrued the woman's intentions, the touch clarified matters considerably. Furthermore, these reactions suggest that he was tempted (shame) and knew that he shouldn't be (anger). There are, in this description, echoes of the ancient hatred of the body that permeated so much of patristic writing, along with the monastic fear of women's touch. Hugh's cutting out of the contaminated flesh harkens back to the gospel admonition to cut off an offending member.[54] Furthermore, this is a clear analogy to castration as the excision of an offending member. The author wanted his readers to see that even as a young man Hugh could withstand the temptations posed by his interaction, as a member of the parish clergy, with the women to whom he ministered. Yet, despite this assertion of Hugh's triumph over temptation, the young man must, nevertheless, have been shaken by the experience because, not long afterward, he fled parochial work for the austere and hermetical life of a Carthusian monk.[55]

Fleeing the world and daily interaction with female parishioners did not mark the end of Hugh's battle to control his lust. Following in the long line of monks who struggled with the flesh, Hugh once again experienced temptation when he was about forty years old and about to be made prior of a Carthusian community. Unlike the story of Hugh's temptation and flight from the world, reported in one source only, his second and more spectacular struggle with the flesh is amply attested by various sources. According to Adam of Eynsham, by this time Hugh had "a body well tamed by his many austerities and a heart purified by assiduous meditation and continuous contemplative prayer."[56] Nevertheless, Adam reported that Hugh's sexual temptations were so strong that "he would have preferred to endure the torments of Hell, rather than the violence of his own desires."[57] The *Metrical Life* states that: "The furnace of the enticement set his vitals on fire, and the very depth of his heart was challenged by overpowering heat."[58] Gerald of Wales, more succinct but more explicit, wrote that he endured "the struggle between the flesh and the spirit."[59] So, as a mature man and an experienced monk, Hugh was once again assailed by sexual temptation, as he had been as a young man in the world.

The sources provide dramatic descriptions of Hugh's struggle and turmoil. They present him as fighting evil angels in hand-to-hand combat. The language of military prowess is invoked to describe his resistance. After warding off temptation, according to Adam, Hugh was visited in a vision by Basil, a deceased Carthusian prior, who asked him what he wanted. Hugh replied:

> "My loving father and venerable master, the law of sin and death which is in my members torments me to the death, and unless you assist me as you were wont to do, your disciple will assuredly die." He had scarcely uttered these words when the holy man said briefly "It is well, I will aid you." He immediately cut open his bowels with a knife which he seemed to be holding in his hand, and extracting something resembling red hot cinders, he flung it out of the cell a long distance away.[60]

Adam's report is somewhat more opaque than that found in the *Metrical Life,* which states that Basil "was seen holding an unsheathed knife. Opening up and probing Hugh's vital parts, he severed the inflamed gland of the flesh and flung it away like a deadly poison, outside the protecting wall of the cloister. This done, the physician disappeared, and carnal temptation . . . ceased."[61]

Both these versions leave room for interpretation. For example, the "red hot cinders" could be understood to be the fires of lust, although the "gland" referred to in the *Metrical Life* certainly leads toward the genitals. Gerald of Wales, however, did not mince words in his description of Hugh's deliverance from sexual desire. He wrote: "At length an angel appeared to him in the semblance of a man and seemed to cut off his genitals in an instant with a pair of forceps he was holding in his hands."[62] Thus, Gerald unequivocally presented a description of Hugh having been mystically castrated.

All three of the main sources, Adam of Eynsham, Gerald of Wales and the author of the *Metrical Life,* agree that from that time forth Hugh no longer experienced sexual temptation. The author of the *Metrical Life* wrote that "carnal temptation and sleep ceased to simultaneously oppress the patient . . . from that time on he did not feel any movement of the flesh strong enough to prevent him from easily checking it."[63] Gerald of Wales reported that "Hugh was given a divine remedy [for lust], and from that time on he never experienced any strong temptations or (and this is the greater miracle) hardly ever the slightest attraction."[64] Adam of Eynsham recounted that Hugh "rejoiced exceedingly at the vision, . . .

and realized that he had been completely cured both in spirit and body."[65] Thus, the immediate result of Hugh's mystical surgery was chastity and the control of the flesh.

These reports about Hugh of Avalon recall the earlier example of Equitius, who was similarly castrated in a dream. The details of the reports about the two men bear remarkable similarity, even though the more cautious twelfth-century authors seem to have hesitated to be as blatant in their descriptions of the mystical castration.[66] Nevertheless, just as mystical castration had subsequently allowed Equitius to teach women as well as men, so, too, after his mystical surgery, Hugh was able to consort with women with impunity. Adam of Eynsham wrote that:

> The confidence given him by this exceptional favour caused him to imitate the other bishops and occasionally invite devout matrons and widows to eat at his table. He used to lay his holy hands on their heads and make the sign of the cross and even sometimes reverently embrace them.[67]

Adam did not include the story that Hugh had been tempted by a woman parishioner in his early life. The only mention of Hugh's battles with chastity are those he experienced as a fully mature Carthusian monk. Yet, it was not as a monk but as a bishop, active in the world, that Hugh would have encountered women in his daily life. Significantly, this fact is recognized by Adam. He linked Hugh's "amazing gift of chastity" with his ability, as a bishop, to teach women, dine in their company and, one may hazard to suggest, be their friend. As with the earlier example of Equitius, mystical castration provided a holy man with the opportunity to be in women's company and to teach them, without being subject to sexual temptation or accusations of impropriety.

The notion that castration—mystical or otherwise—was a means to ensure chastity was problematic. Clearly, stories about Hugh's castration circulated widely and must have engendered some controversy or scandal because Adam of Eynsham was at pains to deny the story. After recounting his version of events, the excision of the red hot cinders by prior Basil, Adam stated:

> Hugh briefly narrated this to me many times in private conversations. The full and detailed account which I have now given I heard from his own lips in his last illness. . . . I have written thus about this, because I have heard that someone else gave another version in which our Lady,

the blessed virgin mother of God, appeared to him and made him a
eunuch, so that he was completely cured and did not thereafter experience the slightest carnal inclination. I have therefore set down truth-
fully what I heard from his mouth about the circumstances of the
healing and who healed him.[68]

There is, however, some ambiguity in Adam's denial. We cannot be certain which distressed him more, the suggestion of mystical castration
itself, or the thought it might have occurred at the hand of the Virgin
Mary. The author of the *Metrical Life* was more effusive in his evaluation
of events. He concludes that: "Thus Hugh won a golden trophy of victory
over his own flesh." This is similar to Abelard's understanding of castration as a divine gift that had freed him from the struggle to control his
body. It was Gerald of Wales, however, who seemed to display the most
positive and open understanding of castration. In an exhortation to
chastity, he wrote that: "No one is obliged to castrate himself, nor should
we make ourselves eunuchs (but to do so out of fervent faith and devotion is laudable)."[69] Thus, Gerald adhered to the Nicaean prohibition
while still promoting metaphorical castration as meritorious.

The persistence of stories of mystical castration may suggest that it
may have been considered a viable solution, if not a divine grace, by
devout men seeking to control a seemingly uncontrollable body. Even
Thomas Aquinas, himself, was believed to have had his genitals bound in
a girdle of chastity by two angels, who came to him in his sleep. Henceforth, his hagiographer claims, Thomas abhorred the sight of women and
avoided their company.[70] This abhorrence of women on Thomas's part, is
a distinct departure from the earlier examples in which mystical castration allowed men to be in the company of women with impunity. Nevertheless, it would seem to follow in the pattern of mystical castration as a
viable means by which to achieve perfect chastity.

In all of these examples, castration, mystical or actual, was linked to
the religious man's ability to withstand lust and reject the carnal temptations posed by women. Mystical castration was a divine gift, a sign of
God's grace and something praiseworthy. It was a powerful symbol, yet
also a means of locating the site of a man's spiritual struggle and his
identity in his genitals. While physical castration was forbidden, or too
horrible to contemplate, men, nevertheless, sought the security of mystical castration. Indeed, the depth of comfort inherent in the notion of a
body in which sexual desire had been completely eradicated was so profound that even Peter Abelard was able to gain solace and, ultimately, see

the benefits of his ordeal. Significantly, in the examples of Abelard and Hugh of Lincoln, like Origen and Equitius before them, we see men who liked women and enjoyed their company. But their very attraction to women in the intellectual or spiritual realm was inhibited by their bodies and overshadowed by their uncontrollable sexual desire. For a man who liked women, castration, mystical or actual, would appear to have been one means by which soul and body could remain pristine. Anxiety about the deleterious effects of women's company was not, then, always the result of misogyny. There is a sense in which both Peter Abelard and Hugh of Lincoln can be seen to have disliked or feared their own bodies more than they disliked or feared women. This fear of the body and its propensity to irrational sexual desire led men to do violence to themselves. In Abelard's case this violence was in the act of reinterpreting his physical mutilation. In Hugh's case, it was in his own psychological response to sexual desire and his envisioning of his own violent castration. Each, however, achieved the desired effect of being able to teach women and be in their company without accusations or the threat of impropriety. It is not perhaps startling that in a society which propagated such hatred of the physical world and the body, castration would appear as a reasonable solution to the problem of the body and sexual desire, especially among men who could not or would not avoid women.

NOTES

1. Anne Llewellyn Barstow, *Married Priests and the Reforming Papacy: The Eleventh-Century Debates* (New York: Mellen, 1982), 19–104.

2. In the course of the twelfth century, the practice of confession spread at the grassroots level, while in the schools a more refined sacramental theology was being developed. The increased need for the parish clergy to interact with and instruct the laity was recognized in twelfth-century pastoral manuals. Leonard E. Boyle, "The Inter-Conciliar Period 1179–1215 and the Beginnings of Pastoral Manuals," in *Miscellanea Rolando Bandinelli Papa Alessandro III* (Siena: Accademia Senese degli Intronati, 1986), 45–56. Canon 21 of the Fourth Lateran Council made annual confession obligatory for both men and women. *Decrees of the Ecumenical Councils,* ed. Norman P. Tanner, vol. 1, *Nicaea I to Lateran V* (London: Sheed and Ward, 1990), 245. While women may have been equally liable to confess and participate in the sacraments, the question of whether they received equitable pastoral care remains moot. See Jacqueline Murray, "The Absent Penitent: The Cure of Women's Souls and Confessors' Manuals in Thirteenth-Century England," in *Women, The Book and the Godly,*

86 *Conflicted Identities and Multiple Masculinities*

ed. Lesley Smith and Jane H.M. Taylor (Cambridge, Eng.: D.S. Brewer, 1995), 13–26.

3. For an overview of monastic rules governing chastity and restricting contact with women see Aaron W. Godfrey, "Rules and Regulation: Monasticism and Chastity," in *Homo Carnalis. The Carnal Aspect of Medieval Human Life,* ed. Helen Rodnite Lemay, Acta, 14 (Binghamton: CMERS/SUNY, 1990), 45–57. Jo Ann McNamara provides a discussion of the process by which monastic values, including the separation of men and women, came to dominate and be projected onto the secular clergy in "Canossa and the Ungendering of the Public Man," in *Render Unto Caesar. The Religious Sphere in World Politics,* ed. Sabrina Petra Ramet and Donald W. Treadgold (Washington: American University Press, 1995), 131–50. There is some debate as to just how sheltered medieval monastics were. For example, Sally Vaughn has argued that Anselm of Bec's world "encompassed women as well as men," and that he regarded friendships with women as appropriate for a prior and abbot. "St. Anselm and Women," *Haskins Society Journal* 2 (1990): 83–84.

4. Ruth Mazo Karras, "Sharing Wine, Women, and Song: Masculine Identity Formation in the Medieval European Universities," in *Becoming Male in the Middle Ages,* ed. Jeffrey Jerome Cohen and Bonnie Wheeler (New York: Garland, 1997), 187–202.

5. For a discussion of the development of the theology of scandal, particularly in the twelfth century, see Lindsay Bryan, *"Vae Mundo a Scandalis:* The Sin of Scandal in Medieval England" (Ph.D. diss., University of Toronto, 1998).

6. Eusebius, *The History of the Church from Christ to Constantine,* trans. G.A. Williamson (1965; reprint, Harmondsworth: Penguin, 1981), 8.5, 247–48. For a discussion of Origen see Peter Brown, *The Body and Society. Men, Women, and Sexual Renunciation in Early Christianity* (New York: Columbia University Press, 1988), 161–69.

7. This verse tends to be glossed over in modern translations, losing some of its power in the process. This more literal translation of Jerome's Vulgate, the version with which medieval people were familiar, is my own.

8. Eusebius, *History of the Church,* 247. This ambivalent reaction is seen in Justin Martyr's praise of a young man who sought castration to avoid sexual temptation. The incident is discussed in James A. Brundage, *Law, Sex, and Christian Society* (Chicago: University of Chicago Press, 1987), 65.

9. 1 Nicaea (325) c. 1 in *Decrees of the Ecumenical Councils,* ed. Tanner, 1.6.

10. Jerome, Letter 22, *Ad Eustochium,* CSEL 54. The english translation is from *The Letters of Saint Jerome,* trans. Charles Christopher Mierow, Ancient Christian Writers (Westminster, MD: Newman Press, 1963), 1.150.

11. For an excellent overview of Jerome's life, including his relationships with women and his devotion to Origen's theology, see Brown, *Body and Society,* 366–86.

12. Augustine, *Confessions,* CSEL 33, The English translation is from *Confessions,* vol. 5, trans. Vernon J. Bourke, Fathers of the Church 21 (New York: Fathers of the Church, 1953), 2.2.3.

13. Gregory the Great, *Dialogorum Liber I, Patrologia Latina* 77:165. Gregory's use of the verb *eunuchizari* leaves no ambiguity as to what occurred. The translation is from Gregory the Great, *Dialogues,* trans. Odo John Zimmerman (New York: Fathers of the Church, 1959), 16.

14. Gregory the Great, *Dialogorum, Patrologia Latina* 77:165; trans. Gregory the Great, *Dialogues,* 16.

15. Ibid.

16. Ibid.

17. Jean Leclercq, "Modern Psychology and the Interpretation of Medieval Texts," *Speculum* 48 (1973): 484; and Greti Dinkova-Bruun, "Cruelty and the Medieval Intellectual: The Case of Peter Abelard," in *Crudelitas. The Politics of Cruelty in the Ancient and Medieval World,* ed. Toivo Viljamaa, Asko Timoren and Chritian Krötzl (Krems: Medium Aevum Quotidianum, Gesellschaft zur Erforschung der materiellen Kultur des Mittelalters, 1992), 119. On the authenticity of the letters see Barbara Newman, "Authority, authenticity, and the repression of Heloise," *Journal of Medieval and Renaissance Studies* 22 (1992): 121–157; reprinted in Barbara Newman, *From Virile Woman to WomanChrist. Studies in Medieval Religion and Literature* (Philadelphia: University of Pennsylvania Press, 1995), 46–75.

18. There is a vast literature available on Peter Abelard. The story of his life and relationship with Heloise is so well known that it has entered the western collective consciousness of romantic love. Accordingly, the events of his life will not be rehearsed here. The most recent and comprehensive study is M.T. Clanchy, *Abelard. A Medieval Life* (Oxford: Blackwell, 1997).

19. For recent studies that examine how Heloise came to define herself in the aftermath of the scandal and her subsequent entry into religious life see Glenda McLeod, " 'Wholly Guilty, Wholly Innocent': Self-Definition in Héloise's Letters to Abélard," in *Dear Sister. Medieval Women and the Epistolary Genre,* ed. Karen Cherewatuk and Ulrike Wiethaus (Philadelphia: University of Pennsylvania Press, 1993), 64–86; Catherine Brown, "*Mulierbriter:* Doing Gender in the Letters of Heloise," in *Gender and Text in the Later Middle Ages,* ed. Jane Chance (Gainesville: University of Florida Press, 1996), 25–51; and Elizabeth Freeman, "The Public and Private Functions of Heloise's Letters," *Journal of Medieval History* 23 (1997): 15–28.

20.   Mary M. McLaughlin, "Abelard as Autobiographer: The Motives and Meaning of his 'Story of Calamities,'" *Speculum* 42 (1967): 475.

21.   "A Second Ajax: Peter Abelard and the Violence of Dialectic," in *The Tongue of the Fathers: Gender and Ideology in Medieval Latin,* ed. David Townsend and Andrew Taylor (Philadelphia: University of Pennsylvania Press, 1998), 14–34.

22.   Martin Irvine, "Abelard and (Re)writing the Male Body: Castration, Identity, and Remasculinization," in Cohen and Wheeler, *Becoming Male in the Middle Ages,* 87–106; the quotation is from 101–102.

23.   Bonnie Wheeler, "Origenary Fantasies: Abelard's Castration and Confession," in Cohen and Wheeler, *Becoming Male in the Middle Ages,* 107–28.

24.   A summary of these views is found in Yves Ferroul, "Abelard's Blissful Castration," in Cohen and Wheeler, *Becoming Male in the Middle Ages,* 135.

25.   Ibid., 135–36.

26.   Ibid., 135.

27.   Guillaume de Lorris and Jean de Meun, *The Romance of the Rose,* trans. Charles Dahlberg (Hanover and London: University Press of New England, 1983), lines 8800–8801, 160–61.

28.   Ferroul, "Abelard's Blissful Castration," 136.

29.   Ibid., 140. As Ferroul points out, according to canon law, a legitimate and consummated marriage was not nullified by subsequent castration (131). Some interesting reflections on the public and private nature of desire and the effect of Abelard's castration on his marriage to Heloise are found in Peggy Kamuf, "Marriage Contracts: The Letters of Heloise and Abelard," in eadem, *Fictions of Feminine Desire. Disclosures of Heloise* (Lincoln: University of Nebraska Press, 1982), 1–43.

30.   Claire Nouvet, "La castration d'Abélard: impasse et substitution," *Poétique* 83 (1990): 261, 269; and Dinkova-Bruun, "Cruelty and the Medieval Intellectual," 119.

31.   Pierre Abélard, *Historia Calamitatum,* ed. J. Monfrin (Paris: J. Vrin, 1959), 71. The translation is from *The Letters of Abelard and Heloise,* trans. Betty Radice (Harmondsworth: Penguin, 1974), 66.

32.   Monfrin, 70; trans. Radice, 66.

33.   Monfrin, 73; trans. Radice, 67–68.

34.   Monfrin, 80; trans. Radice, 75.

35.   Monfrin, 80; trans. Radice, 76.

36.   Fulk of Deuil, *Epistola 16, Patrologia Latina* 178:373. Fulk is discussed in Peter Dronke, *Abelard and Heloise in Medieval Testimonies* (Glasgow: University of Glasgow Press, 1976), 27; and Irvine, "Abelard and (Re)writing the Male Body," 92–93.

37. Monfrin, 75; trans. Radice, 70.
38. Monfrin, 75; trans. Radice, 70.
39. J.T. Muckle, "The Personal Letters Between Abelard and Heloise," *Mediaeval Studies* 15 (1953): 47–94. See Muckle, 88; trans. Radice, 146.
40. Muckle, 89; trans. Radice, 147.
41. Muckle, 88; trans. Radice, 146.
42. Muckle, 89; trans. Radice, 147. For a discussion of Abelard's sexual violence see Kamuf, "Marriage Contracts."
43. Monfrin, 102; trans. Radice, 98
44. Muckle, 88; trans. Radice, 146.
45. Muckle, 89; trans. Radice, 148.
46. Muckle, 89; trans. Radice, 148.
47. Muckle, 89; trans. Radice, 148.
48. Leclercq, "Modern Psychology and the Interpretation of Medieval Texts," 484.
49. The most authoritative information about Hugh comes from the life written by his friend, Adam of Eynsham, in 1212. Adam of Eynsham, *The Life of St. Hugh of Lincoln (Magna Vita Sancti Hugonis),* ed. and trans. Decima L. Douie and Hugh Farmer, 2 vols. (London: Thomas Nelson, 1961). Another life, written in verse sometime during Hugh's lifetime, likely in the 1190s, was revised after his death. *The Metrical Life of Saint Hugh of Lincoln,* ed. and trans. Charles Garton (Lincoln: Honywood Press, 1986). Gerald of Wales also wrote about Hugh in the *Gemma ecclesiastica. Giraldi Cambrensis. Opera,* ed. J.S. Brewer, Rolls Series 21 (London: Longman, 1862) , vol. 2. This has been translated in Gerald of Wales, *The Jewel of the Church. A Translation of Gemma ecclesiastica,* trans. John J. Hagen (Leiden: Brill, 1979).
50. The most recent biography of Hugh is by David Hugh Farmer, *Saint Hugh of Lincoln* (Kalamazoo, Mich.: Cistercian Publications, 1985); and idem, "Hugh of Lincoln, Carthusian Saint," in *De Cella in Seculum. Religious and Secular Life and Devotion in Late Medieval England,* ed. Michael G. Sargent (Cambridge, Eng.: D.S. Brewer, 1989), 9–15. Older studies that allude to his struggles with the flesh but glide over many of the details or implications include: George G. Perry, *The Life of St. Hugh of Avalon. Bishop of Lincoln* (London: John Murray, 1879); Herbert Thurston, *The Life of Saint Hugh of Lincoln. Translated from the French Carthusian Life* (London: Burns and Oates, 1898); Reginald Maxwell Woolley, *St. Hugh of Lincoln* (London: Society for Promoting Christian Knowledge, 1927); Joseph Clayton, *St. Hugh of Lincoln. A Biography* (London: Burns Oates and Washbourne, 1931).
51. *Metrical Life,* lines 165–166; 16, 19. The ensuing description of the woman could stand as an example of medieval men's ideals of female beauty.

52. *Metrical Life*. lines 229–235; 20–21.

53. *Metrical Life,* lines 245–260; 20–23.

54. Matt. 5:30. See the perceptive and provocative discussion by Vern Bullough and others of the links between pain and sexuality, with reference to the desert ascetics. Vern L. Bullough, Dwight Dixon and Joan Dixon, "Sadism, masochism and history, or When is behaviour sado-masochistic?" in *Sexual Knowledge, Sexual Science. The History of Attitudes to Sexuality,* ed. Roy Porter and Mikuláš Teich (Cambridge: Cambridge University Press, 1994), 47–62.

55. *Metrical Life,* lines 261–281; 22–23. Hugh's abrupt departure from parochial life led earlier historians to conclude he was afraid of women. I would argue, on the contrary, that because Hugh actually liked women, he was afraid of himself and doubted his ability to control his bodily and emotional desires. For this earlier interpretation see Woolley, *St. Hugh of Lincoln,* 7; Clayton, *St. Hugh of Lincoln,* 18.

56. Adam of Eynsham, *Magna Vita,* 2.2, in Douie and Farmer 1:49.

57. Ibid.

58. *Metrical Life,* lines 360–361; 26–27.

59. Gerald of Wales, *Gemma,* 2.17; trans. Hagen, 188.

60. Adam of Eynsham, *Magna Vita,* 2.2, in Douie and Farmer 1:51–52.

61. *Metrical Life,* lines 394–398; 28–29.

62. Gerald of Wales, *Gemma,* 2.17; trans. Hagen, 188. Substantially the same view is presented in his *Vita S. Remigii* in *Giraldi Cambrensis. Opera,* ed. James F. Dimock (London: Longman, 1877), 7.76.

63. *Metrical Life,* lines 398–402; 28–29.

64. Gerald of Wales, *Gemma,* 2.17; trans. Hagen, 188.

65. Adam of Eynsham, *Magna Vita,* 2.2, in Douie and Farmer 1:52.

66. Note that none of the sources use the verb *eunuchazari* which Gregory the Great employed to such effect.

67. Adam of Eynsham, *Magna Vita,* 4.9, in Douie and Farmer 2:48. Hugh's easy familiarity with women, including married women, has caused discomfort even among modern historians. For example, Herbert Thurston explained that Hugh was likely almost sixty years old when he would have shown such "paternal tenderness." He attributed Hugh's behavior to the "greater external demonstrativeness which allowed grown men to embrace each other and to shed tears in public without shame, [which] must have had some influence also upon the behaviour of priests and religious persons towards women. . . . Still there seems no doubt that the holy Archbishop used a freedom in his dealings with women whose saintly conduct was known to him, which in our days would rightly be deemed unbecoming." Thurston, *Life of Saint Hugh,* 613–14. In light of this, it is small wonder that the issue of Hugh's mystical castration has traditionally been ignored by historians.

68.   Adam of Eynsham, *Magna Vita,* 2.2, in Douie and Farmer 1:52.

69.   Gerald of Wales, *Gemma,* 2.20; trans. Hagen, 203.

70.   William de Tocco, *Ystoria sancti Thome de Aquino de Guillaume de Tocco (1323),* ed. Claire le Brun-Gouanvic, Studies and Texts, 127 (Toronto: PIMS, 1996), Cap. 11. The language of this passage calls to mind the practice of castration by tying a ligature around the genitals. See Emmanuel Le Roy Ladurie, "The Aiguilette: Castration by Magic," in idem, *The Mind and Method of the Historian,* trans. Siân Reynolds and Ben Reynolds (Chicago: University of Chicago Press, 1981), 84–96.

Medieval Masculinities and Modern Interpretations
The Problem of the Pardoner

VERN L. BULLOUGH
WITH GWEN WHITEHEAD BREWER

What we now call gender differences were very apparent in the Middle Ages. In general, medieval people attempted to explain these, as many moderns do, by turning to the medical explanations of the day. For the most part, medieval concepts can be traced back to Greek and Roman medicine which had become part of the accepted belief patterns of the western world. Put simply, men were warmer and dryer than women, and even the most masculine woman was not as warm and dry as the most feminine man.[1]

It was these differences in warmness and dryness that resulted in the primary sex characteristics (penis and vagina) and what we now call the secondary sexual characteristics: body shape, hair, skin touch, but which medieval people believed also affected such things as disposition. The popular medieval explanation that females were males turned inside out coincided with this explanation, as did the fact that males had more body hair than females. The growth of the beard, along with the ability to produce semen, were the key signs of virility.[2] There was worry, however, that the growing refinements and restraints of civilization might somehow feminize men, and this belief, perhaps, was a factor of the increasing frequency of the stories of hairy wild men in the later Middle Ages.

Probably the most extended medieval treatment on the difference between the sexes was by Peter Abano in the twelfth century. He held that the male spirit was livelier, given to violent impulses but slower to anger and slower to calm. The male was long-suffering at tasks of labor, eager in deeds, able, noble, magnanimous, fair, confident et al.[3] But medieval writers recognized that there were variations in the sexes and even in what might be called gender behavior, as well as in physical form. These properties have been summarized by Joan Cadden, and are important to any discussion of male stereotypes. A feminine man is tenderhearted, envious, emotionally unstable, intolerant of physical work, bitter, deceitful and timid—characteristics which are usually described as feminine in medieval writings. Such a man has less body hair than a masculine man, and he exhibits certain additional unspecified feminine behaviors. A man whose hairline starts high on his neck is womanly, shy, slow and irascible, and a man with straight eyebrows is feminine, malicious and flexible.[4]

Women with masculine qualities were highly praised, but only a limited number of feminine qualities were considered even potentially desirable in men. Caroline Bynum has pointed out some of these.[5] Certainly the nurturing qualities of the mother were projected onto Jesus and some of the apostles, and during the twelfth century Cistercian monks symbolically used feminine symbols to describe human relationships with God.[6] In general, however, praise for men with feminine qualities is not a mainstay of medieval literature as is praise for women with masculine qualities. Underlying this medieval prejudice was the belief that it was men who were superior and women who were subordinate.[7] In spite of the fact that the role of the cleric was in itself sometimes described in femininized terms, men were supposed to be men, and if they did not meet the stereotypes, medieval society expressed considerable ambivalence toward them.

This ambivalence can be illustrated in several ways. The case of hermaphrodites is a good example. Aristotle, in his discussion of such individuals, had held that hermaphrodites were really either male or female but that some sort of material accident, perhaps tumors, caused them to possess secondary organs of the opposite sex, thus causing confusion. Still, the true sex and principal genitals were consistent with the underlying complexion. Medieval writers were less certain than Aristotle, and Albertus Magnus, for example, held that sometimes it was impossible to determine which sex should prevail.[8]

Joan Cadden, in her examination of the medieval reaction to such individuals, found that hermaphrodites were often pejoratively described as rebellious or disruptive. Sometimes, and more subtly, the traits and behaviors of the individuals in question were at once identified and suppressed by attempting to reduce them to permutations of the conventional categories of masculine and feminine. As a result, hermaphroditic anatomical features, transvestite acts and homoerotic behavior became associated, and there was no real separation between them in medieval language.[9] All, in a sense, were a threat to the traditional masculine image that men had of themselves.

It is with this background that I would like to turn to an examination of a particular example of gender confusion in medieval literature, namely the character of the Pardoner in Chaucer's *Canterbury Tales*. First, a caveat. I am not a Chaucer scholar and my attempt here is to use a character to illustrate ambiguous masculinity in Chaucer's time. Then I will explore how later generations of scholars, individuals who no longer accepted the Greek humoral theory, tried to come to terms with such a character. I think such a study poses a cautionary warning to us as medievalists because it illustrates just how much our own cultural prejudices influence our interpretations of the past and emphasizes how strong the assumption was, in both medieval and modern times, that there was somehow something wrong with being an effeminate man.

Chaucer set the pattern in his general prologue to the *Canterbury Tales* by going as far as he possibly can in picturing the Pardoner as somehow defective. He emphasized the vanity of the Pardoner: "Hym thoughte he rood al of the newe jet" (A. 682).[10] His physical characteristics are described in negative terms:

> By ounces henge his lokkes that he hadde,
> And therwith he his shuldres overspradde;
> But thynne it lay, by colpons oon and oon.
> (A. 677–79)

> A voys he hadde as smal as hath a goot
> No berd hadde he, ne nevere sholde have;
> As smooth it was as it were late shave.
> I trowe he were a geldyng or a mare.
> (A. 688–91)

The Pardoner's view of himself is quite different. In fact, he seems quite proud of what he is.

> "Lordynges," quod he, "in chirches whan I preche,
> I peyne me to han an hauteyn speche,
> And rynge it out as round as gooth a belle,
> For I kan al by rote that I telle."
> (C. 329–32)

He is not ashamed of his small voice, which Chaucer compares to a goat's, but revels in it, indicating that he has spent some time perfecting it. Even his appearance he finds useful.

> "I stonde lyk a clerk in my pulpet,
> And whan the lewed peple is doun yset,
> I preche so as ye han herd bifoore
> And telle an hundred false japes moore.
> Thanne peyne I me to strecche forth the nekke,
> And est and west upon the peple I bekke,
> As dooth a dowve sittynge on a berne.
> Myne handes and my tonge goon so yerne
> That it is joye to se my bisynesse."
>
> (C. 391–399)

But it is not just the effeminate appearance of the Pardoner which sets him apart, but the entire negative portrayal of his behavior by Chaucer. Something that resulted in making the Pardoner one of the least admirable, if not the most repulsive, characters in the *Canterbury Tales*. Chaucer emphasizes that the Pardoner, even though a cleric, is anxious to promote his youthfulness, associating himself with young lovers to learn womanly ways (D.187). He is boastful of a "joly wenche in every toun" (C. 453). The Pardoner tells the other pilgrims that the theme of his sermons is always the sin of avarice, yet he also openly announces that he preaches, not "for correccioun of synne," but for money: "al my preching is [to make people give their money] . . . unto me." His skillful, manipulative preaching is extremely effective for he says one sermon to a parson's congregation elicits more money for him than the parishioners give the poor parson in a year. He carries with him a glass box "[y]crammed ful of cloutes [rags] and of bones" which he falsely sells as sacred relics that can perform miracles. The Pardoner lives well, with "moneie, wolle, chese, and whete" even though his soliciting and accepting such money means that the children "of the povereste wydwe in a village . . . sholde . . . sterve for famyne." He brags to the pilgrims that by such tricks he has "wonne, yeer by yeer, an hundred mark sith I was pardoner" (C. 345–451). In sum, in creating the Pardoner as such a repulsive character who even boasts of his hypocrisy, of his avarice and of his cruelty to the innocent poor, Chaucer established a negative prototype of the effeminate male in Western literature.

What Chaucer did not do is explain how the Pardoner came to be so effeminate. It is this question which modern scholars have tried to answer and, in the process, they have continued to perpetuate a negative stereotype of the effeminate man even as they attempted to explain the character in terms of modern attitudes and current knowledge.

INTERPRETATIONS

Most of the attention to the Pardoner has come in the twentieth century since earlier critics did not see the need for any explanation. A good example of earlier scholars is perhaps the attitude of George Lyman Kittridge, considered the "father " of American historical literary criticism. He would have insisted that Chaucer, "the gentleman," could not have meant anything vulgar about the Pardoner, especially since he wrote for an audience of both men and women.[11] Others simply labeled the pardoner as "grotesque, " as did Donald R. Howard.[12] Many agreed. Walter C. Curry wrote that the Pardoner was provided by nature with a warped mind and soul.[13] A.F. Scott called the Pardoner a "consumate hypocrite."[14]

THE PARDONER AS EUNUCH

But increasingly Chaucer scholars sought to explain why the Pardoner appeared as he did and why he might have acted as he did. One of the earliest scholars to make such an attempt was Walter Curry, who hypothesized that the Pardoner was a eunuch from birth, born without testicles. Curry summarized the popular medieval belief about such individuals:

> Born a eunuch and in consequence provided by nature with a warped mind and soul, he is compelled to follow the urge of his unholy impulses into debauchery, vice, and crime. Being an outcast from human society, isolated both physically and morally, he satisfies his depraved instinct by preying upon it. His character is consistent throughout both with itself and with nature, as described in the physiognomies. And Chaucer, the artist and a man of deep human sympathy, has shown by the infinite care with which he has developed the Pardoner's character that he is able to appreciate, without judging too harshly, the point of view of even a eunuch *ex nativitate*.[15]

Obviously, Curry felt that somehow there was something wrong about an effeminate male, but admired Chaucer for his empathy with his characters. Curry tried to make Chaucer's task easy by labeling the Pardoner a eunuch, something that the character himself could not help. The question we have to ask is whether this portrait of the eunuch or feminized male is a realistic one for the medieval period? Curry held that Chaucer was greatly influenced in his portrait by the scientific literature of physiognomy dating back to classical times. To document this, Curry relied heavily on the writing of Antonius Polemon Laodicensis who lived in the second century C.E.[16] Though Polemon's description existed in a few manuscript copies, none widely circulated, most medieval medical treatises intermixed ideas about physiognomy with astrological information. Chaucer probably had no knowledge of Polemon's description of a eunuch and instead relied upon such medieval medical writings on the subject by the pseudo-Aristotle,[17] Michael the Scot,[18] Gilbertus Anglicus,[19] the *Secretus Secretorum*[20] and Constantine the African.[21]

Medically, the most complete explanation of eunuchs available to a person of Chaucer's background was in the writings of Constantine the African, an authority whom Chaucer indicates his physician would have read.[22] Constantine included his description of eunuchs under his explanation for male sterility, something he attributed as due to at least one of four factors: (1) those whose ducts leading from the brain to the testes had been severed; (2) those who had had intercourse too often; (3) those with healthy semen but who could not have erections; and (4) those who had neither desire nor potency.[23] This last condition he links with an effeminate appearance, and it is possible that this description might fit the portrait that Chaucer wanted to draw. Certainly, it was a safe one for Curry to use because then he did not have to deal with the problems of sexuality.

Even if Constantine had furnished the base for Chaucer's portrait, a word of caution would have been necessary about the implications. Medieval writers, while accepting the influence of physiognomy and astrology to delineate character, also looked to other factors as well, since otherwise there would be no place for free will and all action would have been predetermined. This is illustrated by an example which Albertus Magnus derived from the pseudo-Aristotle. According to accepted medieval legends about Hippocrates, his disciples had made a perfect image of him and submitted it to an excellent physiognomist, who declared it to be the likeness of a man given to luxury, deceit and lustful desires of the body. The disciples, angered at what they felt was a slur upon the character of their master, reported what had been said to Hippocrates. Hippocrates calmed them, by explaining that the physiognomist had judged his natural traits correctly and that it had only been his love of philosophy and his own integrity, combined with a life of study and effort, that enabled him to triumph over nature.[24] The point to emphasize is that physiognometric predictions are a potential guide to character, but not the final determinant, and there had to be other factors which remained unexamined.

Why would Curry select this particular image of a eunuch, since the eunuch in Christian culture had a number of different images? Deeply imbedded in Christian thinking about the subject is the concept of the spiritual eunuch, a figure with whom Chaucer would have been familiar. The Gospel of Matthew, for example, includes a dialogue between Jesus and his disciples on the subject of divorce and remarriage. In the discussion, Jesus implied that remarriage after divorce was adultery, a statement which the disciples questioned. Upset at the harshness of such a judgment, some of his followers declared that if remarriage posed such dangers, it probably would be better to remain unmarried. Jesus replied:

> All men take not this word, but they to whom it is given. For there are eunuchs, who are born so from their mother's womb: and there are eunuchs, who were made so by men: and there are eunuchs, who have made themselves eunuchs for the kingdom of heaven. He that can take, let him take it.[25]

Generally, this statement was interpreted to mean that service to God demanded a self-imposed continence. But this is not the portrait of the eunuch that Curry had. Some early Christians, however, went so far as to interpret this literally. In the third century, Origen, for example, castrated himself in order to meet the standards of continence, and others followed his example.[26] Such acts of self-mutilation, however, soon came to be forbidden by the early Councils of the Church.[27] Still the Christian ideal of a eunuch, if only a scriptural eunuch in R.P. Miller's term,[28] remained. Such a person, however, would not fit the Pardoner's description either literally or allegorically.

It is hard to imagine that Chaucer would have been hostile to a "scriptural eunuch," but such a person would have had to be symbolized by a celibate and spiritual-ethical Pardoner, a character quite different from that of the Pardoner portrayed by Chaucer. Rather, the sexual state of the Pardoner is depicted in somewhat hostile terms. This, however, might also be a historical depiction, since it could have been brought about by the influence of returning crusaders, who had had contact with the Byzantine Empire and the Islamic world, where eunuchism was widespread,[29] and where eunuchs were often identified in the popular mind with both passive homosexuality and lechery. Still, Chaucer's Pardoner does not fit the exaggerations associated with the characteristics of the Byzantine eunuchs. Nor does it seem likely he was *castrati,* a person castrated to preserve his voice, since this was not a practice in England at that time.

A FEMALE TRANSVESTITE?

The ambiguities of the Pardoner probably are symbolic of the ambiguities in the medieval mind about effeminate males. The Pardoner, for
example, with the same description, could be described as a female
transvestite, although apparently no one as yet has done so. In the hagio-
graphic literature, the female who donned male garb and acted the role of
a male was a much admired figure. Many such individuals became saints
when it was discovered, at their death, that they were really female.[30]
Starting in the early Church, with St. Pelagia and St. Margarita, and continuing through St. Marina, St. Athanasia, St. Dorotheus, St. Eugenia, St.
Euphrosyne, St. Theodora and St. Anastasia Patricia, up to the twelfth-
century St. Hildegunde, such male impersonators seem to have been
much admired once their true sex became known. St. Hildegunde, who
died in 1188 and whose day is celebrated on 20 April, was the closest of
these "beardless saints" to Chaucer's own time, and Chaucer might well
have been acquainted with her story.[31] Such an explanation would also
conform to the confusion that medieval people had about various gender
dysphorias. Perhaps one of the reasons this explanation has not yet been
considered by modern scholars is that, for the most part, transvestism
was not a medical diagnosis until the 1960s. Still, it fits equally well with
Constantine's description of a eunuch.

A HERMAPHRODITE?

Another possible description for the feminized Pardoner is that he was a
hermaphrodite. Like female transvestism and eunuchism, this category,
too, has a mixed tradition. In classical culture, the hermaphrodite was an
idealized figure of which there are many surviving examples. The literature about the hermaphrodite is equally idealized.[32] For this reason,
Howard W. Jones, a modern specialist in hermaphroditism, concluded
that the classical hermaphroditic figures were not based upon any kind of
reality, but rather on an ideal, perhaps of bisexuality, since the "type of
abnormality" depicted is "but rarely observed in the examining room."[33]

    Beryl Rowland, a Chaucer scholar, advanced the idea that the Par-
doner might have been anatomically bisexual, an example of what she
called testicular pseudohermaphroditism,[34] but the person with this syndrome usually presents as a female. Moreover, since medieval midwives
usually examined infants to see that they were physically normal, any
child to survive would have had to have had only slight variations at
birth. From our present knowledge, if the Pardoner was not a hermaphro-

dite, a more likely diagnosis is that he had Klinefelter's syndrome. In such individuals (XXY), the external genitalia of the infant are male and there are testes, but as an adult both the penis and testes are smaller than normal. The somatic development through infancy and childhood is quite normal, and the disorder is often not recognized prior to puberty. Often the person lacks a beard and has a high-pitched voice. They usually are tall since, even though their upper torso is "normal," they have extra long legs. They often have breasts as adults and, although they can usually ejaculate, they lack sperm. The changes that they undergo in puberty often lead to unsatisfactory adjustments and many in today's world have opted for surgical transformation into females.[35]

Other kinds of hormonal or chromosomal imbalances are possible if we look only to biological explanations, since the range of possibilities is large. Though the appearance of the Pardoner is closest to that of Klinefelter's syndrome, the description of his sexual activities tends to present a problem. The Klinefelter's syndrome person normally would not have a sufficient sex drive to account for this conduct. The Pardoner brags about his sexual promiscuity but this might well have been fictional deceit made in an effort to appear normal. Although it is difficult and hazardous to generalize from current conditions, we know that large numbers of those individuals with sexual anomalies try to disguise themselves, try to appear similar to the ordinary person, rather than apart from them. Often such individuals today have poor self-images and take great pains not to call attention to themselves. Chaucer's Pardoner, however, is portrayed as being deliberately provocative, flaunting his sexuality in a caricature of sexual ambiguity. This conduct seems to be quite contrary to the biological explanations or even to female transvestism.

THE PARDONER AS HOMOSEXUAL

Another possible explanation for the Pardoner's conduct is that Chaucer was caricaturing an effeminate male homosexual. Whether or not Chaucer was caricaturing someone in attendance at the royal court, as Manly has argued, is beyond our ability to know.[36] We do know that Chaucer was not unacquainted with same-sex activities, now categorized as homosexuality. The term "homosexual" is a nineteenth-century one and implies a more modern connotation than Chaucer would have had. Nonetheless, religious authorities were concerned about same-sex activities in the later Middle Ages.[37] Often, in Chaucer's time, the person attracted to individuals of the same sex was described under such catchall terms as "sodomist" or as one who engaged in activities "contrary to nature." Both terms mean many other things besides same-sex contacts including, for example, masturbation. Occasionally, the classic term "pathic" was used. Other times such individuals are described simply as effeminate. A good example of this occurs in the *Roman de la Rose*, where the young lover is told not to rouge or paint his face because such a custom belonged only to ladies or to men of "bad repute" who have had the misfortune to find a love contrary to nature.[38]

Same-sex orientation appears in various fabliaux,[39] in Dante,[40] in Boccaccio[41] and in such English works as those by the Pearl Poet. The latter claimed that the descendants of Adam and Eve had turned filthy by fleshly deeds:

> Contriving practices contrary to nature, using them basely, each on the other, harming one another by their bad habits. They fouled their flesh strangely, till the friends saw the daughters of noblemen were delightfully fair, and formed fellowship with them in human fashion, thus engendering giants by their evil jesting.[42]

Self-degradation, for the Pearl Poet, was equated with same-sex activities, since men had learned the lust of the flesh where each man took for a mate "a man like himself and they join filthily in the female way" and thereby established an unclean custom.[43]

Chaucer himself elsewhere classified sexual relations between members of the same sex as a primary sin,[44] although he regarded any discussion of such sins as venturing into a forbidden area. Still, he nonetheless argued that since the Bible spoke about it, then men should also be able to discuss it. It seems clear that Chaucer was knowledgeable about sex and sexual sins.[45] In fact, the Pardoner becomes a symbol for sexual ambiguity and Chaucer makes frequent aspersions that he is not quite a man. The term "mare" or "gelding" which appears in Chaucer's description of the Pardoner, and which Curry used to make the case of the Pardoner being a hermaphrodite, are also terms then used to describe individuals who engaged in same-sex activities. Derrick Sherwin Bailey, in his analysis of the Vulgate and its English versions, pointed out that there was often an equation of "effeminate" with same-sex activity in biblical literature.[46] This usage was carried over into both Latin and English literature. A Latin poem by the twelfth-century satirist, Walter of Chatillon, for example, described a group of men who apparently engaged in same-sex activities as effeminate and also as "mares."[47]

SOME PROBLEMS

This raises two sorts of questions. If the Pardoner was homosexual why did Chaucer not simply say so? Secondly, why did it take so long for modern scholars to examine the question of homosexuality in the "Pardoner's Tale"? The easy answers are that the effeminate male was a catchall category and homosexuality itself was not a medieval term and neither was it a simple diagnosis. Moreover, medieval people often threw several categories of behavior under the concept of sin against nature, as well as under the term "sodomy." Similarly, homosexuality was not a subject much discussed in literary criticism until comparatively recently and, though hinted at, full discussion was more or less socially forbidden. While informal discussion might have taken place, it is doubtful that any scholarly journal would have printed a full discussion on the topic. Neither homosexuality nor transvestism could really be considered as a possible explanation because they were outside the purview of scholarly discussion. In fact, it was not until the 1950s that the possibility of the Pardoner being a homosexual entered into the scholarly debate, and not until 1980 did it fully reach the attention of scholarly critics.[48] Since then it has continued to be an issue.[49] It might now even be called a fashionable interpretation.

But the answer is also more complicated, at least as far as Chaucer is concerned. Chaucer represents himself as a reporter who gives us a catalog of the other pilgrims. He represents himself as a naif, a retiring, bashful, elfish rhymer to whom everything is bright, fresh and superficially superlative. He agrees with the outrageous opinion of the Monk about monastic labor; he accepts the Friar's claim to be the best beggar in his house; he calls the Maunciple "gentil," a term he extended to the red faced Summoner ["a gentil harlot and a kynde" (Prologue 647)].[50] In other words, we are expected, or at least invited, to see behind and around this often naive praise. In rhetorical terms, we are asked to consider the *effectio* as it may point to the *notatio,* the external portrayal as it may point toward the inner character, the outward and visible as it manifests the inward and invisible. And we are drawn to this possibility because Chaucer makes no overt, absolute judgments beyond superficial naive praise.

It might well be, as Manly argued,[51] that the character of the Pardoner was based on a real-life court figure and to do more than hint at sexual ambiguity would have been not only libelous but dangerous. We do know that same-sex relationships, which had been somewhat tolerated earlier in the Middle Ages, in spite of denunciations by such individuals as Peter Damian,[52] came in for increasing hostility in official Church circles in the twelfth, thirteenth and fourteenth centuries. With the development of canon law and the formalization of theological assumption, the Augustinian view of same-sex relationships became enforced. In secular society, there was a growing tendency during this period to move such relationships from the category of sin against nature, a religious issue, to the category of crime against nature, a state issue. A too obvious reference might make listeners hostile. In spite of all this, however, Chaucer's picture of the effeminate male, whether we describe him as bisexual, transvestite, homosexual, eunuch, hermaphrodite or what have you, has served as a negative literary model for the ambiguous male. Even in the twentieth century, as our knowledge of sexual development has expanded, the negative model established by Chaucer still carries great influence.

In Chaucer's defense, however, it might be argued that if the subsequent English tradition of the "swishing queen" came from the Pardoner, it was by taking him unpardonably out of context. That was done by ignoring both the tale told by him and the end of Chaucer's tale about him, and instead, letting the earthy Harry Bailey's response be the final determinant. This occurs when, after finishing his tale, the Pardoner invites Harry to "unbokele" his purse and be the first to buy, to literally "kisse," the relics offered. This is too much for Harry.

> "Nay, nay!" quod he, "thanne have I Cristes curs!
> Lat be," quod he, "it shal nat be, so theech!
> Thou woldest make me kisse thyn olde breech, And swere it were a
>   relyk of a seint, Though it were with thy fundement depeint!
> But, by the croys which that Seint Eleyne fond, I wolde I hadde thy
>   coillons [testicles] in myn hond
> In stide of relikes or of seintuarie.
> Lat kutte hem of, I wol thee helpe hem carie;
> They shul be shryned in an hogges toord!"

> (C. 946–955)

This abusive answer silences the Pardoner, who is so angry he cannot speak.

That the Pardoner's tale should be taken out of context is not surprising. That, after all, is what the Pardoner himself does; his sales pitch comes after his admission of hypocrisy and his boasts about his ability to sell false relics for his own gain. He is a hypocrite who preaches against the very vices he himself flagrantly practices (avarice, cupidity, verbal fraud). It should also be emphasized that the moral *exemplum* he preaches—the ironic tale of the three rioters who seek death and find it in their own corrupt natures and actions—is one of the most popular tales of the Canterbury sequence, and the one most often set by itself outside the frame of the Prologue and the final sales pitch and rebuke.

Moreover, the sequence about the Pardoner does not end with Harry's rebuke, but with the Knight's intervention:

> "Namoore of this, for it is right ynough!
> Sire Pardoner, be glad and myrie of cheere;
> And ye, sire Hoost, that been to me so deere,
> I prey yow that ye kisse the Pardoner.
> And Pardoner, I prey thee, drawe thee neer,
> And, as we diden, lat us laughe and pleye."
> (C. 962–967)

Though Harry will not kiss the false relics of the Pardoner, which he equates with excrement—a nice homoerotic allusion—he is made to kiss the Pardoner (kiss of peace) and make up for his gross (though perhaps accurate) insult. Thus, whether or not the Pardoner has testicles, and exactly what he would and does do with them, is less important than the reestablishment of the social order.

Clearly, the Pardoner is obviously an effeminate male, and as such seems physically aberrant if not abhorrent to Harry, and perhaps to the other pilgrims. He is, however, still recognized as a member of the social community moving toward Canterbury, and through the pilgrimage of life. Unfortunately, this aspect of the story is often forgotten, and the Pardoner has come to be a stock character for describing the effeminate male, the stock figure of the foppish, effete, "gay blade," set off from society. This is not, however, what Chaucer intended and he ended this tale with: "Anon they kiste, and ryden forth hir weye" (C. 968).

The best summation of the tale might well be that medieval people, although confused about describing gender dysphoria, and unable fully to explain it, were willing, at least, to tolerate it and to accept the differences of the socially unusual, the sexually and medically unique. While later commentators tried in various ways to explain what the Pardoner was, it might be that Chaucer was ahead of us. What does it matter, in the long run, what moderns think the real explanation for the Pardoner was? He was an effeminate male, not a pleasant situation to be in, but one that obviously existed in the medieval period. Perhaps "existed" is the correct word. We need more studies of what constituted masculinity in the Middle Ages to go beyond such a description.[53] All we can say now is that the lot of those males who were effeminate must have been a hard one in the Middle Ages. We can also add that modern commentators are only now beginning to understand the implications of gender ambiguity.

NOTES

1. This idea was developed at considerable length in terms of female differences by Vern L. Bullough, "Medieval Medical and Scientific Views of Women," *Viator* 4 (1973): 485–501. It has often been reprinted. For a more recent survey see Joan Cadden, *Meanings of Sex Difference in the Middle Ages* (Cambridge: Cambridge University Press, 1993).

2. Cadden, *Meanings of Sex Difference,* 181, citing *Secretum mulierum minor,* Cambridge University, Trinity MSS O.2.5, fols. 130–31r, and R.14–45, fol. 25r; Hildegard, *Causae et curae,* ed. Paul Kaiser (Leipzig: B.G. Teubner, 1903), 1:18.

3. Richard Foerster, ed. *De translatione Latin Physiognomicorum quae ferentur Aristotelis* (inaug diss. Kiel: Libraria Academica, 1884), 10–11. See also Petrus de Padua, *Liber compilationis physionomie,* Bibliothèque Nationale, MS lat. 16089, fol. 99a, cited in Cadden, *Meanings of Sex Difference,* 188.

4. Cadden, *Meanings of Sex Difference,* 170–212.

5. Caroline Walker Bynum, "Jesus as Mother and Abbot as Mother: Some Themes in Twelfth-Century Cistercian Writing," chap. 4 in *Jesus as Mother: Studies in the Spirituality of the High Middle Ages* (Berkeley: University of California Press, 1982), 110–69.

6. Caroline Walker Bynum, *Holy Feast and Holy Fast: Religious Symbolism of Food* (Berkeley: University of California Press, 1987).

7. Vern L. Bullough, Brenda Shelton, and Sarah Slavin, *The Subordinated Sex* (Atlanta: University of Georgia Press, 1988).

8. Albertus Magnus, *De animalibus,* 26, ed. Herman Stadler, Beiträge zur Geschichte der Philosophie des Mittelalters 15 and 16 (Münster: Aschendorf, 1916 and 1920), Bk. 18.2.3.66, 1225.

9. Cadden, *Meanings of Sex Difference,* 212.

10. The quotations are from *The Riverside Chaucer,* 3rd ed. Larry D. Benson, gen. ed. (Boston: Houghton-Mifflin, 1987).

11. George Lyman Kittridge, *Chaucer and His Poetry* (Cambridge: Harvard University Press, 1915).

12. Donald R. Howard, *The Idea of the Canterbury Tales* (Berkeley: University of California Press, 1976), 339 ff.

13. Walter Clyde Curry, *Chaucer and the Mediaeval Sciences,* rev. 2nd ed. (New York: Barnes and Noble, 1960), 70. The first edition of Curry's book appeared in 1926.

14. A.F. Scott, *Who's Who in Chaucer* (New York: Tapplinger, 1974), 44–45.

15. Curry, *Chaucer and the Mediaeval Sciences,* 54–70. The quote is from 70.

16. Polemon was a rhetorician and historian who flourished in the second century C.E. His *Physiognoman* survives in at least three manuscripts. Lynn Thorndike and Pearl Kibre, *Incipts: A Catalogue of Medievial Scientific Writings in Latin* (Cambridge, Mass.: Medieval Academy, 1937). It was edited by I.G.Z. Franzius, *Scriptores physiognominae veteres* (Altenbury, 1780), 169–310.

17. For a discussion of this, see Lynn Thorndike, *A History of Magic and Experimental Science During the First Thirteen Centuries of Our Era,* 2 vols. (New York: Columbia University Press, 1923), 2:246–78. See also George Sarton, *Introduction to the History of Science,* 3 vols. in 5, (Baltimore, Md.: Williams and Wilkins, 1927), 1:556–57. The pseudo-Aristotle probably dates from the ninth century C.E. and there are many incunabula editions. The part dealing with physiogonomy was edited by Richard Förster, "Physiognomonige secreti secretorium pseudo aristotelici versiones latinae" in *Scriptores physiognomonici graeci et latini* (Leipzig: Teubner, 1892), 2:181–222. There is an Early English Text Society edition, John Lydgate and Benedict Burgh, *Secrees of old philisoffres,* ed. by Robert Steele (Early English Text Society, 1894), extra series 66. Lydgate (1370- 1451) began the translation in *rime royal* and it was finished by Benedict Burgh (fl. 1472). There are other English prose editions. For a continuation of this, see Vern L. Bullough, "An Early American Sex Manual or Aristotle Who?" *Early American Literature* 7 (1973): 236–46.

18. Michael Scot, *Physionomia.* Thorndike, *History of Magic,* 2:308, reports eighteen editions of this between 1477 and 1660. "Physionomia" is found in Michael Scot, *De Secretis naturae* (Amsterdam, 1740), 204–328. See also Lynn Thorndike, *Michael Scot* (London: Thomas Nelson, 1964), 85–92.

19. Gilbertus Anglicus, *Compendium medicinae* (Lyons: Im. Jacobum Sacconum, 1510). An English summary of this can be found in H.E. Handerson, *Gilbertus Anglicus* (Cleveland, Ohio: Cleveland Medical Library Association, 1918), 34–36.

20. Albertus Magnus [pseud.], *Book of Secrets of Albertus Magnus,* eds. Michael R. Best and Frank H. Brightman (Oxford: Clarendon Press, 1973).

21. Constantino l'Africano, *Il Trattatao di fisiologia e igeniene sessuale,* eds. Marco T. Malato and Umberto de Martini (Rome, 1962), 14–20.

22. "Prologue," line 433. For other references see the "Merchant's Tale," lines 1810–11.

23. Constantine the African, *Il Trattatao di fisiologia e igeiene sessuale*,14–20. See also Edward I. Congren, "The Pardoner's Bid for Existence," *Viator* 4 (1973): 177–206.

24. Quoted by Thorndike, *History of Magic*, 2:575. There is a similar story in Lydgate's and Burgh's *Secrees of old philifosoffres*, st. 2486–2520; 79–80, but minus the succeeding explanation of Hippocrates.

25. Matt. 19:11–12

26. Eusebius, *Ecclesiastical History*, ed. and trans. Kirsopp Lake (London: William Heinemann, 1926), 6.8.

27. See the discussion by Derrick Sherwin Bailey, *Man-Woman Relation in Christian Thought* (New York: Harper, 1959), 72, note 11.

28. Robert P. Miller, "Chaucer's Pardoner, The Scriptural Eunuch, and the Pardoner's Tale," *Speculum* 30 (1955): 18–99. Reprinted in *The Pardoner's Tale*, ed. Dewey R. Faulkner (Englewood Cliffs, N.J.: Prentice Hall, 1973), 43–69.

29. For a discussion of eunuchs in the Byzantine system, see J.B. Bury, "Dignities and Offices of Eunuchs," in *The Imperial Administrative System in the Ninth Century* (1911; reprint, New York: Burt Franklin, 1958), 120–29; for a general discussion of eunuchs, see Vern L. Bullough, *Sexual Variance in Society and History* (1976; reprint, Chicago: University of Chicago Press, 1978).

30. See Vern L. Bullough, "Transvestites in the Middle Ages," *American Journal of Sociology* 79 (1974), reprinted in Bullough, *Sex, Society and History* (New York: Neale Watson, Science History Publications, 1976), 60–73. For a more comprehensive discussion see Vern L. Bullough and Bonnie Bullough, *Cross Dressing, Sex, and Gender* (Philadelphia: University of Pennsylvania Press, 1993).

31. I have summarized her story in the various books and articles cited above, and an easily available account is in Alban Butler, *Lives of the Saints*, revised and supplemented by Herbert Thurston and Donald Attwater, eds., 4 vols. (New York: P.J. Kennedy, 1956), 2:135.

32. Marie Delcourt, *Hermaphrodite: Myths and Rites of the Bisexual Figure in Classical Antiquity*, trans. Jennifer Nicholson (London: Studio Books, 1956).

33. Howard W. Jones Jr., "Hermaphroditism in Graeco-Roman Culture," in *Hermaphroditism, Genital Anomalies and Related Endocrine Disorders*, 2d ed., eds. Howard W. Jones and William Wallace Scott (Baltimore, Md.: Williams and Wilkins, 1971), 15.

34. Beryl Rowland, *Blind Beasts: Chaucer's Animal World* (Kent, Ohio: Kent State University Press, 1971), 100. I am not entirely sure what Rowland meant by her term since it is one no longer used in the literature. The best description of testicular feminization in male pseudohermaphrodites is by John McLean Morris, "The Syndrome of Testicular Feminization in Male Pseudohermaphrodites," *American Journal of Obstetrics and Gynecology* 65 (1953):

1192–1213. These infants, however, have female external genitalia. In fact, most hermaphrodites have external genitalia that would classify them as females as infants, although perhaps the strong emphasis on male children might have led any ambiguous child to be classed as a male.

35. Harry J. Klinefelter Jr. "Klinefelter's syndrome," in Jones and Scott, *Hermaphroditism,* 178–89.

36. John Manly, *Some New Light on Chaucer* (New York: H. Holt, 1926); and *Canterbury Tales,* ed. John Manly (New York: H. Holt,1929).

37. Bullough, *Sexual Variance,* 380–93. The increased hostility of the Church and its concern with it is argued by John Boswell, *Christianity, Social Tolerance, and Homosexuality* (Chicago: University of Chicago Press, 1980). I disagree with Boswell's main thesis in that I think the Church was always hostile to homosexuality, but I do agree with him that enforcement of prohibitions against same-sex activity became more effective during and after the twelfth century, as did public concern about it.

38. Guillaume de Lorris and Jean de Meun, *Le Roman de la Rose,* ed. Ernest Langlois (Paris: Librairie de Firmin-Didot, 1920), lines 11–12. See also the English translation by Charles Dahlbert (Princeton: Princeton University Press, 1971), 60–61.

39. See, for example, Robert Harrison, *Gallic Salt: Eighteen Fabliaux* (Berkeley: University of California Press, 1974), 366–69.

40. Dante Alighieri, *Divine Comedy, Inferno,* Canto XV, lines 106–08; *Purgatory,* Canto XXVI, lines 40–42, 76–93. Dante did not spell out exactly what constituted violence against nature or unnatural lust or sodomitical activities. Most of those assigned to the lower levels by Dante were his political enemies. Dante also grouped in Purgatory those whose transgression was "hermaphrodite."

41. See, for example, Boccaccio, *Decameron,* Tale 10 of Day 6 in which Friar Cipolla described a pilgrimage to acquire relics. G.H. McWilliams in his translation of *The Decameron* (Baltimore, Md.: Penguin, 1972), 511, claims that the passage uses code language to describe homosexual experiences.

42. "Cleanness," in the *Pearl Poet,* ed. and trans. Margaret Williams (New York: Random House, 1967), 131.

43. "Cleanness," 147–52.

44. The subject of sex and sin against nature in Chaucer began receiving attention in the 1950s and the topic has continued to attract attention. For some of the early works see Paul F. Baum, "Chaucer's Puns," *PMLA* 71 (1956): 232; P.J.C. Field and George Williams, "Chaucer's Best Joke—The Tale of Sir Thopas," chap. 8 in *A New View of Chaucer* (Durham, N.C.: Duke University Press, 1965); and Helen Storm Corsa, *Chaucer, Poet of Mirth and Morality* (South Bend, Ind.: University of Notre Dame Press, 1964).

45. "Parson's Tale," lines 577–78; "Merchant's Tale," lines 1839–49, for example.

46. Derrick Sherwin Bailey, *Homosexuality and the Western Christian Tradition* (London: Longmans, Green, 1955), 38–39; 48–53.

47. Jill Mann, "Chaucer and the Medieval Latin Poets, Part B: The Satiric Tradition," in *Writers and Their Background: Geoffrey Chaucer,* ed. Derek Brewer (Athens, Ohio: Ohio University Press, 1975), 172.

48. This was the result of an article by Monica E. McAlpine, "The Pardoner's Homosexuality and How It Matters," *PMLA* 95 (1980), 8–22. Probably the first to hypothesize on the homosexuality of the Pardoner was Muriel Bowden, *A Commentary on the General Prologue to the Canterbury Tales (*New York: Macmillan, 1948), 274–76. Others include, in order of publication date, Gordon Hall Gerould, *Chaucerian Essays* (Princeton: Princeton University Press, 1952), 58–60; Beryl Rowland, "Animal Imagery and the Pardoner's Abnormality," *Neophilologus* 48 (1964): 56–60; Jill Mann, *Chaucer and the Medieval Estates Satire: The Literature of Social Classes and the General Prologue to the Canterbury Tales* (Cambridge: Cambridge University Press, 1973), 145–51; John Gardner, *The Poetry of Chaucer* (Carbondale: Southern Illinois University Press, 1977), 30–33.

49. Since McAlpine's article, others have entered the discussion. Noteworthy have been C.D. Benson, "Chaucer's Pardoner: His Sexuality and Modern Criticism," *Medievalia* 8 (1985 for 1982): 337–49; Steven Kruger, "Claiming the Pardoner: Toward a Gay Reading of Chaucer's Pardoner's Tale," *Exemplaria* 6 (1994): 115–39; Carolyn Dinshaw, "Chaucer's Queer Touches/ A Queer Touches Chaucer," *Exemplaria* 7 (1995): 243–64.

50. Gentil and harlot, however, are an unusual pairing of the words and it might be a pun. If the Summoner is a gentleman, using the term "harlot" lowers his status. If he is of lower birth, "gentil" is also insulting to him.

51. Manly, *Some New Light on Chaucer; Canterbury Tales.*

52. Peter Damian, *Liber Gomorrhianus,* cap. vii, *Opera omnia,* ed. Constantini Cajetan, in *Patrologia Latina* 145: 167. See for example, Bullough, *Sexual Variance,* 347–414; and Boswell, *Christianity, Social Tolerance.*

53. It is hoped that this volume will contribute more to understanding this as have two other recent volumes: *Medieval Masculinities,* ed. Clare Lees with the assistance of Thelma Fenster and JoAnn McNamara (Minneapolis: University of Minnesota Press, 1994); and *Becoming Male in the Middle Ages,* ed. Jeffrey Cohen and Bonnie Wheeler (New York: Garland, 1997). Two additional studies on gender in Chaucer should also be included: Elaine Tuttle Hansen, *Chaucer and the Fictions of Gender* (Berkeley: University of California Press, 1992); and Carolyn Dinshaw, *Chaucer's Sexual Poetics* (Madison: University of Wisconsin Press, 1989).

Triangularity in the Pagan North
The Case of Bjǫrn Arngeirsson and Þórðr Kolbeinsson*

JENNY JOCHENS

Among the some forty Old Norse narratives classified as the sagas of Icelanders (or family sagas), is a subgroup labeled "skald sagas" because in
each the chief character is an Icelandic *skald* or poet.[1] The group contains a core of four, in which the major theme, expressed in several stanzas, is the poet's unhappy love for a woman. At least four other narratives
focus on a hero for whom love and poetry are found among his many pre-
occupations.[2] These men are presumed to have lived in the ninth century,
their poetry kept alive orally until the thirteenth century, when prose
authors wrote their biographies and inserted the poetry into the texts. The
consequence of this theory, if correct, would postulate that expressions
of romantic love and longing in the north predated by several centuries
similar articulations emanating from France.

These articulations of heterosexual love in the skald sagas and their
dating have long preoccupied Old Norse scholarship. Of no less interest
is the possibility that these narratives can also be used to explore other
aspects of sexuality. A growing awareness of men's bisexuality in the
classical Greek civilizations has inspired scholars to look for similar
manifestations elsewhere.[3] Increasingly it appears that, in the premodern
world, a man's sexual choice was not an either/or but a both/and.[4]

MALE BONDING IN OLD NORSE

Initially, it would seem that the Germanic/Nordic world might furnish
apposite settings for a wide spectrum of same-sex relations among men.
As the first manifestation of the *Männerbund,* the *comitatus,* identified

by Tacitus among the ancient Germans, was the first social group of nonkin. In our time, it is difficult to believe that the bonds of affection between chieftain and warriors, which extended to a willingness to die for the leader, would have excluded homoerotic feelings. Perpetuating the *comitatus*, the Viking band, which was the Nordic version of the *Männerbund*, was in decline by the time of the saga age, but the old system of male bonding persisted in royal circles, where it was expressed in affection of court poets for their king and leader. References to love or friendship [*kærleikr*] between and among men are numerous in all saga genres (although rare between a man and a woman), but these do not seem to carry homoerotic connotations. At best, only the telltale sign of jealousy raises its head. Thus, Þjóðólfr, King Haraldr Sigurðarson's chief skald, became jealous [*ǫfundsjúkr*] of the other men surrounding the king because he and Haraldr had "the greatest love and friendship [*kærleikr*]" for each other.[5]

From saga passages and legal texts it is, nonetheless, obvious that the Norse world was familiar with homosexual acts. If such activity became known, little opprobrium accrued to the person who had played the active role, but the passive partner was so despised that the mere accusation by a third party that one male had been penetrated by another was sufficient to allow the victim of the words to kill his accuser, who also could expect outlawry by the community. Most often appearing in the form of sexual libel, references to homosexual acts reflect power struggle and domination rather than eroticism and affection. As evidence of phallic aggression, some of the alleged cases may have existed only in the accuser's imagination, and others may be classified as male rape, but sufficient evidence remains to suggest that Norse men did engage in homosexual acts.[6] The category of *cinaedus,* the male who was willing to be penetrated, has not been identified in Norse culture.[7] It is likely, therefore, that a man alternated between the active and the passive role, but since the latter was despised, any man engaging in same-sex activities ran the risk of exposure. For this reason, the problem may largely have been suppressed in the sources, and rumors of passive homosexuality emerged only when sufficient hostility had accumulated.

Although best known for their love poetry, the poets in the skald sagas also had careers as court poets, but it is difficult to identify homoerotic feelings between them (or the other court poets) and the king. Since the skald sagas portray the poet's unhappy love for a woman, the situation often involves a triangle where the poet loses to a rival. Recently, gay and lesbian scholars, working under the label of "queer theory," have revived René Girard's idea of triangularity in the modern novel. A generation ago Girard proposed that the modern novel was dominated by the systematic metaphor of the triangle, within which two rivals compete for the same object, often a woman. Despite the competition, the bond between the men is as intense as that which links either of the rivals to the desired object.[8] Focusing entirely on the erotic aspect of the triangle, Eve Kosofsky Sedgwick has coined the term "homosocial desire" to identify a continuum of bonding between men.[9] The seeming contrast between "homosocial" and "desire" is intended to draw the social and political relations back into the area of the erotic and to suggest that men—whether married or not—enjoyed the former as well as the latter. The triangular scheme lends itself well to an analysis of this bonding because it allows a comparison of male/male and male/female relations at close quarters.

TRIANGULARITY IN *BJARNAR SAGA HITDŒLAKAPPA*

The theme of triangularity can be pursued in several of the skald sagas, but most successfully in *Bjarnar saga Hítdœlakappa*.[10] The story deals with two male poets, the older Þórðr and the younger Bjǫrn, and their love for the woman Oddný. I want to show that the two men's love was fueled initially by Þórðr´s erotic attraction to Bjǫrn. Although Bjǫrn may have had relations with other men later in his life, at this time he spurned Þórðr, and Þórðr, thus humiliated, turned to revenge. When Bjǫrn turned his attention to Oddný—arranging their engagement before he left for Norway—Þórðr decided to compete for her. The young man did not return within the time specified in the engagement contract, and Þórðr spread the rumor that Bjǫrn had died and married Oddný himself. Initiated in Bjǫrn´s youth, the rivalry between the two men passed through three phases for which I shall use the internal chronology of the narrative, as suggested by Sigurður Nordal.[11] The problem between Bjǫrn (born in 989) and Þórðr occurred while Bjǫrn was in his early teens. It is mentioned briefly in the first chapter and several times later.

The first phase (chs. 2–9) extended from Bjǫrn's departure in 1007 to his return in 1019. When Þórðr made a trip abroad several years after his marriage, Bjǫrn caught up with him and took revenge by robbing him of his belongings but spared his life. Later, the case between the two men was settled by King Óláfr. The second phase (chs. 10–14) covers the winter 1019–1020, which Bjǫrn spent with Þórðr and Oddný on their farm at Þórðr´s invitation. Þórðr´s gesture was intended to demonstrate that the two rivals were now able to keep the agreement negotiated by King Óláfr before Bjǫrn's return. The host quickly became irritated, however, when he noticed his wife's continued affection for, and flirtation with, Bjǫrn. The third phase (chs. 15–34), extended over the last four years of Bjǫrn's life (1020–1024), a period during which he married and settled on a farm near Þórðr. Their rivalry escalated to accusations of homosexuality, bestiality and—as I shall argue—recitation of the forbidden *mansǫngvar* aimed at each other's wives, as well as ambushes and manslaughter, culminating in Þórðr's killing of Bjǫrn.[12]

INITIAL TROUBLE

My suspicion of Þórðr's attraction to Bjǫrn is prompted by the description of the two men's appearance and physique. Already, in the first chapter, the reader is told that "Bjǫrn grew to great size early and became very strong; he was manly and handsome to look at" (1:112). Later, before his final battle, when he was thirty-five, he was described as "a very large man, handsome, freckled, red-bearded, curly-haired, and although weak of eyesight, still the best fighter" (32:197). In both his own saga and in that of Grettir, he was compared favorably with the notoriously strong protagonist of the latter narrative with whom he competed in swimming (19:163).[13]

In contrast, Þórðr was regularly referred to as a small man. Twice in poetry Bjǫrn described him as "the little fellow" [*lítill sveinn* (st. 6, 9)]. Here it may be poetic license substituting for the previous and no less flattering expression "the coward" [*sveinn enn hvíti* (st. 3)]. Prior to their final showdown, however, Bjǫrn repeated the expression *lítill sveinn* in prose (32:201), suggesting that Þórðr indeed was a small man. It is also worth noticing that when Þórðr brought Bjǫrn's severed head to Þórdís, Bjǫrn's mother, she asked him to give it to his own wife, instead, assuring him that Oddný would prefer it to "the small and miserable head that dangles from your neck" (33:205).

Þórðr's looks, therefore, did not correspond to the Norse norm for male beauty.[14] Instead, he was known as "a great skald." He put his poetic gift to good use in the service of Earl Eiríkr, but ordinary people did not like him because he "was insulting and malicious toward those he thought easy to deal with" (1:112). As a mere youth, Bjǫrn had—"as many others"—been exposed to Þórðr's "spite and *áleitni.*" Whatever may be implied by this last term, it was so severe that Bjǫrn moved away from his parents (or was sent away) and spent time with his relative Skúli, thinking

that "he was better off there than with his father because of the *áleitni* of
Þórðr Kolbeinsson" (1:112). The standard translation of *áleitni,* used
twice in close proximity, is "getting too close."[15] A passage in *Vatnsdœla
saga* suggests the form such "closeness" might take. After Þorsteinn had
redeemed himself through a valorous act, his father, Ketill, apologized for
the *frýja* [inciting] or *áleitni* he had hurled at his son earlier; he had
blamed Þorsteinn for not going to war and earning fame but, instead,
spending time by the evening fire [*bakeldr*] at home, filling his stomach
with beer and mead. Reflecting on these words, Þorsteinn remembered
his father as having asserted that he was no better than a daughter or any
other woman in using arms, and that he was a shame for the family.[16] It
seems that Ketill's *frýja* was intended to spur Þorsteinn to manly deeds
and the *áleitni* specified effeminacy as the explanation for his inaction. If
this reading is applied to the text under consideration, it must be concluded that, although Þórðr composed poems of praise both to Earl Eiríkr
and King Óláfr, in Iceland he was best known as *níð* poet.[17] In his dealings
with Bjǫrn his poetry may have contained sexual innuendoes. In addition
to "obstrusiveness" and "importunity," *áleitni* is one of the words used in
recent years to indicate sexual harassment in modern Icelandic.

The text makes four other references to the original trouble between
the two men. Immediately after having reported that Bjǫrn moved in
with Skúli, the author added: "I do not intend to dwell on the quibbles
[*smágreinir*] which occurred between Bjǫrn and Þórðr before Bjǫrn
came to Skúli because they do not concern this story" (1:112). *Bjarnar
saga* survives only in fragments, and among the lost passages was the
original beginning. A version of the (almost) first five chapters, including
the passage just quoted, was inserted into *Bœjarbók* of *Óláfs saga
helga.*[18] While it is true that the quarrel did not concern the story of King
Óláfr, readers of *Bjarnar saga* can only regret the omission in this passage on which they rely for Bjǫrn's story.

The next three references occurred in Norway. When Þórðr arrived
at the court of Earl Eiríkr, Bjǫrn was already there. Apparently the young
man did not refer to their earlier disagreement when Þórðr arrived, but
the author noted specifically that Þórðr "did not let it be known that the
relationship between him and Bjǫrn had not always been good" (3:117).
While Bjǫrn's silence was noble, Þórðr had other motives, as I shall
show. He suggested that they forget their earlier "disagreement" [*mis-
sœtti*], but when he tried to persuade Bjǫrn to let him—Þórðr—transmit
a ring to Oddný—the earl's gift to Bjǫrn—the young man answered that
had Þórðr been as "fair" [*jafnvel*] to him in Iceland as he appeared to be

at this moment, he might have trusted him now (3:117). (Nonetheless, he did ask him to convey the ring to Oddný.) The last reference to the previous trouble occurred back in Iceland. When Þórðr had made his first snide remark in poetry to Bjǫrn during the winter visit, before responding in kind, Bjǫrn commented: "You still make the kind of poem [*bragarháttinn*] you did in the old days" (12:141).

In other words, it seems that Bjǫrn in his youth had been insulted so seriously by Þórðr's poetic utterances that he preferred to avoid his company. Unfortunately, there is little evidence of the exact nature of the insult, but from legal evidence it is known that *níð*, especially expressed poetically, often involved erotic libel. Immediately following the ring episode, Þórðr asked the earl whether he was aware of Bjǫrn's age, and he proceeded to inform him that the young man was only eighteen. The subtext suggests that he appeared much older, and the author later revealed that Þórðr was fifteen years his senior.

I submit that, while in his late twenties, the small Þórðr had been smitten by the young and handsome teenage Bjǫrn, before the latter grew to full stature, and had suggested a relationship. When he was rebuffed, he began to tease and abuse the young boy in taunts undoubtedly of a sexual nature. Unwilling to comply with Þórðr's solicitations, and as yet unable to respond to his verbal challenges poetically, Bjǫrn found the situation so difficult that he moved away. Now frustrated by Bjǫrn both sexually and verbally, Þórðr was so deeply hurt that he never forgave the young man.

FIRST PHASE 1007–1019

While staying with Skúli, Bjǫrn grew into manhood and fell in love with a neighboring girl named Oddný, nicknamed "Island Candle" [*Eykyndill*] for her beauty.[19] The author reported that Bjǫrn "visited her regularly and often sat and talked with her" (1:113). These two features belong to the topos of the illicit love visit and are often a shorthand for sexual intercourse.[20] Scholars who have debated the authenticity of Bjǫrn's poetry have noted that his first stanza—which includes a reference to "the beautiful woman Eykyndill who will sleep with me as my wife" and which he allegedly recited after he had been wounded in Russia—would make more sense if it referred to an episode back home; Bjǫrn might have composed it to irritate Þórðr who had already begun to exhibit jealousy.[21] The theory is attractive because it would make Bjǫrn's physical and poetic maturity coincide.

Normally, a woman's family tried to prevent a young man from making unwanted visits by using force, if necessary. This did not happen in Bjǫrn's case, undoubtedly because Bjǫrn—in contrast to all other uninvited visitors—asked for Oddný in marriage before he left for Norway. They were engaged in an arrangement that specified that her father must wait for three years before giving her to another. If Bjǫrn was unable to return by this time, he was to send word himself (2:114).

Apparently, Þórðr could not stay away from Bjǫrn, and later the same summer he also went to Norway.[22] Here he pretended to become reconciled with Bjǫrn, but his motive was to discover the young man's future plans and, if possible, move in on Oddný. One evening, when both men were drunk, "but Bjǫrn more so," Þórðr inquired into Bjǫrn's plans before offering his own advice. He elicited from the young man the information that he intended to go on Viking expeditions before returning to Iceland, because he would not want to leave once he had married. Knowing this, Þórðr could now afford to give the opposite advice, that he thought it unwise for Bjǫrn to go abroad, not knowing "whether you will return or not;" instead he should go home and proceed with his marriage. Repeating, in passing, the uncertainty of the future, Þórðr commented that "if you return to Iceland, as we expect," but we may guess that he hoped for the opposite. He showed his own interest in Oddný by stating that "no other marriage in Iceland could be as good as with Oddný" (3:118). Against his better judgment, Bjǫrn handed to Þórðr the ring he had received from the earl and asked him to give it to Oddný, admonishing him to "do well with my errand" (3:119).

Upon his return, Þórðr did give Oddný the ring, reporting that Bjǫrn would settle the marriage later. Þórðr added, however, that Bjǫrn had transferred the marriage arrangement [*ráðahaginn*] to himself in case of Bjǫrn's death or failure to return, despite the fact that Bjǫrn had made it clear that he had commissioned other men [*sette men*] to take care of such an emergency.

Bjǫrn was seriously wounded in Russia. It took him so long to recover that all the ships had departed for Iceland when he returned to Norway, at the end of his third year of absence. When Þórðr had heard from merchants that Bjǫrn had been wounded already at the end of the second year, he paid them to spread the rumor that the young man had died. Þórðr, himself, spoke of Bjǫrn's death, even adding that he knew his burial place. Pressing to obtain Oddný in marriage, Þórðr was told by her relatives to wait until Bjǫrn's deadline for return had passed, but with no word from the young man the following year, Oddný was married to Þórðr.

When Bjǫrn learned of this, he refused to return to Iceland; instead, he joined the service of the English king and later spent three years on Viking expeditions in Denmark and Sweden, but he did not forget Oddný. While in England, he recited a stanza (st. 2) remarkable for its sexual frankness.[23] After several years Bjǫrn's opportunity for revenge appeared when Þórðr traveled to Denmark to retrieve a legacy from his uncle. On route, Þórðr first stopped in Norway to pay respect to the new king, Óláfr helgi, where he asked privately about Bjǫrn and was told that he was on expedition with many men.

The two rivals finally met near the small Brenn Islands in Sweden, in an encounter that surely must be one of the most unheroic in Norse literature. Þórðr at first tried to hide his identity by changing his name. When this scheme failed, he instructed his men to tell Bjǫrn that he had remained in Denmark and had not yet obtained his property. Realizing that Bjǫrn wanted only him and not his men, he decided to hide under a bush, covered by his cloak and a blanket, although one of his men told him that this behavior was a "great shame" [*mikil svíverðing*]. Within the Brenn Islands, the two parties had anchored by the two small islands, named Þrælaeyrr (Slave Island) and *Oddaeyrr* (Point Island), respectively. At this moment the island on which Þórðr was hiding is not indicated, but later, in Iceland, Bjǫrn referred to their meeting on "the Slave island" in a stanza. Since the name is known only from this text, it seems intended to add to Þórðr's shame. Þórðr, nonetheless, pretended that hiding under a bush was a normal way in which to encounter an enemy, because, as Bjǫrn approached, he jumped up and "greeted him well." When Bjǫrn made it clear that he knew all about Þórðr's deceitful behavior concerning Oddný, Þórðr offered compensation. Declaring that Þórðr deserved to die, Bjǫrn nonetheless spared his life because he had been the king's guest, but Bjǫrn robbed him of his property (7:127–30). Eventually the king negotiated a settlement between them and urged them to keep peace after their return to Iceland.

SECOND PHASE 1019–1020

Þórðr returned to Iceland immediately but Bjǫrn remained with the king for two more years. When he finally arrived, at first staying with his parents, Þórðr decided—against his wife's advice—to invite Bjǫrn to spend the winter with them to "test his mind and his faithfulness to me" (11:136).[24] His hidden agenda of aggression, or at least his ambivalence, is suggested by the semiotics of the blue cape which he wore on the trip to extend the invitation.²⁵ When Bjǫrn arrived, Þórðr at first "received him well, placed him next to himself and especially asked his men to treat them equally." During the first half of the winter on the farm, the two men, nonetheless, engaged in a series of escalating confrontations provoked by the sexual tension within the triangle. Worried by dwindling supplies as the winter deepened, Þórðr became petty and complained that Bjǫrn and his animals consumed too much food.

Þórðr's own tension surfaced immediately upon Bjǫrn's arrival and manifested itself toward Oddný. Irritated that the guest did not work, Þórðr assigned tasks to everybody and ordered Oddný to milk, one that was beneath the housewife's dignity. When she refused and ordered Þórðr to clean the animals' stalls, he slapped her (12:139–40). When Bjǫrn witnessed this episode, it prompted him to recite several stanzas in which he, as mentioned earlier, referred to Þórðr's small stature both in mind and body. His first stanza also suggested that Oddný wished to talk to him, and this encounter initiated a series of flirtations between Bjǫrn and the women on the farm. The prose stated that when Þórðr came home one night he discovered his guest was busy "talking to the women" [*átti tal vid konur*] and that he was "happy" [*kátr*], again, two expressions frequent in the topos of the illicit love visit and redolent with sexual overtones. Responding in verse, Þórðr referred to Bjǫrn's "flirtation . . . with the servant women" [*gleymr þinn . . . við griðkonur* (12:140, st. 4)]. Although Oddný may not have been implicated in this scene, Þórðr was suspicious. Later one evening, he came into the house very quietly to find out what was going on. Hearing voices, he thought them to belong to Bjǫrn and Oddný and attempted to eavesdrop. When Bjǫrn became aware of it, he told Oddný, who left angrily (12:141–42).

The sexual tension mounted one evening when Þórðr staged an affectionate scene with his wife, intending to test Bjǫrn's reaction. Placing Oddný on his lap, he was gentle, kissed her and recited a stanza in which he asserted his rights to her (12:142). Responding with no less than four stanzas (st. 8–11), Bjǫrn reminded Þórðr that at their encounter in Sweden he—Bjǫrn—had avenged himself for being deprived of marrying Oddný when he caused Þórðr to lose both honor and possessions. Apparently not fully convinced himself that this was sufficient, Bjǫrn "made an additional insult" [*sǫðlar því á ofan*], a stanza which intimated that he still enjoyed Oddný's favors to the extent that he had fathered one of her sons (st. 12).²⁶

When such sexual insults could escalate no further within the confines of the private household, Þórðr shifted down into another register and complained to Oddný that Bjǫrn's dog and horses ate too much. Closing the winter in the same manner in which it had begun, Þórðr displayed irritation against his wife by not sharing their bed equally and forced her to sit up, a scene which Bjǫrn related in a stanza. At the winter's end Bjǫrn took leave; he and Oddný wished each other well.

THIRD PHASE 1020–1024

Although Bjǫrn settled nearby and eventually married, the enmity between the two rivals continued to further heights and involved sexual accusations, court cases, ambushes and killings. Fifteen episodes can be identified, of which three occurred immediately after Bjǫrn's departure and twelve more followed after an interlude of two years.[27] No longer confined to Þórðr's farm, the poets appeared to have broadcast their compositions to wider audiences, despite the danger inherent in such poetry. After Bjǫrn had crafted a particularly humiliating stanza about Þórðr having been bitten by a seal, Þórðr retaliated in kind and described an episode of his rival picking up a calf from the barn floor (15:152, st. 18; 16:153, st. 19). (The degrading character of this scene eludes the modern reader.) When Bjǫrn decided to prosecute the case, friends attempted to arrange a compromise, but Þórðr insisted on taking it to the *þing* where Þórðr, nonetheless, was forced to pay an enormous fine of a hundred silver (16:154).[28] In these fifteen encounters Bjǫrn gained more honor in ten, the two men were about equal in four, but Þórðr triumphed in the final showdown, when he overwhelmed and killed Bjǫrn with twenty-four men. Eight of the encounters contained sexual insults and/or accusations classifiable as *níð*.[29] For my purposes four of these are worth examining in detail.[30]

The first of these episodes (the third in the sequence) concerns the discovery on Þórðr's property of a carving, later referred to as a *níðreising* (a raised *níð* pole), which depicted "two men, one wearing a blue hood, who stood bent over, one behind the other. Considered a bad discovery, men said that the situation was not good for either of the men, but it was worse for the one who stood in front."[31] Bjǫrn immediately composed a stanza whose transmission is corrupt, undoubtedly because of its obscenity. It is possible, nonetheless, to determine that Bjǫrn identified Þórðr by name, as the one on whom injury was inflicted by a "warrior" or "phallus," probably Bjǫrn himself. In other words, by standing in front, Þórðr was identified as the passive partner in a homosexual act. Accusing Bjǫrn of both the sculpture and the stanza, Þórðr took him to court where he was sentenced to pay a fine of three marks (17:154–56), far less, however, than the hundred silver which Þórðr had been forced to pay earlier. The passage has received a great deal of critical comment.[32] I would argue that Bjǫrn deliberately represented himself as the aggressor, both in the carving and in the stanza. He had earlier avenged Þórðr's deceit concerning Oddný, but he had never forgotten the insults suffered in his youth from Þórðr's *áleitni*. He now presented himself as doing to Þórðr what the older man had tried to do to him when he was a boy. Emphasizing aggression, he portrayed himself in a blue hood—the color of violence—humiliating Þórðr bodily and visually, as well as verbally and emotionally.

By then, Bjǫrn may no longer have been a stranger to homosexual relations since he could have gained experience abroad. The attentive reader cannot help but notice that during four of his twelve years of absence from Iceland (1013–1017) he established a close relationship [*félag*] with a certain Auðunn, a man from Vík in Norway but of Danish ancestry. Auðunn bore the unique nickname *bakskiki* [Backflap]. The name suggests that he wore a coat [*skiki*] whose length was limited to the body and thus short in the rear [*bak*]. Equally important, he was an outlaw. He and Bjǫrn passed the following three years harrying in Denmark. The following year, Bjǫrn interceded with the Norwegian king and obtained permission for Auðunn to settle in Vík again. Icelandic law decreed full outlawry on a man who accused another of being the passive partner in a homosexual relationship. It is likely that the author thought a similar law obtained in Norway, although none has been recorded.[33] Furthermore, one assumes that the same penalty applied to the passive partner, as well. It is, therefore, possible that Auðunn's nickname and his outlawed status reflect his past sexual preferences, now placed at Bjǫrn's service.

The sculpture episode provided a temporary lull in the rivalry, but after two years Þórðr started up again, this time resorting to physical violence. Bjǫrn's superior strength, however, assured his survival.[34] Bjǫrn, himself, reinstated their conflict within the sexual realm, this time not human, but bestial.[35] Bjǫrn had composed a poem about Þórðr's mother which became known as *Grámagaflím*. In it he told a story of Þórðr's conception, alleging that his mother had become pregnant by eating rotten fish [*grámagi*, gray-maw] found on the shore (20:168–69).[36] Norse bestiality normally referred to a man and a horse, with the latter playing the active role. Appearing mainly in the form of libel, such references

were intended to humiliate further a man who had been accused of playing the passive role within the same-sex couple.[37] A man's active genital
activity with four-footed animals, the bestiality understood by Christian
canonists and theologians, is not mentioned in the Norse sources, but its
occurrence in Iceland, as in all rural societies, cannot be discounted.[38] At
any rate, both sexual and gender roles were reversed in Bjǫrn's poem,
since a woman conceived actively by eating a dead animal. The obscenity in the situation is increased by the second stanza, which contains a
detailed description of a pregnant woman which is unique in Norse literature ("The belly of the bride / grew beneath the breast / the woman
walked with a lean / heavy in the womb / too large around her gut"). The
prose author stated that, because of his origin, Þórðr "was not completely human from either of his parents," and the last stanza included the
now familiar accusation of cowardice.

    The prose author admitted that Bjǫrn had composed the poem, but
he shielded the author by employing a double indirection when he
inscribed it into his text. Driving sheep up into the mountains, Bjǫrn and
his workers came upon a certain Þorkell and his farmhand busy producing charcoal in a hut. Bjǫrn listened stealthily to their conversation outside, as they discussed the quarrel between himself and Þórðr and the
poetry [*verki,* a word with libelous overtones] they had composed about
each other. The two charcoal burners disagreed as to who had been more
insulting. Referring to Bjǫrn's newest composition, the prose author
reported that it was now "known to some men by word of mouth." He
proceeded to insert the poem, thereby allowing the reader to judge the
farmhand's opinion that he had never heard anything worse. In other
words, neither Bjǫrn nor the charcoal burners recited the poem, but the
author, nonetheless, inserted it into his prose.

    Þorkell immediately retorted that Þórðr's poem *Kolluvísur* [Cattle
Verses] about Bjǫrn was far worse.[39] The farmhand had not heard it.
Although urged, Þorkell at first refused to recite it because it was forbidden, but eventually he complied.[40] The author did not insert this poem,
but we must imagine that Bjǫrn let Þorkell finish his performance,
because he immediately rushed into the hut, blamed him for transgress-
ing the law, and killed him (20:170).

    Both Þorkell and Bjǫrn applied the restrictions which the *þing* ear-
lier had imposed only on the two rivals (after episode 2), that is, not to
compose poetry about each other, now extended to all other reciters as
well. It may have been in Bjǫrn's interest to do so at this moment, but
Þorkell's initial compliance—although not required specifically of

him—is understandable in view of the general prohibition against verbal affronts, especially when articulated poetically. According to the Icelandic law, *Grágás,* a man risked outlawry or at least a fine if he composed or merely recited even a few lines of any poem that contained blame [*lostr*] or disgrace [*háðung*].[41]

This legal background is important for the third episode.[42] Having been bested by Bjǫrn on two more occasions, Þórðr decided to return the conflict to the arena of the erotic.[43] At a horse *þing*—a social occasion where entertainment was furnished by fights between horses—Þórðr was invited to recite poetry. Immediately, "he recited a poem he called *Daggeisli* which he had composed about Þórdís, Bjǫrn's wife, whom Bjǫrn himself called *Landaljómi.*" The meaning of "sun" in both nicknames assures Þórdís's identity, although the information that Bjǫrn had married is lost in a lacuna in the manuscript. The prose author continued: "Listening carefully to this amusement, Bjǫrn did not need to be encouraged to respond in kind. As soon as Þórðr had finished, he recited the poem he called *Eykyndelsvísur* for further amusement" (23:174). Identification in this case was not necessary since Eykyndill, Oddný's nickname, was apparent to all.

Since nothing is known about the poems except their titles, these might indicate that they praised the two women. I shall argue, however, that they belong to the forbidden genre of *mansǫngr,* for which full outlawry was the penalty. A passage to this effect was included in both principal manuscripts of *Grágás,* in a chapter "On Poetry" and in the "Manslaughter Section" respectively.[44] The original meaning of the word itself would seem to be "a song about a *man* or female slave," but in the later genre of *rímur,* and in modern Icelandic, it is defined as a poem praising a woman or describing a poet's emotions. When the full chapter "On Poetry" is considered, however, it is clear that the lawmakers had not *mansǫngr i*n the form of love poem—a subject they could ignore—but erotic libel in mind. By suggesting the sexual use of a woman, a poet insulted the man who controlled her or was responsible for her marriage. Because *mansngvar* (the plural) belonged to a complex of verbal insults and libels that aroused anger and produced violence, they had to be controlled.

We can only guess the contents of Þórðr's *Daggeisli,* dedicated to Bjǫrn's wife, Þórdís. No indication survives, however, of a sexual relationship between her and Þórðr. Þórdís was a supportive wife who remained perfectly aware of her husband's continued affection for Oddný. When Kálfr, one of the men responsible for Bjǫrn's death, brought the victim's necklace to her, she asked Þórðr to give it to Oddný instead as a keepsake, thereby increasing his public humiliation (33:205). Bjǫrn also loved his wife, calling her *Landaljómi* [Land-Light; 23:174].[45] Beginning with this nickname, Þórðr composed his *Daggeisli* [Day-Beam] as ironic praise of his opponent's wife, doubtlessly including explicit insults against Bjǫrn, perhaps of a sexual nature.

It will be recalled that Bjǫrn had composed two love stanzas about Oddný (st. 1, 2) during his absence from Iceland, at the time she was his legal fiancée. They may not have been included as part of the *Eykyndilsvísur* he now recited, but they clearly indicate that he and Oddný had consummated their love before his departure. Since Þórðr was not involved with Oddný at the time, such suggestions may not have bothered him, even if they were now repeated, but at least one prominent husband was known to have become jealous by poetic references to his wife's previous affair.[46] Little doubt remains about Bjǫrn's continued love for Oddný, since it will be recalled that he had spent the winter with the couple and had suggested that he was still enjoying Oddný's favors, even having fathered one of her sons. If these stanzas were now part of the *Eykyndilsvísur,* their explicit references to Oddný would have angered Þórðr. But if Bjǫrn composed new stanzas for the occasion, he would hardly have missed the opportunity to remind Þórðr of the former relationship.

Briefly stated, it may be conjectured that the two poets intended to slander each other at the horse *þing.* Both labeled by the wives' affectionate nicknames, the poems may have appeared to praise the two women. Perhaps this was an effort to hide the real libelous content which undoubtedly contained suggestions of the poet's enjoyment of the other's wife or innuendoes of his sexual deficiency. Although the author of the saga had been bold enough to include poetic bestiality, the genre of *mansǫngr* was considered too dangerous, and therefore only the titles have survived.

This interpretation is reinforced by the reaction of Oddný's two sons who were present at the *þing.* Asked by Þórðr about the *skemmtan,* the older, Arnórr, who later became a famous poet himself, strongly objected and declared that it should not be tolerated. The younger, Kolli, however, thought that the two poems were fair game, because "one *verki* cancelled out the other" (33:174–75). The insinuation of the incriminating word *verki* is reinforced when the different parental status of the two boys is understood. Arnórr was provoked by Bjǫrn's insult to both his parents in the poem last recited, whereas his father's earlier poem about Þórðís and

Bjǫrn did not bother him because he knew the latter merely as a recent visitor. In contrast, Kolli was not troubled by Þórðr's humiliation, but supported Bjǫrn. At this point in the narrative, Kolli was unaware of his own paternity, but since both narrator and reader were already informed, the author allowed the young boy to support his real father at this early moment.[47] Instinctively, Kolli was not disturbed by the revelation of the relationship between Bjǫrn and his mother since he, himself, was its product. Þórðr's insult of Bjǫrn, at the beginning of the contest, may have faded from his memory or been amply matched by Bjǫrn's verse against Þórðr. In short, although the genre of *mansǫngr* was not explicitly linked to these two poems, they most probably belonged to this category of erotic libel. Bjǫrn's *Eykyndilsvísur* may have included a genuine expression of love because of his continued affection for Oddný.[48]

The final showdown between the two rivals is also worth examining.[49] Having ascertained that Bjǫrn was home alone, Þórðr organized a party of twenty-four men, whom he distributed in four groups of six, each stationed strategically around Bjǫrn's farm, waiting for him to appear (31–32:195–203). Exiting to attend to the horses, Bjǫrn was met by the four groups. Bjǫrn greeted Þórðr, the last to arrive, with the scathing remark: "You are late in arriving at such an encounter, little boy," to which Þórðr assured him—with a significant (Freudian) slip—that he would be standing close enough to give him a *klækishǫgg* [a stroke by a coward]. Before the author could explain that Þórðr "had made a slip of the tongue" [*mismælt*] and had wanted to say that he was going to give Bjǫrn a *klámhǫgg* [a stroke of shame], Bjǫrn retorted that a *klækishǫgg* was the only stroke of which Þórðr was capable.

These two terms, *klámhǫgg* and *klækishǫgg,* reveal Þórðr's true nature. The former was a stroke received on the behind which sliced off the buttocks. In *Grágás* it was used in parallel with gelding, and both were assigned to the "greater wounds" for which perpetrators risked full outlawry.[50] Its emasculating connotations are made clear from a passage in *Kormáks saga.* The word was not used directly here, but it was clearly the stroke which had wounded Bersi in the buttocks [*þjóhnappar*]. As a result he was divorced by Steingerðr who bestowed on him the obscene nickname *Raza-Bersi* [Ass-Hole Bersi].[51]

That accusations involving the word *klám* were not limited to heterosexual relations, is suggested by the term *klámyrði* [obscene language] used twice in *Sneglu-Halla þáttr.* King Haraldr was reputed to take "foul language" [*háðyrði*] as well as he gave it, absorbing even *klámyrði* "when he was in a good mood" (9.1:264). He demonstrated this receptivity one day with the poet Halli, with whom he often engaged in bawdy conversation. When Halli greatly admired a beautiful ax, the king asked him whether he was willing to allow himself to be penetrated [*ser-ðask*] to obtain it. Halli declined but added that he "could appreciate" [*várkunn þykki mér*] that the king wanted to dispose of the ax the same way he had obtained it. Pretending not to understand the gravity of the insult, the king offered the ax to Halli, stating that since it had been given to him as a gift, he would part with it in the same way. Queen þóra, however, had understood and later blamed Haraldr for having rewarded Halli for his *klámyrði* (9.10:293–94).[52] This was not the first time Halli had referred to rumors of the king's role as a passive partner. When the two first met, the king had asked whether Halli had been penetrated by the monster Agði on his way to Norway [*sarð hann yðr eigi Agði?*]. Halli retorted that he and his men had suffered "no shame" [*enga skǫm*] because Agði was waiting for better men; "he is expecting you tonight" (2:265).[53]

In other words, both *klámyrði* and *klámhǫgg* suggest effeminacy and emasculation.[54] The latter was precisely what þórðr wanted to do to Bjǫrn, most likely in retaliation for the young man's refusal many years earlier. One may wonder whether a *klámhǫgg* could be performed when the two opponents were facing each other, as Bjǫrn and þórðr clearly did in the beginning of this encounter. In another story—in which Ketill hit the Swedish king, a woman in male disguise, across the backside with his sword, adding insult to injury by declaring: "Madame, this is how we cure the itch in your crotch and I call it a *klámhǫgg*"—the body postures suggest that Ketill may have attacked from behind.[55] At any rate, in the case at hand, when Bjǫrn, already badly wounded, was on his knees, armed with only a pair of scissors, and surrounded by many men, þórðr positioned himself better to "cut off his buttocks, and Bjǫrn fell there" (32:203). Although þórðr finally succeeded in his *klámhǫgg,* the Freudian slip which produced the other word *klœkishǫgg,* a stroke by a coward, summed up Bjǫrn's opinion of his rival as a *hvítr* and *lítill sveinn.*[56] Briefly stated, Bjǫrn and þórðr were not homosexuals in the modern sense. Both were married and had fathered children, but they had also experienced homosocial desire, and may have engaged in homosexual acts.

ODDNÝ

Although this essay focuses on the two men, a few words must be said about Oddný, the object of their rivalry. Her love for the young Bjǫrn cannot be doubted. She seemed to have enjoyed his early visits and was one of the few women to whom the sagas of Icelanders granted the right of consent in marriage.[57] When her father approached her about Bjǫrn's proposal she willingly agreed because "she knew him beforehand and they had loved each other for a long time" (2:114). When Bjǫrn did not return, however, she apparently married Þórðr without complaint. The author suggests that people thought it a more prestigious marriage than with Bjǫrn. She and Þórðr "got along well" (6:125), and later she remarked that she had believed her husband to be "a good man." She changed her mind, however, when she learned that he had deceived her by hiding Bjǫrn's survival, declaring in the same breath that she now realized he was nothing but "lies and looseness" (10:135). She suspected that Bjǫrn had made him pay for his deceit and was against Þórðr's invitation, but after Bjǫrn arrived, she enjoyed his company. She became upset over the men's quarrels (13:147), but defended Bjǫrn against Þórðr's complaints (13:148). After Bjǫrn had recited the stanza about Þórðr not giving her space in bed, she asked them to stop composing about her. Before Bjǫrn's departure she offered one of her daughters in marriage as recompense for his having lost her (14:150). After Bjǫrn's death she became seriously ill. Only then did her husband show a redeeming feature by taking care of her during her last years. Þórðr finally voiced his regret that the three protagonists had ever crossed paths.

CONCLUSION

In the triangle consisting of Þórðr, Bjǫrn and Oddný the heterosexuality of the two men, vying for the same woman, cannot be doubted. Bjǫrn's love for Oddný is never in question, and although Þórðr may have been inspired by jealousy and the desire for revenge against Bjǫrn in the beginning, he gave her a good married life for ten years, eventually loving her deeply, as indicated by his behavior after Bjǫrn's death (which had removed the justification for his jealousy). Nonetheless, the men's rivalry was more intense than their love for Oddný. Antedating their relationship with her, the men's bonding may have been of a sexual nature. The expression of homoerotic relations in Old Norse was restricted to libel. Although the passive partner received the worst opprobrium, "the situation was not good for either of them," as was stated in the *níð* pole episode. Þórðr could never have articulated his interest in the young Bjǫrn in positive terms. The authorial description of the two men, and

Þórðr's never flagging interest in Bjǫrn's physique, suggest that he had been smitten by the beauty of the young man. Although Bjǫrn had refused to play the passive partner with Þórðr, he was not beyond envisioning himself in the active role, an experience he may have gained during his four years with Auðunn. The story of these two poets demonstrates familiarity with homosocial desire in the Norse world.

NOTES

*Different versions of this essay were presented at a conference on the skald sagas arranged by Theodore M. Andersson at Stanford University in 1995 and at the University of Iceland, 1996. I am grateful to Bjarni Guðnason for a critical reading.

1. For the most recent treatment of the genre, see *Poets and Poetic Personality in the Icelandic Sagas,* ed. Russell Poole (Berlin: de Gruyter, forthcoming).

2. The first four consist of *Kormáks saga, Hallfreðar saga, Bjarnar saga Hítdælakappa* and *Gunnlaugs saga.* The other four include *Fóstbrœðra saga, Gísla saga, Grettis saga* and *Egils saga.*

3. Among the abundant and growing literature, see David M. Halperin, *One Hundred Years of Homosexuality: And Other Essays on Greek Love* (New York: Routledge, 1990); John J. Winkler, *The Constraints of Desire: The Anthropology of Sex and Gender in Ancient Greece* (New York: Routledge, 1990); David Cohen, *Law, Sexuality, and Society: The Enforcement of Morals in Classical Athens* (New York: Cambridge University Press, 1991); and idem, *Law, Violence, and Community in Classical Athens* (New York: Cambridge University Press, 1996).

4. For the English Renaissance, see Alan Bray, *Homosexuality in Renaissance England* (London: Gay Men's Press, 1982); and Jonathan Goldberg, *Sodometries: Renaissance Texts, Modern Sexualities* (Stanford: Stanford University Press, 1992).

5. Unless indicated otherwise, the Norse texts will be quoted from the series Íslenzk fornrit (ÍF) (Reykjavík: Hið íslenzka fornritafélag, 1933–), giving volume, chapter and page. In this case, see Sneglu-Halla þáttr, 9.1:263–64. The sagas of Icelanders and the short stories are now available in English translation in *The Complete Sagas of Icelanders Including 49 Tales,* gen. ed., Viðar Hreinsson, 5 vols. (Reykjavík: Leifur Eiríksson Publishing, 1997). Þjóðólfr made his last stanza about Haraldr´s fall at Stamford Bridge in 1066, and based on a comment in *Hemings þáttr,* it is generally assumed that he also fell in this battle. (But see 28.3:190, note). As a further sign of intimacy between the two men, the story

also reported that after the king had been wounded, he asked Þjóðólfr to let him rest his head in the poet's lap. This part of the story is found in *Hauksbók* (Copenhagen: Det kongelige nordiske oldskrift-selskab,1892–96), 344–45. See note 53 for further suggestion of the relationship between Haraldr and Þjóðólfr. For the relationship between King Óláfr *helgi* (St. Óláfr) and the poet Sighvatr Þórðarson, see Jenny Jochens, "From Libel to Lament: Male Manifestations of Love in Old Norse," in *From Sagas to Society,* ed. Gísli Pálsson (Enfield Lock, Middlesex, Eng.: Hisarlik Press, 1992), 247–64, esp. 247–48.

    6. Jenny Jochens, "Old Norse Sexuality: Men, Women, and Beasts," in *Handbook of Medieval Sexuality,* eds. Vern Bullough and James Brundage (New York: Garland, 1996), 369–400.

    7. On the *cinaedus in* the Roman world, see Amy Richlin, "Not Before Homosexuality: The Materiality of the *Cinaedus* and the Roman Law against Love between Men," *Journal of the History of Sexuality 3* (1993): 523–73.

    8. René Girard, *Deceit, Desire, and the Novel: Self and Other in Literary Structure,* trans. Yvonne Frecero. (Baltimore, Md.: The Johns Hopkins University Press, 1966).

    9. Eve Kosofsky Sedgwick, *Between Men: English Literature and Male Homosocial Desire* (New York: Columbia University Press, 1985).

    10. Text in ÍF 3:111–211. References will be given in the text to chapter and page in this edition. W. Bryant Bachman Jr. provides an English translation in *Four Old Icelandic Sagas and Other Tales* (Lanham, Md.: The University Press of America, 1985), 151–222; and Alison Finlay, in *The Complete Sagas,* 1:225–304. For the most recent treatment of the saga, see Bjarni Guðnason, "Aldur og einkenni Bjarnarsögu Hítdœlakappa," in *Sagnaþing helgað Jónasi Kristjánssyni sjötugum 10. apríl 1994* (Reykjavík: 1994), 1:69–85. See also Bjarni Einarsson, *Skaldasögur: Um uppruna og eðli ástaskáldasagnanna fornu* (Reykjavík: Bókaútgafa Menningarsjóðs, 1961), 234–56. (This part is not included in the Danish translation of the work, 1976). For other studies of triangularity in medieval literature, see Christine Marchello-Nizia, "Amour courtois, société masculine et figures de pouvoir," *Annales E.S.C.* 36 (1981): 969–82; and Jane Burns, *Bodytalk: When Women Speak in Old French Literature* (Philadelphia: University of Pennsylvania Press, 1993), 209–27.

    11. See Introduction to ÍF 3, lxviii-xcvii, esp. lxxxvi-lxxxvii.

    12. On the verses, see John L. Simon, "Some Aspects of the Verses in Bjarnar Saga," *Parergon 22* (1978): 25–39; Laurence de Looze, "Poet, Poem, and Poetic Process," in *Bjarnarsaga Hítdœlakappa a*nd *Gunnlaugssaga ormstungu," Journal of English and Germanic Philology 85* (1986): 479–93; and W.H. Vogt, "Die Bjarnar saga hítdœlakappa. Lausavísur, frásagnir, saga," *Arkiv för nordisk filologi 37* (1921): 27–79.

130   *Conflicted Identities and Multiple Masculinities*

13. See *Grettis saga,* ÍF 7.58:187.

14. On this issue, see Jenny Jochens, "Before the Male Gaze: The Absence of the Female Body in Old Norse," in *Sex in the Middle Ages: A Book of Essays,* ed. Joyce E. Salisbury (New York: Garland, 1991), 3–29.

15. It appears several times in the translated saints' lives. For references, see Johan Fritzner, *Ordbog over det gamle norske sprog,* 3 vols. (Kristiania, Oslo: Den norske Forlagsforening, 1886–1896), 1:31.

16. See ÍF 8.4:11, 2:4, 3:8. On *áleitni,* see Hermann Pálsson, *Úr hugmyndaheimi Hrafnkels sögu og Gretlu,* Studia Islandica 39 (Reykjavík: Bókautgafa Menningarsjóðs, 1981), 105–10.

17. On *níð* in general, see Preben Meulengracht Sørensen, *The Unmanly Man: Concepts of Defamation in Early Northern Society,* trans. Joan Turville-Petre (Odense, Den.: Odense University Press, 1983), with references. On *Bjarnar saga* specifically, see Patrick Guelpa, "Le concept de níð à partir de *Bjarnar saga Hítdœlakappa,*" *Études germaniques* 38 (1983): 442–53. See also Carol Clover, "Regardless of Sex: Men, Women, and Power in Early Northern Europe," in *Studying Medieval Women,* ed. Nancy Partner (Cambridge, Mass.: The Medieval Academy of America, 1993), 61–85.

18. See ÍF 3: lxiii–lxx, xcv–xcvii.

19. On her name, see Kari Ellen Gade, "Penile Puns: Personal Names and Phallic Symbols in Skaldic Poetry," in *Essays in Medieval Studies: Proceedings of the Illinois Medieval Association* (Urbana: University of Illinois Press, 1989), 57–67.

20. See Jenny Jochens, "The Illicit Love Visit: An Archaeology of Old Norse Sexuality," *Journal of the History of Sexuality* 1 (1991): 357–92.

21. See Sigurður Nordal's Introduction, ÍF 3:lxx-lxxiv and Vogt, "Die Bjarnar saga hítdœlakappa."

22. The author's comment that the purpose was to retrieve an inheritance in Denmark does not fit this trip but one he undertook ten years later.

23. For commentary and translation, see Roberta Frank, *Old Norse Court Poetry: The "Dróttkvœtt" Stanza,* Islandica 42 (Ithaca, N.Y.: Cornell University Press, 1978), 161–63.

24. On this passage, see Fredrik J. Heinemann, "Intertextuality in *Bjarnar saga hítdœlakappa,*" in *The Audience of the Sagas: The Eighth International Saga Conference. Preprints* (Gothenburg, Swe.: Gothenburg University Press, 1991), 1:193–200. The author's use of words also suggests Þórðr's hidden agenda; Þórðr claimed he wanted to *reyna skap Bjarnar,* echoing the expression *skapraun* which carries the meaning of provocation.

25. Saga authors regularly present a character in blue (or black) clothing when they want to indicate danger. For analysis and a list (incomplete) of such pas-

sages, see Paul Acker's introduction to his translation of *Valla-Ljóts saga* in *Comparative Criticism: An Annual Journal* 10 (1988): 207–37; esp. 208–10. In conformity with the female role as the whetter of men, Bjǫrn's mother was not only the first to notice the blue cape, but she advised him not to accept the invitation, thus refusing reconciliation, whereas Bjǫrn's father thought it would serve the purpose Þórðr stated. Young men had greater difficulty resisting female goading than older; in this case Bjǫrn first accepted his mother's advice by stating that he wanted to stay with his father and only later gave in to Þórðr's entreaties and his father's persuasion (11:136–38). I do not agree with Heinemann's translation of this passage and, therefore, draw a conclusion opposite from his (previous note, 195). Bjǫrn might not have gotten into trouble if he had stayed at home. If this is the case, his father's advice led to his downfall. Consonant with this interpretation, we notice that prior to the the the final showdown with Þórðr, Bjǫrn's father had borrowed his son's weapons, leaving him defenseless during his last battle (30:192–93). On the female whetter in the saga world, see Jenny Jochens, "The Whetter: Brynhildr" and "The Nordic Whetter," chaps. 7 and 8 respectively, in *Old Norse Images of Women* (Philadelphia: University of Pennsylvania Press, 1996), chs. 7 and 8.

26. On the similarity between this stanza and st. 28 in *Eyrbyggja saga,* see Introduction to this text, ÍF 4:viii and the Introduction to *Bjarnar saga,* lxxiii-lxxiv. On a later occasion Bjǫrn met the young Kolli and in a stanza remarked on his likeness to himself (21:171–72, st. 29; this is episode 7 in the third phase; see following note). This stanza resembles st. 27 in *Eyrbyggja saga.*

27. The episodes can be identified as follows: (1) Þórðr bitten by a seal and Bjǫrn recited *níð* stanza; (2) Þórðr recited *níð* stanza and paid fine; (3) Bjǫrn raised *níð* pole, recited *níð* stanza, and paid fine; (4) two of Þórðr's kinsmen ambushed Bjǫrn but were killed; (5) a killer in Þórðr's pay was strangled by Bjǫrn; (6) Bjǫrn composed *Grámagaflím,* Þórðr *Kolluvísur* and Bjǫrn killed the reciter of the second; (7) Bjǫrn recited a stanza about his paternity to Oddný's son Kolli; (8) Bjǫrn paid fines for employing two outlaws, but killed two others who worked for Þórðr; (9) Þórðr and Bjǫrn each recited a poem about the wife of the other; (10) Bjǫrn captured two men sent by Þórðr to kill him; (11) attacked by six men, Bjǫrn killed one; (12) attacked by nine men, Bjǫrn killed two; (13) Bjǫrn persuaded Þorsteinn to arbitrate the case between him and Þórðr; (14) Þórðr and Bjǫrn recited one last stanza; (15) final showdown in which Bjǫrn killed three men before being killed by Þórðr.

28. Episodes 1 and 2.

29. Episodes 1, 2, 3, 6, 7, 9, 14 and 15.

30. Episodes 3, 6, 9 and 15.

31. For a fuller analysis of the following, see Jenny Jochens, "Poets and Passion: Gender Relations in the Skald Sagas," in Poets and Poetic Personality in the Icelandic Sagas.

32. See Bo Almqvist, *Norrön niddiktning: Traditionshistoriska studier i versmagi. 1: Nid mot furster* (Stockholm: Almqvist & Wiksell, 1965), 177, n. 68; and Sørensen, *The Unmanly Man.* In this English translation (56–57) Sørensen has changed his mind from the Danish original (1980, 69–70) and argues for Bjǫrn as the active partner.

33. On this issue, see Kari Ellen Gade, "Homosexuality and Rape of Males in Old Norse Law and Literature," *Scandinavian Studies* 58 (1986): 124–41.

34. Episodes 4 and 5. Þórðr exhibited his usual strain of cowardice by using a numerically superior force against his enemy; 18:157–59.

35. On bestiality in general, see Joyce E. Salisbury, "Bestiality in the Middle Ages," in *Sex in the Middle Ages: A Book of Essays,* ed. Joyce E. Salisbury (New York: Garland, 1991), 173–86.

36. *Grámagi* is also identified as *rauðmagi,* the male of *hrognkelsi* (Cycloperus lumpus), whereas the female is known as *grásleppa.* On the poem, see Joseph C. Harris, "Satire and the Heroic Life: Two Studies (*Helgakviða Hundingsbana* I, 18 and Bjǫrn Hítdœlakappi's *Grámagaflím),*" in *Oral Traditional Literature: A Festschrift for Albert Bates Lord,* ed. John Miles Foley (Columbus, Ohio: Slavica Publishers, 1981), 322–39.

37. See Jochens "Old Norse Sexuality."

38. See John Liliequist, "Peasants against Nature: Crossing the Boundaries between Men and Animals in Seventeenth- and Eighteenth-Century Sweden," *Journal of the History of Sexuality* 1 (1991): 393–423.

39. Þórðr had earlier composed a single stanza in which he accused Bjǫrn of having picked up a calf from the floor, a task unworthy for the farmer himself (episode 2; 16:153, st. 19). Since this stanza was known and had been cited, the *Kolluvísur* referred to now must be a different and longer poem on a similar subject.

40. A poem with the same name is referred to in *Sneglu-Halla þáttr,* but likewise not cited; see ÍF 9.6:276.

41. See *Grágás: Lagasafn íslenska þjóðveldisisins,* eds. Gunnar Karlsson, Kristján Sveinsson and Mörður Árnason (Reykjavík: Mál og menning, 1992), 273–75.

42. Episode 9 in the sequence (note 27).

43. Episodes 7 and 8. In the former, Bjǫrn publicly announced that Oddný's son Kolli looked like himself and, in the latter, he killed two more of Þórðr's men. Bjǫrn recited the stanza about his paternity about three years after he left Þórðr's farm, when Kolli was "a few years old" (21:171). When Þórðr

and Oddný were married, the saga author reported that they eventually had five sons and three daughters (6:125). The six years of marriage (1010–1016) before Þórðr's second departure for Norway would barely be enough for the birth of eight children, and as stated here, Kolli's age would suggest that he could have been conceived by Bjǫrn during his stay on Þórðr's farm. See also note 26 and 47.

44. See *Grágás* 274. On this issue, see Jochens, "From Libel to Lament," especially 250–53.

45. Scholars have discussed who gave her the nickname. Finnur Jónsson assumed it was Þórðr [see his *Den oldnordiske og oldislandske litteraturs historie,* 2nd ed., 3 vols. (Copenhagen: Gad, 1920–24), 1:563], but Bachman, *Four Old Icelandic Sagas and Other Tales,* 192, attributes it to Bjǫrn himself. The text is ambiguous, but the latter suggestion makes more sense.

46. See King Óláfr's reaction to the story of his wife's previous relationship with the poet Óttarr, as told in *Óttars þáttr svarta.* The various versions are conveniently found in *Íslendinga sögur,* eds. Bragi Halldórsson et al. 3 vols. (Reykjavík: Svart á Hvítu, 1987), 3:2201–06. For treatment, see Jochens, "From Libel to Lament," 255–57.

47. During the final battle between the two poets, Kolli fought hard against Bjǫrn, but when Bjǫrn revealed that Kolli was not Þórðr's son but his own, the young man left the battle immediately (32:200–202). See note 43 for his age. It seems difficult to reconcile the episode at the horse *þing* with his tender age and impossible to make his role in the battle fit this chronological frame. This may suggest that both stanza 21 and the setting were borrowed from *Eyrbyggja saga;* see note 26.

48. Mediated through horses, the two men's hostility at the meeting took not only verbal but also physical form.

49. Episode 15.

50. *Grágás,* 211.

51. See ÍF 8.12:250 and 13:254. For another use of the word, see *Samsons saga fagra,* ed. John Wilson (Copenhagen: Samfund til udgivelse af gammel nordisk litteratur 65, 1953), 25.

52. Haraldr's interest in sex was notorious. After various flirtations in Byzantium, he became the only king who openly was a bigamist. In Russia he married Ellisif and brought her to Norway, where he also married Þóra.

53. See also Halli's obscene poem about the king's horse (10:294–95). On this stanza, see Michael Minkov, "Sneglu-Halli, 2:11: *Dróttinserðr,*" *Saga-Book of the Viking Society* 22 (1988): 285–86. Since the horse was a gift from the poet Þjóðólfr, Halli's poem may illuminate the relationship between the king and Þjóðólfr, his favorite poet; see note 5.

54. See also the use of the word *klámorð* by which Þórarinn referred to a previous characteristic of himself as a person whose gender it was difficult to determine; see st. 10 in *Eyrbyggja saga,* ÍF 4.19:43.

55. The scene is found in *Hrólfs saga Gautrekssonar;* text in *Fornaldar sögur Norðurlanda,* ed. Guðni Jónsson, 4 vols. (Reykjavík: n.p., 1954), 4.13:95. In retaliation the disguised king hit Ketill "with an ax under the ear so hard that he fell down head over heels"; his spill suggests that he was behind the king.

56. Þórðr's preoccupation with Bjǫrn's backside is noticeable in the failed attempt at reconciliation (episode 14). Despite Þorsteinn's valiant efforts, arbitration failed because Þórðr insisted on counting all the verses he and Bjǫrn had made. When he discovered that Bjǫrn's list contained one stanza more than his own, he demanded to compose a last verse in which he referred to Bjǫrn's broad behind. As might be expected, Bjǫrn retaliated in a stanza in which he reiterated his accusation of Þórðr's cowardice (29:189–90, st. 31, 32). For further analysis of this episode, see Jochens, "Poets and Passion," in *Poets and Poetic Personality in the Icelandic Sagas.*

57. On this issue, see Jenny Jochens, *Women in Old Norse Society* (Ithaca, N.Y.: Cornell University Press, 1995), 24–29, 44–52.

Steel Corpse
Imaging the Knight in Death

RACHEL DRESSLER

Thirteenth- and fourteenth-century England was the site of a thriving effigy industry, and prominent among its carved products were representations of knightly patrons.[1] In 1980, H.A. Tummers published a study of English secular tomb figures in which he cataloged 143 surviving military effigies from the thirteenth century alone.[2] The sheer number of armored tomb figures speaks to the increasing self-promotion among English knights during this period: their proliferation points to their protoypes' struggles to achieve autonomy from, and social parity with, the nobility. In this dynamic social process, the military effigy acted as the site for a gendering unique to the knight, and in contradiction to lived experience.

The armored figure's visual construction of an idealized masculinity operated along three trajectories: status, lineage and physical attributes. Of these categories, social status determined the articulation of the other two, both of which served the knight's social agenda. The methods employed to make visible these concerns involved costume and pose: the wearing of mail, the display of heraldic insignia and the foregrounding of the powerful male body. Behind many of these representational strategies lay the knight's growing consciousness of himself as a member of an elite, yet not a part of the highest echelon. In effect, his tomb effigy laid false claim to a status comparable to that of the highest magnates in medieval England.

Like other nonclerical figures, the knight's effigy made a relatively late appearance in medieval England. Lay burial within the church had been a controversial issue since the early Christian period. The Council of Mainz (813) forbade the burial of any within the church but bishops and abbots, worthy priests and faithful laymen.[3] Nevertheless, the *Anglo-Saxon Chronicle* indicates at least one instance of a lay burial in preconquest England.[4] Yet, lay church burial seems to have been restricted to peripheral spaces such as the *porticus* until the twelfth century.[5] Questions about the practice persisted to the end of the thirteenth century, when, in 1292, the Statutes of Chichester limited lay church burial to lords of the village, patrons of the church and their wives.[6] Church burial thus came to signify high status.

While lay tombs may have found a relatively early place within the church precinct, three-dimensional representations of them did not, at least in England.[7] The earliest three-dimensional effigies were ecclesiastical: abbots, bishops and archbishops. This representational practice dates back to the mid-twelfth century. It was not until 1230–1240 that the first military effigy made an appearance in the figure of William Longespée, now located in the south aisle of Salisbury cathedral (Figs. 1 and 2).

Scholars have arrived at the date for this figure based upon its stylistic affinities with some of the facade sculpture from Wells cathedral.[8] It is thought that the workshop responsible for the Wells figures eventually established itself in the west of England, specifically Bristol, from which its funeral products were disseminated across the country throughout the decades of the fifties and sixties.[9] There was also an active southeastern, possibly London, group working in the 1260s, as well as one or two ateliers active in Yorkshire in the first half of the fourteenth century.[10] The distinctive traits of these workshops will be discussed at various relevant points in this essay.

THE EFFIGIES' CONSTRUCTION OF CLASS

The thirteenth- and early-fourteenth-century English military effigies are chiefly characterized by the wearing of chain mail indicating a knightly status. In choosing to have themselves or their ancestors portrayed in this costume, knightly patrons were following the practices of churchmen, who earlier chose to represent themselves in the vestments of their ecclesiastical office. On the tomb of Archbishop de Gray in York cathedral, for example, the effigy is shown wearing mitre, alb and dalmatic, and holding the bishop's staff (Fig. 3).[11]

Royalty followed ecclesiastical practice in representing themselves by their office in life. They are most often shown in royal regalia. King John, buried in Worcester cathedral, is depicted lying on top of his tomb

Figure 1. "William Longespée," Salisbury Cathedral, ca. 1240s, right side (photo by author).

Figure 2. "William Longespée," Salisbury Cathedral, ca. 1240s, left side (photo by author).

Figure 3. Archbishop de Gray, York Cathedral, ca. 1255 (photo by Evelyn Lane; used by permission).

wearing an ankle-length tunic, with a crown on his head and what was probably a scepter in his right hand (Fig. 4).[12]

The knights' choice of mail has been of most interest to costume and military historians, who have mined the effigies for information about the evolution of medieval dress or military technology.[13] While the correspondence between the effigies' costume and actual armor may not be absolute, we can observe certain changes in types of armor occurring within the corpus of knights' figures. The earliest effigies, such as William Longespée, wear a mail coif, hauberk with sleeves ending in mittens and mail chausses covering the lower legs and feet.[14] A few effigies wear the great helmet, cylindrical and flat-topped with a horizontal eyeslit and bar across the front. In addition to the mail suit, knights' fig-

Figure 4. King John, Worcester Cathedral, 1225–30 (photo by author).

ures also wear long surcoats with split skirts, cinched with a belt or cingulum. Most seem to be equipped with spurs, although the particular form of spur, whether prick or rowel, is impossible to determine due to damage.[15] Finally, many of these figures also possess swords and shields, the latter being some variation of the long, narrow, concave, kite shape, as on the Salisbury effigy, or a shorter, wider, heater shape. The type of shield seems to have little relation to date.

Effigies dating after the mid thirteenth century wear somewhat shorter surcoats and show added defenses, perhaps corresponding to the plate or *cuir bouilli* additions to mail in actual armor. At Rippingdale, the figure seems to have thigh defenses, or cuisses (Fig. 5).

By the turn of the century, effigies might wear greaves on their shins, brassarts on their upper arms and other plate or *cuir bouilli* additions. Eventually, effigies, whether stone, alabaster or brass, will be dressed totally in plate armor.[16]

The choice of costume for all male effigies, whether archbishops or knights, speaks the medieval conception of identity. The twelfth-century degree of individualization has been debated by numerous scholars. Colin Morris, for example, has argued that the period between 1050 and 1200 can be characterized as a time of self-discovery during which individuals began to reflect on the relationship between their particular

Figure 5. Unknown Knight, Rippingdale, early fourteenth century (photo by author).

thoughts and experiences and the larger society.[17] Yet, Carolyn Bynum has objected to such an anachronistic interpretation, arguing that Morris et al. have applied modern criteria to a medieval phenomenon. She contends that twelfth-century self-identity was grounded in a collective sense: one understood oneself as a member of a socially recognized group, not as an autonomous individual.[18]

As their tomb effigies suggest, elites in thirteenth- and fourteenth-century England conceived of themselves more in accordance with Bynum's model than Morris's. Clerics, knights or royals, all are represented as members of a social group, rather than discrete individuals. The knight's effigy seems particularly strong in its institutional allegiance. While careful attention is paid to details of armor, which identify the figure as a knight, there seems to have been little interest in individualized portrayal. The faces are generalized and the poses conventional: straight-legged, cross-legged, devotional, sword-handling. In all, there is little to suggest a desire to capture the prototype's particular features or personality.[19] Rather, the choice of costume, the presence of swords, shields and spurs, all locate the individual within the order of "those who fought," and fought on horseback. Possession of a warhorse, or destrier, was a distinguishing mark of knighthood, and helped promote the knight's elite status. By having themselves portrayed as armored, armed and prepared to mount, the patrons of the military effigies laid claim to an elevated position in thirteenth- and fourteenth-century English society.

The strenuous visual argument for status and function on the part of the knights' effigies results from the checkered history of the chivalric institution in England. As Jean Scammel has demonstrated, thirteenth-century English knights had shed the taint of servility only relatively recently.[20] Until the second half of the twelfth century, there was no true permanently established knightly class: knights performed as such by virtue of equipment often provided to them on a temporary basis by the lord. Without arms and a horse, there was little to distinguish the knight from the agricultural worker. According to Scammel, even as late as 1197 knighthood could still be a temporary state dependent on the lord's need for military support. Witness the case of William of Upton, whose lord agreed to provide him with equipment and three-tenths of a knight's fee as long as William was in service at Wallingford Castle.[21] William was an occasional knight, who would shed this identity at the end of his service. In this instance, as in many others, knighthood meant simply the possession of weapons, and endured only as long as those weapons were available.[22] Occasional knights, as Scammel has termed them, could be called upon to undertake farmwork—carting, reaping, and mowing—during crucial agricultural periods.[23] Possession of land entailed no coherent social class, since land could or could not be tied to military service, and could be free or unfree. In short, from the Norman Conquest through the first half of the twelfth century, the social divide in England was between great landholders, or magnates, and everyone else, not between knights and agrarian workers.

Even in the later twelfth century, landholding knights occupied a precarious social position. If it could be demonstrated that they had performed seasonal labor, or had been subject to such demands from their lord, these occasional knights could find themselves reduced to villein status and dispossessed of their lands by those magnates.[24] It was only an action by the English crown that granted the knight permanent stature. In 1166, Henry II put forth *novel disseisin,* a petty assize that allowed plaintiffs to recover land simply by proving dispossession. He also established the petty assize of *mort d'ancestor,* which protected secure inheritance of land. With these two procedures Henry provided for hereditary tenure, and guaranteed a class of permanent landholders and self-arming warriors answerable directly to him and his royal successors.[25] The great lords found themselves cut out of the equation.

Evidence indicates that, by the later twelfth century, lesser landholders or county knights were enjoying some recognition as a coherent
social group. The Assize of Clarendon (1166) refers to knights as a segment of society distinct from barons and other freemen; the Assize of
Northhampton charges knights of each hundred to report suspected
crimes in their neighborhood to the crown.[26] In the thirteenth century, the
Magna Carta drew a distinction between great barons, mentioned by
name, and lesser men holding their lands directly from the crown, who
were referred to collectively.[27]

The knight's relationship with the king afforded them not just security from dispossession but also an increasingly aristocratic status. In all
probability this relationship, with its attendant social enhancement, also
led to a decrease in the numbers of knights in the first half of the thirteenth century. A survey of the eyre rolls for the thirteenth century suggests that at any one time there were between one thousand and two
thousand knights in England, excluding barons, landless knights and
those avoiding grand assize service.[28] Henry III's institution of distraint
of knighthood indicates that the crown perceived insufficient numbers to
support its military endeavors. The remedy was to require all laymen of
full age who held one or more knight's fees, to be knighted.[29] The first
distraint was ordered in 1242, and again in 1253/4 and 1256. The situation was dire enough that the king began to offer incentives such as
equipment and dress to convince those qualified to undergo the increasingly expensive dubbing ceremony.

One possible reason for the thinning of knightly ranks at this time
was the cost involved in keeping up appearances. As lesser knights
became more aristocratic they began to adopt many of the great lords'
attributes.[30] Knights laid claim to numerous elite trappings: heraldic
devices, titles, great seals, prestigious manor houses.[31] The magnates
reacted with resentment and with attempts to distance themselves from
those they considered social upstarts. When the knight Gilbert de
Bailleul adopted a great seal featuring a mounted warrior, hitherto an
image limited to kings and lords, he was sharply reprimanded by Richard
de Lucy, justiciar of England.[32] In the twelfth century, magnates tended
to reject the mounted warrior device in favor of a representation of a
shield bearing their arms; they may have hoped in this way to distinguish
themselves from lesser knights.[33] Eventually, knights adopted the
heraldic seal as their device of choice. Tournaments, and the expensive
spectacles associated with them, were another way of demonstrating
one's wealth and status. An increasingly threatened baronage may have

raised the stakes too high for the least well off lesser knights, causing their ejection from knighthood's ranks.[34] By the 1270s England seems to have recovered somewhat from its knights' decimation, but the lower ranks were now gone for good.

Chief among the aristocratic practices taken over by the lesser knights was the tomb effigy. By the second decade of the thirteenth century, the custom of representing oneself or a distinguished ancestor on a tomb had filtered down from the highest ecclesiastics to royals and then to magnates. Geoffrey Plantagenet's enamel image was produced around 1152, Henry II and Eleanor of Aquitaine's effigies at Fontevrault date around 1200 and King John's figure in Worcester cathedral dates 1225 to 1230. As noted, the earliest military effigy is probably that of William Longespée. In the Temple Church in London the earliest knight's effigy, alleged to be that of William Marshall, dates ca.1250.[35] By the third quarter of the thirteenth century, there seems to have been an explosion of military effigies as lesser knights strove to associate themselves with the highest levels of society. As has been noted by others, there is little to distinguish the effigies of the minor knights from those of their social betters; they display the same poses, armor and attributes.[36]

Despite appearances, these effigies dissemble; thirteenth-century county knights were not the social or political equals of magnates. They were a territorial elite with cultural connections to the great lords, but with equal or stronger links to their own localities. In other words, county knights were more local than national in their orientation.[37] The Assize of Northampton's charge to county knights as representatives of their neighborhoods is but one demonstration of lesser knighthood's localized character in the twelfth century. Thirteenth-century knights retained this territorial orientation. It was as representatives of their county that knights were summoned to parliament to deliberate issues of taxation. And they were summoned as commons, not peers.[38] An account of the parliament held at York in September 1268 indicates that while all nobles, *nobiliores,* were present, *maiores Angliae* had excused themselves from attendance. J.R. Madicott has interpreted the latter group to mean the commons, the knights and possibly the burgesses.[39] Thus, in the eyes of one chronicler, knights were socially inferior to magnates.

In addition to making exaggerated claims about status, the knights' effigies engage in other visually deceptive strategies. Their costume and martial attributes suggest that the prototypes for these figures were warriors first and foremost. Yet, at the time that the majority of these figures were produced, county knights served more in civil than military capacities.[40] Peter Coss has noted that already, in the second half of the twelfth century, the number of knights who rarely fought was increasing.[41] By King John's reign in the early thirteenth century, barons were deciding for themselves the appropriate size of their retinue rather than observing the full service quota. While desiring a reduction in their own military obligations to the crown, magnates were also faced with resistance to service by their subtenants. On all sides "those who fought" were begging off and hiring replacements.[42]

If not warfare, what was occupying the county knights? One of their main obligations seems to have been serving in the grand assize, the Angevin-inspired alternative to trial by battle. When called to serve by the sheriff, knights acted as witnesses, investigators, electors and jurors before the royal justices. Eyre rolls indicate that knights were expected to have a territorial interest in the county for which they were serving.[43] This, again, demonstrates the localized character of the county knight. Such knights were also active in county courts. In the fourteenth century, participation in the grand assize decreased as other judicial processes took hold, but knights were still very active in local administration.[44]

If making war was not the knight's main obligation, why did their effigies make such emphatic militaristic claims? The progressive independence of the knightly class from the magnates produced tensions and anxieties on both sides of the social divide. The magnates feared losing their superior status in the general leveling of the aristocracy that occurred in the late twelfth and early thirteenth centuries. Thus, they took measures to ensure their distinction from their perceived social inferiors. At the same time, the county knights, now more autonomous in relation to their overlords, desired social parity with them, and imitated the magnates' customs to achieve that end. Since the great lords were employing the military ethos of chivalry, especially the tournament, to articulate their social status, county knights must have felt compelled to adopt the same vocabulary. To have themselves represented as warriors was to achieve an association with the great lords that might serve to erase the last traces of servility still clinging to the English version of the knightly institution.

THE EFFIGIES' CONSTRUCTION OF LINEAGE

The commission and display of effigies was one strategy adopted by county knights in their struggle to achieve autonomy and even social parity with England's magnates. As we have seen, the effigies' martial costume and attributes served to claim elite status. The visual construction of a distinguished lineage also worked to justify pretensions to a superior social position. Heraldic devices on shields and surcoats served to demonstrate an illustrious (even if specious) family heritage. These motifs provided a site where collective social identity, specific familial descent and gender converged. The effigy of William Longespée (Fig. 2), for example, features a blazon of six lions rampart carved in low relief on the figure's shield. John of Marmoutier recounted in his chronicle that at the knighting of William's grandfather, Geoffrey Plantagenet, Henry I placed a blue shield painted with six gold lioncels around his neck.[45] Thus, William's effigy demonstrates to all informed viewers its prototype's aristocratic and knightly heritage. The three water bougets can still be detected on the shield of the figure thought to be William, second Lord Ros of Hamlake, in the Temple Church (Fig. 6).

While these figures are among the rare cases where the arms are still visible, Henry Lawrence cataloged close to two hundred military effigies prior to 1350, for which coats of arms were present at one time.[46] In all likelihood, most military effigies had arms carved or painted on their shields, and perhaps their surcoats, when new, but these have disap-

Figure 6. "William, Second Lord Ros of Hamlake," Temple Church, London, early fourteenth century (photo by author).

peared over the centuries. On a number of effigies traces of pigment are still visible and surface conditions suggest that formerly details of armor had been stamped into or painted on a layer of gesso. The same process might have extended to heraldic devices.[47]

Howard Bloch has linked the emergence of heraldry in twelfth-century France to the changeover from clan to lineage as the operative familial unit. Such a change of orientation seems to have been brought about by the progressive dispersal of familial lands in the post-Carolingian era.[48] Prior to the eleventh century, lords had dispersed the family holdings horizontally, across the extended clan: family, friends, neighbors. The fact that men and women could inherit equally accelerated the fragmentation of the patrimony. Subtenants identified themselves with their lord as a kind of extended family group. Scholars have noted that sometime around 1000 families began to think of themselves as tied to a specific geographic location, rather than to a lord. "Family" came to denote the holders of a certain property, more than those connected to a lord through feudal obligations. The family wealth came more in the form of an inheritance of this property than a grant from the lord. Consequently, the outer boundaries of the clan shrank to encompass only those eligible to inherit the property: the heritable fief ensured the transformation of the horizontal clan to the vertical family descent.[49]

By the eleventh century, grants of land were becoming transmissible through generations. In the second half of the century, the heritable fief was a more frequent contributor to the family patrimony than was a grant from an overlord. Ultimately, having a heritable patrimony became a marker of status. Contemporaneously, the practice of primogeniture worked to ensure the integrity of that patrimony through time. It also intensified the association between patrimony, status and vertical blood relationship already initiated by the narrowing of the extended clan to the consanguineous family. This was the lineage mentality: having noble status required the possession of a patrimony, which itself required demonstrating an ancestry of male fief holders from whom to inherit.

The Anglo-Norman aristocracy practiced both heritability of the patrimony and primogeniture, along with their continental counterparts.[50] The lineage mentality devolved upon both magnates and county knights. All lands in England had been forfeit to William I as penalty for Harold's rebellion. The Norman ruler parceled out his newly gained lands among his followers, who further divided these territories among their vassals in accordance with feudal practice. As described previously, *novel disseisin* and *mort d'ancestor* eventually ensured the local elites, the county knights, both secure possession of a fief and the right to transmit it to their ancestors.[51] Indeed, by 1200 their holdings had become fully heritable.[52]

This group adopted a number of strategies for safeguarding their hard-won, and always precarious, social gains.[53] One of these was the issuance and preservation of written records or charters, which stressed the hereditary rights to patrimony by virtue of the issuant's descent. County knights' families may have also encouraged a stress on lineage in certain twelfth- and thirteenth-century forms of literature. Philip Morgan suggests that such family concerns operated in the works of Ordericus Vitalis and the romances of *Fouke le Fitzwaryn* and *Guy of Warwick*.[54] The adoption of toponymic surnames also reinforced the hereditary link between a family and its heritable estates.[55]

Heraldry became the visual marker of the required lineage. Its origins are to be found in the symbols appearing on individual's banners, such as those visible in the Bayeux Embroidery associated with William the Conqueror.[56] By the mid-twelfth century the shield was favored as the field for heraldic display. After the conquest, the Anglo-Norman aristocracy of England made prominent use of symbols on banners and, by the twelfth century, certain designs were already associated with particular individuals and their families. Issues of lineage were intersecting the developing practice of heraldry.[57] Magnates were the first to employ heraldic devices in this manner.[58] Designs seem to have been deployed horizontally, through the kinship group and vertically, through the lord's dependents. So, for example, the checky device displayed on the banner held by Ralph I, Count of Vermandois, on his first seal also appears as part of the arms of his cousins, the earls of Leicester, Warenne and Warwick.[59] In the early twelfth century, heraldic devices were the exclusive privilege of the magnates; a knight was expected to bear the arms of his overlord, not his own distinctive design. In this period, heraldry for the knight signified his servitude to the magnate.

With the increased elitism of knighthood in England, knights began to bear their own devices. Coats of arms proliferated on knightly seals, domestic objects, liturgical vessels and on architecture. As noted previously, in seals the arms appear on the heraldic type, which had replaced the equestrian figure for the lower ranks of knighthood. In other media the arms denoted the identity of the benefactor.[60] The craze for devices accelerated when knights became cognizant of the symbols' prestige value as a marker of status. By the 1250s, so many new heraldic designs had been invented that lists began to be kept in order to maintain a coherent record of what device belonged to whom. The Glovers Roll, ca.1250, records 215 shields with arms.[61] Heraldry was becoming a discipline.

For the county knight, displaying a heraldic device on his effigy reinforced his claims to elite status within his locality. Through these symbols he announced his elevated social position, as well as its justification by virtue of his lineage and patrimony. He also shored up his status by aping the signifying practices of the higher aristocracy: his arena might be smaller than that of a magnate, but his heraldic insignia claimed similar power over his own locality.

Yet, the claims to ancient aristocratic rank made by the heraldic devices on many military effigies were essentially false. By the time of Henry III's distraint of knighthood, membership in this institution was fluid enough to accept anyone with the means equal to a knight's fee. It was income and goods, not lineage, that determined one's knightly position.[62] And there are indications that marriage was an equal, if not greater, factor in acquiring, retaining and enhancing the patrimony than the male line of descent.[63] The wealth and position of the fifteenth-century Pierrepont family of Holme Pierrepont, for example, was primarily due to the marriage between a male ancestor and Annora de Manvers, in the late thirteenth century. She brought to them the knight's fee at Holme, which became their patrimony, a fact the family's late-fifteenth-century cartulary chooses to ignore. It is recorded, however, in the cartulary of the Augustinian priory at Felley. The status of a wife's lineage might also be adopted as the family history if it were more likely to ensure continued possession of estates. In all, heraldic devices on knights' effigies had less credibility than might be supposed.

THE EFFIGIES' CONSTRUCTION OF THE KNIGHT'S BODY

One of the outstanding characteristics of the knights' effigies is the emphatic physicality of many of the carved figures. Longespée's body is slender, but powerful: the volumes of the limbs are readily perceived beneath their mail covering (Figs. 1 and 2). At Rippingdale, the figure's athletic body evidences his physical prowess even more: the shoulder and arm muscles swell as they pull the hands into the prayer position; the heavy mass of the right leg cuts through the surcoat's split in one strong crossover motion (Fig. 5). Most astonishing of all is the Dorchester Abbey knight (Figs. 7–10).

The figure is husky and solidly built, with heavily muscled arms and legs. These brawny members twist and turn, thrusting themselves into the viewer's space and awareness.

Figure 7. Unknown Knight, Dorchester Abbey, ca. 1260, left side (photo by author).

Figure 8. Unknown Knight, Dorchester Abbey, ca. 1260, right side (photo by author).

Figure 9. Detail of Figure 7 (photo by author).

Figure 10. Detail of Figure 8 (photo by author).

As the Salisbury, Rippingdale and Dorchester effigies demonstrate, pose has much to do with the heightened corporeal presence of some armored figures. The cross-legged attitude characterizes the majority of thirteenth- and early-fourteenth-century military effigies in England.[64] Indeed, with the exception of a few much later figures in Spain, only English knights' figures display this attitude.[65] The effects of crossed legs are visible at Rippingdale and Dorchester when contrasted to the effigy of William Longespée. With no motion to activate them, William's straight legs lie quietly on the tomb slab, and the rest of his figure follows suit. The upper and lower body reside in the same frontal plane, only his turned head breaks out of alignment. William's figure possesses the potential for action, not the reality of motion. At Rippingdale, on the other hand, the right leg swings over the left causing the right hip to tilt up and the lower body to twist in a slightly corkscrew manner. The upper leg emerges from the surcoat as a broad, muscular arc. While the upper remains static, the lower body declares the knight's readiness for action. In the Dorchester effigy, upper and lower body both come to life in a powerful twisting pose that engages the entire figure. The figure's dynamism is intensified by its sword-handling gesture, a pose present in many of the cross-legged figures from England.[66] Thus, as the hips twist to the right, propelling the right leg over the left, they are countered by the action of the arms. The left arm moves left across the torso to grab the scabbard, while the right arm swings over the chest to grab the sword hilt, preparatory to withdrawing it. The most active members of the knight's body, his legs, hips and arms, are marked by muscles bunched with effort.

Several scholars have credited workshop practices with the degree of activity in military effigies. Prior and Gardner assigned the most active, cross-legged and sword-handling figures, such as the Dorchester knight, to Bristol or centers influenced by Bristol, while attributing the more serene, praying figures to London or its circle.[67] Alfred Fryer and Lawrence Stone concurred in localizing the most vigorous figures to Bristol and West Country workshops, but added London shops under influence of the west to the list.[68] Hurtig and Tummers both agree with Fryer and Stone.[69] It is true that workshop practices can help us understand the dissemination of the vigorous effigy, but its origin may lie in issues that go beyond simple stylistic preferences.

Of course, it is the costume of the military effigy that allows such a precise understanding of the body's disposition, hence the impression of active physicality. The mail in which these figures are clad conforms to the rounded volumes of arms and legs. On Longespée, for example, the mail clings to the length of the slightly bent left arm and gives the illusion of hanging off the thinner lower limb. At Rippingdale, the sculptor has carefully indicated the way the mail sleeve of the hauberk creases when the lower arms draw up to the chest in prayer. At the same time, the mail is made to conform without a wrinkle to the swelling upper arm. At Dorchester the mail sleeve faithfully articulates the way the shoulder muscle contracts and the tricep extends, as the right arm withdraws the sword.

The treatment of the lower body in many of these figures is equally effective at conveying the body's physicality. As discussed previously, the knights of the later thirteenth and early fourteenth century wear short mail hauberks, which frequently end above the knees, mail leggings and surcoats with split skirts. This costume allowed sculptors to emphasize potent parts of the male body: the hips and legs. While his legs are still, Longespée's calves receive a certain definition from the chausses encasing them. We have already seen how at Rippingdale the sculptor employed the cross-legged pose to accentuate the powerful right limb, as it surges through the bunched folds of the surcoat. The hauberk's skirt and the chausses articulate the strong contours of this figure's thigh and calf. Similar effects are visible on the Dorchester knight: its mail covering again helps to define and emphasize the figure's muscular responses to movement. In addition, the sculptor has fashioned a softer, sheerer surcoat, which participates in the corporeal articulation. On the left leg, the S-shaped folds of cloth call attention to the contraction of the thigh muscle as the leg bends back underneath the right limb. At the figure's rear, parabolic folds emphasize the breadth of the right hip as it tilts upward.

The impact of the knight's costume is apparent when one examines other surviving contemporaneous effigies. Nonknightly figures include ecclesiastics, here represented by Archbishop de Gray (Fig. 3), kings such as King John (Fig. 4) and other male civilians (a small group) and female effigies, like that of an unknown lady from Worcester cathedral (Fig. 11).

While all of these figures wear the clothing denoting their station in life—mail, vestments, royal regalia and mantle—the knight's costume has one striking difference from the rest: its high degree of corporeal display.[70] I have discussed in detail the way sculptors employed mail to foreground the knight's powerful, muscular body, especially its lower portions. By contrast, those who carved the figures of churchmen, kings and women strove for the opposite effect. In these effigies drapery is

Figure 11. Unknown Lady, Worcester Cathedral, ca. 1250 (photo by author).

used to conceal the lower body. Archbishop de Gray's figure is swathed in heavy vestments whose drapery pattern—the dalmatic's parabolic folds against the vertical lines of the alb—create a lively surface but no corporeal definition. Indeed, the only indication of a body beneath the archbishop's costume is his feet. King John's body appears to have more bulk than the archbishop's, but any definition is lost beneath the vertical pleats of his gown and mantle. The woman's body is not dissimilar to King John's, although her arms, in their tight fitting-sleeves, are more apparent, but her lower body is not discernible beneath the fluted folds of her heavy gown.

At the level of corporeal display, the effigies seem to draw a distinction between knights and members of other social and gender groups. It is interesting that this occurs in the period in which, according to Anne Hollander, European men and women began to dress very differently from one another.[71] The difference amounted to the degree of corporeal definition, for as we have noted, a mail suit of armor defined the body in a way that a heavy gown could not. Thus, the mailed/male body assumed a totality of presentation, a unity, which the female body lacked. But within the corpus of effigies not all males wear armor; that is a distinction reserved for knights. Ecclesiastics and kings are closer to women in their bodily display. This suggests that medieval gender definition was more complicated than a simple matter of biological sex. In other words, the visual evidence of the effigies implies that gender was as much or more a matter of social construction than biology, and that medieval knights perceived themselves, and were perceived by others, as a special kind of man.

The key to that specialness lies, once again, in the choice of costume for the tomb effigy. In deciding to have themselves, or their ancestors, portrayed in mail, medieval knights were bent on representing themselves by a physically powerful and active ideal. The heightened corporeal definition and display achieved through costume and pose was inextricably tied to the practical function of mail: defense in war. As articulated through the effigies, the warrior was muscular, vigorous and (in many examples) skilled at swordplay. A vigilance and penchant for action signified by the visible, and visibly powerful, legs, especially when crossed, and sword-handling of so many of the knights' effigies set them apart from the composed serenity of the praying clerics, kings and women with whom they share the sacred space of the church.

Chivalric literature privileges physical prowess much as the effigies do. In the *chansons des gestes,* heroes are invariably brave and skillful fighters, and they are fierce to the point of bloodthirstiness. The eponymous hero Roland refuses to sound his horn for help, inviting the ensuing bloody disaster. The poem provides a laundry list of slaughter by the Franks; over and over Roland's men strike brutal blows that tear through protective armor, dismembering the enemy. Sanson cuts his opponent down through the heart and liver, Anseï impales an enemy through his steel hauberk and casts the body a spear's length away, Roland himself wields Durandel against Chernuble and cleaves his adversary through the spine.[72] The epic knight is then described as piling corpse upon corpse. In *The Song of William* all the knightly protagonists progress through the various battle scenes cleaving through breasts and bodies, lopping off arms and heads. Girart is described as lancing an enemy through the back, spitting him well until dead.[73] William's nephew, Gui, although very young, insists on joining his reluctant uncle in battle and shows himself as fierce as any of the more experienced fighters. In his first encounter, Gui splits an enemy's buckler in two, rends the hauberk and kills his opponent with heavy blows of his sword.[74] All of these knights are vigorous, strong and active, almost to the point of absurdity.[75]

The knightly heroes of medieval romance are also celebrated for their vigor and military might. In *The High Book of the Grail,* Sir Gawain engages in numerous feats of arms, which he wins every time. While fighting for the shield of Machabeus, the Arthurian hero impales an adversary on his lance and sends him tumbling over his horse.[76] Later on, he is described at tournament as enthusiastically unhorsing or wounding every opponent, including the Lord of the Fens, whom he subdues with furious blows of his sword.[77] Sir Gawain's physical prowess takes a backseat to that of another warrior in *Sir Gawain and the Green Knight.* When the Green Knight makes his dramatic entrance into Arthur's hall, readers are provided with a vivid description of his appearance. Green from his head to his feet, the title character is described as huge and brawny with long, great legs; he is, indeed, half a giant.[78] In the *Green Knight,* as in all these tales, fictional knights look and behave with all the vigor idealized in the effigies of their real counterparts.

Books of chivalry also emphasize the knight's need for physical vigor and military skill. Geoffroi de Charny's *Book of Chivalry* harps on themes of prowess and hardiness.[79] The author singles out for praise those men-at-arms who exhibit strength, agility and eagerness for tourney or battle.[80] He applauds the knights whose physical skills have earned them renown and condemns cowards who place concern for their lives over valor.[81]

Chivalric literature not only parallels the effigies' idealization of the active knight, it also engages in drawing distinctions between knights and other gender and social groups. Simon Gaunt has recently analyzed two constructions of masculinity in medieval romance: monologic and dialogic.[82] The former construction pits man against man and leaves little or no functional role for women in the narrative.[83] Monologic masculinity characterizes *chansons de geste* such as *The Song of Roland, Ami et Amile* and *Raoul de Cambrai,* which privilege the relationship between men, whether good or bad, and more or less exclude women from the male world of war.[84] Female characters are confined to the domestic sphere where their role is to urge their men on to greater feats of battle.

In addition to isolating the man's world from the presence of women, the chansons' monologic masculinity also pits chivalric ideals against royal wrongdoing, setting knights in opposition to kings. King Louis deprives Raoul de Cambrai of his rightful territorial inheritance and then compounds his original misdeed by granting Raoul other lands taken away from the legitimate heirs. The king's actions lead to the eventual destruction of Paris. In *Daurel et Beton,* Charlemagne supports the words of a traitor and murderer against those of his sister, for financial gain. It would appear that chivalric literature contains a structural parallel to the knights' effigies: it sets apart knights and kings.

The gender isolation of epic is less apparent in romance. Gaunt has noted that twelfth- and thirteenth-century romances do not exclude women as significant characters, as in the *chanson de geste,* but make good use of women in constructing a complicated model of masculinity. In the *Roman d'Eneas,* for example, the major role of Eneas's love interest, Lavine, ensures that the hero will focus his attentions and desires on a women, not on another man. The male solidarity of epic, such as the bond between Roland and Oliver, carried the threat of homosexual bonding. Romance works to ensure an exclusively heterosexual masculinity, but without sacrificing the solidarity of the battlefield.[85] At the same time, the warrior bonding evident in epic remains intact but is controlled by the female presence in the story. The knight is socially bonded to other knights but sexually bonded to a woman.[86] The knight does not identify with a female character; she merely operates as the foil for his masculinity. Romance constructs a masculine subject out of a female other and a male ally. Gaunt calls this dialogic masculinity.[87]

Other forms of medieval literature present more overtly misogynist attitudes when examining knighthood. Knights were routinely criticized for various signs of effeminacy.[88] Odericus Vitalis assailed the knights of his day for being faddish, fawning and addicted to women. According to him, the real knight was he who wore decently fitted clothing, displayed skill at horsemanship and other physical endeavors and remained ready for action.[89] William of Malmesbury criticized the young men of the court for emulating a feminine model of behavior: mincing gait, loose gestures and seminakedness.[90] Both of these writers roundly condemned what they saw as a willingness to be dominated socially by fashion and sexually by women. Such weakness rendered the knight like a woman, a fit object for scorn.

It is likely that the aggressive corporeality and militarism of the knights' effigies responds to these clerical charges. By emphasizing well-developed musculature, physical action and the warrior's role, the knight's figure counters accusations of effeminacy such as those cited above. At the same time, these features work to differentiate the military effigy, and its prototypes, from any possible resemblance to a woman.

Thus far we have been considering the divisions drawn between different social and gender groups in medieval effigies and medieval literature. We have seen how the knight's image in both sculpture and literature was that of a strong, vigorous fighter, distinct from the king and the lady. In the effigy, the display of muscular arms and legs, the presence of mail and frequently, shield and sword, speak to the knight's warrior ideal. In epic, romance and books of chivalry, the detailed and gruesome accounts of endless battles and the physical descriptions of hearty knights accomplishes much the same purpose. In the effigies, the articulation and revelation of the knight's body contrasts with the concealment of the king's or the woman's. In epic and romance, the king's misdeeds and the lady's isolation from the battlefield likewise divide all these groups.

Within the complex social and gender configurations articulated in the effigies and in literature, clerics also have a part to play. Within the effigies, they are allied to the kings and women because of the concealing nature of their costume. In literature, their social role often opposes that of the knight. Above we saw two clerics attacking the knights of their day for gender failings: Odericus Vitalis and William of Malmesbury both condemned knighthood for its perceived effeminacy. These attacks suggest that relations between clergy and knights were not always completely cordial.

Both these clerics were critical of the knight's fondness for court life over the field of action; therefore, it is something of a paradox that clerics also routinely condemned the tournament, one of knighthood's favorite venues for displays of physical and military prowess.[91] The Church condemned tournaments officially at the Council of Clermont in 1130, and clerical hostility to the chivalric display persisted throughout the course of the thirteenth century. Caesarius of Heisterbach told stories of knights condemned to damnation for their fondness for the sport.[92] The English monk and chronicler, Matthew Paris, recounted the legend of a dead knight who revived briefly in order to warn his brother about the spiritual threat of tournaments.[93] Since tournaments were so extraordinarily popular, especially among English knights, it is to be expected that clerical opposition to them could only drive a wedge between these two groups of men.

There are other literary indications of an alienation between knights and clerics, or at least a belief that the two were and should play different roles. This evidence comes not from clerics, but from a knight. Geoffroi de Charny makes it quite clear that the order of knighthood and the order of priesthood should remain quite distinct. In a section of the *Book of Chivalry,* in which he compares knighthood to other orders, de Charny discusses the proper role for the clergy: living in abbeys and cloisters, praying and fasting in service of Christ. He makes a point of noting that

What about the cult of the [?]
(from Virgin Mary)
the Crusades, and
Knights Templar [?]

clergy are spared the physical danger and strenuous effort of battle.[94] A little later he returns to the theme and reiterates that priests have a noble office to perform and should not undertake other duties.[95] But de Charny goes further than distinguishing the role of knight from priest. He suggests that of the two orders, knighthood is superior. He insists that because their vocation is the most dangerous for soul and body, knights must maintain a clearer conscience than that of any other order. Furthermore, he calls knighthood the most rigorous order of all and says that there is no religious order whose members have to endure as much suffering as that endured by knights.[96]

As with kings and ladies, the sense of difference between knights and clerics resonates with the visual characteristics of their respective effigies. The knight, especially the cross-legged, sword-wielding figure such as the Dorchester knight, glories in the physical potential of the body and the military role. The cleric, such as Archbishop de Gray, conceals the body and dwells on the emblems of ecclesiastical office. In observing the difference between the two groups' representations (and self-representations), it is noteworthy that English military effigies display one further difference. Hurtig pointed out that, unlike their continental counterparts, English knights' effigies show no signs of what she termed the liturgical tradition—hands folded in prayer and head flanked by angels—until the end of the thirteenth century.[97] This tradition was associated with the figures of clerics and some royalty. Its absence in the earliest military figures underscores the social division articulated in the visual representation.

CONCLUSION

The knightly effigies of England remind us of an important fact: the medieval construction of gender was fluid and determined as much or more by social function as by biological sex. The idealized masculinity proffered by these armored tomb figures speaks to the social tensions between three categories of male: knights, kings, clerics. Scholars have speculated that the alienation of knights from their rulers, evident in literature, had its origin in the changing position of knighthood in the face of increasing monarchic power.[98] I have argued that the struggle between knights and magnates was equally significant in the former's visual representation. Wearing armor and displaying heraldry worked to claim a parity with the highest nobility. Furthermore, the effigies' e corporeal spectacle, with its assertion of the male body's most members, served to distinguish the knights' figures from all other effigies, male or female. Such assertive corporeality visually promoted the knight as a fierce and effective warrior, an identity also permeating chivalric literature but not reflecting daily experience, as we have seen. Ultimately, the armored effigies of England constructed an elite, warrior masculinity that was more fantasy than fact.

NOTES

1. Parts of this essay were originally presented as a paper in the "Visual Constructions of Masculinity" session sponsored by the Medieval Feminist Art History Project at the annual meeting of the International Congress on Medieval Studies, Kalamazoo, Michigan, 1997, and the International Medieval Congress, University of Leeds, 1997. I would like to thank Paula Gerson and Pamela Sheingorn for their support of this project. I am grateful to my colleague Sarah Cohen for her cogent comments on my work. This research was partially funded by a Faculty Research Assistance Program award from the University at Albany, State University of New York, 1996.

The question of patronage is difficult to answer for effigies of the thirteenth and early-fourteenth centuries. To my knowledge, almost no contracts survive for these commissions, nor are there descriptions in wills or other documents. The only fourteenth-century contract I know of dates from 1376 and refers to a figure in plate armor, not mail. See J. Blair, "Henry Lakenham, Marbler of London, and a Tomb Contract of 1376," *Antiquaries Journal* 60 (1980): 66–74.

2. H.A. Tummers, *Early Secular Effigies in England* (Leiden: E.J. Brill, 1980), 135, 143. The other recent fundamental source is Judith Hurtig, *The Armored Gisant Before 1400* (New York: Garland, 1979). Both authors are concerned primarily with dating the effigies and determining the sequence of stylistic transmission within the corpus of works. Tummers includes an invaluable typology for the knights' effigies, other male civilians and ladies; in addition, he provides an extensive bibliography that includes numerous treatments of figures in publications of county and national antiquarian and archeological societies. These will be cited when relevant for secular figures. Readers should also consult Kurt Bauch, *Das mittelalterliche Grabbild: figürliche Grabmäler des 11. bis 15. Jahrhunderts in Europa* (Berlin: de Gruyter, 1976); Erwin Panofsky, "The Early Christian Period and the Middle Ages North of the Alps," chap. 3 in *Tomb Sculpture: Its Changing Aspect from Ancient Egypt to Bernini* (London: Thames and Hudson, 1964); and Henriette Jacob, *Idealism and Realism: A Study of Sepulchral Symbolism* (Leiden: E.J. Brill, 1954).

3. Christopher Daniell, *Death and Burial in Medieval England* (London: Routledge, 1997), 186; and Paul Binski, *Medieval Death: Ritual and Representation* (London: British Museum Press, 1996), 72.

4. Daniell, *Death and Burial,* 186–87.

5. Binski, *Medieval Death,* 72.

6. Daniell, *Death and Burial,* 186.

7. Panofsky (*Tomb Sculpture,* 51–52) notes several three-dimensional effigies of laypersons from the Continent: the bronze plaque of Rudolph of Swabia (d. 1080), Cathedral, Merseberg; Duke Widukind, ca. 1130, Church at Enger.

8. Hurtig, *Armored Gisant,* 118–21; Tummers, *Early Secular Effigies,* 79.

9. Tummers, *Early Secular Effigies,* 120–21. The original attempt to date and localize military effigies is to be found in Edwards Prior and Arthur Gardner, *An Account of Medieval Figure Sculpture in England* (Cambridge: Cambridge University Press, 1912), 553–69, 580–90.

10. Hurtig, *Armored Gisant,* 134, 148.

11. On the effigy of Archbishop de Gray see Patricia Bolin Pepin, "The Monumental Tombs of Medieval England, 1250–1350" (Ph.D. diss., University of Pittsburgh, 1977), 84–85.

12. Matthew Bloxam, "The Sepulchral Remains and Effigies in the Cathedral Church of Worcester," *The Archaeological Journal* 20 (1863): 345.

13. Most recently Michael Prestwich used knightly brasses rather than stone effigies to illustrate his discussion of medieval armor. See *Armies and Warfare in the Middle Ages, the English Experience* (New Haven: Yale University Press, 1996), 18–27. He also used other visual sources such as aquamaniles, miniatures and misericords. Prestwich is not alone in his use of visual images to support discussions about armor development. Tummers (*Early Secular Effigies,* 52) warns against considering effigies as accurate reflections of reality. The author points out quite rightly that funerary art is more conventional than other categories of image and that the dress on effigies may have been slower to change than actual fashion. Reservations about iconography as an index of reality with regard to armor were voiced by Zdzislaw Zygulski in "Armour as a Symbolic Form," *Waffen und Kostumkunde Zeitschrift der Gebel* 26 (1984): 77.

14. The method for depicting the chain links does vary among the effigies. In some cases mail takes the form of bands of curved lines running vertically down the length of a limb, while in others it runs around the circumference. In addition, some mail seems to be composed of interlaced rings. As far as can be determined, these differences do not represent different types of mail, just different ways of depicting the same material. This is also true in the case of so-called banded mail. See Tummers, *Early Secular Effigies,* 66–68. Some scholars have looked at mail depiction as a way of localizing figures. Thus, the longitudinal band style has been considered characteristic of Bristol or Bristol-influenced workshops. See A.C. Fryer, "Monumental Effigies Made by Bristol Craftsmen,

1240–1550," *Archaeologia* 74 (1923–24): 25–26; and A. Andersson, *English Influence in Norwegian and Swedish Figure Sculpture in Wood* (Stockholm: Wahlstrom and Widstrand, 1950), 52–54. Tummers believes that no such conclusion should be drawn.

    15. Only one figure has preserved its spurs intact and those are of the prick variety; there are no surviving rowel types. See Tummers, *Early Secular Effigies,* 68.

    16. The study of stone and alabaster figures in plate armor is badly needed. Brasses have been examined recently by John Coales, ed., *The Earliest English Brasses: Patronage, Style, and Workshops 1270–1350* (London: Monumental Brass Society, 1987).

    17. Colin Morris, *The Discovery of the Individual 1050–1200* (Toronto: University of Toronto Press, 1987). Other scholars taking the same position include John Benton, "Individualism and Conformity in Medieval Western Europe," in *Individualism and Conformity in Classical Islam,* ed. Amin Banami and Speros Vryonis Jr. (Wiesbaden: Harrassowitz, 1977), 145–58; Robert W. Hanning, *The Individual in Twelfth-Century Romance* (New Haven: Yale University Press, 1977); Peter Dronke, *Poetic Individuality in the Middle Ages* (Oxford: Clarendon Press, 1970); Richard Southern, "Medieval Humanism," in *Medieval Humanism and Other Studies* (New York: Blackwell Press, 1970), 29–60; idem, *The Making of the Middle Ages* (New Haven: Yale University Press, 1959), 219–57; Walter Ullman, *The Individual and Society in the Middle Ages* (Baltimore: Johns Hopkins Press, 1966).

    18. Caroline Bynum, "Did the Twelfth Century Discover the Individual?" in eadem, *Jesus as Mother. Studies in the Spirituality of the High Middle Ages* (Berkeley: University of California Press, 1982), 82–109.

    19. So concludes Albert Hartshorne in *Portraiture in Recumbent Effigies, and Ancient Schools of Monumental Sculpture in England, Illustrated by Examples in Northhamptonshire* (Exeter: William Pollard, 1899), 8. My own observations of numerous effigies throughout England have led me to concur with Hartshorne's opinion.

    20. J. Scammel, "The Formation of the English Social Structure: Freedom, Knights, and the Gentry, 1066–1300," *Speculum* 68 (1993): 591–617.

    21. Ibid., 596–97.

    22. Ibid., 591. Scammel (597–601) has distinguished four broad categories of "knight" in the late eleventh century of which only two represented knights for life. The other two were occasional knights.

    23. Ibid., 605.

    24. Ibid.

    25. Ibid., 606.

26. Ibid., 595.

27. Peter Coss, *Lordship, Knighthood and Locality, a Study in English Society c. 1180-c. 1280* (Cambridge: Cambridge University Press, 1991), 3.

28. J. Quick, "The Number and Distribution of Knights in Thirteenth-Century England: the Evidence of the Grand Assize Lists," in *Thirteenth-Century England 1,* ed. Peter R. Coss and Simon D. Lloyd (Woodbridge, Eng.: Boydell Press, 1986), 114–23.

29. Peter R. Coss, *The Knight in Medieval England 1000–1400* (Phoenix Mill, Eng.: Alan Sutton Publishing, 1993), 60–62.

30. David Crouch, *The Image of the Aristocracy in Britain 1000–1300* (London: Routledge, 1992), 136.

31. Ibid., 15.

32. Ibid., 139.

33. Ibid., 244. Brigitte Bedos Rezak observes that magnates retained the equestrian image between 1250 and 1350, but lesser knights adopted a simple heraldic device in place of the mounted figure. See "Medieval Seals and the Structure of Chivalric Society," in Howell Chickering and Thomas H. Seiler, eds. *The Study of Chivalry, Resources and Approaches,* (Kalamazoo, Mich.: Medieval Institute Publications, 1988), 338–39. Evidence presented by P.D.A. Harvey and Andrew McGuinness supports the idea of a change in seal imagery in the late thirteenth century. These two authors note that the two copies of Barons' Letter of 1301 have between them ninety-five surviving seals. Of these eighty-one are of the heraldic rather than the equestrian type used by those below the rank of earl. They also cite the higher percentage of heraldic seals on deeds from the duchy of Lancaster from the thirteenth and fourteenth centuries. See *A Guide to British Medieval Seals* (Toronto: University of Toronto Press, 1996), 55–56.

34. Coss (*Knight in Medieval England, 67–71*) suggests that there were other reasons for the decline in numbers in addition to prohibitive costs associated with the knightly lifestyle. He lists inflation leading to a loss of real income and the burden of civil obligations on the knights as contributing factors.

35. In 1598 the Temple Church effigies were already associated with William Marshall and his sons William the Younger (d.1231), and Gilbert (d.1241). See J. Stow, *A Survey of the Cities of London and Westminster and the Borough of Southwark* (London, 1598). Later authors included Geoffrey de Mandeville (d.1140) among the figures represented. See William Burton, *Description of Leicestershire* (London, 1622). These names have persisted in association with the Temple Church effigies until the present day. Henry Lawrence notes that J.G. Nichols disputed the identification on the basis of the heraldry. See Henry Lawrence, *Heraldry from Military Monuments before 1350 in England and Wales* (London: Harleian Society, 1946), 51. Tummers (*Early Secular Effigies,*

19) acknowledges the weight of tradition concerning these figures and says that the link with the Marshall family must be taken seriously. One should also consult the restoration studies of these effigies: Edward Richardson, *The Monumental Effigies of the Temple Church with an Account of their Restoration in the Year 1842* (London: Longman, Brown, Green and Longmans, 1843), 10–15; C.G. Addison, *The Temple Church* (London: Longman, Brown, Green and Longmans, 1843); W. Burge, *The Temple Church: an Account of its Restoration and Repairs* (London: Pickering, 1843); and A. Eisdale, *Temple Church Monuments* (London: G. Barber and Son, 1933).

36. Philip Morgan, "Making the English Gentry," in *Thirteenth-Century England 5,* ed. Peter R. Coss and Simon D. Lloyd (Woodbridge, Eng., Boydell Press,1993), 22; Tummers, *Early Secular Effigies,* 20.

37. Morgan, "Making the English Gentry," 21; Coss, *Lordship, Knighthood and Locality,* 308–09. Both authors acknowledge the affinities between county knights and great lords but stress that the lesser group never lost their ties with their neighborhoods or their social inferiors.

38. Scammel, "The Formation of the English Social Structure," 613, 616–17.

39. J.R. Madicott, "The Crusade Taxation of 1268–70 and the Development of Parliament," in *Thirteenth-Century England 2,* ed. Peter R. Coss and Simon D. Lloyd, (Woodbridge, Eng., Boydell Press, 1987–88), 96–97. This account is from the Furness continuator of William of Newburgh's mid-thirteenth-century *Historia rerum Anglicanum.* Madicott notes another possible, but unlikely, interpretation: the *maiores* refer to the nobles who excused themselves from granting the tax.

40. Tummers, *Early Secular Effigies,* 20–21.

41. Coss, *Knight in Medieval England,* 44.

42. Morgan, "Making the English Gentry," 26.

43. Quick, "Number and Distribution of Knights," 116–17.

44. Coss, *Knight in Medieval England,* 113.

45. This episode is included in many studies of heraldic evolution. See R. Howard Bloch, *Etymologies and Geneologies. A Literary Anthropology of the French Middle Ages* (Chicago: University of Chicago Press, 1983), 76 and Maurice Keen, *Chivalry (*New Haven: Yale University Press, 1984), 126.

46. Lawrence, *Heraldry.* Not all of the figures he lists are stone effigies. In the cases where he was not able to see the arms, he relied on antiquarian descriptions of the figures.

47. The figures of William Longespée and that of a second effigy, usually identified as William's son, in Salisbury cathedral both bear traces of paint. See Tummers, *Early Secular Effigies,* 18.

48. Bloch, *Etymologies,* 66. I am indebted to Bloch's analysis of kinship and heraldry, 67–83, for most of what follows.

49. Bloch, *Etymologies,* 68–69. Bloch notes that the different conception of family is reflected in the Church's modifications to the rules of consanguinity. The new criteria shrank the forbidden degrees from seven to four and were implemented by the Fourth Lateran Council (1215). In changing its marriage laws the Church acknowledged the narrower conception of family.

50. John Hudson, *Land, Law and Lordship in Anglo-Norman England* (Oxford: Clarendon Press, 1994), 66, 109. For an in-depth analysis of the medieval English notion of the family see J.C. Holt, "Feudal Society and the Family in Early Medieval England," parts 1 and 2, *Transactions of the Royal Historical Society* 32 (1982): 193–212; 33 (1993): 193–220.

51. On lineal anxiety see M. David, "Le mariage dans la société féodal, note critique," *Annales E.S.C.* 36 (1981): 1053.

52. Hudson, *Land, Law and Lordship,* 67.

53. Morgan, "Making the English Gentry," 22–23.

54. Ibid., 23.

55. Ibid., 24.

56. I use "embroidery" here instead of the traditional "tapestry" in deference to Madeline Caviness's interpretation of the gender politics at work in this textile and the scholarship on it. Her ideas will appear in her book *Triangulating Medieval Art: Object History Feminism* now in preparation.

57. Crouch, *Image of the Aristocracy,* 222.

58. Coss, *Knight in Medieval England,* 79. Crouch (*Image of the Aristocracy,* 223) suggests that the royal use of coats of arms may have been in imitation of aristocratic practice and not the reverse as might be expected.

59. See Crouch, *Image of the Aristocracy,* 222, 227, fig. 8, and 231, fig. 9a. See also P.D.A. Harvey and Andrew McGuinness, *Guide to British Medieval Seals,* 47.

60. J.J.G. Alexander and Paul Binski, eds., *The Age of Chivalry. Art in Plantagenet England 1200–1400* (London: Royal Academy of Art), 56–57.

61. Crouch, *Image of the Aristocracy,* 235; Coss (*Knight in Medieval England,* 82) cites, in addition, Matthew Paris's illustrations in his *Chronica Maiore,* Occasional Rolls, General Rolls and county rolls. For more information on the rolls of arms see N. Denholm-Young, *History and Heraldry, 1254–1310: A Study of the Historical Value of the Rolls of Arms* (Oxford: Clarendon Press, 1965).

62. Scammel, "Formation of the English Social Structure," 612–13.

63. Morgan, *Making the English Gentry,* 24–25.

64. Tummers cataloged 143 knights' effigies from the thirteenth century and found that 109 had crossed legs. See his chart in *Early English Effigies,* 135–43.

65. Ibid.

66. Tummers counts at least seventy among his cross-legged examples.

67. Prior and Gardner, *An Account of Medieval Figure Sculpture,* 553–54, 591–93, 601, 610–12. Prior and Gardner refer to the more serene group as the "composed London type."

68. Fryer, "Monumental Effigies," 2; and Lawrence Stone, *Sculpture in Britain, The Middle Ages,* 2nd ed. (Harmondsworth: Penguin Books, 1972), 149–50.

69. Hurtig, *Armored Gisants,* 124–26, 134–36; and Tummers, *Early Secular Effigies,* 107.

70. Tummers (*Early Secular Effigies,* 55) suggests that the lack of a mantle on female effigies may suggest lower rank. Additionally, the figure's gesture, with her right hand resting on her breast, may be associated with aristocratic status. For this figure, as well as King John, see Bloxam, "Sepulchral Remains and Effigies," 273–74; 347–48.

71. Anne Hollander, *Sex and Suits* (New York: A.A. Knopf, 1995), 33.

72. *The Song of Roland,* trans. Robert Harrison (New York: New American Library, 1970), 91–93.

73. *The Song of William,* trans. Edward Noble Stone (Seattle: University of Washington Press, 1951), 20.

74. Ibid., 71.

75. Richard Kaeuper has described prowess as the core of chivalric ideology as evidenced in chivalric literature. He developed this idea in "Chivalry and the Problem of Violence" (paper presented at the annual meeting of the International Congress on Medieval Studies, Kalamazoo, Mich., May 1997).

76. *The High Book of the Grail: a Translation of the Thirteenth-Century Romance of Perlesvaus,* trans. Nigel Bryant (Cambridge, Mass.: D.S. Brewer; Totowa, N.J.: Rowman and Littlefield, 1978), 38–39.

77. Ibid., 47–48.

78. *Sir Gawain and the Green Knight,* trans. Marie Borroff (New York: W.W. Norton, 1967), 4.

79. Richard W. Kaeuper and Elspeth Kennedy, *The* Book of Chivalry *of Geoffroi de Charny: Text, Context, and Translation* (Philadelphia: University of Pennsylvania Press, 1996).

80. Ibid., 85–91.

81. Ibid., 129.

82. Simon Gaunt, "Monologic Masculinity: the *chanson de geste,*" and "The Knight Meets his Match: Romance," chaps. 1 and 2 respectively, in *Gender and Genre in Medieval French Literature* (Cambridge: Cambridge University Press, 1995).

83. Ibid., 22–26.

84. Ibid., 62–63. Gaunt acknowledges that others have considered the role of women in the *chanson* as critics of the dominant male ideology; he notes, however, that these women are frequently ignored, attacked or suppressed, so that their critique lacks impact. For scholars interested in this issue see S. Kay, "Compagnonnage désordre social et hétérotextualité dans 'Daurel et Beton'," in *Actes du XIe congrés de la Société Rencevals,* 2 vols. (Barcelona, 1990), 1:352–67; idem, "Investing the Wild: Women's Beliefs in the Chansons de Geste," *Paragraph* 13 (1990): 147–63; and idem, "La Composition de Raoul de Cambrai," *Revue de Philogie et d'Histoire* 62 (1984): lxxi.

85. Gaunt, *Gender and Genre,* 76–77. Dido's homophobic rantings about Eneas reinforce the heterosexual agenda of the story.

86. Ibid., 83.

87. Ibid., 22–23, 73–74.

88. Susan C. Shapiro, "Sex, Gender, and Fashion in Medieval and Early Modern Britain," *The Journal of Popular Culture* 1 (Spring 1987): 114–15.

89. Odericus Vitalis, *The Ecclesiastical History,* ed. and trans. Marjorie Chibnall (Oxford: Clarendon Press, 1973), 4:189.

90. William of Malmesbury, *The History of the Kings of England,* trans. John Sharpe (London: H.G. Bohn, 1854), 278–79.

91. Coss (*Knight in Medieval England,* 120) notes that the tournament was an increasingly important part of chivalric culture from the thirteenth century on. Within the tourneying milieu lavish display was imperative as evidence of wealth and power. Also see Richard Barber, *The Knight and Chivalry,* rev. ed., (Woodbridge, Eng.: Boydell Press, 1995), 162–66; and Richard Barber and Julie Vale, *Tournaments: Jousts, Chivalry and Pageants in the Middle Ages* (Woodbridge, Eng.: Boydell Press, 1989).

92. Barber, *The Knight and Chivalry,* 375.

93. Keen, *Chivalry,* 95. Matthew Paris was obviously somewhat ambivalent as he produced some of the earliest visual records of the heraldic devices associated with tournaments in his chronicles. See Antony R. Wagner et al., *Aspilogia II: Rolls of Arms Henry III* (London: Society of Antiquaries, 1967). Also see Coss, *Knight in Medieval England,* 73–76.

The English royal response to tournaments was as ambivalent as the St. Albans monk's. Generally, a king's response was geared to the amount of political unrest present at any given time. Richard I recognized the legitimacy of the tournament and approved it as a good training ground for young knights, but also acknowledged its potential for destruction. In 1194, he attempted to exert control over the activity by licensing only five places in England as tourneying grounds. Knights who wished to participate had to obtain a license and pay a fee. Non-English knights were excluded from these gatherings in the hopes of avoiding violent political rivalries. In Henry III's reign, tournaments were forbidden during his minority, during the struggle with the French and during the unrest leading up to the de Montfort rebellion. Edward I was a passionate tourneyer but forbade them during his Welsh, Gascony and Scottish campaigns in the 1290s. See Barber, *The Knight and Chivalry,* 162–64; Coss, *Knight in Medieval England,* 53–56; and Keen, *Chivalry,* 96–97.

94. de Charny, in Kaeuper and Kennedy, *Book of Chivalry,* 167.

95. Ibid., 175.

96. Ibid., 167, 175–77.

97. Hurtig, *Armored Gisants,* 115, 138–51.

98. In particular, Gaunt cites the following studies: Erich Köhler, "Quelques observations d'ordre historico-sociologique sur les rapports entre la chanson de geste et le roman courtois," in *Chanson de geste und höfischer Roman: Heidelberger Kolloquium 30. Januar 1961* (Heidelberg: C. Winter, 1963), 21–30; idem, *L'aventure chevalresque: Idéal et réalité dans le roman courtois,* trans. Eliane Kaufholz (Paris: Gallimard, 1974); D. Boutet, "Les Chanson de geste et l'affermissement du pouvoir royal (1100–1250)," *Annales E.S.C.* 37 (1982): 3–14; A. Gérard, "L'Axe Roland-Ganelon: valeurs en conflit dans la Chanson de Roland," *Le Moyen Age* 75 (1969): 452–65; Peter Haidu, *The Subject of Violence: The Song of Roland and the Birth of the State* (Bloomington: Indiana University Press, 1993), 101–19; and Judith Kellogg, *Medieval Artistry and Exchange: Economic Institutions and Literary Form in Old French Narrative* (New York: P. Lang, 1989), 88–91.

Chivalric Conversation and the Denial of Male Fear

ANDREW TAYLOR

> *"[B]eing a man" . . . is an unceasing effort, a*
> *tense and vigilant posture of the will, ever on the*
> *alert against the terrible, the unthinkable humil-*
> *iation of being unmasked, in an unguarded*
> *moment, as a cissy, a pansy or a weed.*
>
> JANET BATSLEER[1]

In 1388 Jean Froissart came to stay with the Gaston Phébus, count of Foix and viscount of Béarn, in his court on the edge of the Pyrenees, where he was received graciously. One night, while he was sitting by the fire after supper and waiting for the count to appear, Froissart and a tough mercenary leader called the Bascot de Mauléon fell into conversation "in the way one does talk about arms and warfare" [*et tout ainsi que l'on parle et devise d'armes*]:

> The Bascot began to speak and to tell of his life and of the deeds of arms that he had been at, enduring as much loss as profit. Then he asked me, "Sir John, have you anything at all in your history of this business that I am speaking of?" And I answered and said, "I do not know. Either way, give me your account, for I will gladly hear you speak of arms, and as well I cannot have been told everything."[2]

So the Bascot tells his story, which runs for several pages and covers several campaigns. At Poitiers, his first battle, he captured one knight and two squires, which won him three thousand francs. When the English and French made peace he joined a group of over twelve thousand mercenaries by the banks of the Loire. These men, companions in the so-called Free Companies, proceeded to dominate central France, raiding, sacking, or demanding protection money. They fought against the constable of France and threatened the pope in Avignon, who bought them off for sixty thousand francs. By the time the Bascot came to fight in the

169

battle of Cocherel he had his own castle and led forty lances. His career was not without its setbacks, however. Bernard de Tharide, who was actually a cousin, captured him and ransomed him for a thousand francs. What might well have been one of the most dangerous and frightening moments—although fear is not a word that the Bascot ever uses—occurred during an abortive raid on Sancerre, when the Companions were ambushed after crossing the Loire. This is an episode that the Bascot describes at particular length.

From time to time other knights at the count of Foix's court join in or Froissart prompts the Bascot, until the signal is sounded summoning those knights who are in town to attend the count at his midnight supper. Under similar circumstances, talking of arms and warfare "in the way one does," Froissart would have first heard the stories of the Hundred Years' War from which he formed his *Chronicles.*

The relation of these reported conversations to any social reality is not easy to determine. Froissart's poetry participates in the elaborate play of self-reflexivity that makes French court poetry of the late Middle Ages seem almost postmodern in sensibility. In his *Fonteine amoureuse,* for example, Froissart depicts a narrator who is both lover and poet writing to his lady, who writes poems in reply. Her identity becomes ever more elusive until her very existence becomes questionable, as if she were but a poetic fiction serving to generate further poetic fictions, which ultimately become the poem itself .[3] When, in *L'Espinette amoureuse,* Froissart's poet/narrator encounters the young woman who will be his love interest, she is reading one of Froissart's own sources, the romance *Cléomades* of Adenet le Roi. This is a poetry of mirrors. Froissart's encounter with the Bascot might be seen as another such self-referential moment, where the chronicle shows its author gathering the material that will become the chronicle, and read as an elaborate play on codes of verisimilitude. What we see is not Froissart himself on a particular historical evening, but an idealized narratorial figure. This narrator reconciles the roles of clerk and knight so often set in opposition in Froissart's poetry; he is cherished by the Count, who orders him to read aloud each night from his long romance, the *Méliador,* and he is on good terms with the knights, whose deeds he saves for posterity by gathering them into his great compendium.[4] All this leaves the value of the *Chronicles* as a historical source highly questionable. But the encounter with the Bascot points outward to some social reality nonetheless, since Froissart authenticates his account by reconstructing common speech patterns of his day. Even if the conversation never occurred or has been extensively reshaped, it suggests established social norms for conversation between men and evokes a broader circulation of courtly discourse. As Peter Ainsworth concedes in his persuasive treatment of the literary shaping of this passage, "much of [Froissart's] military lexis and style must have been derived from years of listening to soldiers' tales."[5]

Lengthy and elaborate conversation on love and on war had long been a feature of court culture, praised by some, censured by others.[6] John of Salisbury expresses the hostility of many clerics, when he lashes out at the practice of braggart soldiers:

> The more boastful they are in the hall, the more certain it is that when it comes to the issue of an actual battle, they will send ahead their ser-vants into the fight in droves under the lead of Sanga [a character in the *Eunuchus* of Terence], while they themselves, to save their skins, trail behind the rear guard in company with the slingers and others whose aim is rather to hurl missiles against the foe from a distance than to meet them in hand-to-hand conflict. But afterwards, when they return home without a wound or a scratch (as generally happens)
>
> > "They sing of battles hard fought and weary war;
> > There contends Eacides, and yonder Achilles;
> > And they paint the whole Trojan war in flowing wine":
>
> and each boasts that about his temples he narrowly missed a thousand deaths. Indeed never thereafter will you be able to endure the dazzle of their glory. A tale of this kind will be handed down to the hundreth year; their sons who will be born and grow up, will tell it over to their sons. If they break any lances, which their artful laziness has contrived to have made as fragile as hemp, if the gold leaf or red-lead or other coloring matter has been knocked off their shields by some chance blow or other accident, their garrulous tongue, if they find any to listen, will make the incident memorable from century to century.[7]

John of Salisbury's hostility toward the military conversation of his day emerges strongly from beneath his classical allusions and references to Roman warfare, but he shows little understanding of the social function of this conversation. In chivalric literature such boasting was crucial in building a knight's identity, and it probably was so in real life as well. Sandra Hindman notes that in the romances of Chrétien de Troyes, "[w]hile the lady attempts to shape the knight as she reads aloud to him, offering role models for his behaviour out of romances, the bachelor

knight creates his own public image in the stories he recites at court."[8]
The thirteenth-century prose romance *Merlin* describes how Merlin
instituted this practice at Camelot:

> And one should, as you well know, be able to distinguish the good
> from the bad and honor each according to who he is. For this reason, I
> recommend that the moment a knight takes up a quest you have him
> swear as he is about to leave that when he returns he will recount all the
> things that happened to him in his quest, whether they are to his glory
> or his shame.[9]

The need to reward bravery and military accomplishments and to punish
cowardice and acts of military weakness by having them retold is a continual theme in chivalric literature, and was one of the major functions of
heralds, chroniclers and minstrels.[10]

Elaborate vows, which became ever more heavily ritualized in the
late Middle Ages, provided another means of publicly committing the
knights to extreme bravery.[11] *Les Voeux du héron,* a poem that describes
vows allegedly made by the knights of Edward III in 1338, captures
something of the coercive force of these rituals. At a royal banquet a
heron is served, and each of the knights swears by the bird to perform an
act of daring. The count of Salisbury goes first, asking his countess to
place her hands on his eyelid and close it and then vowing that he will not
open his eye until he has invaded France. Others follow. However, one of
the knights, Jean de Beaumont, expresses his reservations at their extravagant promises:

> . . . I am astonished by so much talk.
> Boasts that are not accomplished mean nothing.
> When we are in taverns, drinking strong wines,
> And being watched by ladies
> With firm breasts in tight bodices
> And with bright eyes that sparkle with smiling beauty,
> Nature makes us desire
> To do battle—only to want mercy later on.
> Thus we conquer Yaumont and Agoulant,
> And others defend Oliver and Roland.
> But when we are in the field on our swift horses,
> Our shields hanging from our necks, our lances lowered,
> And the terrible cold is chilling us,
> And all our limbs fail us entirely,

And our enemies are approaching us,
Then we would rather be hidden in a cellar so deep
That no one could ever find us.
I would not give one besant for such boasting![12]

This is as close as chivalric literature will get to acknowledging what the knights actually felt on the field of battle or the extent to which their behavior was being constricted by the predetermined roles imposed upon them. Chivalric culture required that knights assume these roles as a matter of duty and had little tolerance for their questioning.

Household ordinances formally encouraged the kind of conversation Froissart had with the Bascot. As the household book of Edward IV specifies, the squires are to immerse themselves in chivalric lore:

[The squires] of old be accustomed, wynter and somer, in after nonys and in euenynges, to drawe to lordez chambrez within courte, there to kepe honest company aftyr theyre cunyng, in talkyng of cronycles of kinges and of other polycez or in pyping or harping, synging, other actz marciablez, to help occupy the court and acompany strauungers, tyll the tym require of departing.[13]

The "talking of chronicles" mentioned here might refer to the public reading from chronicles or equally to conversation about what had been read.[14] Both were common and they formed a continual circle.

Conversation was important because it allowed the squires to assess the models presented to them, comparing what they heard from a variety of veterans and moral advisers, reconciling conflicts between different branches of the code of chivalry, and preparing themselves as best as possible for an experience that no account could really convey. In this regard, the conversation of Edward's squires would have had much in common with the anxious conversation of military cadets at Sandhurst reported by John Keegan. For these cadets, the central question is what is a battle really like?:

That this—or its subjective supplementary, "How would *I* behave in a battle?"—is indeed the central question reveals itself when it is raised in a roomful of cadets—and probably any gathering of young men any-where—in a number of unmistakable ways: by a marked rise in the emotional temperature, in the pitch of voices, and in what a sociologist might call "the rate and volume of inter-cadet exchanges"; by signs of obvious physical tenseness in the ways cadets sit or gesticulate—

unless they assume, as some do, a deliberately nonchalant attitude; and by the content of what they have to say—a noisy mixture of slightly unconvincing bombast, frank admissions of uncertainty and anxiety, bold declarations of false cowardice, friendly and not-so-friendly jibes, frequent appeals to fathers' and uncles' experience of "what a battle is really like" and heated argument over the how and why of killing human beings, ranging over the whole ethical spectrum from the view that "the only good one is a dead one" to very civilized expressions of reluctance at the prospect of shedding human blood at all.[15]

Here, at last, we begin to get a sense of the range of male anxiety that underlies chivalric and heroic discourse and the wealth of dissimulation this anxiety produces. What Keegan's account suggests, and others confirm, is soldiers are afraid not just of battle itself, of being killed or mutilated, but of failing to pass the test, of letting others down or disgracing themselves.[16] To avoid this, they must exercise a rigorous self-control, suppressing the natural instinct to flee from danger. Their military training allows them to practice this self-control and self-suppression, and disciplines not just their bodies but their emotional responses and their speech. The conversation of cadets and squires is perforce disingenuous.

Chivalric conversation was institutionally sanctioned because it enforced chivalric ideology. Through their discussions, young men learned genealogical history, heraldry and court ceremonial; they learned the complexities of feudal obligation; they learned appropriate model speeches; and they learned crucial chivalric values. These values, of which courage and loyalty were perhaps the most important in war, had to be so deeply ingrained that a knight would ignore common sense and natural instinct and persistently risk his neck instead of simply running away. So, from an early age, the future knight was raised on tales of military glory and taught a certain stance toward violence and toward fear— the one thing chivalric literature virtually never mentions directly.

Like most chivalric writings, Froissart's *Chronicles* rarely discuss fear, unless to attribute it to women. Instead, the *Chronicles* coalesce around moments of individual courage and loyalty, even when the evidence indicates that some knights panicked or fled. Froissart's long account of the Battle of Otterburn is a case in point. The story of Otterburn was often retold and it generated an enduring ballad tradition. The battle was particularly memorable because it centred around the personal rivalry of the two famous border warriors, James Douglas and Henry Percy, and led to the capture of one and the death of the other. It was a story that had from the very beginning the plot of a romance. But the battle was also, according to Froissart, unusually hard fought and provided a general chivalric exemplar. Froissart was informed by both parties "that it was as hard a struggle and as well fought as any battle ever has been."[17] He agrees with this judgment:

> Of all the struggles, battles, and encounters, both great and small, that I have written of above in this history, this one that I am speaking of at the moment was one of the hardest and best fought without cowardice, for there was neither man, nor squire, nor knight who did not acquit himself well and do his duty and all hand-to-hand.[18]

It is this harsh hand-to-hand struggle that Froissart notes in particular.

> The knights and squires on both sides were close together and fought valiantly and ardently as long as their battle-axes and lances lasted. Cowardice had no place there, but hardiness reigned and the knights and squires displayed great courage. And the two sides were so closely joined together and crowded that neither side could use archers, for they were so closely joined that they fought together hand-to-hand, and nobody gave way but all held firm to their place.[19]

The resulting casualties testified to this courage: "So, consider if it was not a mixed and hard business and well fought, when there were so many dead and captured on one side and on the other."[20] The ideological function of the *Chronicles* emerges clearly in this description. Froissart writes: "in order that the honourable enterprises, noble adventures and deeds of arms which took place during the wars waged by France and England should be fittingly related and preserved for posterity, so that brave men should be inspired thereby to follow such examples."[21]

The *Chronicles* set forth a code based on a single opposition: bravery versus cowardice. Yet the actual behavior of the men at Otterburn cannot have been as consistently indifferent to fear as Froissart implies. Although the two sides are described as pressing each other hard for a long time, there is a huge disproportion between the light Scottish casualties, which Froissart gives as about a hundred killed and two hundred taken prisoner, and the heavy English casualties, which Froissart gives as 1,860 killed. The light Scottish casualties suggest that in the initial stages, when the battle was more or less balanced, the soldiers did not engage with each other anything like as ferociously as Froissart claimed.

The disproportionately heavy English casualties suggest that many of those who died were slain as they ran. This was a common pattern in early warfare,[22] and Froissart does specifically mention the long chase after the English, but he strongly implies that the casualties occurred before the retreat, elevating the battle on account of the courage of both sides as "one of the hardest fought" in his day.

Froissart's account covers any English weakness. He offers excuses for the English defeat, stressing that they were tired from the long march and that fortune turned against them, and insisting that they had fought bravely. Above all, when he comes to the critical moment where the English break (and probably, although Froissart never quite admits this, flee in panic), Froissart avoids any direct reference to their emotional condition:

> And as fortune shifts, though the Englishmen outnumbered the Scots, and were valiant and experienced fighters, and attacked their enemy valiantly, and had at first pushed the Scots back, yet in the end the Scots took the place and all the aforesaid Englishmen were taken, and a hundred more, except Sir Mathew Redman, the Captain of Berwick.[23]

Froissart concentrates on the Scottish who thrust forward, rather than the English who begin to drop back. He allows the squires and knights who retreat to remain anonymous, except for Redman, whose behavior he depicts not as an act of panic but as a *decision,* taken reluctantly after the unarmed others had fled: "when he perceived the setback and that there was no remedy and that the English were fleeing and opening up before the Scots on all sides, and that the knights and squires surrendering, and the Scots taking them prisoner, he mounted his horse because he wanted to save himself and departed."[24] This careful veiling of human but embarrassingly unchivalric behavior spares not just the English but the entire chivalric class from shame. Froissart tells of men who are tired and pushed back but one can read his entire account of Otterburn without ever once encountering a man who is afraid.

The Bascot's laconic description of his career adheres to the same code of silence, never once acknowledging fear, even when recounting the disastrous raid on Sancerre. The party rode to the Loire by night, crossed in a fleet of small boats and set up a rear guard, but things soon began to go wrong. It is worth considering this passage in some detail:

And because it was nearing dawn, we left a hundred lances behind to guard the horses and the boats, and set out ourselves and rode past the palace where the ambush was. They never once came out, but once we had passed by and were about a quarter of a league down the road, they emerged and attacked those who had stayed by the river, who were all killed or taken, and the horses and boats seized, and then they mounted our horses and spurred on so that they reached the city almost as we did. They all cried out "Notre-Dame! Sancerre!" for the count was there with his men and Sir Louis and Sir Robert who had set the ambush and there was a great crush of lances, and those of them who were on horseback, as soon as they arrived, dismounted and attacked us fiercely. And what harmed us most was that we could not spread out because we were riding down a road which had high hedges and vines on both sides. And as well, a number of them who knew the land and the road well had got up among the vines with their men, and were throwing rocks and stones down on us so much that they were smashing us up. We could not retreat and we found it very difficult to push on toward the town which was on a steep hill. We were much worked-over and Sir Aimery was mortally wounded . . . And I tell you it was a very hard battle and brutal, and we held on and defended ourselves as best we could while, on one side and another, many were killed or smashed, and, as they showed, they would have preferred to take us alive rather than dead.[25]

The account offers a detailed and plausible account of a raid that had suddenly become unusually dangerous. Hemmed in, on the enemy's side of the river, with their line of retreat cut off, and their plans obviously betrayed, the Companions ran a grave risk not just of being captured but of being killed. In this tight space, with rocks being hurled down from above, the Bascot and his companions would not necessarily have been able to surrender, and this disrupted the mechanism of ransoming, one of the main limitations on the death toll among knights. In fact their leader, Aimery is captured, but although his captor arranges for him to be led away, the guard does not take sufficient care of him and he bleeds to death.

All in all, it was a brutal engagement, but the language is restrained. The Bascot notes that what most troubled or harmed them [*ce qui trop nous greva*] was that they were so enclosed, that they suffered "*grant paine*" and were "*mult traveillés*"; and he ends with a general assessment: the battle was very hard [*mult dure*] and brutal [*felon*], with many killed and smashed up or wounded [*navré*]. He describes only the bare essentials, as he might if he were reporting the event to a superior officer. Above all, he never mentions how he felt personally. This spare style is a common one. As one modern veteran notes, "Generally, the telling of war stories is direct and undecorated, which is the way soldiers seem to prefer it."[26]

It is not unreasonable to wonder how much the Bascot's laconic account is concealing. If we think of this account as a version of an actual report, with the voice of the soldier more or less reproduced in Froissart's text, then the Bascot's concentration on this episode and the precise sequence of events suggests that it stayed in his mind and that he exorcised it in the retelling. His account becomes a kind of "talking cure."[27] At the time, the Bascot's iron self-control may have slipped, but he imposes order upon the episode retroactively, reestablishing himself in the brotherhood of men who feel no fear.

Whether the Bascot is speaking is, however, in some sense, beside the point. Chivalric discourse was part of a sustained exercise in role-playing and in self-censorship, in which unacceptable emotions were replaced with appropriately noble speeches. These speeches served to maintain the knight's public status, to hearten his friends and to intimidate his enemies, and they also became his memorial. Carefully recorded and embellished by chroniclers, heralds and minstrels, the speeches of defiance were passed on to succeeding generations, in the manner John of Salisbury scorns. Young knights would endeavor to model their behavior on these heroic forerunners, behaving and speaking in appropriate manner. If an actual soldier such as the Bascot described his campaigns he would have observed the same codes that are presented throughout Froissart's *Chronicles*. Indeed, he would have learned how to speak from hearing chronicles and romances read aloud, just as his own words would furnish material for the chronicles that would come after him.

The Bascot's account adheres to a code of silence, but the code is more intense on the field of battle itself, where the hero must demonstrate his indifference to pain, danger and death in his presence. Here suppression becomes a kind of language game, a heroic litotes. The best speeches are self-deprecating, ironic and lapidary. Douglas's death speech at Otterburn offers a good example. His close companion, Sir John Sinclair, asked him how he fared, and he replied:

> Poorly, . . . thanked be God. One could not find many of my ancestors who have died in their beds. I tell you, think how to avenge me, for I consider myself but dead, for my heart is stopping too often.[28]

The phrase "strong silent man" evokes, but not quite accurately, the code of heroic litotes. The emotional resonance of the code lies in the hero's ability to rebuke fear and pain not with silence but with measured speech and sardonic amusement, with the jest with which a man greets death. The code can be traced out in a wide variety of popular men's writing in different cultures, and its coercive power is easily recognized in the popular writing that still shapes our attitudes today. What these defiant speeches share with the plain style of the simple "soldier's tale" is the suppression of any personal weakness.

Balancing such elaborate displays of self-censorship, however, are gushes of ritualized abuse and swearing. A form of aggressive posturing, this language serves both to intimidate an opponent and to sublimate one's own fear in self-induced rage as one "works oneself up." Posturing also keeps casualties down since it is an alternative or lengthy preliminary to actual combat.[29] Such posturing takes the form of extreme verbal license; the speeches are boastful, hyperbolic, rhetorically extravagant and defiant of taboo. The two forms of speech, stoical, heroic understatement and aggressive vaunting or abuse, one repressive, the other expressive, appear to interact in a psychological drama of containment and release that recurs across many cultures. As Robert Graves suggests, "Silence under suffering is usually impossible. The nervous system demands some expression that does not affect towards cowardice and feebleness and, as a nervous stimulant in a crisis, swearing is unequalled."[30] Heroic litotes shows considerable stability. Douglas does not sound that different from the soldier described by Castiglione who, when pierced by a lance, remarked that a fly had bit him.[31] Heroic abuse, on the other hand, is protean. Being copious of speech, it allows greater scope, takes a variety of poetic forms and demands verbal sophistication as well as self-control.[32] However, abuse, by its very nature, eludes full recording. Since its ability to provoke anger and vent fear comes in part from breaching taboo, it is no longer likely to be completely effective when it can be written down. Only occasionally will traces of this pre-combative abuse survive.[33] The language that comes after, decorous, self-controlled and socially sanctioned, replaces the curses, obscenities, yells and screams of the battlefield.

The essential suppression of heroic litotes is the suppression of what men actually feel when confronted with pain and danger: the visceral, degrading, brute sensation that this code systematically denies. The code is a form of emotional blackmail, enforcing itself by an implicit threat of ostracism. Raised on a litany of heroes who are never afraid, men can only silence their own feelings by emulating the dry wit of these terse pronouncements. To lapse from this standard of rigid self-control is to be consigned to the others: feminized men and lower foreigners; to fulfill its demands is to be fully instated in the homoerotic group of loyal friends meeting worthy foes. The fifteenth-century biographical romance *Le Jouvencel* shows the code at its most seductive:

> It is a joyous thing, is war . . . You love your comrade so in war. When you see that your quarrel is just and your blood is fighting well, tears come to your eyes. A great sweet feeling of loyalty and of pity fills your heart on seeing your friend so valiantly exposing his body to execute and accomplish the command of our creator. And then you prepare to go and die or live with him, and for love not to abandon him. And out of that there arises such a delectation, that he who has not tasted it is not fit to say what a delight it is. Do you think that a man who does that fears death? Not at all; for he feels so strengthened, he is so elated, that he does not know where he is. Truly he is afraid of nothing.[34]

This rhapsody comes from a semifictionalized account of the life of Jean de Bueil, who had fought under Joan of Arc and had it composed in his own honor by three of his personal clerks. It enshrines its hero in a quasi-religious fraternity, a brotherhood of men for whom death is the ultimate union.[35] To give in to fear or even to admit its existence is to risk banishment from this company of true men for whom war is "a joyous thing."

In keeping with such speech codes, Froissart's works are not an expression but a repression of male experience, and this is a crucial part of their social function. They set out not just examples of what men must do to count as men, but how they must speak, offering a series of implicit conventions which force inappropriate emotions into silence. Similar codes govern much masculinist writing to this day; popular fiction, movies and television, thrillers, cowboy stories, war stories and the like, are as systematically misleading as Froissart, describing a world of men for whom bloodshed and violence is a simple joy.[36] From Froissart to the public-school literature of heroism is but a step. Sidney Lanier, the editor of *The Boy's Froissart,* notes, "In reading him the young soul sifts out for itself the splendor, the hardihood, the daring, the valor, the generosity, the boundless conflict and unhindered action, which make up the boy's early ideal of the man."[37] Lanier does not quite go so far as to say that the perfect American man should behave like a medieval knight—for him, full adult masculinity lies not just in military courage but in meeting the emotional challenges of later life—but he never repudiates the code of valor.

Nor is the distortion confined to popular culture. Much military writing also systematically obfuscates the human reality of war. For one thing, the writers are often closely linked to the military institutions of their day, as Froissart was. Knowledge requires complicity. As Alfred Vagts argues, "A very large part of military history is written, if not for the express purpose of supporting an army's authority, at least, with the intention of not hurting it, not revealing its secrets, avoiding the betrayal of weakness, vacillation, or distemper."[38] But the problem extends further. Since war is a form of male testing, we cannot expect men to present it honestly. To do so would be a fatal "unmasking," a humiliating revelation of one's own lack of true manhood. There will always be dissimulation, whether it is the deliberate nonchalance, bombast and bold declarations of false cowardice of the Sandhurst cadets as reported by Keegan, or the dehumanizing conventions of much military writing, in which abstract formations push forward or get pushed back: waves are launched, squares hold, lines break.[39] To this day, our understanding as a society of how men behave in battle is highly limited. S.L.A. Marshall shocked military officials in the late forties when he discovered that less than 20 percent of American infantrymen in World War II actually fired at the enemy and that most of them shot wide or did not shoot at all.[40] French officers a century earlier had known this, and evidence of the reluctance to shoot to kill can be found elsewhere, including the numerous undischarged muskets on the field of Gettysburg, but it apparently came as a surprise to American military authorities, who modified their training programs accordingly.[41] Yet, as Dave Grossman suggests, the explanation is simple enough, though it took him numerous interviews with American veterans to discover it:

> I began to realize that there was one major factor that was missing from the common understanding of killing in combat, a factor that answers this question [why men fail to fire] and more. That missing factor is the simple and demonstrable fact that there is within most men an intense resistance to killing their fellow men. A resistance so strong that, in many circumstances, soldiers on the battlefield will die before they can overcome it.[42]

The intense physical resistance to being killed is even further from being addressed. The very word "fear" is striking by its absence in writings of many military psychologists, who prefer to write about "stress," just as Froissart preferred to write about fatigue.[43]

In his classic study of medieval warfare, J.F. Verbruggen concludes that in the essentials medieval knights were no different from men today—they were often afraid: "Despite their great and sometimes wholly admirable gallantry, the knights were still human beings who feared for their lives in the presence of danger, and who behaved as men have always done in battle—in fear of death, mutilation, wounds and captivity."[44] Why should we believe it was otherwise? The "flight or fight" mechanism can be seen in military engagements across cultures and throughout history, just as it can be observed throughout the animal kingdom. It makes biological sense; "The posturing, mock battle, and submission process is vital to the species."[45] A fighter who was completely devoid of fear or who actually enjoyed killing would, under many circumstances, be an intolerable hazard to both parties. It is true that medieval knights formed a socialized cast to endure danger. It is true also that the experience of battle or severe danger can work extreme changes in people's character, so that all sense of danger is temporarily lost; many modern soldiers do report enjoying the intensity of war and even pining for it during peace, and often these accounts do seem remarkably frank.[46] But this does not mean that the knights ever reached the stage of total indifference to death or pain attributed to them in chivalric literature. If they had, it would not have taken them long to kill each other off completely.

Why, then, has the depiction of the knightly class as one that feels no fear seldom been challenged? Perhaps it is because the Middle Ages provides the greatest repository of martial rhetoric for Western culture and the chivalric code its most influential idealization. For nineteenth-century Europe, the Middle Ages evoked a simpler time free from the complexities of industrial and secular society, a time symbolized by the simple but courageous knight. For Léon Gautier, the "simple, vigorous, almost brutal" faith of the knight, was matched by his simple enjoyment of sung epic; the knight could not read, and his spirit was untouched by the sophistry and scepticism that Gautier saw in his own society.[47] Chivalry also provided a terminology and set of attitudes to enoble modern war. Writing within a few years of the end of World War I, Johan Huizinga found in the hero of the *Le Jouvencel,* who is "afraid of nothing" and finds war "a joyous thing," a testimony to manly courage for his own age:

> This could just as well have come from a modern soldier as from a
> knight of the fifteenth century. It has nothing to do with the knightly
> ideal *per se,* but reflects the emotions constituting the background of

> pure fighting courage itself: the trembling stepping away from narrow
> egoism into the excitement of facing mortal danger, the deeply touch-
> ing experience of the bravery of one's comrades, the enjoyment of loy-
> alty and self-sacrifice.[48]

Huizinga perseveres in a tradition of idealizing combat that was already
beginning to be challenged as the experience of the trenches entered
broader public consciousness. Once again chivalry served to veil the hor-
rors of actual warfare. His praise for *Le Jouvencel* as a true expression of
a courage that transcends egoism and even his use of the term "primitive"
to characterize this "ascetic excitement" are in harmony with the views
of Gautier. They share a vision of medieval chivalry as a moral touch-
stone for the modern world.

   The late medieval code of chivalry is an extreme example of a code
of aggressive masculinity. Reflecting a society's military needs, it
enforces a rigorous censoring of human expression which is imposed
through a system of representation so pervasive and so comprehensive
that no individual can expect to loosen its emotional hold completely.
This system of representation can be seen in romances, in chronicles and
in idealized memoirs like *Le Jouvencel* or quasi-historical poems like
Les Voueux du héron. The core values that these works taught, loyalty
and courage, were internalized through the endless discussion of battles
and deeds of arms that formed a standard part of court custom—"*tout
ainsi que l'on parle et devise d'armes.*" Both the conversation and the
writings made it very clear what a knight should feel but never quite
revealed what he felt.

NOTES

   1. Janet Batsleer et al., *Rewriting English: Cultural Politics of Gender
and Class* (London: Methuen, 1985), 78.
   2. "[The Bascot] le mist en voye de parler et de recorder de sa vie et des
armes où en son temps il avoit esté à tant de pertes comme de prouffis, et trop
bien luy en souvenoit. Si me demanda: 'Messire Jehan, avés-vous point en vostre
histoire ce dont je vous parleray?' Je luy respondi: 'Je ne sçay. Aye ou non, faittes
vostre compte, car je vous oy voulentiers parler d'armes, et il ne me puet pas de
tout sovenir, et aussi je ne puis pas de tout avoir esté infourmé.'" *Oeuvres de
Froissart: Chroniques,* ed. Kervyn de Lettenhove (Brussels: V. Devaux,
1867–1877; reprint, Osnabrück: Biblio Verlag, 1967), 11 (1383–1386): 108. The
translations are my own.

3. Sylvia Huot, *From Song to Book: The Poetics of Writing in Old French Lyric and Lyrical Narrative Poetry* (Ithaca, N.Y.: Cornell University Press, 1987), 305–11. Recent discussion of Froissart's reflexivity include Rosemary Morris, "Machaut, Froissart, and the Fictionalization of the Self," *The Modern Language Review* 83 (1988): 545–55; Philip E. Bennett, "The Mirage of Fiction: Narration, Narrator, and Narratee in Froissart's Lyrico-Narrative *Dits*," *The Modern Language Review* 86 (1991): 285–97; Laurence de Looze, "From Text to Text and from Tale to Tale: Jean Froissart's *Prison amoureuse*," in *The Centre and Its Compass: Studies in Medieval Literature in Honor of Professor John Leyerle*, ed. Robert A. Taylor et al. (Kalamazoo, Mich.: Medieval Institute, 1993), 87–110; Michel Zink, "L'Amour en fuite: *L'Espinette amoureuse* et *Le Joli Buisson de Jeunesse* de Froissart ou la poésie comme histoire sans objet," in *Musique naturele: Interpretationen zur französischen Lyrik des Spatmittelalters,* ed. Wolf-Dieter Stempel (Munich: W. Fink, 1995), 195–209; and William Calin, "Narrative Technique in Fourteenth-Century France: Froissart and His Chroniques," in *Studies in Honor of Hans-Erich Keller: Medieval French and Occitan Literature and Romance Linguistics,* ed. Rupert T. Pickens (Kalamazoo, Mich.: Medieval Institute,1993), 227–36.

4. For such a reading, see Peter F. Ainsworth, *Jean Froissart and the Fabric of History: Truth, Myth, and Fiction in the Chroniques* (Oxford: Clarendon, 1990), 144–45.

5. Ibid., 150.

6. The classic study of courtly conversation during this period is Richard Firth Green, *Poets and Princepleasers: Literature and the English Court in the Late Middle Ages* (Toronto: University of Toronto Press, 1980).

7. *The Statesman's Book of John of Salisbury, being the Fourth, Fifth, and Sixth Books and Selections from the Seventh and Eighth Books, of the Policraticus,* trans. John Dickinson (New York: Russell and Russell, 1963), 6.3, 184–85. The verses are from Ovid, *Heroides* 1.31 with echoes of *Metamorphoses,* 12.161.

8. Sandra Hindman, *Sealed in Parchment: Rereadings of Knighthood in the Illuminated Manuscripts of Chrétien de Troyes* (Chicago: University of Chicago Press, 1994), 86.

9. ". . . il convient, che sés tu bien, connoistre les bons des mauvais et hounerer chascun selont chou qu'il est, pour chou te loc jou que si tost que chevaliers se metera en queste des armes on li fache jurer si tost coume il s'en partira de court qu'il dira voir au revenir de toutes les choses qui li seront avenues et qu'il avra trouvé en sa queste, ou soit s'ounour ou sa honte." *Merlin: Roman en prose du XIIIe siècle,* ed. Gaston Paris and Jacob Ulrich, 2 vols. (Paris: Firmin Didot, 1886), 2:98. There is a modern French translation by Henri de Brel, *Le Roman de Merlin l'Enchanteur* (Paris: C. Klincksieck, 1971), 260.

10. See Andrew Taylor, "Songs of Praise and Blame and the Repertoire of the *Gestour,*" in *The Entertainer in Medieval and Traditional Culture: A Symposium,* ed. Flemming G. Andersen, Thomas Pettitt, and Reinhold Schröder (Odense, Den.: Odense University Press, 1997), 47–72.

11. Maurice Keen, *Chivalry* (New Haven: Yale University Press, 1984), 212–16.

12. ". . . de tant de paroles me vois moult merveillant./ Vantise ne vaut nïent qui n'achievement./ Quant sommes es tavernes, de ches fors vins boevant,/ Et ches dames de les, qui nous vont regardant,/ A ches gorgues polies, ches colieres tirant,/ Chil oeil vair resplendissent de beauté sourriant,/ Nature nous semont d'avoir ceur desirant/ De contendre, a le fin de merchi atendant;/ Adont conquerons nous Yaumont et Agoulant,/ Et li autre conquerant Olivier et Roland./ Mais quant sommes as camps sur nos destriers courans,/ Nos escus a no col et no lanches baissans,/ Et le frodure grande nous va tous engelans,/ Li membre nous effond[r]ent, et derrier et devant,/ Et nous anemis sont envers nous approachant,/ Adont vauriemes estre en un chelier si grant/ Que jamais ne fuissons veü ne tant ne quant./ De si faite vantise ne donroie .j. besant!" *The Vows of the Heron (Les Voeux du héron): A Middle French Vowing Poem,* ed. John L. Grigsby and Norris J. Lacy, trans. Norris J. Lacy (New York: Garland, 1992), 52–53, lines 359–76. On the historicity of this acount, see John L. Grigsby, "Intertextualité interrompue par l'histoire: Le Cas des *Voeux du Héron,*" in *Courtly Literature: Culture and Context,* ed. Keith Busby and Erik Kooper (Amsterdam: John Benjamins, 1990), 239–49.

13. Alec R. Meyers, ed. *English Historical Documents: 1327–1485* (London: Eyre and Spottiswoode,1969), 128–29.

14. On public reading of chronicles as part of court ceremonial, see Joyce Coleman, *Public Reading and the Reading Public in Late Medieval England and France* (New York: Cambridge University Press, 1996), esp. 117–21.

15. John Keegan, *The Face of Battle* (New York: Viking Press, 1976), 17–18.

16. Dave Grossman, *On Killing: The Psychological Cost of Learning to Kill in War and Society* (Boston: Little, Brown, 1995), 51–53; Samuel Hynes (*The Soldiers' Tale, Bearing Witness to Modern War* [New York: Allen Lane, 1997], 64), notes that the "fear of fear" was particularly debilitating for those World War I officers raised on the public school code of fearlessness.

17. "Que ce fut une aussi dure besoingne et aussi bien combatue que bataille peust oncques estre." Froissart, *Chroniques,* 13 [1386–1389]: 219.

18. "De toutes les besoingnes, batailles et rencontres qui sont icy-dessus contenus en ceste présente histoire dont je traittie et ay traitté, grandes, moyennes et petites, ceste-cy don't je parle à présent en fut l'une des plus dures et des

mieulx combatues sans faintise, car il n'y avoit homme, chevalier ne escuier, qui ne s'acquitast et fesist son devoir et tout main à main." *Chroniques,* 13: 222.

19. "Moult estoient prests et ententifs et de bonne voulenté chevalliers et escuiers d'un costé et d'autre à faire armes et euls combatre très-vaillamment et ardamment tant que lances et haches leur durroient. Là n'avoit point couardise de lieu, mais hardement ryoit en place des belles appartises d'armes que ces jeunes chevalliers et escuiers faisoient; et estoient si joints l'un à l'autre et si attachiés que trait d'archiers de nul costé n'y avoit point lieu, car ils estoient si près assamblés que main à main et l'un dedens l'autre, et encoires ne bransloit nulle des batailles, mais se tenoient ferme et fort chascuns sur son pas." *Chroniques,* 13: 220.

20. "Or regardés se ce fut une dure besoigne et bien combatue, quant si grant nombre en y ot de mors et de pris de l'une partie et de l'autre." *Chroniques,* 13: 240. One of the other manuscripts notes the discrepancy directly, adding "mais l'une l'eut pieurre que l'autre." See, *Oeuvres de Froissart, Chroniques,* ed. Albert Mirot (Paris: C. Klincksieck, 1975), 15 [1387–1389]: 171.

21. "Affin que li grant fait d'armes qui par les guerres de Franche et d'Engletre sont avenu, soient notablement registré et mis en mémore perpétuel, par quoy li bon y puissent prendre exemple, je me voeil ensonnier de les mettre en prose." *Chroniques,* 2 [1322–1339]:1.

22. John Keegan, *A History of Warfare* (New York: Alfred A. Knopf, 1993), 105, 250–51, 271.

23. "[M]ais ainsi que les fortunes tournent, quoyque les Anglois feussent le plus et tous vaillans hommes et usés d'armes, et qu'ils assaillissent leurs enemis moult vaillamment, en les reculant et reboutant de première venue bien avant, les Escots obtindrent la place, et furent tous prins les chevalliers deussus nommés, et encoires plus de cent aultres, excepté monseigneur Mahieu Rademen, capitaine de Bervich." *Chroniques,* 13: 228.

24. "[Q]uant il perceut la desconfiture et que nul recouvrir n'y avoit, et que leurs gens s'enfuioient et se ouvroient devant les Escots à tous lés, et chevalliers et escuiers se rendoient, et Escots fiançoient, iceulx Anglois, il monta à cheval et se party de là pour soy cuidier sauver." Ibid.

25. "Et pour ce que il adjournoit, nous ordonnasmes cent lances des nostres à demourer derrière pour garder les chevaulx et la navie, et le demourant de nous meusmes le bon pas et passames tout oultre l'embusche. Oncques ne s'ouvry sur nous, et quant nous feusmes oultre environ le quart d'une bonne lieue, ils saillirent hors, et tantost vindrent sur ceulx qui estoient au rivage et se boutèrent entre euls, et les desconfirent de fait; et tous furent ou mors ou prins, et les chevaulx conquis, et la navie arrestée; et monterènt sur nos chevaulx, et férirent à pointe d'esperons tellement qu'ils furent aussi tost à la ville comme nus. On crioit partout 'Nostre-Dame! Sancerre!' car le conte si estoit là avec ses gens et messire Loys et messire Robert avoient fait l'embusche, et là ot grant pousseis de

lances, ca ceulx qui estoient à cheval, aussi tost qu'ils furent à nous, ils misrent piet à terre et nous aissilirent fièrement. Et ce qui trop nous greva, ce fut que nous ne pouvions eslargir; car nous estions entrés en ung chemin, lequel à deux costés estoit enclos de haultes hayes et de vignes. Et encoires entre eulx qui congnoissent le pays et le chemin, une quantité d'eulx et de leurs varlets estoient montés amont les vignes, qui nous jettoient pierres et caillous, tellement qu'ils nous froissent et rompoient tous. Nous ne povions reculer, et si avions grant paine au montrer contre la ville qui siet sur une montagne. Là fusme-nous moult traveillés, at là fut navré ou corps tout oultre messire Aymery . . . Et vous dy que ce fut une bataille moult dure et ung rencontre moult félon, et nous tenismes de defendismes tant qu nous peusmes et tant que d'un costé et d'autre en y ot plusieurs occis et navrés, et, à ce qu'ils monstroient, ils nous avoient plus chiers à prendre en vie que mors." *Chroniques,* 11: 116–17.

    26.   Hynes, *Soldiers' Tale,* xv.

    27.   The term was coined by Bertha Pappenheim (Fräulein Anna O.), a patient of Josef Breuer, an early collaborator of Freud. See Jeffrey Berman, *The Talking Cure: Literary Representations of Psychoanalysis* (New York: New York University Press, 1985), 1–32.

    28.   "Petitement, . . . Loenges à Dieu, il n'est gaires de mes ancisseurs qui soient mors en chambre, ne sur lits. Je vous dy: pensés de moy vengier, car je me compte pour mort. Le cuer me fault trop souvent." *Chroniques,* 13: 224

    29.   John Keegan provides numerous examples in *A History of Warfare,* noting also that not all early or pretechnological warfare is harmless and its ritualization should not be idealized (99).

    30.   Robert Graves, *Lars Porsena or the Future of Swearing and Improper Language* (London: Kegan Paul, Trench, Trubner, [1927]), 32.

    31.   Baldesar Castiglione, *The Book of the Courtier,* trans. George Bull, 2nd ed. (Harmondsworth: Penguin, 1976), 59.

    32.   For examples see Alan Dundes et al. "The Strategy of Turkish Boys' Verbal Duelling Rhymes," in *Parsing Through Customs: Essays by a Freudian Folklorist* (Madison: University of Wisconsin Press, 1987); John Dollard, "The Dozens: The Dialect of Insult," *American Imago* 1 (1939): 3–24; Roger D. Abrahams, "Playing the Dozens," *Journal of American Folklore* 75 (1962): 209–20; William Labov, "Rules for Ritual Insults" and Thomas Kochman "Toward an Ethnography of Black American Speech Behaviour," 241–64, esp. 258 ff., both in *Rappin' and Stylin' Out; Communication in Urban Black America,* ed. Thomas Kochman (Urbana: University of Illinois Press, 1972); and Ashley Montagu, *The Anatomy of Swearing* (New York: Macmillan, 1967), 11, on the "kul kentanak" (anger make-for) swearing in Australia.

    33.   I discuss some examples of late medieval battlefield abuse in "Songs of Praise and Blame."

34. Quoted in Johan Huizinga, *The Autumn of the Middle Ages,* trans. Rodney J. Payton and Ulrich Mammitzsch (Chicago: University of Chicago Press, 1996), 81–82.

35. The eroticization of death as a form of male bonding was particularly strong among the Knights Templar. See Bruce Holsinger, "The Color of Salvation: Desire, Death, and the Second Crusade in Bernard of Clairvaux's *Sermon on the Song of Songs,*" in *The Tongue of the Fathers: Gender and Ideology in Twelfth-Century Latin,* ed. David Townsend and Andrew Taylor (Philadelphia: University of Pennsylvania Press, 1998), 156–86.

36. The code of genteel violence in men's writing of the nineteenth and twentieth centuries has been studied extensively. See Colin Watson, *Snobbery With Violence: Crime Stories and Their Audience* (London: Eyre and Spottiswoode, 1971); Paul Fussel, *The Great War and Modern Memory* (New York: Oxford University Press, 1975); and Batsleer et al., *Rewriting English,* which compares the patterns of masculinist fiction to those in women's writing.

37. Sidney Lanier, ed., *The Boy's Froissart, being Sir John Froissart's Chronicles of Adventure Battle and Custom in England France Spain etc.* (New York: Charles Scribner's Sons, 1901), v.

38. Quoted in Grossman, *On Killing,* 34.

39. Keegan offers a powerful critique of this tendency in military writing in *Face of Battle.*

40. Samuel Lyman Atwood Marshal, *Men Against Fire: The Problem of Battle Command in Future War* (Washington, D.C.: Combat Forces Press, 1947), 56–57.

41. Charles J.J.J. Ardant du Picq, *Battle Studies,* trans. John N. Greely and Robert C. Cotton (Harrisburg, Pa.: Military Service Publishing Company, 1946). See also Richard Holmes, *Acts of War: The Behaviour of Men in Battle* (New York: Free Press, 1985), both discussed in Grossman, *On Killing,* 9–12.

42. Ibid., 4.

43. See, for example, Reuven Gal and A. David Mangelsdorff, eds., *Handbook of Military Psychology* (Chichester, Eng.: Wiley, 1991).

44. J. F. Verbruggen, *The Art of Warfare in Wester Europe During the Middle Ages, from the Eighth Century to 1340,* trans. Sumner Willard and S.C.M. Southern (Amsterdam: North-Holland, 1977), 41.

45. Grossman, *On Killing,* 6.

46. Hynes, *Soldiers' Tale,* 28–30, 39–40, 99–100.

47. Gautier, *Les Épopées françaises: Étude sur les origines et l'histoire de la littérature nationale,* 2nd ed., 4 vols. (Paris, 1878–1892), 1:10–11.

48. Huizinga, *Autumn of the Middle Ages,* 81–82.

Separating the Men from the Goats
Masculinity, Civilization and Identity Formation in the Medieval University

RUTH MAZO KARRAS

Medieval society was a society of collectivities in which identity came from membership in particular groups.[1] Many of these groups—knights, monks, apprentices, guildspeople—underwent particular initiation ceremonies that marked their selection or separation from the rest of society.[2] In knighthood, for example, the ritual of dubbing admitted one into a military elite. For men of the aristocracy, it also marked a coming of age, the attainment of manhood. The entrance into a university, into the elite intellectual world, also marked the acceptance into a masculine subculture. The ritual process of initiation into that subculture reveals a great deal about medieval ideas of what it meant to be a man—as distinguished from a boy, from a woman and also from a beast.

Rituals of initiation into university life appear in only a few sources; the most detailed depiction comes in a book of Latin dialogues for the use of students at German universities in the late fifteenth century. The *Manuale Scholarium* was presumably intended for students whose Latin was not up to the standard they would need at the universities, where not only all instruction but also all conversation among students was to be in Latin.[3] Historians have taken the dialogues as illustrative of actual situations in which students might find themselves, and the appropriate linguistic responses to those situations.[4] This text, however, is more than an antiquarian's dream of vignettes out of everyday life at the university. Particularly in its depiction of an initiation ceremony for freshmen, it provides insight into the meaning of a university education for those not destined to go on to be great scholars. In today's debates over the role of universities in North American society, where legislators who want to improve their constituents' employment opportunities at the least cost are pitted against those who speak from the ivory tower for the life of the mind without considering the needs of the world outside, it is useful to be reminded that these issues are not new. In the age in which the European university began, intellectual inquiry was only peripherally relevant to many or most undergraduate students, who were concerned with where the education would get them.[5] This particular text indicates the role of university education in the civilizing process and the creation of an elite masculine identity, crucial features of what education could do for the average student.

The classic studies on initiation rituals, by Arnold van Gennep and Mircea Eliade, offer typologies that are helpful in analyzing the ritual from the *Manuale Scolarium*. For van Gennep an initiation ceremony is just one example of a "rite of passage," an important event in one's life marked by special rituals and having a wide social significance. Although they often do not coincide with biological puberty, initiation rituals constitute a sort of social puberty: they mark the separation from the asexual category of child and the incorporation into the group of adult men and women.[6] The rite of initiation is often quite different for men and for women. Many societies need such a ritual for men more than for women, since for women marriage fulfills the same functions. Men must derive their identity from other adult men rather than from their household status.[7] For women, menarche is a biological indicator of maturity and marriageability (although these may need a complementary social recognition as well), while men, lacking such a clear indicator, must prove their maturity and manhood by undergoing various tests.[8]

For women, too, marriage often separates them from the natal family, whereas men may need a special ritual to separate them from the mother who raised them. This ritual can involve giving them a status above that of women; in many societies the initiation means not just becoming an *adult* male, but an adult *male*. The distinction between a man and a woman is more important than that between a man and a boy.[9] Various components of male initiation rituals in different societies have been interpreted as rejection or domination of the feminine.[10] David Gilmore, an anthropologist who has focused on the construction of masculinity, denies that "male initiations are uniformly or even primarily concerned with inculcating male dominance." He suggests, instead, that manhood acts as a social barrier against human enemies, forces of nature, time and human weaknesses that endanger group life.[11] Yet if some of these dangers—notably forces of nature and human weakness—

are identified with the feminine, then achieving manhood must mean triumphing over womanishness. The process of initiation for young men often, if not always, involves the creation of a binary opposition between masculinity and femininity.

Rites of passage like puberty rituals are societywide, applying to all men (or all women) of a certain age within the culture. Mircea Eliade identifies other kinds of initiation in addition to those that apply to everyone: those that bring the initiate into a secret society or brotherhood, and shamanistic initiations, which bring their subject into a particular vocation.[12] In all forms, the initiate dies and is reborn as a new man (Eliade discusses men almost exclusively), with special knowledge and spiritual power: "Initiatory death signifies the end at once of childhood, of ignorance, and of the profane condition."[13] Entrance into the medieval university was clearly not a rite of passage that applied to all men of a certain age group. It falls between Eliade's two other categories. It certainly was an exclusive, if not a secret, society within medieval culture more generally. But since medieval students were considered members of the clergy (even if they had not taken orders), and since the universities were among other things vocational schools for future clergymen, entrance into the university could be seen as a step on the road to special spiritual powers, as with Eliade's shamanistic initiations.

The third major anthropological theorist who has dealt with initiation rituals, Victor Turner, focuses on the bonding that emerges from the initiation, which he calls *communitas. Communitas* is obviously of the utmost importance for secret societies or fraternities, as well as the community of students at the medieval university, and is much the same sort of phenomenon that is discussed today as "male bonding." For Turner, this bonding, which is more fraternal than hierarchical, is created through various means which include ritual humiliation: "In the liminal phase of Ndembu rites of passage, and in similar rites the world over, communitas is engendered by ritual humiliation, stripping of signs and insignia of preliminal status, ritual leveling, and ordeals and tests of various kinds, intended to show that 'man thou art dust!' "[14]

When anthropologists have turned to study initiation rituals in contemporary Western society, they have tended to focus not on rituals common to all members of a society or a given subculture, but rather on particular, exclusive groups. It should not be surprising that one of these groups is the college fraternity: it fulfills Eliade's description of a secret society, and it is also relatively accessible to anthropologists, who can find native informants right on their own campuses. These studies are relevant to a consideration of medieval initiation rituals in that they involve young men at approximately the same stage of life, in approximately the same social situation (at an educational institution, possibly away from home for the first time). Medieval students may on average have been slightly younger than modern ones, but not much—the average age of university entrance may have been as low as seventeen—and in any case people assumed adult responsibilities at a younger age in that era.[15] Without suggesting some essential component of the masculine psyche that makes young men in groups behave in certain ways no matter what the historical context, we can still compare the rituals of modern fraternities and medieval student groups to identify differences based on the historical frameworks.

Descriptions of modern fraternity initiations give varying accounts of what constitutes manhood and brotherhood. One study based on field-work in the late 1950s describes the process of separation from the community outside the fraternity through the heavy time requirements placed on pledges; the deliberate disorientation of the pledges during the transition phase; the cutting of the pledges' hair to create equality and to remove an association with the past, a purification as well as a disorientation; the reintegration into the new ritual system and reconfirmation of the hierarchical social structure of the fraternity.[16] Gender issues are entirely absent in this analysis. The author never even specifies whether the (unnamed) campus is all male or coeducational. There is also very little emphasis on masculinity in the hazing of the pledges: occasionally they are referred to as "girls" but the main focus does not seem to be on what it means to become a man.[17] And there is no mention at all of sexual prowess as a standard of manhood. This lack of emphasis, which may be due to the fact that the fraternity members knew they were being observed, stands in stark contrast to other accounts, for example, Larry Colton's memoir of his membership in Pi Kappa Alpha fraternity at the University of California at Berkeley in the mid-1960s. There, pledges were constantly referred to as "cunts" and challenged to be "man enough" to join the fraternity. Manhood was measured by the ability to withstand physical torture, humiliation and large amounts of alcohol, and also by the pledges' sexual history and current behavior.[18] The emphasis on sex also emerges in accounts of gang rapes that have taken place in fraternities in recent years. This behavior takes male bonding to its extreme: men prove their manhood through drinking and sex, and their brotherhood through drinking and raping together. Peggy Reeves Sanday's account of fraternity gang rape places the practice squarely

within the context of the fraternities' other customs. According to Sanday, the fraternity initiations she describes are rituals in which the
pledges cleanse themselves of effeminacy. The pledges must kill the
inner woman and deny all femininity within them; this is done "by first
stressing sexual differences and then representing these differences as
hierarchical: part of the same psychic process, manhood and brotherhood are represented as infinitely superior to the despised and dirty feminine. The ritual inducts pledges into the brotherhood by first producing
and then resolving anxiety about masculinity."[19] The bonding as brothers
risks a homoeroticism that must be denied through the aggressive assertion of heterosexuality.

The sexual practices of contemporary fraternity men cannot, of
course, be extrapolated back into the Middle Ages. More directly relevant to the medieval experience of initiation rituals and the construction
of masculinity is the process that Sanday describes. Young men come to
a university: they are in a new place, not sure what to expect, worried that
they do not belong. They need to become members of a group or community. To become members they must deny their previous identity through
a process of ritual humiliation. Having achieved this denial, they can
begin to construct their new—adult, masculine—identity. In contemporary fraternities this is done through the rejection of the feminine. As we
shall see, in the medieval university it was accomplished through a rejection of the bestial and uncivilized, though the bestial still carried with it
overtones of femininity.

For most medieval students, who did not pursue higher degrees, the
university was a place to acquire skills, credentials and connections that
would help them in their career path, whether within the church or without. The time spent at the university acculturated them into a world of
shared experience that set them off from the uneducated perhaps even
more than their actual learning. This was even more true of students at
the German universities of the later Middle Ages than it was, for example, of Paris in its thirteenth-century heyday. The universities were
beginning to become finishing-schools for the sons of the nobility; they
were also part of the expected path for the sons of petty knights, small
merchants or prosperous artisans as well as the wealthy. In effect, the students were there to learn a system of behavior as well as a body of
knowledge.

The types of student behavior prohibited in the statutes of the
medieval universities indicate what modes of life students were learning.
In effect, they were learning from their peers to live like the elites they

hoped to become. They wore fashionable clothing rather than prescribed academic dress, carried and used weapons, drank, gambled and consorted with prostitutes.[20] Carrying weapons, although it was not a feature only of aristocratic society in the later Middle Ages, fit in with a pseudochivalric ethos. The need to demonstrate one's masculinity through fighting might seem incongruous in a population where so many were clergy or presumed to be preparing for a life in the church. However, that circumstance may have been exactly what made students so ready to defend their honor by force. Someone who by reason of his tonsure, or expected future tonsure, might be expected not to fight back might be seen as fair game for frauds or insults. Students, therefore, had to show their willingness to stand up for themselves manfully. Heterosexual activity may in part have been motivated by the same factors.

These student behaviors, which can be seen as imitations of aristocratic masculinity, coexisted uneasily with another ideal of masculinity, that of the lettered man whose education brought with it wisdom and moderation. At the same time, as they functioned as finishing schools for students who would not enter holy orders, the universities were also vocational schools for the clergy and professional schools for scholars. The initiation ritual of the *depositio* as presented in the *Manuale Scolarium* mediates between these different ideas of masculinity, symbolically stripping the initiate of his animalistic nature, which might express itself in the pursuits of drinking, whoring and fighting, and yet, at the same time, concluding with a feast that comports well with the aristocratic virtue of largesse.

The readiness to gamble and to spend on clothing and on banquets signifies, above all, that one can afford to do so. Largesse was also considered a virtue within the university context. This largesse was often displayed by individuals' providing (voluntarily or not) feasts for their colleagues, often on celebratory occasions marking milestones in a university education.

The first milestone was entrance into the university. The new student or *beanus* was often made to provide a feast for other students.[21] At Orléans in 1367, for example, the authorities were very concerned because this practice was impoverishing many students, who had only a little money laboriously acquired by their parents and relatives. These students were being bullied into providing a banquet for their fellows, led to the tavern "like sheep to the slaughter."[22] For the students involved, it was a question of demonstrating one's suitability for membership in the community through one's largesse. A student might also be expected or required to provide a feast for his colleagues, examiners or the whole nation (at Paris and other universities, an organization of students and masters coming from the same geographical region) when he determined as a bachelor (achieved his degree by taking the leading role in a public disputation) or when he incepted as a master (gave his first lecture) or took up an office in the nation.[23]

Both of these features—hazing of the freshman or *beanus,* and the use of a feast to mark (or to pay for) one's entrance into the community of scholars—are found in the statutes of the German universities. For example, according to a decree of the Heidelberg arts faculty in 1419, a bachelor who had just been examined for his license was not to invite anyone to a bath or a feast after the bath, except the dean and his fellow examiners, because "in such excessive and abundant banquets poor men are greatly harmed."[24] Inviting the examiners, however, seems to have been routine, and the bathhouse as venue might imply that the examinee hired the services of prostitutes as well. There was a similar provision at Vienna, requiring the bachelor to spend not more than thirty pence for bath and feast.[25]

Although financial hazing of new entrants was prevalent at the German universities, it was not the only form. The 1447 statutes from Erfurt required that "from a *beanus* for the removal [*depositio*] of his *beanium* no more than a third of a Rhenish florin shall be exacted, unless permission to spend more has been obtained from the rector of the University and the Secret Council."[26] Presumably such permission could be obtained in the case of a wealthier student. The use of *beanium* as a noun, representing the status of freshman as a thing that could be removed by a specific act or ceremony, indicates that being a *beanus* was not just a question of newness but a matter of having some taint from which one had to be purified. Hazing could also take the form of taunting or other harassment. At Vienna in 1385, students were prohibited from exacting money from or insulting the *beani;* at Leipzig they were told not to harass them during the procession of Corpus Christi. Other university and college regulations provided a penalty for students who threw urine or feces at *beani* or otherwise physically molested them.[27] Clearly, the ritual humiliation aspect of initiation was present here.

The most detailed account we have of the initiation of a *beanus* is from the *Manuale Scholarium.* The relation of this account to social practice, however, is not unproblematic. The *Manuale Scholarium* was probably first published in Heidelberg, sometime in the 1480s; there were seven editions in various cities before the end of the fifteenth century. It consists of eighteen dialogues between two students, Bartoldus and Camillus, about various aspects of student life. Because the titles of many of the chapters begin with "How students talk about . . . ," commentators have taken the *Manuale* as a guide to the kind of everyday Latin a student would need to know. The learning of Latin, indeed, was a major part of what set university men off from other people in the late Middle Ages; it was not only the language of scholarship, but also a sign of membership in a particular elite.[28] The *Manuale* also has been taken as a general guide to student life.[29] Some aspects of it can be substantiated from other sources: the giving of gifts to examiners (which was, of course, prohibited), the disputations, the regulations about clothing. It is still not entirely clear, however, whether it was meant, or can be taken, as a direct reflection of practice, or whether it is in part tongue-in-cheek, depicting stereotypes that have some truth to them but are, nevertheless, stylized or exaggerated.

The authorship of the *Manuale,* as we have it, is not known. Most of the work, however, also appears in a book by Paul Schneevogel (Paulus Niavis) of Leipzig. Scholars at first suggested that Schneevogel had simply plagiarized the work, claiming it as his own; more recent work, however, gives priority to Schneevogel and considers the *Manuale* a revised version of his book.[30] Schneevogel's work was entitled "Conversational Latin for New Students," and if the work was, in fact, originally written for this purpose, it probably bears the same relation to social practice as a tourist phrasebook does today—close enough to make it useful, but not a reliable description. It seems most likely that the book was originally written at Leipzig, but then reworked for a Heidelberg audience, and as it stands, probably refers to practices that would have been recognizable to students at most German universities, even if they did not correspond in precise detail to the practices at any one. The *Manuale* covers a wide range of topics: matriculation, the initiation ceremony, lectures, the clash between the philosophical schools of the *via antiqua* and the *via moderna,* the law faculty, the beauties of nature, meals, student quarrels, examinations, the requirement of speaking Latin, the disposal of chamberpots, proper academic dress, disputations, lending money, news from home, women and love, jugglers and traveling players, inviting one's masters to the baths or feasts.

The section that concerns us here is the description of the *depositio cornuum* or removal of the initiate's horns. One of the two students comments to the other about a horrible stink in the room: "there's either been a corpse rotting here, or a goat, filthiest of all beasts." They find it to be a horrible monster: "for this beast is horned, has ears like an ox, and his teeth, sticking out in both directions from his jaw, threaten to bite like a wild boar. He has a nose curved like an owl's beak, and red and bleary eyes threatening rage." They then discover that the monster is actually a *beanus*. When they offer him wine and he attempts to drink, they call him venomous and say that he "ought to drink water, muddy water, at the brook with the cattle." They then speak of how his mother would be sad if she knew how he was being treated, and accuse him of weeping when he hears his mother mentioned. They address him: "O *Beanus,* o ass, o stinking goat, o smelly female goat, o toad, o zero, o figure of nothing, o you nothing at all! May the devil shit all over you and piss on your stomach and feet!" They discuss cutting off his horns, pulling out his teeth, cutting his beard and nose hairs; one student goes to get implements and returns with a salve as well, made from goat excrement. They saw off the horns, pull out the teeth and shave the beard using water with fragrant herbs picked from the garden by the outlet of the privy. They threaten to hang him by a rope in the privy. They then force him to confess to a variety of crimes, from theft to rape to perjury. As "penance" for these offenses, they order him to buy them a generous dinner with fine wine. They all then wish him luck; he has become a member of the community.[31]

To what extent was this ritual of deposition actually practiced? It is well attested from the sixteenth century on, as a more or less official ritual of the German universities.[32] The initiate wore a hat with horns which were sawn off, had false teeth pulled, had his head shaved and underwent other indignities. It is not so clear what was actually practiced in the later medieval period. Heidelberg records from 1454 contain a list of students who "put off [*deposuerunt*] their *beanium*."[33] This phrase, however, may not refer specifically to the removal of the horns, because the same phrase is used as in Erfurt, in the statute limiting the amount a *beanus* could be made to pay. It could mean simply "removal of freshman-ness" rather than "removal of horns." There are two other texts from Erfurt, however, which, when read in conjuntion with the *Manuale,* seem to support the existence of a practice similar to that described there. One is Goswin Kempgyn of Neuss's *Trivita Studentium,* written at Erfurt sometime in the mid-fifteenth century. This text is a long poem describing various aspects of student life and study. In the one manuscript that has survived, it is heavily glossed, so even where the poem itself is cryptic, the glosses explain what is happening to the *beanus*. The whole ritual is called the *vexatio beanum* (harassment of the *beanus)*. The *beanus* is to be transformed by the use of ragged clothing, basin and blade and to be bathed. He is advised to bear the ritual patiently rather than fight it.[34] There is no reference to horns, but the shaving and bathing are similar, and the use of excrement is implicit in references to the buttocks and farting.[35]

The other text is a pamphlet from 1494, the *Monopolium der Schweinezunft* by Johannes Schram.[36] This parody of a quodlibetal disputation discussed the *beanus* as follows: "Of *beani*, whether they can be received in our society, I decree: they must be cleansed of their *beanium* before they are received. And the way they must be cleansed is clear from the third part of Alexander, distinction 23ff., *on horned animals,* line *beasts,* verse *full of stench; A sea, a wave, a body of water purge forth that which makes a shameful sound, and feminine filth; these likewise are good for a beanus, honey, liquid, water, wine (there's some good Latin), the drinking of which pleases the one being purified and the one helping.* Cups, *gantz volle* [completely full], drinking, *das sie werden tolle* [so they get happy], because the *depositio* alone is not enough, but that there be a feast for his colleagues, of good wine (according to others, good beer), which I prove thus . . ."[37] Clearly, the feast itself is connected with the purging of the *beanus*'s taint and accompanies, rather than consititutes, the *depositio.*

As to what exactly is the taint that must be purged, the *Manuale* is our best clue. There we must look for exactly what sort of transition the *beanus* is in fact making. The *beanus* is in a liminal state between the status of unlearned child and that of university student, but what are the features that distinguish those statuses?

One thing that is happening to the *beanus* is the transition from an animal—an especially bestial one—into a human. This transition represents the process of civilization: the bringing of the rude, unlearned, rough new entrant within the pale of acceptable society. The unlearned man is compared to a human beast. Indeed, such an image of bestiality corresponds well to medieval literary depictions of peasants. The image of the uneducated person as bestial is found in the writings of university men throughout the High and late Middle Ages.[38] Jacques LeGoff notes with reference to this particular text:

> Thus the future intellectual abandoned his original condition, which strongly resembled the images of the peasant, the country bumpkin found in the satirical literature of the time. From bestiality to humanity, from rusticity to urbanity, these ceremonies, in which, degraded and

practially emptied of its original content, the old primitive essence
appeared, recall that the intellectual had been extracted from a rural
environment, from an agrarian civilization, from a rude, uncivilized
life on the land.[39]

But it was not an abstract or essential medieval intellectual who was
being cleansed of the taint of bestiality or rusticity; it was students in
fifteenth-century German universities. And, in fact, a comparison with
the treatment of peasants in fifteenth-century German literature reveals
that the connection of this ritual with rusticity is not nearly as direct as
one might expect.

Peasants in late-medieval German literature were depicted as stupid,
boorish, violent and with an affinity for excrement, but they were not
particularly depicted as bestial. Violence was a more important theme in
depictions of peasants than animal nature.[40] Peasants were criticized for
laziness and for ambitions beyond their station, but these criticisms did
not for the most part use animal imagery. In the Shrovetide plays that
were performed in a number of towns, peasants are shown as unrestrained in sex, excretion and gluttony.[41] It is precisely this unrestrained
behavior that the university student is being asked to give up as he
becomes a member of the learned community. Yet, although peasants are
indeed shown as foolish, immoral and bestial in their appetites, they are
not often described as bestial in appearance or directly compared to animals. They do appear likened to animals in the stories of the Neidhart tradition, a collection of tales which appeared in a variety of forms in
late-medieval Germany.[42] In the Neidhart Fuchs chapbook, the peasants
are compared to bears, cranes, swine, wild boars, oxen and dogs. Yet,
even here, the comparison is behavioral; they are not grotesque as in
some earlier French literature.[43]

Although the representation of the *beanus* as a horned beast does not
resonate with particular texts of fifteenth-century German literature representing peasants, the taint of rusticity still remains as part of the pollution from which the *beanus* must be cleansed. Even if fifteenth-century
German peasants are not depicted as goats, they are shown as filthy and
hypersexual, characteristics connected with the *beanus* (as well as with
Jews and women).

The connection of the *beanus* with rusticity was largely independent
of the actual demographics of the medieval university. A study of the
social origins of university students in medieval Heidelberg shows that
although there was a high percentage (ranging up to 45 percent in one

year) of *pauperes,* or students whose income was low enough that they were exempt from matriculation fees, these were not mainly rural dwellers. Only 11 percent of all students in a sample between 1386 and 1450 were from villages. And not all of these, of course, would be peasants in any economic sense; they were the sons of the village elite, although they still might be considered *rustici* simply because of their rural origins.[44]

Only a small segment of the university population in fifteenth-century German then, came from rural origins. Nevertheless, the *beanus* may have been considered a rustic in a figurative rather than a literal sense, simply because he had not yet entered into the community of the educated. The learning of Latin, in particular, was taken in medieval universities to distinguish between rustics and others: a statute of the Collège de Foix at the University of Toulouse in 1429, for example, spoke of the "rudeness, swineherdishness and viciousness" of the vernacular, which "plowmen, swineherds and rural dwellers" speak.[45] Even so, peasants or rural dwellers were a small enough segment of the university population, and the relation of the goat imagery to depictions of peasants is indirect enough to suggest that a rejection of rusticity is not all that is going on in the initiation ritual of the *depositio.*

If we focus on the goat, "filthiest of beasts," it becomes apparent that the ritual is connected with sexuality and abjection as well as rusticity. The goat is the animal mentioned most prominently in the text; it is also the one which is characterized by horns and beard, the features which must be removed. Goat excrement also appears prominently. The general function of excrement in the text (which is not all goat excrement) is to connect the initiate with filth. But goat excrement was also thought to have medicinal properties. According to Albertus Magnus, "the fat of a goat, mixed with the excrement of a goat, rubbed on gout, eases the pain; the excrement of female goats, burned, mixed with vinegar or a mixture of vinegar and honey, rubbed in vigorously, cures baldness."[46] Vincent of Beauvais, in his magisterial compilation *Speculum Naturale,* gives more recipes involving goat excrement, which was efficacious for wasp stings, uterine flux, snakebite, scrofula, hemorrhage, baldness, excoriation, burns, gout, arthritis and abcesses.[47] Both baldness and gout are characteristic of men rather than women; baldness is a sign of maturity and gout of luxurious living, both presumably to be obtained in the future by the prospective student.[48] Yet, in the name of healing, and following commonly accepted healing practice, the initiators were going to smear the initiate with feces. The prohibition from Heidelberg from 1466 (above) indicates that feces were used in hazing *beani.*[49]

The goat was connected in medieval culture not only with physical but also with spiritual filth. Goats appear in the Old Testament, especially in Leviticus, as sin-offerings. They are sacrificed for the sins of the people, or sent out into the wilderness with the sins of the people upon them (the scapegoat).[50] Old Testament images of sacrifice to redeem sin were interpreted as types of Christ, and the goat was seen in this connection by Augustine, Hrabanus Maurus, Rupert of Deutz and others.[51] Even when the New Testament directly contrasts the sacrifice of Christ with that of an animal—"Neither by the blood of goats and calves, but by his own blood he entered in once into the holy place, having obtained eternal redemption for us" (Heb. 9:12)—the goat was still identified as a type of Christ.[52] More often, however, medieval traditions about goats drew more on another Biblical theme, that of Christ as the shepherd separating the sheep from the goats (Matt. 25:32), than on the goat as a type of Christ. Many commentators made the direct connection between the goats and sinners and between the sheep and saints. The sheep on the right hand and goats on the left became a theme in early Christian art. But the sin here connected with the goat was not just any sin, but the sins of the flesh and the impurity of the body.[53]

The connection of the goat with the sins of the flesh is also found in the bestiary tradition. Bestiaries described various animals and gave moral explanations for their characteristics; they were intended not just to convey knowledge about nature but also to edify. Many of the Latin and vernacular bestiaries were more or less direct translations from the Greek Physiologus, which did not include the goat, but some supplemented this with information from elsewhere, notably from Isidore of Seville, the sixth/seventh century encylcopedist. Isidore had this to say about the goat:

> The male goat [*hircus*] is a lascivious animal, and wanton, and always eager for sexual intercourse, who looks sideways because of libidinousness, from which it gets its name: for *hirqui* are the corners of the eyes, according to Suetonius. Its nature is so hot that its blood alone will dissolve the stone adamant, which neither fire nor iron will vanquish.[54]

Isidore also discussed the *caper* and *capra* (another word for male and female goat), the *haedus* [kid], and wild goats [*agrestes caprae* or *capreae*] who live on the heights of mountains and have especially good vision. The goat's sharp eyes are taken in some bestiary texts to symbolize the all-seeing God, and the wild goat's discernment of good herbs on mountains is like that of priests who seek out Jesus to cure people. Some bestiary illustrations show a goat pasturing on the mountains, or looking into the distance, but others depict the lascivious male goat, bearded and with long horns.[55] One text quotes a reference to male goats in the Psalms and interprets: "The he-goats are those who follow the depravities of the devil and clothe themselves in the shaggy hide of vice."[56] Another interprets the blood that dissolves adamant as corruption in the law of God.[57]

The goat's connection with the libido is also found outside the bestiary tradition. One of the most extreme examples is *Moriuht,* an eleventh-century Latin poem by Walter of Rouen, about an extremely libidinous Irishman who is constantly referred to as a *caper* (and his wife as a *capra)*. The modern editor of this poem suggests that its connection of goats with filth, odor and sex is drawn from classical sources.[58] In medieval art, the personification of Luxuria (Lust), one of the seven deadly sins, is often shown riding on a goat.[59] The natural philosopher Albertus Magnus thought enough of the sexual power of goats to claim that "whoever eats two goats' testicles and has intercourse, from the surplus of the digestion of this meal will engender a male child, unless there is an impediment in the woman with whom he has intercourse."[60]

The goat, especially as a symbol of sin, was also associated with the Jew in the Middle Ages. Jews were sometimes depicted with horns. The direct link was with the devil rather than the goat, but the diabolical horned Jew was sometimes shown together with a goat whose horns were identical to his. Since the goat was the devil's chosen animal, Jews were often depicted riding goats or with goatlike beards. The odor attributed to Jews in the Middle Ages further links them to the *beanus* of the dialogue.[61] It is not likely that the *Manuale*'s intent was to portray the *beanus* as a Jew. However, the association with the Jew would have resonated for medieval readers, and would have identified the *beanus* with the imagined character of the Jew as filthy, depraved and nonhuman.

The sexual aspect of the goat, and its odor, are both clearly present in the *Manuale* dialogue. The aroma that Camillus smells brings a goat immediately to his mind, and he calls the *beanus* an *olens capra,* echoing the way classical sources describe the *hircus,* but making the *beanus* into a female rather than a male goat. Part of the *beanus*'s preinitiate status, his not knowing how to behave properly or his lack of civilization, is his libido as well as his smell.

One possible reading of the *Manuale* text is that the *beanus* is being feminized, rather than cleansed of the feminine. The cutting off of the horns, the shaving of the beard and the transformation of the odor into a sweet smell might point in this direction. Given the status hierarchy of the university, and the lack of actual women, the new students, the youngest members, could be effectively cast in the feminine role (with possible homoerotic implications). However, while perfumes and unguents might be connected with women or effeminacy, strong odors could also be connected with women, and often were, in medieval misogynous discourse. The horns, too, are not distinctively masculine— the female goats raised in northwestern Europe in the Middle Ages also had horns. Nor can the cutting off of the horns be a simple castration symbol. Horns, of course, were a sign of cuckoldry; their removal might indicate that the *beanus* was no longer to be a figure of ridicule. The language of the ritual clearly points to a cleansing of the feminine, not a feminizing of the *beanus.* The Erfurt mock quodlibet, which refers to "feminine filth" (*lutum femineum*) as that which must be purged along with the foul odor, makes this connection as well.[62]

Rather than feminizing, the ritual was initiating the student into an alternative form of masculinity. It rejected the bestiality of uncontrolled sexuality. Yet, it is not likely that a student-initiated ritual would be attempting to turn the prospective student into an asexual celibate. The authorities at medieval universities might have preferred their students have nothing to do with women, and several of the other dialogues in the *Manuale* suggest that this ought to be the case, but it is clear enough from other sorts of records that this was never accepted by the students themselves. Rather, the ritual would seem to be taking away not the initiate's sexuality, but his uncontrolled and indiscriminate sexual impulses. He is now to be civilized, a gentleman.[63]

For those who did come from an aristocratic background, and were not intended for a life in the church, the *depositio* might also perform the function of making the entrance into the intellectual world acceptable. In making explicit the rejection of the feminine, the ritual in effect denied that study or latinity was effeminate, that it was incompatible with knighthood and honor. If the uneducated man is like a female goat, then to enter the university was not to deny one's masculinity but to affirm it.

The civilized student might be sexually active but not lascivious and wanton, which were the characteristics both of women and of animals. Many medieval medical scholars, after all, recommended moderate coitus as productive of good health for men; it was the Aristotelian idea of balance and moderation rather than the Christian idea of chastity that controlled in their work.[64] Rational and controlled sexual desire was associated with humans, as opposed to irrational, lustful animals.[65] Uncontrolled, animal lasciviousness was also associated in many medieval discourses with femininity; the initiate here is becoming not only human, but masculine.[66] The masculinity is one which mediates between the church's demand of celibacy (not often honored) and total sexual abandon. University students might emulate aristocratic practices in taking their pleasure where they could find it, but they were not to be controlled by it.

The rejection of the feminine along with the animal resonates with contemporary fraternity practice. Fraternity boys become men through rejection of the feminine. Pledges are humiliated by being called girls, pussies, cunts; by surviving the hazing they prove they are men (not women). The medieval student was proving he was a man (not animal). But the medieval student, in rejecting animality, also rejected feminine weakness and, indeed, modern fraternity initiations also cast the pledges as animals who need to be humanized.[67]

Both medieval and modern initiations also share an emphasis on separation from the mother. Bartoldus refers to the *beanus* as too "softly reared" for the harsh treatment they are giving him: "What if his mother, who loves him alone, should know this? Oh how many tears she would weep, how her heart would feel saddened! . . . Hey, look at his face. He's not weeping, is he? Certainly his eyes are wet. When he heard his mother mentioned, he was moved"[68] Compare this to Sanday's account, in which the pledges are called "mama's boys," and told: "Listen up, girls. . . . All your life you've been a bunch of nerds. You always went home from school to your mom, and she cooked for you, did your wash, made your beds, and told you what to wear. . . . We're going to cleanse the weak, dependent pussy out of you, and maybe then you won't look so wretched."[69] The idea of independence would not be expressed the same way in the medieval context—many of the students would be expected to have servants, even at the university—but the parallel remains in the cleansing of the weak and feminine.

The medieval university was a men-only system. The world of power, for which it was supposed to prepare its graduates, was a world without women. Where the modern ritual may be intended to reassure young men, who are insecure about their masculinity, by providing tests for them to pass and a confirmation that they have cleansed the feminine (and the homoerotic) from their identity, there was less need for this in the medieval system. That system was already so gendered that the exclusively masculine nature of the university was not in question. The rejection of the feminine is, therefore, much less explicit in the medieval ritual, but it still lurks behind this text. Women are already excluded from the university setting, but the masculine members of the university community still had to expunge the feminine from within themselves.

The student entering the university was becoming a man. What sort of man? This question is partly one of social status, or status-linked behavior: he was to act not like a rustic, but like a gentleman. It was partly a question of adherence to certain standards of propriety. He was to follow the advice of his rational mind and not his animalistic desires. To follow those desires would make him not only unsuitable for education, but, in fact, like a woman. The question of whether women had rational souls was open for debate in this period; following Aristotle, they were held to be much weaker than men, and more prey to their emotions.[70] The student was to be of a higher sort.

Despite a greater presence of women in late medieval universities than in earlier (as servants, and even, in Germany, as wives of masters[71]) misogynistic views were still prevalent. The *Manuale* repeats a number of misogynist commonplaces. Bartoldus has seen a particular girl in church, for whom he is aflame with love; Camillus tells him that she is poisonous because she is menstruating. Camillus is going to a dance; Bartoldus dissuades him, arguing that it is better to stay home and study than associate with women, for "the roses seem to blossom on the cheek and there is all that is beauty on the surface, but inside there is an ulcer, full of madness, and foulness, and poison." He also refuses to accompany his friend to a party, even though the women there will be decent as well as beautiful, because "in one hour you are bound to be so inflamed that in a fortnight you'll have no kind of appetite for study."[72] Women are distracting as well as dangerous. Bartoldus falls in love with the daughter of a judge, who sends him a ring as a gift; Camillus warns him against becoming entrapped, as she is already pregnant by another and looking for someone on whom to father her child. The common stereotype of women as fickle and lustful rears its head once again.

Medieval students would have little opportunity to interact with women as social equals. Even if prohibitions against bringing women into the colleges were frequently disregarded, it would not be the respectable women of the town who would be brought into students' rooms in this manner, but rather prostitutes, who were ubiquitous in university towns.[73] Students would, of course, have occasion to do business with women, landladies or retailers, as well as prostitutes. But these would generally not be women of their own social class. The *Manuale,* along with other medieval misogynist texts, seems dedicated to maintaining women as the social Other. A man might consort with them but they could not be his peers; women of his own class, potential marriage partners, were to be discouraged. This attitude toward women would have had an effect on the student's postuniversity career. And it was perhaps the informal education in appropriate masculine and civilized behavior, given in an all-male environment, rather than the content of the curriculum, that would have most shaped his behavior. In this, too, medieval student society resembled the contemporary university fraternity.

This initiation ritual marks not only a stage in life, or a stage in one's vocation or career, but an assertion of identity, and an identity that is specifically masculine, since women are by definition excluded. The ceremony itself creates a cultured, civilized, elite if not aristocratic masculine identity. The initiate is incorporated into a society of the shaven and bathed, the sweet-smelling, in other words the society of those who can afford a comfortable life and are ready to assume the privileges that go with it. It is also a society of those who can control their sexual impulses. They may still carouse with their companions, as the feast at the end of the ritual indicates, but they share higher goals as well.

The *depositio* marked a student's entry into the university, not his graduation from it. It, therefore, conferred no specific transition into a particular career. But it did mark the beginnings of the student's formation as an educated man, and all the social cachet that went along with it. He was marked as the right kind of person, whatever his actual academic accomplishments. He could emulate some aristocratic practices, but he was more than a knight because he was educated. Simply the fact of being a university man, regardless of what he knew or could do, was important in the medieval context, as it is often important today. And the text from Heidelberg reveals to us what kind of man that was: constructed through a rite of passage as a member of an elite group who could moderate their animal natures and live like gentlemen. By transcending the bestial and feminine, the medieval university student could become a man.

NOTES

1. An earlier version of this paper was presented at the conference on "Animals and Human Society: Medieval and Early Modern Europe" at the Shelby Cullom Davis Center for Historical Studies, Princeton University, on 24 October 1997. I thank William Chester Jordan, the Director of the Center, and the

audience, especially Peter Brown, Sharon Farmer, Mary Fussell, Jón Haukur Ingimundarson, Ken Mills, John Murrin and Mary Voss-Henninger, for their suggestions. I also thank Martha Davis for her assistance.

2. See, for example, Maurice Keen, *Chivalry* (New Haven: Yale University Press, 1984), 64–82; Benjamin R. McRee, "Unity or Division? The Social Meaning of Guild Ceremony in Urban Communities," in *City and Spectacle in Medieval Europe,* ed. Barbara A. Hanawalt and Kathryn L. Reyerson (Minneapolis: University of Minnesota Press, 1994), 189–207.

3. The *Manuale Scholarium* is edited in Friedrich Zarncke, *Die deutschen Universitäten im Mittelalter* (Leipzig: T.D. Weigel, 1857), 1–48.

4. Hastings Rashdall, *The Universities of Europe in the Middle Ages,* 2nd ed., ed. F.M. Powicke and A.B. Emden (Oxford: Clarendon Press, 1936), 3:378, n. 3.

5. Alan B. Cobban, "Reflections on the Role of Medieval Universities in Contemporary Society," in *Intellectual Life in the Middle Ages: Essays Presented to Margaret Gibson,* ed. Lesley Smith and Benedicta Ward (London: Hambledon Press, 1992), 227–41; Stephen C. Ferruolo, "'Quid dant artes nisi luctum?' Learning, Ambition, and Careers in the Medieval University," *History of Education Quarterly* 28 (1988): 1–22.

6. Arnold van Gennep, *The Rites of Passage,* trans. Monika B. Vizedom and Gabriella L. Caffee (Chicago: University of Chicago Press, 1960), 65–68.

7. T.O. Beidelman, "Containing Time: Rites of Passage and Moral Space or Bachelard among the Kaguru, 1957–1966," *Anthropos* 86 (1991): 453; Marie-Paule Ferry, "Mariage des femmes et initiation des hommes: Beliyan et Bedik du Sénégal oriental," *Journal des Africanistes* 55 (1985): 75–83.

8. James L. Brain, "Male Menstruation in History and Anthropology," *Journal of Psychohistory* 15 (1988): 313 (although his argument that all forms of bloodletting in men are imitations of menstruation is pushing the evidence a bit far).

9. Jean-Claude Muller, *La Calebasse Sacrée: Initiations Rukuba (Nigéria central)* (Montreal: Presses Universitaires, 1989), 206–09; William M. Schneider and Mary Jo Schneider, "Selako Male Initiation," *Ethnology* 30 (1991): 285–88.

10. Filip De Boeck, "Of Bushbucks Without Horns: Male and Female Initiation Among the Aluund of Southwest Zaïre," *Journal des Africanistes* 61 (1991): 56–57; Gilbert Herdt, "Transitional Objects in Sambia Initiation," *Ethos* 15 (1987): 46.

11. David D. Gilmore, *Manhood in the Making: Cultural Concepts of Masculinity* (New Haven: Yale University Press, 1990), 168, 226.

12. Mircea Eliade, *Rites and Symbols of Initiation: The Mysteries of Birth and Rebirth,* trans. Willard R. Trask (New York: Harper & Row, 1958), 2.

13. Eliade, *Rites and Symbols,* x, xii.

14. Victor Turner, *Dramas, Fields, and Metaphors: Symbolic Action in Human Society* (Ithaca, N.Y.: Cornell University Press, 1974), 53.

15. Although the statutory minimum age at many universities was fourteen, entrance at that age does not seem to have been typical. There are only a few places for which there is good data, but at New College, Oxford, in the fifteenth century, the average age at entrance was 17 1/2 years old. At Oxford in the sixteenth century the median age was seventeen, and two-thirds of undergraduates entered between the ages of sixteen and eighteen. At Wittenberg in the mid-sixteenth century the typical age of matriculation was seventeen. T.A.R. Evans, "The Number, Origins, and Careers of Scholars," in *History of the University of Oxford,* ed. T. Aston, vol. 2 (Oxford: Clarendon Press, 1992), 499–500; Owen and Miriam Gingerich, "Matriculation Ages in Sixteenth-Century Wittenberg," *History of Universities* 6 (1986–87): 135–37.

16. Thomas A. Leemon, *The Rites of Passage in a Student Culture: A Study of the Dynamics of Transition* (New York: Teachers College Press, 1972).

17. "What do you think this is, a girl scout camp?" Ibid., 120; also 152, 153.

18. Larry Colton, *Goat Brothers* (New York: Doubleday, 1993), 3–185.

19. Peggy Reeves Sanday, *Fraternity Gang Rape: Sex, Brotherhood, and Privilege on Campus* (New York: New York University Press, 1990), 171.

20. Léo Moulin, *La Vie des étudiants au moyen âge* (Paris: Bibliothèque Albin Michel de l'histoire, 1991), is the best general account. For the regulations from fifteenth-century German universities: Rudolf Kink, *Geschichte der kaiserlichen Universität Wien* (Vienna: Carl Gerold & Sohn, 1854), vol. 2; J.C. Hermann Weissenborn, ed., *Acten der Erfurter Universität,* vol. 1 (Halle: Otto Hendel, 1881); H. Ott and J.M. Fletcher, eds., *The Medieval Statutes of the Faculty of Arts of the University of Freiburg im Breisgau* (Notre Dame, Ind.: Mediaeval Institute, 1964); Friedrich Zarncke, *Die Statutenbücher der Universität Leipzig* (Leipzig: S. Hirzel, 1861); Eduard Winkelmann, *Urkundenbuch der Universität Heidelberg* (Heidelberg: Winter, 1886).

21. The word *"bejanus"* or *"beanus"* first appears in France and is thought to derive from *bec-jaune.* Early modern German texts explained the term as an acronym: *B*eanus *E*st *A*nimal *N*esciens *V*itam *S*tudiosorum, "A beanus is an animal that does not know the life of the scholarly." Wilhelm Fabricius, *Die Akademische Deposition* (Frankfurt a. M.: L. Lichtenberg, 1895), 34. This is, of course, a false etymology. Several people have asked me whether the "beanies" worn by freshmen at some U.S. universities earlier in this century could have any possible relation to "beanus," but the *Oxford English Dictionary,* 2nd edition, derives this from "bean" as slang for "head."

22. Marcel Fournier, *Les Statuts et privilèges des universités françaises depuis leur fondation jusqu'en 1789* (Paris: Larose et Forcel, 1890), 1:125–26;

see also Heinrich Denifle and Emile Chatelain, *Chartularium Universitatis Parisiensium* (Paris: Delalain, 1891), 2:523–24.

23. Examples abound in *Auctarium chartularii universitatis Parisiensis,* vol. 1, *Liber Procuratorum Nationis Anglicanae (Alemanniae) in Universitate Parisiensi 1333–1406,* ed. Heinrich Denifle and Emile Chatelain, 2nd ed. (Paris: Didier, 1937).

24. Winkelmann, *Urkundenbuch der Universität Heidelberg,* 117. On the sociability of baths see Georges Duby and Philippe Braunstein, "The Emergence of the Individual," in *A History of Private Life,* vol. 2, *Revelations of the Medieval World,* ed. Georges Duby, trans. Arthur Goldhammer (Cambridge: Harvard University Press, 1988), 600–610.

25. Kink, *Geschichte der kaiserlichen Universität Wien,* 1:55 (1427).

26. Weissenborn, *Acten der Erfurter Universität,* 18. There are earlier (fragmentary) statutes from the 1370s or 1380s or perhaps after 1395 that do not include this provision, which may thus be new in the mid-fifteenth century.

27. Kink, *Geschichte der kaiserlichen Universität Wien,* 2:77; Zarncke, *Die Statutenbücher,* 111, 102; Winkelmann, *Urkundenbuch der Universität Heidelberg,* 183.

28. Walter Ong, "Latin Language Study as a Renaissance Puberty Rite," in *Rhetoric, Romance, and Technology: Studies in the Interaction of Expression and Culture* (Ithaca, N.Y.: Cornell University Press, 1971), 115–19.

29. For the ways different scholars have used it, see the introduction to the English translation by Robert Seybolt, *The Manuale Scholarium: An Original Account of Life in the Mediaeval University* (Cambridge: Harvard University Press, 1921), 9–12. More recent scholarship has treated it in much the same way.

30. Gerhard Ritter, "Über den Quellenwert und Verfasser des sogennanten 'Heidelberger Gesprächbüchleins für Studenten' (manuale scholarium, um 1490)," *Zeitschrift für die Geschichte des Oberrheins* N.F. 38 (1923): 4–32; Gerhard Streckenbach, "Paulus Niavis, 'Latinum ydeoma pro novellis studentibus'—ein Gesprächsbüchlein aus dem letzten Viertel des 15. Jahrhunderts," *Mittellateinisches Jahrbuch* 6 (1970): 152–91; 7 (1971): 187–251.

31. Zarncke, *Die deutschen Universitäten,* 6.

32. Fabricius, *Die Akademische Deposition,* 41–69; Johann Friedrich Hantz, *Geschichte der Universität Heidelberg,* (Mannheim: J. Schneider, 1862), 1:86. Tools for the *depositio,* including knives and pliers, are depicted in Rudolf Kittel, *Die Universität Leipzig und ihre Stellung im Kulturleben* (Dresden: Heligsche Verlagsanstalt GMBH, 1924). Luther gave a spiritual interpretation of the *depositio* in one of his *Tischreden* (vol. 4, no. 4714, cited in Almuth Märker, *Geschichte der Universität Erfurt 1392–1816* [Weimar: Böhlau, 1993], 31).

33. Gustav Toepke, ed., *Die Matrikel der Universität Heidelberg* (Heidelberg: Carl Winter, 1884; reprint, Nendeln: Kraus Reprint, 1976), 1:278.

34. Michael Bernhard, *Goswin Kempgyn de Nussia Trivita Studentium: Eine Einführung in das Universitätsstudium aus dem 15. Jahrhundert,* Münchener Beiträge zur Mediävistik und Renaissance-Forschung, 26 (Munich: Arbeo-Gesellschaft, 1976), 61–62.

35. Shaving also appears in the records of New College, Oxford, from 1400; it was apparently a "vile and horrible" ritual inflicted upon new masters of arts the night before their inception. *Statutes of the Colleges of Oxford,* vol. 1, New College (Oxford: J.H. Parker, 1853), 47.

36. Johannes Schram of Dachau, as he is identified in the pamphlet, matriculated at Erfurt in 1490 and became a Master of Arts in 1494. The matriculation is in Weissenborn, 435, and the list of masters is in Erich Kleineidam, *Universitas Studii Erffordensis: Überblick über der Universität Erfurt im Mittelalter, 1392–1521* (Leipzig: St. Benno-Verlag, 1964), 1:386.

37. Johannes Schram, *Monopolium der Schweinezunft,* in Zarncke, *Die deutschen Universitäten,* 111.

38. Alexander Murray, *Reason and Society in the Middle Ages* (Oxford: Clarendon Press, 1978), 237–44.

39. Jacques LeGoff, *Intellectuals in the Middle Ages,* trans. Teresa Lavender Fagan (Cambridge, Mass.: Blackwell, 1992), 80.

40. I rely here on Paul Freedman, *Savagery and Sanctity: The Image of the Medieval Peasant as Alien and Exemplary* (forthcoming, Stanford University Press). I am grateful to Professor Freedman for making the chapter on German literature available to me in advance of publication.

41. John E. Tailby, "Peasants in Fifteenth-Century *Fastnachtspiele* from Nuremberg: The Problems of their Identification and the Significance of their Presentation," *Daphnis* 4 (1975): 178. See also Hagen Bastian, *Mummenschanz: Sinneslust and Gefühlsbeherrschung im Fastnachtspiel des 15. Jahurhunderts* (Frankfurt: Syndikat, 1983), 72; Samuel Kinser, "Presentation and Representation: Carnival at Nuremberg, 1450–1550," *Representations* 13 (1986): 8; James A. Parente Jr., "Empowering Readers: Humanism, Politics, and Money in Early Modern German Drama," in *The Harvest of Humanism in Central Europe: Essays in Honor of Lewis W. Spitz,* ed. Manfred P. Fleisher (St. Louis: Concordia, 1992), 270.

42. Eckehard Simon, *Neidhart von Reuental* (Boston: Twayne, 1975).

43. Freedman, *Savagery and Sanctity.*

44. Christoph Fuchs, *Dives, Pauper, Nobilis, Magister, Frater, Clericus: Sozialgeschichtliche Untersuchungen über Heidelberger Universitätsbesucher des Spätmittelalters (1386–1450)* (Leiden: Brill, 1995), 17, 75–76.

45. Fournier, *Les Statuts et privilèges des universités françaises,* 1:828.

46. Albertus Magnus, *De Animalibus Libri XXVI,* ed. Hermann Stadler, Beiträge zur Geschichte der Philosophie des Mittelalters, Texte und Untersuchungen, 15–16 (Münster i. Westf.: Aschendorff, 1916), 22:2:1, 1369.

47. Vincent of Beauvais, *Speculum Naturale* (Nuremberg: Anton Koberger, 1485), 19:31, fol. 124r.

48. This use of excrement for male ailments contrasts sharply with Hippocratic writings which associate excrement with the ailments of women. Heinrich von Staden, "Women and Dirt," *Helios* 19 (1992): 7–30.

49. Or perhaps their use was merely threatened or implied. Contemporary fraternity initiation rituals (although with their emphasis on alcohol, they tend to focus on vomiting more than on excreting) sometimes involve making the initiate believe that he is eating feces and drinking urine, when this is not actually the case. The purpose, according to Sanday, is to build trust and teach the initiate to obey unquestioningly. Sanday, *Fraternity Gang Rape,* 160, 169; Colton, *Goat Brothers,* 48.

50. Lev. 4:23, 16:15, 16:21–22.

51. L. Wehrhahn-Stauch, "Bock," in *Lexikon der christlichen Ikonographie* (Rome: Herder, 1968), 314.

52. *Glossa Ordinaria* to Heb. 9:13, in *Patrologia Latina* 114:658: "Hircus Christum significat, per similitudinem carnis peccati."

53. Wehrhahn-Stauch, "Bock," 314–15.

54. Isidore of Seville, *Etymologies,* Book 6, ed. Jacques André (Paris: Les Belles Lettres, 1986), 1:13–15, 46–49.

55. Florence McCulloch, *Medieval Latin and French Bestiaries* (Chapel Hill: University of North Carolina Press, 1962), 121–23; Robert Reinsch, ed., *Le Bestiare: Das Thierbuch des normannischen Dichters Guillaume le Clerc,* Altfranzösische Bibliothek 14 (Leipzig: 1892; reprint, New York: A.M.S. Press, 1973), 298.

56. Richard Barber, trans., *Bestiary* (Woodbridge, Eng.: Boydell Press, 1993), 83.

57. Emmanuel Walberg, ed., *Le Bestiare de Philippe de Thaün* (Lund: Hj. Möller, 1900), 105.

58. Walter of Rouen, *Moriuht: A Norman Latin Poem from the Early Eleventh Century,* ed. Christopher J. McDonough (Toronto: Pontifical Institute, 1995), 130. I thank Jan Ziolkowski for this reference.

59. William M. Voelkle, "Moran Manuscript M. 1001: The Seven Deadly Sins and the Seven Evil Ones," in *Monsters and Demons in the Ancient and Medieval Worlds,* ed. Anne E. Farkas, Prudence O. Harper and Evelyn B. Harrison (Mainz: Philipp von Zabern, 1987), 106; Wehrhahn-Stauch, "Bock," 316; Beryl Rowland, *Blind Beasts: Chaucer's Animal World* (Kent, Ohio: Kent State University Press, 1971), 19.

60. Albertus Magnus, *De Animalibus Libri XXVI,* 22:2:1, 1369.

61. Joshua Trachtenberg, *The Devil and the Jew: The Medieval Conception of the Jew and its Relation to Modern Antisemitism* (Philadelphia: Jewish Publication Society, 1961), 46–47.

62. Zarncke, *Die deutschen Universitäten,* 111.

63. I am not suggesting that the "civilizing process" going on in this initiation ritual is the same thing described by Norbert Elias: *The Civilizing Process,* vol. 1, *The History of Manners,* trans. Edmund Jephcott (New York: Urizen Books, 1978); vol. 2, *Power and Civility,* trans. Edmund Jephcott (New York: Pantheon, 1982). Elias is talking about the process of civilization on a societal rather than on an individual level. Elias suggests that "civilized" behavior became important at the time of the Renaissance and the rise of the state, as a centralized monopoly on violence replaced a system in which the individual nobleman could basically do as he pleased. But the story here about university initiation has little directly to do with state power.

64. John W. Baldwin, *The Language of Sex: Five Voices from Northern France Around 1200* (Chicago: University of Chicago Press, 1994), 184–86; Joan Cadden, *Meanings of Sex Difference in the Middle Ages: Medicine, Science, and Culture* (Cambridge: Cambridge University Press, 1993), 273–76; Danielle Jacquart and Claude Thomasset, *Sexuality and Medicine in the Middle Ages,* trans. Matthew Adamson (Princeton: Princeton University Press, 1988), 136.

65. Joyce E. Salisbury, *The Beast Within: Animals in the Middle Ages* (New York: Routledge, 1994), 78–80.

66. The literature on the connection of femininity and lasciviousness is vast. I have discussed it in various places, including "Gendered Sin and Misogyny in John of Bromyard's 'Summa Predicantium,'" *Traditio* 47 (1992): 233–57. See also R. Howard Bloch, *Medieval Misogyny and the Invention of Western Romantic Love* (Chicago: University of Chicago Press, 1991). Salisbury (*The Beast Within,* 155–58) discusses the association of women with animals.

67. At Colton's fraternity, pledges were known as "goats" and members of one's pledge class were one's "goat brothers." Colton recounts being harangued: "You're a fucking goat, that's what! A *goat!* You're the dumbest species on earth . . ." Colton, *Goat Brothers,* 42. Richard Ford reported of his Michigan State Sigma Chi pledge class in 1963: "You had to bray like a donkey, buzz like a fly, bleat like a goat, be scorned, scourged, ridiculed, and insulted until they let you join them." Richard Ford, "Rules of the House," *Esquire* 105.6 (June 1986): 234.

68. Zarncke, *Die deutschen Universitäten,* 6.

69. Sanday, *Fraternity Gang Rape,* 167. This was followed by the actual "cleansing," which involved anointing each pledge's scrotum with Ben-Gay.

70. Prudence Allen, *The Concept of Woman: The Aristotelian Revolution 750 B.C.-A.D. 1250* (Montreal: Eden Press, 1985).

71. J.M. Fletcher, "Wealth and Poverty in the Medieval German Universities," in *Europe in the Late Middle Ages,* ed. J.R. Hale, J.R.L. Highfield, and B. Smalley (Evanston, Ill.: Northwestern University Press, 1965), 418–19. See

John M. Fletcher and Christopher A. Upton, " 'Monastic enclave' or 'open society'? A consideration of the role of women in the life of an Oxford college in the early Tudor period," *History of Education* 16 (1987): 1–9, for discussion of the roles of women within the university.

72. Zarncke, *Die deutschen Universitäten,* 35–41.

73. See, for example, Grosse Fürstenkolleg, Leipzig, in Zarncke, *Statutenbücher,* 196; Johannes Kerer, *Statuta Collegii Sapientiae. The Statutes of the Collegium Sapientiae in Freiburg University. Freiburg, Breisgau, 1497,* ed. Josef Hermann Beckmann (Lindau: Jan Thorbecke, 1957), 28, 38. For prostitutes and students generally, see Ruth Mazo Karras, "Sharing Wine, Women, and Song: Masculine Identity Formation in the Medieval European Universities," in *Becoming Male in the Middle Ages,* ed. Jeffrey Jerome Cohen and Bonnie Wheeler (New York: Garland, 1997), 187–202 .

Gravitas and Consumption

SUSAN MOSHER STUARD

Why "signification between material objects and social station . . . strives to remain relatively uncomplex and controlled" Daniel Miller does not reveal. But he is well aware of the consequences when this breaks down: people lower in a given hierarchy will fulfill their aspirations by changing their behavior, dress and consumption "since it now becomes possible to mistake a poor nobleman for a wealthy trader." This is no sooner done than, Miller attests, the privileged, in turn, attempt to maintain differentials, since they have

> access to knowledge about goods and their prestige connotation. By
> this process, fashion emerges as the means for continuing those forms
> of social discrimination previously regulated by sumptuary rulings. In
> other words, demand for goods may flourish in the context of ambigu-
> ity in social hierarchy.[1]

Miller is concerned with issues of class, but his analysis of process may also say something about the social construction of gender. His own investigations in the early modern period found a confusion of signs in regard to class standing: among poor noblemen and wealthy traders. Confusion over signs, I wish to suggest here, broke out much earlier, and among noblemen who were anything but poor, and were most certainly merchant traders themselves. They initiated the earliest medieval sumptuary legislation.[2] These gentlemen stood at the highest levels of urban society; they were the *sapientes,* or grave, wise leaders of Italy's city states, specifically of the greatest of these, Venice and Florence. This confusion over signs appears to date from the early and middle decades of the fourteenth century when certain features of fashion, trend and trendsetting emerged to stimulate demand in Europe's market economy.

Initially, confusion had little to do with class. The sumptuary law that regulated dress, festivities and consumption distinguished among consumers by gender and by age, not by class, and this remained true of sumptuary law in Italian cities through the fifteenth century.[3] In time, with heightened demand for luxury goods, the emergence of a second-hand market and the opportunity for poorer folk to dress in the castoffs of the wealthy, a class dimension to confused signals certainly emerged, but urban sumptuary law's early concern with the consuming habits of members of the lawgivers' own families—their wives and their very own children—suggests different considerations ruled the thoughts of wealthy and grave lawmakers, even when demand may have already begun to creep across class barriers.

Why gender, and its accompaniment, age? Why were these the salient categories in which lawgivers attempted to comprehend, and control, changes in consumer behavior in the markets which had created, and more significantly maintained, their own personal munificence? Two pieces of fourteenth-century legislation, the sumptuary law of 1334 of Venice and a comparable attempt at legislating restraint in 1355 at Florence, can provide a glimpse into current thinking.

First, it is important to understand that sumptuary legislation was drawn, debated and enacted in an atmosphere of high emotion. Gravitas may have prevailed but it was ruffled by what lawmakers saw in the streets and in their own homes. The law of 1334 was an acknowledged failure from the start, so the Venetian Senate deliberations of 21 May 1360 rumbled out: "And thus is noted in our city today, *more than in all other parts of the world,* more vanities and inordinate expenses among wives, and other women . . ."[author's emphasis].[4] Could Venetians, who had gone to great lengths to make their markets premier in luxury trade in Europe, be so aghast at the local inhabitants' response to those markets? Women's fashions brought torrents of complaint on the issue of expenses. Whether too bold or too retiring, the current fashion was always wrongheaded. Later in 1443 in Venice, Ser Bartolomeo Marcello called the fashion of covering the head and face now favored by women, "abominable."[5] Yet, in Florence, it was immodesty in women's décolletage that offended lawmakers.[6] The dour Latin of Florence's law of 1355 had been translated into the vernacular by Andrea Lancia, with the didactic purpose of acquainting those only literate in the vernacular—

therefore women for the most part—about the provisions of the law in order to avoid just such outrages.[7] In Venice the law of 1334 was to be broadcast every six months in what turned out to be a vain effort to keep women and children informed—and conforming. Feelings ran high about what appeared to be superfluity (the very term was used in the Venetian law of 1334). This accompanied pique at excesses of behavior at weddings and parties, and there was a strong dose of moral outrage mixed into these lengthy laws, particularly in regard to weddings where civic leaders saw extravagance take precedence over due respect for the Holy Sacrament.

The complexity of agendas that surface when reading sumptuary law should caution a modern reader interpreting this legislation. Because women and youth were mentioned most often in Venetian and Florentine laws does not mean that they possessed exclusive right to showcase the family's wealth in the manner which those studying postindustrial society readily recognize. Patriarchs of the family were not expected to be somber producers of wealth in order to assert their probity; they could, and did, consume with zest, a matter to which this study will turn considerable attention. Second, sumptuary laws were catchall enactments, and confusing for that reason. In 1334 in Venice, when Ser Thomas Superancio had a sudden afterthought about the length of women's mantles, proposing to limit women's trains to one *bracchia* (about sixty-eight centimeters), he introduced his measure onto the floor of the Senate and gained immediate, and resounding, approval for it.[8] Sudden notions and remembered affronts to sensibility made grab bags of these laws, so they follow little system and appear to be somewhat incoherent. Third, sometimes the law fined the consumer, sometimes the producer, while enforcement fell to various offices of government in both cities or to the church; in particular, hapless civic notaries charged with spotting violations and granting exceptions sat on a hot spot.[9] They were more likely to get it wrong than right: Venice might wish to limit women's finery but it also wanted women of the doge's family to appear in bright colors even if they were in mourning.[10] Last, a great donna could go right over the heads of local authorities, as did Christine Correr in 1438 in a famous case where she petitioned the pope to wear the clothes and jewels due her because of both her beauty and the status of her family (she specified these wares in great detail).[11] Clearly, her family encouraged her in her effort to skirt civic law, indeed, the wise leaders of cities, the *sapientes* themselves, often appear to be thinking more in terms of exceptions than of the rule when it came to consumption.

The picture of sumptuary law that emerges is one of confused and even contradictory impulses, and thus the Venetian law of 1334 was full of exceptions. Ser Ziani Baduario almost immediately proposed the repeal of the Venetian law of 1334, which indeed did occur later, in 1339. However, Ser Superancio's limit on the length of trains remained the law of Venice, so did limits on women's wearing of two fashions: "*drezatores perlarum*" and "*frexatura de perlis.*"[12] Concern for expenses at home appears to have been a governing motive, as does concern for spiritual values, but the assured measures undertaken by Venetians and Florentines to build successful luxury markets were not in evidence in the regulation of locals purchasing on those markets. Understanding the psychology of consumption, which these wise, grave men assuredly did, failed then to carry over into understanding the psychology of consumption at home, or did it?

At Venice, once the *aurifici* [goldsmiths] established themselves in the Ruga degli Orefici, with shops always open on the Rialto and benches or booths set up on the Campo San Polo and on the Piazza for special market days, can civic officials have been that surprised that local consumers, who could afford the prices, frequented those markets? Venice was the precious metals, that is, the "noble" metals, capital of Europe. Reinhold C. Mueller has argued that by the middle of the fourteenth century, Venice had become a "city of finance" in five areas: with a system of local deposit and *giro* or transfer banks; as a center for maritime insurance; as a money market for short-term loans; as a financial market for "forced" loans or long-term government bonds that were negotiable; and, most significantly, as the premier bullion market of Europe. Values from all five sectors of the interrelated financial markets were quoted daily at the Rialto and showed every sign of being mature, widely frequented and highly rationalized financial markets.[13] Gold and silver wares, in all their attractive forms, tagged after the bullion market quite naturally because the laws that encouraged foreign imports of bullion fed both markets.

The years after 1310 were propitious for the development of a luxury market that used silver in great quantities. Venice was flooded with silver in those years because it had ceased to defend its great silver coin, the grossi, and followed Florence and Genoa to reliance on gold: the gold ducat, in Venice's case. However, old policies that had attracted foreign silver to Venice had not been disassembled, so silver, the essential component of jewelry with gold used only sparingly as embellishment, was available and within means.[14]

Lord Paolo Guinigi of Lucca employed his profits from trading in long-term Venetian government bonds to purchase gems like rubies, pearls and emeralds at Venice early in the fifteenth century, that is, in decades when the integrated financial markets were fully mature.[15] Precious wares could serve as repositories of value for his profits on Venice's financial markets just as well as coin; possibly they served even better. Wealthy foreigners were carefully cultivated where a bench, (or bank [*bancorum*]) devoted to exchange of coin might also display silver wares, which might be gilded or worked with gold and studded with gems. Financial and luxury markets developed hand in hand and they were watched and regulated with every evidence of cultivating the richest foreign customers.

Church sumptuary legislation suggests that the years after 1310 were equally propitious for the growth of a luxury market at Florence. That year in synodal legislation at Florence Bishop Antonio d'Orso Biliotti condemned women's ostentatious dress and regulated the amount to be spent on adornment: what jewelry, including costume jewelry, might be worn, what was absolutely forbidden—enamel work and crowns— and even the number of colors in a woman's ensemble. Modesty was an issue in regard to necklines and formfitting clothing, and no false hairpieces were to be used. Behavior at weddings was controlled and at gatherings to mourn a deceased relative.[16] The prohibitions provide a rundown of the festivities and dress that were most popular for the time, with the important caveat that they reveal information only in regard to the dress and comportment of women.

But sumptuary legislation, it appears, was often doomed to failure. Florence could not expect to display its cunningly woven cloth of silver and gold, its gold-stamped leather and imported ivory and gems without tempting its very own inhabitants to buy. Florence had established itself as the center of production and trade of fine apparel, most notably beautiful fabrics. These products called out to be embellished; they could be shot with silver or gold, embroidered with gems, silver or gold, or stamped with precious metals. While Venetian law described gold, silver and gems in complex terms, Florentine law applied complex descriptions to fabrics and leather—their design, style and color. In both cases lawmakers focused on products of local manufacture. Certainly the great banks of fourteenth-century Florence attracted the sort of customer who could appreciate and afford such luxury wares. The psychology of market behavior, of attraction to those markets, was the business of affluent city fathers and they succeeded at it famously.

But not at home? Wisdom in controlling and promoting their own markets did not apply when members of their own families frequented those markets. This suggests that some answers to the perplexity of sumptuary laws may lie in assessing the consuming behavior of the *sapientes,* the grave, wise lawmakers, themselves. Had consumption become, in Daniel Miller's phrase, "more directly constitutive of social status" and did this disturb the *sapientes* in economic terms, social terms or perhaps both? The munificence of the *sapientes,* themselves, already bordered on the legendary; indeed, it was one factor that explained the attraction of wealthy foreigners to the markets of Florence and Venice. Was this munificence jeopardized by the consumption patterns of women or of youth? Confusion over signs in public display and costume is ever elusive, but perhaps Henry Brod can supply some insight into the behavior of the *sapientes* enacting sumptuary law.

Henry Brod has suggested that in understanding gender scholars have been too ready to assume that a system of hierarchy between men and women is simply constitutive of subordinating women. He notes: "[P]atriarchy institutionalizes not just hierarchy *between* genders, but hierarchy *within* each gender as well."[17] He believes that societies have many easier and more direct ways to differentiate women from men than the elaborate laws and tests that have been written to that ostensible purpose. Thus, such tests and laws may be better understood as differentiating within masculinity, that is to say, a hierarchy of entitlement may be discerned among men. If sumptuary law relates to the economic concerns of the *sapientes,* to their concern over confused visual signs that might affect what foreigners sought out in luxury markets, then there might be an underlying rationality to legislating restraint for women, yes, but also for younger and less powerful men.

At issue here is the historian's tendency to take legislation at face value. Sumptuary legislation defined women as "other" in uncompromising terms. A polar relation was established, in that women were to be limited or restrained whereas men, the *sapientes* themselves, were left unrestrained and might, therefore, exercise their judgment on proper display and attire. Young men were also restrained but it must be assumed that they would outgrow this restraint when gravitas established itself in them. One aspect of sumptuary law has eluded analysis, for the most part: sumptuary law did not forbid consumption and display, it merely limited it. Youth and women were permitted finery, but within specified lines. Perhaps this law served to create a hierarchy of consumption within the community. The laws of both Venice and Florence were based on scales of consumption, and this should be taken as evidence that gradations, often within a hierarchy of masculinity, were of as much concern as legislating public morality, or enlisting the state's help in "holding the line" at home.

For example, in the law of 1334 in Venice, women were permitted a rather generous allowance for finery in apparel. The important consideration is to add it all together: fifteen soldi di grossi for a gold ornament for the hair or neck, seven lira di grossi for other jewelry like necklaces. A belt or girdle could cost up to twelve soldi di grossi and from it a woman might append expensive items like silver knives, purses or needle cases up to a value of ten soldi di grossi. It all adds up: at twenty soldi to a pound a woman might parade around in almost nine lira di grossi worth of silver, gold and gems, and that does not count rich materials in mantles, robes and head coverings, although women were forbidden to wear cloth of gold. A bride might have two dresses, not just one, for celebrating her wedding and they could be costly; she could be accompanied by twenty married women or widows and by ten unmarried women, all suitably decked out, no doubt. This was not a limit on display as such, but a limit on the extent of display and on certain fashions. As noted above, after the appeal of the law, the length of trains in Venice was still limited and two fashions, one in headdresses and one in borders of clothes, were still forbidden.[18]

Matters were not so different in Florence after 1355. Women could not wear cloth of gold or velvet but they were free to wear silk. Trains on robes were limited to less than one *bracchio,* but they were permitted. Fashions, more than precious materials, were forbidden to women, and the law specified that a woman could wear a girdle or belt but it was to be of no greater value than fifteen florins of gold.[19] This was a small fortune, in fact, the limit was so generous that it might be construed as no limit at all, except that there is evidence that girdles or belts of even greater size and value were traded on the markets. Furthermore, this represented a substantial increase over the monetary limit of four florins set on women's belts and fastenings by synodal legislation in 1310.[20] In the civic law of 1355 rich furs were forbidden to all but the wife of a *cavalieri,* and *azzurrata* or enamel work that featured the very precious shade of ultramarine, was expressly forbidden to all.[21]

Youth were more likely to be forbidden to congregate than to consume. Young men could not hold "men only" events on the day of weddings or for fifteen days before or after in Venice. Males above ten could not wear silk or velvet or cloth of gold but they might use "*peroli*" or "*asoleti*"—buttons and fastenings of silver and gold—on their clothes.[22] In the synodal sumptuary legislation of 1310 men had been entirely ignored, but in Florence after 1355 men came under some of the same limits on the cost of their ornaments as women. Still, the greatest attention was directed at men's behavior at public gatherings, so it was young men's conduct, not their apparel, that the law condemned.[23]

In the sumptuary law in Florence in 1325 a careful distinction was elaborated: women were forbidden to dress in men's clothes, and men were forbidden to dress like women: "*nulla mulier . . . vadat induta virilibus vestimentis, vel aliquis vir mulierbribus indumentis.*"[24] The parallel in the phrasing of the law was less than precise. The more outré styles of youth's long hose and short tunics were not intended in this banning of cross-dressing, but rather the now gendered styles in hats, jewelry and fastenings; for example, buttons in a line to the elbow were feminine, but buttons marching up to the shoulder were a masculine privilege.

Generally speaking, men took to the possibilities of cross-dressing with more enthusiasm than women and at Venice in time the law went further than at Florence.[25] By 1443, a Venetian man found wearing a woman's dress or other "*habito desconveniente*" was liable to lose the garment, pay a fine of one hundred lire and go to prison for six months.[26] This economic loss would be significant, however, the fine and the six-month prison term indicated that cross-dressing was regarded as far less serious behavior than reported cases of sodomy, which were serious sex crimes in fourteenth- and fifteenth-century Venice, punishable by death, usually by burning alive.[27] When fornication with nuns commanded only a two-year jail sentence with a fine, and even milder penalties were demanded for adultery, sodomy, with its death sentence, was a very serious matter for the authorities. Nevertheless, Venetian law was more lenient on the passive partner in cases involving two men brought up on sodomy charges, and perhaps the law found no seductive project at all in men's cross-dressing escapades; that is, a sexual invitation signaled through dress remained an unthought assignation of intent. From the evidence at hand, cross-dressing might, at times, hold different and genuinely honorific meanings in Venice: before the festival of the Twelve Wooden Maries was outlawed in 1397, a priest dressed as Mary had been the central figure in the procession to Santa Maria Formosa, and he would have been arrayed in the most precious jewels and fabrics that could be gathered to adorn him. This honor of dressing as Mary fell only to the most worthy among the ordained clergy.

At Florence, Michael Rocke noted that "in hundreds of sodomy

Figure 12. Military-inspired short tunic with buttons, belt and purse emphasized. Silver reliquary from the Treasury of St. Mark. Venice, fourteenth century.

denunciations to the courts and thousands of trial proceedings I have reviewed from the fourteenth to the sixteenth century, not a trace of transvestite boys has yet to come to light."[28] As at Venice, authorities did not associate cross-dressing with seductive intentions in boys or, for that matter, in men. However, San Bernardino would see the matter in a special light by the fifteenth century: boys who were too "spruced up" endangered gender distinctions. Mothers were to blame: "Oh silly, foolish woman, it appears you make your son look like yourself, so that to you he is quite becoming."[29] The problem lay not in rich materials for Bernardino, but in the clever combinations of fastenings, jewels, buttons and trims, perhaps even embroideries, mothers chose for their sons. In Bernardino's eyes it was improper to inflict these feminizing tricks on sons, on the grounds that the results led to confusing gender distinctions in the streets, but, significantly, for Bernardino these primping details of costume did not tempt other men to find young boys sexually alluring. From the evidence that survives, cross-dressing for men was condemned for occasioning uproar in the streets, but it was not understood as scandalous due to any sexual intent, nor did it possess any particular association with the crime of sodomy. Women appearing in masculine styles aroused more scandal and their public acts of transgression through apparel were more generally perceived as dangerous but, again, on the grounds that through details of costume women presumed to men's dignity.

With all who could afford it indulging in fashion and fashionable pursuits, it may help to characterize the *sapientes* in terms of their own consumption behavior. Since they were the unrestrained, that is, ignored in sumptuary laws, it requires studying notarial charters to find what the *sapientes* purchased themselves, and fourteenth-century painting, fresco and sculpture, to see if it is at all possible to ascertain if they kept the articles purchased for their own personal use. First, however, it is helpful to know who the *sapientes* were.

In regard to their political roles, Frederic Chapin Lane pointed out decades ago that where medieval governments served the interests of a noble circle, it was possible to pass with relative ease from private initiatives to public agency because the same persons dictated policy and administered programs in either case.[30] Under these circumstances, private was not the antipode of public, or civic, good nor would the *sapientes* seek solutions to their problems based on such a distinction. Faction might, of course, disturb this fluid translation from private to public sphere and back again, but sumptuary law does not appear to have been a factional issue in civic politics in Italian cities; indeed, it may have been one of the few areas of concurrence for legislators of all political stripes.[31]

In economic and social terms the men who drew up sumptuary legislation (in the case of Venice in 1334, ten *sapientes,* two of them highly trusted *procuratori di San Marco;* in the case of Florence, Thomaso di ser Puccio da Gobio, doctor of law and elected official of the comune of Florence) stood at the highest levels of society and, thus, they were men of the same families that organized principle markets and pursued long-distance trade. In the case of financial markets, in both cities they may be characterized, according to Sir Stanley Jevons's rule to be members of an elite "calculation" community. Jevons argued that most usage of coin, that is, gold and silver, was governed by ignorance and custom but "a small class of money-changers, bullion dealers, bankers or goldsmiths make it their business to be acquainted with differences [in weight and fineness of coins] and know how to derive profit from them."[32] The market for luxury wares was dominated by Venetians and Florentines who belonged to this "calculation" community, and they, or their kin, often held the most powerful civic offices as well.[33]

Indeed, the *sapientes* of these two cities worked together: Florentine banks and their factors were very active on the Venetian money market because they found at Venice the highly efficient markets that facilitated money transactions. In much the same way, the work in ivory and precious gems created in the Ubriarchi workshop at Venice (generally referred to as Embriachi in the art history literature) was directed to Florentine merchants who were resident, or visited, courts and cities in the north because they possessed such opportunity to present fine wares to Europe's most affluent consumers.[34] At the highest social level in both cities, there was a marked sharing of knowledge and a shared purpose; this included the legislating of sumptuary law. Since the market for luxury goods accompanied the bullion market, the luxury trade flourished precisely where financial markets were most efficient, thus, in Venice's integrated financial center and at Florence with its powerful merchant banking houses.

Under these circumstances, it does not stretch credulity to imagine that the most discerning, most magnificent and most prominently attired of all consumers were the wise, grave leaders themselves. In public display they outshone the younger men of their families, and the women of their families as well. There was a message encoded in their public presentation that noble wares denoted noble status. Precious and exotic goods had always conveyed this meaning, as the viewing public knew well. With the increasing popularity of the theme of The Magi or The Three Kings in Florentine and Venetian art, popular awareness was bound to grow. Throughout Europe gems, gold and silver traditionally filled ecclesiastical treasuries, while relics were encased in the most precious repositories obtainable. Scripture was bound in gem-studded silver and gold tablets and, as with Quedlinberg's Gospel of Samuhel, even written in a gold medium. Magnificence was fit for kings as well. Great rulers made even better customers for luxury wares than churches and monasteries, given the evanescence of temporal power and the recycling of stored wealth that accompanied it.[35]

The message conveyed by precious wares was not a message to be tampered with, weakened or in any way diluted. The taste of the most wealthy and most sensitive foreign customers on Venice's and Florence's markets was at stake. The *sapientes,* themselves, might launch a new fashion in luxury goods but if that fashion were flaunted about the streets by mere boys or by a flock of wives, daughters, daughters-in-law, aunts and cousins its message might lead to confusion. Kings and princes were not likely to adopt a fashion displayed so casually in the streets when exclusivity was their right and due.

This story may be told by reference to gold and silver articles of apparel and consumption. With the Balkan silver "strike" of the late thirteenth century, that grew with the opening of more mines in the fourteenth and early fifteenth centuries, even introducing a bit of gold ore [*glama*] onto Italian markets, a trade from point of origin to consumer may be traced in notarial records and civic regulation. Many parties participated: Saxon miners introduced into Serbia for their expertise, Serbian and Bosnian traders, merchants from the Dalmatian city state of Ragusa/Dubrovnik, Florentine factors from the great and smaller banks, *aurifici* trained in Italy or in Dalmatia, mint officials and overseers in Venice, Florentine merchants and their Venetian counterparts and, finally, royal and noble customers from all over Europe, generally represented on the market through their agents.[36]

In 1333 Duccii Puccii, factor of the great merchant banking house of Acciaiuoli of Florence, purchased a silver belt at Ragusa for thirty ducats.[37] Duccii, like other factors of Florentine banks like the Buonocursi, the Bardi, the Peruzzi and the Alberti, visited Ragusa with some regularity and when in town relied on the help of resident Florentines like Benci del Buono, who transacted trade between Ragusa/Dubrovnik and Venice. Ragusa was not only attractive because of the Balkan silver flowing into its port, but also because it was the land terminus of a courier route that linked the Adriatic ports with Constantinople. Banks relied on this courier route to set exchange rates since the two-week trip by land route outpaced the sea voyage by a considerable margin.[38] Duccii Puccii might have been in town transacting grain sales, trading in silver, ascertaining exchange rates on the market at Constantinople or arranging for the transfer of Ragusan wares to the Venetian market. All these activities required knowledgeable factors like Duccii—but why his exchange of gold coin for a hefty silver belt?

This belt, referred to as a *cinctura* or *cintola,* but also referred to as *zonas* in the sumptuary law of 1355 at Florence, and in the records of the

Grazie at Venice, could be made of identical links. It might also be made of decorated or embossed plaques that were linked together. It could be decorated with drawn silver, a craft that is practiced to this day in Dubrovnik, or it might be decorated with gold in any number of cladding processes from beating it into the surface, or spinning out gold thread for a different surface design, or encrusting it with gold or mounting gold settings for precious stones. Belts were unique products of an *aurifici's* skill and valued for their design and cunning workmanship, as well as for their weight in precious metals. They were worn about the hips (in the Eastern style) and provided shape for the flowing robe favored by the *sapientes*. Men's robes fell in expensive folds, weighted down by rich hems often finished with fur. The same belt might also cinch in a heavily padded doublet in the ultramontane style favored by Italian youth, who also showed a considerable length of hose beneath their doublets, but for most of the fourteenth century, the *sapientes* preferred the dignity of the long robe. Accompanied by buttons marching the length of sleeves, great medallions on chains about the neck, attached purses, or more stylishly, *cuslerii*—daggers of silver with elaborate hilts—belts highlighted the dignity of the man. Belts of great heft bespoke wealth—who else but the most affluent could afford to carry their riches about their hips?[39]

When Curzio Mazzi edited a remarkable bundle of charters as a *nozze* [marriage tribute] that he entitled *Argenti degli Acciaiuoli* late in the nineteenth century, he strove to understand the nature of wealth and accumulation in fourteenth-century Florence. The inventories he had found and edited contained charters from 1380 that accompanied a gift of precious articles to a Carthusian church from Madonna Margherita di Vanni degli Spini, wife of Niccolo Acciaiuoli. The list is full of *cinturae*. Finer belts were listed separately—*"Item, una cintura d'ariento isprangata, all'arma degli acciaiuoli"* [Item, one banded silver belt, with the arms of the Acciaiuoli] and *"Item, una cintura con isprangle d'aruenti orata, istrema"* [Item, one belt with gilded silver bands, long and narrow].[40] The inventory grouped others together: *"Item, quatro cinture di perlle"* [Item, four belts of pearl—which may have been glass beads such as those produced at Murano]. There were seven belts [*cincturae* and *cintolae*] listed in this one charter alone. In this small bundle of charters, there were more than twenty belts listed, almost all of silver; two were *cintolettae,* one with mother of pearl, the other banded with gold trim in a style called *franciescha.* This last mentioned belt had a buckle and enamel work as well.[41] The two *cintolettae* were probably smaller belts to be worn by women, like the pearl or beaded belts mentioned above, but most of the belts, including the *cinctura* of the first charter with the Acciaiuoli arms, as well as another *cintola* with gold, enamel and the family's arms, were most likely worn by a man of the family.[42]

It is not altogether out of the realm of possibility that Duccii Puccii, as a bank factor or agent of the Acciaiuoli company in 1333, actually provided the Acciaiuoli family with one or more of these great belts from his travels in Ragusa. Of course, the men of the family might acquire such belts readily elsewhere; still one, as noted above, was worn and could have dated from as early as 1333. The affluent prized their fashionable treasures and willed them down the generations. Whatever the origin of the worn belt, it had not lost value, even if it was no longer worn by the great men of the family. Clearly, the belt was still of worth because it was "recycled" into an endowment for the Carthusian church that had been founded by Madonna Margherita's own husband, Niccolo Acciaiuoli.

The *sapientes* seem to have had it both ways in their consumption of luxury wares. They were a walking display of what nobility should look like, as such they were worthy of emulation by any prince in Europe. But silver and gold articles were fungible assets. Finish wearing them and they did not cease to be repositories of value. Worn or a bit out of style a belt might be used in lieu of cash in certain transactions. Belts were recycled to produce new articles of display, or minted into coin. In this instance adopting a fashion did not result in casting off old finery that had lost all its market value. All silver items could be melted down and refashioned, gems could be reset and gold, even in small quantities, was recoverable.

Consequential consumers from all over Europe bought gold, silver, gems and other precious goods on Italy's great markets. At about the time that Duccii Puccii purchased his great silver belt at Ragusa for 30 ducats, the powerful ruler of Serbia, Dušan, ordered a great belt and a silver ship at Ragusa for 195 ducats. These required thirteen pounds and five ounces of silver.[43] Other belts ordered from goldsmiths at Ragusa were comparably ponderous: one was commissioned in 1313 in filament silver with raised work for over seventy-one ducats and required eleven pounds of silver.[44] Because belts were prestige items they could be fashioned in varying quantity, and quality, of precious metal, with or without gold trim, with or without precious gems, enamel work, intaglio and fancy buckles.[45] The diversity of style, workmanship, precious materials and size encouraged consumption from nobles or royalty of limited or great resources, all of whom looked to Italy for prized possessions.

Figure 13. Sumptuous long robes with embellishment that established a man's gravitas. Italian Fresco. School of Giotto, *Vision of Zachariah,* fourteenth century.

Princes could purchase a diversity of models in line with their pocketbooks.

For the great King, later Emperor, Dušan, or for the Lord Guinigi of Lucca, access to gems and artifacts of silver and gold was comparatively easy. For that matter, most of Europe's royalty, nobility and very wealthy consumers had excellent access to the luxury markets of Venice and Florence. There were two possible approaches: remaining at home and waiting for fashionable goods to be presented, as did King Robert of Sicily, the Black Prince in England and the avid consumers of the Valois dynasty in France. Others traveled to, or through, Italy: Hungarian royalty on a number of occasions and Catalans in pursuit of their Sicilian conquests. Mary Stella Newton argues that it was the appointment of Walter of Brienne as Florentine *conservatore del popolo* that brought French or ultramontane fashions to Italy in the 1340s; this was reinforced by a Genoese presence on the French side at the battle of Crécy.[46] She sees a turn to fashion occurring almost simultaneously in all the major European capitals about 1340; however, many of the articles that created the new fashion had been sold on Italian markets for decades prior to this, while the new ultramontane masculine silhouette, with padded doublet and hose, may not have been either as French, or as new, as Italian chroniclers claimed.[47]

Excellent cooperation of the merchants who staffed luxury markets, be they foreign suppliers or Venetians and Florentines, sustained Italian dominance in luxury trades. The highly rationalized nature of financial markets and banking networks, constructed by Venetians and Florentines in the fourteenth century, supported luxury trades. For example, to bring Ragusan silver and silver wares, to the Venetian market, Florentines arranged shipment, delivery and safe conduct of wares. At least once, these cooperating merchants forgot to pay the required "fifth" on imported silver to the mint, so we meet them in the Venetian *Grazie* (Pardons). Take, for example, the case of the Venetian Peter Reynaldus. In 1337, he failed to report to the Silver Office a purchase of over thirty pounds of Ragusan silver that had been made through a Florentine agent at Venice.[48] Merchants like he, or Duccii Puccii, had fanned out across Europe, reaching northern capitals and stretching their networks across both the English channel and the Irish Sea. Were a northern lord or king unable to visit Italy's great cities, he could rely on the factors or partners of leading banks to bring him the latest fashions; these agents were practically everywhere.[49] Francesco de Marco Datini supplied Avignon, with the assistance of Baldassare Ubriachi, a Florentine merchant banker and, very likely, founder, with his kin, of a great Venetian workshop in precious wares and gems that bore the family name.[50]

In the north, a keener fourteenth-century interest in opulence and display found local goldsmiths unable to fill demand. For example, in

England the Black Prince, son of Edward III, "was frequently abroad and, particularly in his purchases of jewels, had no need of Londoners, little skilled in such matters. He dealt largely with Martin Parde of Pistoia in Italy and Hanekyn, Martin's goldsmith brother."[51] The prince's New Year's gifts were richer than London artisans could supply: an enameled gold cup for the king, jeweled rings, an enameled silver-gilt tabernacle to the bishop of Winchester, a gold mug to the lord of Castelnau of Burgundy, silver gilt cups to German knights who had brought the news of Edward III's election as emperor and a comparable cup to the nurse who guarded the cradle of William, his brother and godson.[52] His need of Italians who could supply opulent gifts, while keeping him informed of what was luxurious and the latest style, made the Black Prince an important customer on the luxury market without ever needing to set foot in Italy. His choice of two brothers from Pistoia, a town twenty miles from Florence and the source of adventurous merchants who had tied their futures to the great merchant banks of Florence, was predictable. But the royal children of Edward III only set the style in consumption, Londoners of means followed, eagerly purchasing stylish wares, as did Margery Randolf. For ten marks of silver she purchased two silver drinking cups, a cup shaped like a coconut, two handled cups with covers, twelve silver spoons, a circlet, a silver girdle [a great belt?] and a gold buckle, two chaplets of pearls, prayer beads and linens all in one shopping spree.[53] Of course, London goldsmiths were swift to stake out a role for themselves, supplying such consumers, but they first needed to learn what the Italian arbiters of fashion dictated.

If consumers at such a distance from Italy spent their wealth so freely for fashions set in Venice and Florence, and for wares that imitated Italian designs, then perhaps there was reason for the Venetians' sense that there were extraordinary luxuries and higher expenses in their city, "more than in all other parts of the world."[54] A cynosure for all consumers who could afford luxury and were inclined to buy, the grave, wise men of Venice and Florence knew they possessed a potent asset in their luxury markets, one that required cultivation, but also careful watching.

The projection of their own public personas through princely consumption connoted both their sense of themselves, as the peers of royalty and high feudal nobility, as well as their canny sense that customers do not buy without some exhibition of how goods convey messages about status. In the interests of newly consequential luxury trades, the *sapientes* needed to grace the piazzas and street corners of Florence and Venice to demonstrate to their customers all the different ways in which a noble or regal station might be conveyed by dress. And they needed to take that message to royal courts throughout Europe. Above all, they needed to instruct kings in the art of costume and fashion where the royal condition was conveyed just as reliably as with the essential, if seldom worn or displayed, regalia of their royal office. Kings would then look like kings not only at coronations and on state occasions, or being depicted as kings on coins and seals; they could also appear kingly in their daily routines at court and their royal progressions at home and abroad.

It is, then, reasonable to ask: when the *sapientes* dressed like kings was this an assertion of status that they were "kings" of a sort themselves, by virtue of their wealth and position at the pinnacle of urban society in sovereign states lacking monarchs?

Over the course of the fourteenth century Italian artists faced their own challenges in iconography when attempting to depict the increasingly popular legend of the Three Kings for their civic patrons.[55] From the School of Giotto's *Adoration of the Magi* of 1306 through the carved ivory Embriachi (Ubriachi) altarpiece of the Certosa di Pavia, with its central panel devoted to the legend of the Magi, until the middle of the fifteenth century when Antonio Vivarini and Giovanni d'Alemagna executed their crowded, but certainly dazzling, *Epiphany* in the so-called International Style, the theme of the Three Kings grew in popularity in Italy's cities.[56] As artists were challenged by the increasing specificity of the legend itself to move beyond the traditional rendering of the Magi as statuesque robed figures with crowns, kneeling or standing before the Christ Child and Virgin, regality was represented more and more frequently through the use of luxurious apparel and rich gifts. In the altarpiece of the Certosa di Pavia kings on horseback, at rest, traveling, in conversation, at prayer and in many other poses, required a variety of costume to depict their regal status. Iconographic messages about kingship represented through costume could become important tools in artists' hands in this context. And a public newly cognizant of wares available on luxury markets might readily grasp their meaning. In Epiphany scenes frames became more crowded with noble retinues for the Three Kings: their robes and accoutrements became more gorgeous, more opulent and varied. They included horses with equipages decorated with precious gems, gold and silver—even, by the time of Vivarini's *Epiphany,* with dogs wearing gem-studded silver collars. All these visual images entered in. It is quite possible that artists had come to rely on the work of their fellow artisans, that is, the *aurifici* and other local luxury craftsmen who were their close associates, for a larger iconographic repertoire. Through using such images artists could tell highly affecting stories about the holy task of bringing gifts of great value to the feet of the Christ Child.

At some psychological level, perhaps, these renderings of the legend of the Magi allowed the *sapientes* who commissioned them to play the coveted roles of grave and wise kings themselves, worshipping at the feet of the Virgin and Child. Donors appeared in luxurious, albeit sober splendor in portraits, and, as in the case noted below, they might even choose to present themselves as one of the Magi. The political ideals of the early Renaissance found little conflict between a princely condition and republicanism in any case, and this abetted new-found satisfactions in assuming a princely guise. A firm sense of hierarchy underlay Renaissance political thought, certainly in Venice, and increasingly, in the later Middle Ages, in Florence, where the idea of "an elite based on blood and social distinction" had achieved maturity.[57] Perhaps the greatest concession to republicanism in this growing social preoccupation with the Magi and regality lay in acknowledgment that great city republics possessed many, rather than only a few, princes. The crowded canvases with the Magi, their retinues and their associates, gave many of the *sapientes* and their sons and brothers the posture of princes. And apparel denoted regality, as did the rare and rich gifts of the Kings. Crowns became fashionable apparel, and if men wore them only when they posed as one of the Magi, their wives and daughters wore crowns more openly in the streets. The regalia of royal power could no longer be claimed as the exclusive domain of a few dynasties. If Italians transgressed sumptuary boundaries they did so at the highest level where the *sapientes,* themselves, appeared in the streets dressed as kings.[58]

Baldassare Ubriachi, possibly the earliest Florentine promoter of the cult of the Three Kings, was possessor of a residence just outside the gates of the city, later cited as the place "where the Magi are." He was also the patron of the church of Santa Maria Novella, and donor of a chapel there dedicated to the Three Kings.[59] In the carved lintel of the chapel "King Balthazar, gift in hand, recommend[s] to the divine pair his protegée Baldassare degli Ubriachi."[60] Richard Trexler argues that Ubriachi brought the cult of the Kings to Florence in the fourteenth century, that is, long before the Medici promoted the civic confraternity of the Company of the Magi to legitimate their own authority.[61] The Ubriachi family may be justly claimed by Venice as well, for in this city, to which they moved over the decades, they revived and built the family's fortunes through importing the most precious materials, then cunningly fashioning them into designs for attire, for use and for display. Their family workshop produced what was arguably the finest work in ivory of the century, the great altarpiece of the Certosa di Pavia where the legend of the Magi took central place.[62]

The Magian theme was very much at home in the aristocratic republic of Venice in the decades after the Closing of 1290. Donor portraits, whether in Florence or Venice, whether posed as Magi or self, allowed great men to display themselves as both regal and devout. Splendor and high seriousness were coupled in a highly conscious manner; whim, fancy and playfulness, so often associated with the emergence of fashion, had little place in this self-aware presentation.

"The dual nature of dress—the tension that can exist between what 'dresses up' reality and the reality underneath" found a resolution of sorts in creating princes of the *sapientes* themselves.[63] Was this a brash and presumptuous assertion of status? Most assuredly yes. However, it was not without some solid foundation in fourteenth-century conditions of life. Italian bankers to kings from Sicily to the Baltic Sea had private knowledge of the financial worth of their royal patrons and, at least before the banking crisis of 1343 to 1345, they could compare royal wealth to their own and to that of their compatriots, with conclusions, most likely, in their own favor. Kings might have enviable assets in land but their bankers knew best how often they flirted with bankruptcy for lack of liquid assets. The *sapientes*' assertions of egalitarian status with reigning monarchs, launched through setting fashions for those rulers, followed quite logically on establishing the financial markets that underwrote princely enterprises, most typically expensive, even bankrupting, wars of aggrandisement.[64] A banker with a king as his debtor might find it quite appropriate to dress as regally as he.

While the *sapientes* readily awarded themselves with princely status, they maintained a discriminating sense of just how many "princes" graced the streets of their towns, and they were sufficiently hierarchical in their judgment to restrict the consuming behavior of their own families. Generally, discussion of sumptuary law disparages the very attempt to control consumption as foolhardy and doomed to failure.[65] This discussion suggests, instead, that fourteenth-century sumptuary legislation was quite cannily directed toward an economically rational, and even realizable, goal: that of maintaining a hierarchy of consumption that would avoid confusion over signals for Italy's most valued and affluent customers: Europe's rulers, princes and lords. It suggests, as well, that sumptuary legislation fed demand. Also, this legislation may have reflected a highly self-conscious understanding of how fashion and trend affected luxury markets, that is, by creating a clientele of a majority of Europe's most privileged and affluent men. It may even have achieved its most serious aims at home, that is, not simply curbing consumption in Venice and in Florence but, instead, setting up a seemly hierarchy of consumption that instructed the rest of Europe in how dress conveys messages about status.

And hierarchy explains a great deal about the new fourteenth-century phenomenon of fashion which chroniclers, storytellers and pundits were so fond of criticizing. Fashion may have been elusive but it was more than the product of whim and fancy. Fashions were often based upon the exotic: the so-called International style which was, in dress at least, a creation of a padded doublet (as large as armor) and form-revealing hose and belts "*franciescha.*" But it was also belts worn low on the hips in the Eastern style, "tartar" hats and robes and bangles "*slavonescha.*"[66] As Diane Owen Hughes has discovered, a fashion like earrings could in time "cross over" from the Jewish community to the Christian community.[67] But all exoticisms depended upon their path of adoption. Only those widely acknowledged to possess high status, that is, status worth emulating, could set fashion. Daniel Miller has asserted that ambiguity in social hierarchy must be present for fashion to flourish, and in a sense that appears to be true in the Italy of the fourteenth century, since poorer consumers could create some ambiguity by copying the less expensive consumption patterns of their social superiors.[68] However, in another sense, no ambiguity existed at all: fashions were only copied when they conveyed proper messages. Those messages linked new fashion to the highest social credentials—regal and lordly credentials. There was a quid pro quo here: if the *sapientes* successfully created fashions that were copied through their clever manipulation of demand, they had come to possess those highest credentials. This is witness to a usurpation of social roles that had far-reaching implications for future economic developments, where the wealthiest, as well as the regal or wellborn, would in time come to arbitrate taste and fashion.

Of course, the project was always in danger of getting out of hand. Markets were, by their nature, largely free and open to any consumer if he or she could pay the price. Fines might limit consumption but many resolved to pay the fines and consume at a higher level and that was legal in sumptuary law. Stimulated demand, a newly important late medieval component of capitalist enterprise, was not easily controlled, but the *sapientes*, who cultivated consumption on their markets, were not the dupes of family members who flaunted the laws. These wise, grave men epitomized their society in their affluence and their consumption, transforming gender in significant ways. Men could become who they appeared to be, and visual signals of wealth and status mattered. Emulation was even desirable but only if differentials, based upon knowledge about goods and their prestige connotations, were respected. Fashion had emerged in Venice and Florence, and it had the power to define a man.

NOTES

1. Daniel Miller, *Material Culture and Mass Consumption* (Oxford: Blackwell, 1987), 135–36.

2. The first laws limiting finery appeared in the last decade of the thirteenth century. The Venetian law of 1299 was almost entirely directed at controlling excess at weddings. In Florence at the end of 1290, a registry to denounce excessive dress was established; the earliest extant law dated from 1307. Subsequent legislation occurred in 1322 and 1324. See Catherine Guimbard, "Appunti sulla legislazione suntuaria," *Archivio Storico Italiano* 150 (1992): 57–81.

3. The sixteenth century represented something of a departure, particularly in Florence where distinction by class became part of sumptuary law. See Carlo Carnesecchi, *Cosimo I e la sua legge suntuaria del 1562* (Florence: Cecchi i Chiti, 1902), 37. There were some intimations of class expressed earlier. Venice exempted the doge's family from sumptuary legislation and the law of 1355 in Florence exempted the spouse of a *cavalieri* from the prohibition against fine furs. Andrea Lancia, "Legge Suntuaria," ed. P. Fanfani, *L'Etruria 1* (1851): 366–83.

4. Venetian State Archives, *Senato, Deliberationes, Miste*, XXIX, fol. 64. See Margaret Newett, "The Sumptuary Laws of Venice," in *Historical Essays*, eds. T.F. Tout and James Tait (London: Longmans Green, 1902), 268–69, note 48: *Et sicut notum est in civitate nostra hodie, plusquam in alique alia parte mundi, fiunt multe vanitates et expense inordinate, circa sponsas et alias mulieres. . . .* The law of 1334 has been published in Giulio Bistort, *Il Magistrato alle Pompe nella Republica di Venezia* (Bologna: Forni, 1912), 329–52.

5. Newett, "Sumptuary Laws of Venice," 268.

6. Diane Owen Hughes, "Sumptuary Law in Renaissance Cities," in *Disputes and Settlements*, ed. John Bossy (Cambridge: Cambridge University Press, 1984), 69–100.

7. Andrea Lancia apparently petitioned the Florentine government in 1355 that a copy of these proclamations be translated for use. Wayne Storey,

Fordham University, is currently studying Lancia's culture of translation and its significance for fourteenth-century Florence.

8. Venetian State Archives, *Senato, Deliberationes,* Reg. 1333–34, fol. 69. Margaret Newett reads his name "Superantia" in the *Deliberationes,* but clearly, we discuss the same Venetian. Newett, "Sumptuary Laws of Venice," 263–72.

9. Richard C. Trexler, *Synodal Law in Florence and Fiesole, 1306–1518* (Città del Vaticano: Biblioteca Apostolica Vaticana, 1971). The Constitution of 1310 regulated artisans who produced luxury wares (230), and introduction (105).

10. Newett, "Sumptuary Laws of Venice," 249–50.

11. C. Foucard, *Lo Statuto inedito delle Nozze Veneziane nell' 1299, nozze* (Venice, 1858). The papacy began regulating "immoderate ornamentation" in 1274, with an edict issued by Pope Gregory X. See Alan Hunt, *Governance of the Consuming Passions* (New York: St. Martins Press, 1996), 26.

12. Venetian State Archives, *Maggior Consiglio, Deliberationes Spiritus,* XXIV, fol. 97. These fashions were headdresses of pearls and borders on robes of pearls. The "pearls" in question might very well have been glass beads. Murano produced lovely ones.

13. Reinhold C. Mueller, "Foreign Investment in Venetian Government Bonds and the Case of Paolo Guinigi, Lord of Lucca, early 15th century," in *Cities of Finance,* eds. Herman Diederiks and David Reeder (Amsterdam: Koninklijke Nederlandse Akademie van Wetenschappen, n.s. 165, 1996), 69.

14. Frederic C. Lane and Reinhold C. Mueller, *Money and Banking in Medieval and Renaissance Venice,* 2 vols. (Baltimore, Md.: The Johns Hopkins University Press, 1985), 1:16–23, 371–73.

15. Mueller, "Foreign Investment in Venetian Government Bonds," 83–84.

16. Trexler, *Synodal Law,* 229–330; and see Introduction, 115–17.

17. Henry Brod, "Constructions of Masculinities in the Canonical Texts of Western Political Theory," (paper presented at the Pacific Division meeting of the Society for Women in Philosophy, Pomona, Calif., 21 May 1994), 3.

18. One lira di grossi = ten ducats. See Lane and Mueller, *Money and Banking in Medieval and Renaissance Venice,* 338, and 338 n. 15; Newett, "Sumptuary Laws of Venice," 264; and Bistort, *Il Magistrato alle Pompe,* 343–48. On cost of living at Venice see Gino Luzzatto, "Il costo della vita a Venezia nel trecento," in idem, *Studi di storia ecnomica veneziana* (Padua: CEDAM, 1954), 285–97; and most recently Donald E. Queller, "A Different Approach to the Pre-modern Cost of Living: Venice, 1372–1391," *Journal of European Economic History* 25 (1997): 441–64. Queller suggests a noble woman's median allowance cost of living, adjusted for housing, would be forty-

two ducats in 1372–77, somewhat after the passage of this law. He also notes that dresses estimated at forty ducats each may be found in the documentary evidence, 461–63.

19. Lancia, "Legge Suntuaria," 370–75. A Florentine *bracchio* contained about fifty-eight centimeters.

20. Trexler, *Synodal Law,* 229 (Constitutions of Florence, 1310).

21. Lancia, "Legge Suntuaria," 373, 377. On women and sumptuary law at weddings see Christiane Klapisch-Zuber, *Women, Family and Ritual in Renaissance Italy,* trans. Lydia Cochrane (Chicago: University of Chicago Press, 1985), 241–46.

22. Newett, "Sumptuary Laws of Venice," 262. Bistort, *Il Magistrato alle Pompe,* 343–45.

23. Lancia, "Legge Suntuaria," 375–81.

24. Cited by Ronald E. Rainey, "The Sumptuary Law of Renaissance Florence," (Ph.D. diss., Columbia University, 1985), 96–97, note 51.

25. On homosexuality at Florence see Michael Rocke, *Forbidden Friendships: Homosexuality and Male Culture in Renaissance Florence* (New York: Oxford University Press, 1996). However, Samuel Cohn notes that over the course of the fourteenth century criminal courts transferred some of the concern over rape from heterosexual cases to homosexual cases. *Women in the Streets* (Baltimore, Md.: The Johns Hopkins University Press, 1996), 29–30.

26. Venetian State Archives, *Senato, Terra,* Reg. I, po. 105, cited by Newett, "Sumptuary Laws of Venice," 206.

27. Guido Ruggiero, *The Boundaries of Eros* (New York: Oxford University Press, 1985), 110. Ruggiero also argues that the passive partner often was treated leniently in prosecutions.

28. Rocke, *Forbidden Friendships,* 38, 109. Michael Rocke found that homosexual liaisons were normal for men in their transition to adulthood and that these relationships were replaced by heterosexual ones when a man reached thirty or so, and married. He does not see sodomy as particularly reprehensible to society, as Ruggiero does for Venice.

29. San Bernardino, quoted in Rocke, *Forbidden Friendships,* 38.

30. Frederic Chapin Lane, "Operation of Merchant Galleys," in *Venice and History* (Baltimore, Md.: The Johns Hopkins University Press, 1966), 216.

31. Few will argue with this assertion for Venice after the Closing of the patriciate in 1290. Anthony Molho, in *Marriage in Renaissance Florence* (Cambridge: Harvard University Press, 1994), argues that Florence possessed an intermarrying elite that created much the same solidarity among the aristocracy.

32. Sir Stanley Jevons, *Money and the Mechanism of Exchange* (New York: D. Appleton, 1893), 78–80. See the discussion of this principle as it applies

to medieval Venice in Lane and Mueller, *Money and Banking in Medieval and Renaissance Venice,* 1:59.

33. See the classic study of Armando Sapori, *La crisi delle compagnie mercantili dei Bardi e dei Peruzzi* (Florence: Olschki, 1926) for the extent of the Florentine banking network before the crisis of the 1340s.

34. See Richard Trexler, "The Magi Enter Florence," *Studies in Medieval and Renaissance History* n.s.1 (1978): 163–85; see also Franco Maria Ricci, *Embriachi, Il trittico di Pavia* (Milan: Bondoni, 1982); and Antonia Bostrom, "Embriachi," *Dictionary of the History of Art,* ed. Jane Turner (New York: Grove, 1996), 10:178–80.

35. Richard Goldthwaite in *Wealth and Demand for Art in Italy, 1300–1600* (Baltimore: The Johns Hopkins University Press, 1993), and in "The Renaissance Economy: The Preconditions for Luxury Consumption," in *Aspetti della Vital Economica Medievale.* Atti del convegno di Studi nel X Anniversario della morte di Federigo Melis (Florence-Pisa-Prato, 10 Marzo, 1984), 659–72, makes the point on fifteenth-century Italian consumption, that the changing of elites in cities through political coups stimulated luxury consumption significantly.

36. Susan Mosher Stuard, "The Adriatic Trade in Silver, c. 1300," *Studi veneziani* 17–18 (1975–1976): 95–143. On the silver mines of the Balkans see Desanka Kovacevic, "Les Mines d'or et d'argent en Servie et Bosnie," *Annales, E.S.C.* 15 (196): 248–58. On gold and silver smiths at Ragusa/Dubrovnik see Cvito Fiskovic, "Dubrovacki zlatari od XIII do XVII stoljeca," *Starohrvatska prosvjeta* ser. 1.3 (1949): 143–249. A Florentine, Puccii, did business in ducats at Ragusa/Dubrovnik. The price could easily keep a nobleman or woman a year in Venice. See Queller, "A Different Approach to the Pre-modern Cost of Living," 455–63.

37. Dubrovnik State Archives, *Diversa Cancellariae,* 10, fol. 27, die xxi Madii, 1333.

38. Barisa Krekic, "Foreigners in Dubrovnik," *Viator 8* (1978): 67–75; and idem, "Four Florentine Commercial Companies in Dubrovnik," in *The Medieval City,* ed. Harry Miskimin, David Herlihy and Benjamin Kedar (New Haven: Yale University Press, 1977), 25–41; see also Susan Mosher Stuard, *State of Deference* (Philadelphia: University of Pennsylvania Press, 1992), 171–202.

39. Boccaccio, Sacchetti, Fra Paolino and Villani all criticize new fashions. Dante singled out belts as representative of the dangerous new trends in consumption. Dante Aligheri, *Divine Comedy,* trans. Charles Singleton (Princeton, N.J.: Princeton University Press, 1975), *Paradiso,* canto 15, lines 97–102, where Dante contrasts the austerity of his ancestor's generation with the ostentation of his own.

40. *Argenti degli Acciaiuoli, nozze, Lungo-Bacci,* ed. Curzio Mazzi (Siena: 189?), 6. *Nozze* were celebratory publications on the occasion of weddings.

41. Ibid., 24.

42. Ibid.

43. Dubrovnik State Archives, *Diversa Cancellariae,* 12, fol. 211, *die xxviii Junii,* 1335.

44. Dubrovnik State Archives, *Diversa Cancellariae,* 5, fol. 41, *die vi Marcii,* 1313.

45. In Ragusa/Dubrovnik there were four grades of silver: *argento plico* (worst or fourth grade of fineness), *argento biancho* (white silver), *argento fino* (fine silver or high grade) and *argento de glama* (gold-laden silver, which was of the greatest fineness). Value differed substantially.

46. Mary Stella Newton, *Fashion in the Age of the Black Prince* (Bury St. Edmonds, Suffolk: Boydell, 1982), 2–6. Rosita Levi-Pisetzky in *Storia del Costume in Italia,* vol. 2 (Milan: Istituto Editoriale Italiano, 1964) sees greater dominance of Italians over the introduction of fashion in costume into Europe.

47. Louise Buenger Robbert, "Twelfth-Century Italian Princes: Food and Clothing in Pisa and Venice," *Social Science History* 7 (1983): 381–404, and Robert Lopez, "Nota sulla composizione dei patrimoni privati nella prima metà del duecento," *Studi sull'economia Genovese nel medioveo,* Documenti e Studi per la Storia del Commercio e del Diritto Commerciale Italiano, 7 (Turin: S. Lattes, 1936), 205–64, both provide examples of such articles of clothing from earlier dates. See also Giovanni Villani, *Cronica* (Florence: Dragomanni, 1845), 12.

48. Venetian State Archives, *Grazie,* R. 7, fol. 59.

49. Kings and great lords could also rely on diplomatic missions to bring back the newest Italian fashion, or agents of the crown sent expressly to buy luxury wares.

50. Trexler, "The Magi Enter Florence," 135. In 1394 Ubriachi reminds Datini of their business dealings in Avignon fifty-five years earlier.

51. T.F. Reddaway, *The Early History of the Goldsmith's Company, 1327–1509* (London: Arnold, 1975), 47.

52. Ibid., 37. Baldassare Ubriachi later served the Black Prince's son, Richard II, probably through Ubriachi's ties with the emperor Charles IV and the empress Elizabeth who were Richard's kin.

53. *Memorials of London and London Life in the XIII, XIV and XV Centuries. 1276–1419,* ed. H.T. Riley (London: Longmans, Green, 1868), 203–04.

54. See note 4 above.

55. See Martin Warnke, *The Court Artist,* trans. David McLintock (Cambridge: Cambridge University Press, 1993), 3–74 for distinctions between civic and court patronage in the fourteenth century.

56. Giotto di Bondone, *Adoration of the Magi,* 1306, Scrovegni Chapel, Padua, Italy; Baldassare Embriachi, *Il Trittico di Pavia* (Milan: Ricci, 1982), 57–76. Antonio Vivarini and Giovanni d'Alemagne, *Epiphany,* ca. 1440, Berlin, Germany. On the legend of the Magi see Joannes of Hildesheim, *Three Kings of Cologne,* ed. C. Horstman, Early English Text Society, 85 (London: M. Trübner, 1886); U. Monneret de Villard, *Le leggende orientali sui Magi evangelici* (Città del Vaticano: Biblioteca apostolica vaticana, 1952); and Luca Beltrami, *La Certosa di Pavia,* 2nd ed. (Milan: Hoepli, 1907).

57. Frank and Fritzi Manuel, *Utopian Thought in the Western World* (Cambridge, Mass.: Belknap Press, 1979) compares the hierarchical utopia of the Renaissance with more egalitarian notions of utopia that emerged in later centuries. For the quotation see Gene Brucker, *The Civic World of Early Renaissance Florence* (Princeton: Princeton University Press, 1977), 30.

58. Trexler, "The Magi Enter Florence," 129–32 . See Levi-Pisetzky, *Storia del Costume in Italia,* 2, 9, pl. 3, *La Famiiglia del Conte Stefano Pooro,* Oratorio, Lentate, fresco, 1370. See Levi-Pisetzky's discussion at the bottom of the page. By 1370 the long belted robe had been replaced by a pleated shorter garment but the belt remained an important component of costume for men. See also her discussion, 77–81.

59. Trexler, "The Magi Enter Florence," 139. See also Trexler, *The Journey of the Magi* (Princeton: Princeton University Press, 1997).

60. Trexler, *The Journey of the Magi,* 119.

61. Trexler, "The Magi Enter Florence,"129.

62. See M.J. Gegnano, "La Bottega degli Embriachi a proposito di opere ignoto o poco note," *Arte Lombardo 5* (1960): 221–28.

63. Reginald Abbott, "What Becomes a Legend Most?: Fur in the Medieval Romance," *Dress* 21 (1994): 5.

64. The great merchant banking houses were precipitated into bankruptcy by the repudiation of loans on the part of their royal debtors, a lesson about regal condition which does not seem to have affected the Florentine fascination with the legend of the Three Kings.

65. This does not mean that women and youth might not, in turn, attempt to accomplish their own purposes through fashion. The *sapientes* did not dress in explicitly sexual clothes. Apparently, at times women tended to display their shoulders and breasts more than in the past and young men appear to have challenged their elders with tight hose, pointed shoes and, later, codpieces. See Lois Banner, "The Fashionable Sex," *History Today 42* (1992): 40; Patricia Simons, "Alert and Erect: Masculinity in Some Italian Renaissance Portraits of Fathers and Sons," in *Gender Rhetorics: Postures of Dominance and Submission in History,* ed. Richard Trexler, Medieval and Renaissance Studies and Texts, 113

(Binghampton: CEMERS, SUNY, 1994), 163–86; and Jacqueline Murray, "Hiding Behind the Universal Man: Male Sexuality in the Middle Ages," in *Handbook of Medieval Sexuality,* eds. Vern Bullough and James A. Brundage (New York: Garland, 1996), 123–46.

66. Stuard, "The Adriatic Trade in Silver," 113.

67. Diane Owen Hughes, "Distinguishing Signs: Ear-rings, Jews and Franciscan Rhetoric in the Italian Renaissance City," *Past and Present 112* (1989): 3–59.

68. Daniel Miller, *Material Culture and Mass Consumption,* 136.

Men and Masculinity in Late Medieval London Civic Culture
Governance, Patriarchy and Reputation[1]

SHANNON McSHEFFREY

In 1489, Thomas Wulley sued Margaret Isot in the Consistory Court of the diocese of London in order to enforce a contract of marriage he claimed had been made eighteen years before. Several witnesses appeared on Thomas's behalf to testify about the circumstances in which marriage vows were exchanged. In 1471, they reported Thomas and Margaret had become sexually involved, much to the consternation of Thomas's parents, who did what they could to break it up. One witness reported that Thomas's mother, finding him and Margaret in bed together one day in Margaret's house, hid Thomas's shoes so that he would have to embarrass himself by walking home in Margaret's footwear.[2] But according to the testimony of John Calton, at that time the local constable, neither his father's nor his mother's influence could deter Thomas from Margaret's company. At length, Thomas's father went to Calton in his capacity as constable and, telling him that Thomas was associating with Margaret "most suspiciously," asked Calton to arrest the pair and take them to the Counter, the London sheriffs' prison. The illicit relations between Thomas and Margaret were not news to John Calton; he reported to the court that he had been hearing for about three months that the neighbors in St. John's Street suspected them of fornication because they spent so much time alone together. Thomas's father told Calton that Thomas and Margaret would be lying together that night in the house of one of Calton's neighbors, John Cracow, if he wanted to catch them in the act.

Later that night at about ten o'clock, Calton went to Cracow's house. As he reported in his deposition, he brought with him four other men, neighbors who had been his dinner guests that evening. When Calton knocked on Cracow's door there was no answer, but the door was open, so he and the other men with him walked into the house and began to search for Thomas and Margaret. Calton found them eventually, in a basement room, both hurriedly trying to put on their clothes—as Calton testified, he spotted Thomas wearing only his doublet, with his gown around his head and his hose and shoes under his arm. Calton took the offending couple, along with Cracow, to his own house to question them in front of the four men who had assisted him in the arrest and some of their wives (still at Calton's house for the dinner party). Cracow, when accused of having harbored fornicators, claimed that he received them in his house because they were, in fact, husband and wife. Calton, now unsure whether he should take Thomas and Margaret to prison, as normal procedure would prescribe, turned to Thomas and asked, "Whi drawyst thou suspiciosly to this woman," when, as he said, "it is not thi faders wil thou shuldest have hir?" Thomas replied, "For i purpose, to wedde hir." To ensure that Thomas was telling the truth, Calton prompted the two of them there and then to exchange vows of present consent to marry again. Even if Thomas had lied about the previous contract, the second contract, before a host of respectable witnesses, itself created an indissoluble union. As marital intercourse was by no means illegal, Calton had no choice then but to let the couple go.[3]

The story that John Calton and the other witnesses told about Margaret Isot and Thomas Wulley, when they appeared before the ecclesiastical court, poses many questions for us about life and relations between the sexes in the late medieval English metropolis. The publicity of and preoccupation with sexual relationships, the openness and permeability of domestic space, the concern shown by Thomas Wulley's parents regarding his irregular relationship with Margaret, and Thomas's father's eventual resort to the local ward official, the constable, to proceed against Thomas when paternal authority failed are all matters of interest to the history of masculinity in the late medieval civic milieu of London.

In this essay, I will explore the nature of masculinity in fifteenth-century London, especially in relation to marriage, sexuality, reputation and political life. At the heart of this inquiry will lie an examination of three key concepts: patriarchy, governance and reputation. The word "patriarchy" is used here in the sense of the ideal of the father-ruled household, an ideal that in the late medieval English urban world extended beyond the family into society as a whole, so that men, rather than women, and particularly older men, were seen as the natural rulers and governors of both family and society. Natural rule depended on status, as well as gender and age: those with the greatest duties and the most considerable power were those defined in medieval documents as "most honorable," "most worthy" or "most substantial." Duties of the patriarch included involvement in civic politics, governance of social relationships in the neighborhood (especially marriage and illicit sexual unions) and responsibility for the conduct of those living in the patriarch's household. These ideals of governance and patriarchy were by no means unproblematic, as historians like Lyndal Roper have pointed out in relation to early modern German cities; they posed difficulties not only for those excluded from natural rule (notably women), but also for those whose duty it was to govern. Sexuality and its relation to reputation, for instance, was a particular site of conflict. Although some historians have recently posited a relatively simple double standard relating to sexual misconduct in late medieval society (for women extramarital sex was clearly wrong and disreputable, whereas for men notions of morality or reputability in relation to fornication or adultery were irrelevant), I will argue that ideas about appropriate male sexual behavior were far more complex than this. Male sexual reputability was contested territory, as notions of self-governance, Christian morality and honor battled with an ethic in which male status and identity were defined by sexual conquest.[4] I will examine two aspects of masculinity in late medieval London: first, the duty and privilege of senior men to regulate marriage and other relationships among those under their governance; and second, the importance of self-rule and sexual propriety in the maintenance of masculine reputation.

MARRIAGE AND REGULATION OF BEHAVIOR

Marriage was, in many ways, the foundation of late medieval patriarchy—not only in the authority the husband was given over the wife and the responsibility the head of the household bore for those who lived under his roof, but in the more diffuse influence that respectable older men, the fathers of the community, exercised over the making of marriages in their families, households, neighborhoods and wards. As part of their larger responsibilities to supervise social relationships among those over whom they had authority, it was the duty and privilege of senior men to ensure that suitable marriages were made, and unsuitable unions prevented or stopped. While there is little evidence to support the old chestnut that all medieval marriages were arranged by fathers or lords—

below elite social levels, at least, late medieval English men and women usually chose their mates themselves—at the same time, a decision as important as the choice of spouse was not made without recourse to the advice, help and sometimes the consent of the important people in a young man's or young woman's life.[5] Women as well as men were involved in the making of marriages, especially women in a position of some authority and responsibility, such as a mistress or a widowed mother, but the roles women played tended to be more informal than those played by men. A man and woman contemplating marriage did not make decisions about this all-important life step in a vacuum but surrounded by families, friends, employers and neighbors who gave advice, acted as go-betweens and witnessed the exchange of vows. The poet William Langland assumed the participation of intermediaries, fathers and friends, as well as the man and woman, themselves in the formation of a marriage:

> And thus was wedloke ywrou3t • with a mene persone;
> First bi the faderes wille • and the frendes conseille,
> And sytthenes bi assent of hem-self • as thei two my3te acorde.[6]

The "mene persone" and the "frendes" in Langland's poem are evinced also in the records of marital litigation from the fifteenth century,[7] their roles frequently proving instrumental in courtship and entry into marriage.

Langland's "mene persone" is represented most clearly in the Latin depositions in ecclesiastical marriage cases by a go-between called a mediator who helped to bring about a marriage between a man and a woman. Both women and men could act as intermediaries, although the scope of the mediator's activity depended somewhat on gender. Women's roles were most frequently informal and especially involved the conveyance of gifts from one partner to the other.[8] Occasionally, mistresses acting on behalf of their female servants played a more substantial role in proposing matches,[9] although this was relatively unusual. Men's roles also included the more subtle and informal aspects of the courtship game, but extended to more formal participation in the making of the marriage. Senior men in a position of authority—frequently with a familial relationship with one of the principals, but often enough simply "interested parties"—played a particularly important role in the process of courtship and marriage. An older male intermediary sometimes prompted couples who were keeping company to take the next step; he might act as a go-between in negotiations before the agreement to marry;

and he might officiate in a formal sense at the exchange of consent.[10] In the context of marriage decisions, the word "friend," by which fifteenth-century people indicated the important people in their lives, both kin and non-kin,[11] most often designated older men from whom a young man or woman could seek advice or even consent. In the case of orphans, for instance, the word might be used to denote guardians.[12] By participating in the formation of the marriage bond, senior men sought to ensure that suitable matches were made, that the proper forms were followed and, ultimately, that the patriarchal social order was maintained.

A typical intermediary's role was played by William Love, an embroiderer and parish clerk of St. Botolph, London. He testified in the 1469 case of Robert Pope c. Lucy Bragge that he had been "a mediator between them, and he had made efforts to induce them to contract marriage between them, having been asked to do so by both parties."[13] William Love, whose status as parish clerk no doubt made him an authoritative figure, was evidently not related to either Robert Pope or Lucy Bragge[14]—indeed, intermediaries were ideally disinterested or at least equally interested in both parties. At Pope's request, Love privately asked Lucy Bragge if she was committed to any other man and if she was interested in Pope. He then relayed her reply back to Pope—she was free of commitments and she was agreeable to speak and drink with him. Soon after, according to Love, the pair formally contracted marriage following a Sunday dinner in his house, Love himself acting as witness. He testified that his young stepdaughter and servant also heard the contract, eavesdropping from a balcony overlooking the hall where Love, Lucy and Robert were eating. Love's wife Alice deposed that after this contract, she also participated in the courtship, albeit in a more informal capacity, bringing gifts from one to the other.[15] This sponsorship of a marriage by an older married man, sometimes with the help of his wife, was characteristic of the path many couples followed toward matrimony.

The rituals performed and the signals sent during a courtship often involved and sometimes required the participation of other parties besides the principals, bearing gifts, questions and information. John Miller, for example, a seventy-year-old weaver, went one morning to visit his widowed stepdaughter, Joan Cardif of Walthamstow, Essex, at the request of an admirer, John Brocher; Miller brought with him a gift of fish from Brocher and the message that Joan was to cook the fish for dinner, because Brocher was bringing some people to her house to dine. Cardif received the fish happily and then asked Miller if this gift indicated that John Brocher wanted to marry her. Miller replied "that if she could find it in her heart to love him as her husband, John would be hers forever."[16] Miller and Cardif then discussed how much money Brocher had and what his debts were, and Cardif offered her stepfather forty shillings to give to Brocher to pay off his debts.[17]

This must have been prearranged, at least to some extent; Cardif and Brocher obviously knew one another and had probably engaged in some courting, although apparently they had not directly discussed marriage. But Brocher's conveyance, through Miller, of food for Cardif to prepare (a customary duty of a wife) served as a signal that he was ready to ask the question. Cardif picked up the signal and asked her stepfather what Brocher's intentions were, expecting Miller to know the answer. Indeed, he did: he was not only aware that John Brocher wished to "be hers forever" but also knew all about his goods and debts. Both Brocher and Cardif had thus separately discussed the possibility of marriage with Miller before they discussed it with each other. Use of a go-between in the delicate matter of proposing marriage prevented at least some of the humiliation and embarrassment that a rejection might cause. Miller, presumably privately, conveyed Cardif's response to Brocher when Brocher arrived for dinner. When the question was later formally and more publicly asked, the answer was already known.

But the mediation in this and many other cases did not end at this point. Depositions indicate that often—perhaps commonly—vows of present consent (creating a canonically indissoluble marriage) were exchanged by a couple in a domestic setting, before witnesses, in a ritualized ceremony. These technically private or clandestine marriages were probably not performed to escape ecclesiastical involvement but rather, as Richard Helmholz has suggested, as a prelude to solemnization of the marriage in a church.[18] A fifteenth-century wedding was not a discrete event but a process;[19] after the exchange of vows in a home, "the public voice," as the depositions say, often held the couple to be husband and wife, although they would sometimes not cohabit until after a church wedding.[20] Canonically, of course, they *were* in fact and indissolubly husband and wife if they had properly exchanged vows of present consent; if they had exchanged vows of future consent, the union could be dissolved if unconsummated, but only by mutual agreement.[21] The exact words spoken were thus very important. Because of this, the formal exchange of consent in a private home was often arranged and directed by a senior man, who knew the rituals and the correct words to ensure a proper, canonically correct marriage.[22]

The responsible party in the case of John Brocher c. Joan Cardif was a local yeoman named John Monk of Enfield, one of the friends Brocher brought over for dinner the day he sent Cardif some fish. Monk himself testified that after they had dined and were all sitting together in the hall of Joan's house, Monk questioned Joan before all the witnesses (there were five there altogether, all men except for Joan), asking her if she was free from all contracts of marriage and whether she could find it in her heart to love John Brocher as her husband. She responded that she was indeed free and that she wished to take Brocher as her husband, because since the death of her first husband she had not seen any other man she so loved. Monk then asked Brocher whether he wished to have Joan as his wife, and he also answered yes. At this point they were ready to exchange formal consent: John Brocher, following John Monk's instructions [*secundum informacionem eiusdem Johannis Monk*], took Cardif by her right hand and said to her, "I, John, take the, Johan, to my weddid wif, the to love and kepe and as a man owght to love his wife, and therto I pliʒt the my trowth." And then Cardif, again at Monk's instruction, took Brocher's right hand and said to him, "'I, Johan, take the, John, to my weddid husband, the to love and to kepe as a woman ought to do her husband and therto I pliʒt the my feith." But, as Monk interjected, she had not used the proper matrimonial words [*verba matrimonialia*]—she should say "ther to I pliʒt the my feith *and trouth.*" Joan, presumably making a distinction between present and future consent,[23] refused to plight her troth without consulting her mother first. A week later, the couple repeated their vows before Joan Cardif's mother, who gave her consent.[24]

John Monk acted as a presider in the exchange of consent, which followed a ritualized pattern that most other such contracts in the depositions also observed.[25] The concern for the exact words spoken was evinced not only by the court, which might be expected to interest itself in canonical form, but also by the lay people conducting the marriages. It was part of Monk's duty to lead the couple to speak the right words, the *verba matrimonialia*, that would make a marriage.[26] The presider, invariably male and usually apparently senior to the others present, took the place of and almost certainly imitated the priest, who solemnized the church wedding in much the same way. Indeed, one couple exchanging vows in a private home were, in fact, directed by a priest, the rector of St. John Zachary, London.[27] The presider was frequently unrelated to either of the principals, and sometimes was of higher social position; John Monk, for example, was a "yoman." There may have been some concern that the man who directed the couple to exchange vows be an objective

party, in order to prevent accusations that one or the other of the principals was suborned. In one case, where the fathers of both parties were
present, each father asked the ritual questions ("Will you, Lawrence, take
Maude . . ."; "Will you, Maude, take Lawrence . . .") in turn, so that the
vows were taken twice, once under the direction of each father, perhaps
to provide a balance of interests.[28] There is no evidence that men such as
William Love or John Monk received or hoped to receive any financial
compensation for their services as mediators or presiders, as might be the
case for nobility or gentlefolk who sometimes used marriage brokers.[29] It
seems that, in relation to marriages of lower-status people, such activities
were viewed as the duty and privilege of men of a certain age and status.

Older men felt it their duty not only to promote marriages between
couples who asked their assistance, but also to prevent relationships from
going too far without benefit of matrimony. Masters, for instance,
queried the intentions of young men too frequently hanging about the
house visiting with female servants. John Ely was courting Agnes Whit-
ingdon when he was confronted by her master, a man named Hawkyn,
who asked him if he wanted to marry Agnes. Eventually Hawkyn pres-
sured Ely to make a contract with her.[30] William Hylle, tailor of London,
similarly testified that William Chapman had frequented his home so
many times that finally he asked Chapman why he came so often. Chapman replied that he came out of love for Hylle's servant, Joan Walter.
Soon after, then, presumably at William Hylle's arrangement, Chapman
came to the house and, in the presence of a number of witnesses gathered
for the occasion, he and Joan exchanged vows.[31] Joan Audely testified
that she had heard her father questioning John Crosby about his numerous visits to his house, and Crosby replied that he wished to marry Isabel
Hamond, Audely's servant. There and then, Hamond and Crosby exchanged consent.[32]

The onus to confirm honorable intentions in the cases cited here was
not on the female servant but on the male suitor. Only rarely were female
servants asked about the nature of their relationship with a man.[33] As
men were assumed to take the initiative, employers occasionally felt it
was necessary to prompt the man's action toward proper ends (marriage), rather than illicit ones (a sexual relationship not leading to marriage). Action was assumed to be in the male sphere, whether it ruin or
protect a woman's good name; women were left with reactive roles. In
this view, young women and their reputations were in need of protection
and it was the responsibility of senior men, especially, to provide it.

The concern of senior men with moral probity went beyond the patriarchal household and the master-servant relationship into the community as a whole. Proper moral standards and publicly acknowledged marriages were of common concern, and senior men, as the patriarchs of the community, felt a responsibility to police relationships outside as well as inside their households. Those only tangentially related to a misbehaving couple could seek to move them onto a straight and narrow path. John Gosnell of the parish of Walthamstow, for instance, testified that he had confronted Richard Heth "because it was publicly said that Richard too suspiciously frequented the home of Agnes [Waltham]." Gosnell said that he told Richard that he would not tolerate such frequent visits unless he knew whether Richard intended to marry Agnes. At length, Richard admitted that Agnes was his wife and Gosnell directed them right there, through the ritual questions, to declare before witnesses their vows of present consent to marry.[34] A putative bigamist in London was urged by one of the witnesses to his first marriage to put aside his second wife and return to his original marriage bed. William Malton, a London ironmonger, told the court that he had "made many entreaties to William Hathewey to take Petronilla as his wife and dismiss the said Margaret Spyndeler, whom he held in adultery."[35] Another example of local outrage apparently prompted one of the few ex officio cases instigated by the London Consistory court.[36] Richard Ellbich had married an excommunicated woman named Alice Trehest clandestinely and outside the parish church and had lived with her and slept with her, even though she was excommunicated. John Cruse, a sixty-four-year-old tailor, reported that "most of the neighbors feel and think that this was and is true, and they speak badly of them."[37] Improper marriages were of wide community concern; they were not only canonically incorrect but also damaging to social relationships. Men like William Hathewey, who married first one woman and then another, often left the first woman in a sorry situation, with a blemished reputation and, perhaps, a child, unable canonically to remarry. It was up to other men to prevent this from happening.

When patriarchal authority was absent, when it failed or when it was insufficient, other resources were available to bolster or stand in for the father's governance. In the case with which I began this essay, Wulley c. Isot, Thomas Wulley's father's own authority was insufficient to dissuade Thomas from his undesirable relationship with Margaret Isot. In such a case, though, Thomas's father was able to make recourse to the local constable, who stepped in and arrested the fornicating couple, and even took the paternal role in the questioning after the arrest, making it clear that Thomas's relationship with Margaret was not in accordance with his father's will.[38]

Thomas Wulley's father was by no means the only man who called upon civic officialdom in his attempts to shape the behavior of his son. While some attempts to influence the marital and sexual behavior of men and women were clearly fairly informal and ad hoc, they were integrally linked to the more official recourses that were available through the civic government. Just as a merchant and citizen of London reasonably expected the mayor and chamberlain of the City to act as guardian for any orphans he might leave,[39] so also did men look to their civic government as an extension of their patriarchal authority in other ways. In particular, the ward moot juries, to whom constables might report wrongdoers such as Thomas Wulley and Margaret Isot after they had been arrested, were active in attempting to shape the behavior of the inhabitants of the local civic districts, the wards.

Ward moot inquests were convened once a year, usually in December or early January. Twelve or thirteen men appointed by the alderman (or, according to some sources, elected by the honest men of the ward from amongst themselves) formed the ward moot inquest jury. One witness before the Consistory court in 1472 described the gathering of such a body: "on a certain day within twelve days immediately following the feast of Christmas, . . . [at] a certain place commonly called Hewlyn's Place," there came "thirteen persons named and elected by Sir George Irlond, Alderman of Cordwainer Street Ward." As the witness explained, their purpose was "to inquire into and investigate crimes perpetrated in the said ward and to expell criminal persons because of their misgovernment and their crimes."[40]

From at least the end of the thirteenth century, these civic bodies had made the sexual activities of the inhabitants of the wards their business, along with such matters as keeping the roads clear and cleaning the ditches. Regulations from the reign of Edward I forward provided that ward moot inquest juries were to present common adulterers, bawds and prostitutes, and that the alderman was to order the removal from the ward of persistent offenders.[41] As the Journal of the Court of Common Council recorded in 1473, inquest juries were enjoined to

> present the names of all common bawdes, common strumpettis, and comon Strumpetmongers, or comon Puters, as well men as women, dwellyng, commyng, or repairyng unto your said Wardis. Ye shall furþeremore present the names of all persones within your said Wardes

which late hath commytted or doon any aduoutry, and the names also
of all suche persones with whom such aduoutry is doon, wheþere thei
be common Aduouterers or not.[42]

In the later fourteenth century, civic officials established more detailed
regulations for the arrest and punishment of such persons and the City
continued to use these provisions through the fifteenth century.[43] The
actual procedure in all cases is not entirely clear, but records indicate that
normally the constable or beadle of a ward arrested offenders and took
them to a jail (usually one of the sheriffs' prisons, called the Counters)
where they remained for a short time while officials decided how to proceed with the case. Some were forwarded to the ecclesiastical courts,
which themselves had a considerable business in the prosecution of sexual offences,[44] but others would later come before their local ward moot
inquest. After an appearance before the inquest, "criminal persons,"
including bawds, prostitutes, fornicators and adulterers, could be presented before the court of the mayor and the aldermen.[45] The juries themselves may have come to the Guildhall to present their findings, at least
until the 1480s, when the mayor and aldermen decreed that henceforth
only the alderman should appear with the inquests' verdicts, "eschewyng
of the grete ieopardie and perellis that haue growen by commyng of the
multitude of the same enquestis to the saide hall in tymes passed."[46] If
convicted before the mayor and aldermen, the miscreants were subject to
a number of punishments, including, for the most egregious cases,
imprisonment and banishment from the city.[47]

The ward moot inquest presentments that survive from the fifteenth
century—the Portsoken ward records for 1465–1482 being the most
extensive—tell us that arrests for sexual misbehavior were by no means
unusual.[48] The Portsoken presentments may tend to mislead us, though,
into thinking that ward officials were only interested in prostitution and
procurement—the juries there presented women, and occasionally men,
as common strumpets, harlots of their bodies, bawds and strumpetmongers. Other records, including the church-court deposition evidence,
make it clear that in other wards beadles and constables also pursued
simple fornicators and, especially, adulterers. This may indicate that
Portsoken had a particular prostitution problem or, more likely, that des-
ignating someone as a "strumpet" or a "harlot of his/her body" was to
mark them as sexually promiscuous rather than, or in addition to, accepting money for sexual favors.[49] The naming of several men as "harlots of
their bodies" in the Portsoken presentments, given the rarity of evidence

for male prostitution and for homosexuality in late medieval London, makes it probable that promiscuity rather than commercial prostitution was at issue.[50]

The laconic civic records of the proceedings give us little sense about how the arrests were made,[51] information that is crucial for understanding how constables and beadles attempted to regulate behavior and in whose interests they were acting. Somewhat ironically, more detailed evidence about how such disorders came to the attention of civic officials comes from ecclesastical court depositions. Witnesses offered testimony regarding civic attempts to control sexual misbehavior in order to impugn the trustworthiness of other deponents, or in suits involving defamation or marriage where actions by ward authorities were part of the case. These records can tell us a good deal about how relatives, neighbors and ward officials handled misbehavior.

One of the remarkable aspects of narratives of arrest, like the story of Thomas Wulley and Margaret Isot, is the apparent acceptance, on all sides, of public intrusion into domestic space.[52] John Calton, by virtue of his office, entered a neighbor's house without his permission, late in the evening, because he had reasonable cause to suspect there were fornicators on the premises. Other constables and beadles also burst into people's houses—even at four o'clock in the morning[53]—to catch offenders in the act. Robert Serle, constable in Aldgate ward, for instance, entered into Margaret Hordley's home at ten o'clock in the evening, where he found Herbert Rowland and Margaret together alone; they, like Thomas Wulley and Margaret Isot, escaped a trip to the Counter by claiming that they were married.[54] In another case, two deponents, seeking to discredit previous witnesses, reported that the beadle of the ward of Farringdon Without had arrested Joan Salman and Walter Haydon, capper, in a certain house situated in the Old Bailey. Here we catch something of the technique of surprise used in these arrests: one man guarded the door while the beadle and another man marched into the house and up into the chamber. In the chamber, they discovered Joan Salman standing next to the bed and Walter Haydon lying on it. Finding them under such suspicious circumstances, the beadle took them from there directly to the Counter.[55] In this case, as in the arrest of Thomas Wulley and Margaret Isot, other men from the neighborhood aided the beadle or constable in the apprehension of the wrongdoers.[56]

In a few cases, we learn how the beadle or the constable came to know that a couple would be engaged in illicit activities at a particular time and place; in Wulley c. Isot, Thomas Wulley's father informed the

constable where the couple would be.[57] In most cases, ward officials
probably came to know about sexual irregularities, and their likely time
and location, through the rumor networks active in every ward and
parish. Some men who came across evidence of wrongdoing did more
than talk about it: they made it their business to inform the appropriate
officials so that the behavior could be corrected or punished. John
Palmer, for instance, witnessed adultery one day in August 1471, when
he entered the house of another man, Horne Tyler (or Horne, a tyler),
between four and five in the afternoon. Going up the stairway leading to
a certain upper chamber of the house, he saw William Stevenes and
Juliana Saunder lying on a bed, having sexual intercourse. Juliana heard
Palmer and came down from the room and asked him to keep what he
had seen there secret; if he did this, she would give him a pair of hose.
Nonetheless, soon after he told the parish chaplain of St. John in Wal-
brook, the holy water clerk of the same parish, the rector of the church of
St. Mary at Hill, and the twelve men of the ward moot inquest jury that
William and Juliana had committed adultery. In John Palmer's mind,
both church and civic officials would be interested in this information.
Because of Palmer's allegations, William Stevenes was indicted before
the ward moot inquest. Witnesses claimed that, although Stevenes had up
to this point been reputed as a man of good fame, afterward his neighbors
held him in little faith.[58] Indictment before the ward moot inquest was
humiliating, embarrassing and damaging.

A ward moot inquest jury could exert considerable pressure on misbehavers to regularize their lives. In early 1472, two fornicators, Joan
Chylde and Thomas Rote, were called before their local ward moot
inquest to answer for their crime. Thomas Rote, examined first, was
asked by one of the twelve members of the jury why he associated with
Joan Chylde in this way, and Rote answered that he wanted to make Joan
his wife. Joan, too, indicated that she wished to marry, so then and there
they exchanged consent in front of those gathered for the inquest. They
kissed, and from then on they were publicly regarded as contracted to
one another.[59] The "community of the ward," as represented by the
twelve men, clearly felt that their illicit relationship was its business. The
pressure brought by the senior men upon the couple did not successfully
effect a valid marriage in this case—we know about it because Thomas
Rote failed to keep the contract. But while Thomas Rote did not wish to
honor his vow (which he later claimed was conditional), he never questioned the jury's jurisdiction in his sexual relationships.

Even when official channels were not actually used, the possibility that they might be invoked gave some men's attempts to shape behavior more authority and force. The threat of an indictment before a London civic court, and the shame that would accompany it, could in itself prove decisive. John Wellys confronted a young man named William Rote with the accusation that Rote had violated his daughter Agnes, insisting that as a consequence Rote had to marry her. When Rote denied any intercourse with Agnes, John Wellys threatened both to harm him physically (and, in fact, attacked him with a knife) and to bring him in front of the mayor and aldermen. Rote later claimed in the consistory court that he contracted marriage with Agnes Wellys that afternoon "as much out of fear for his body as out of shame of appearing before the mayor and aldermen."[60]

All men did not share equally in access to formal means of regulation: status as well as gender was an important factor. Fifteenth-century civic and ecclesiastical documents are full of descriptive phrases that are, to us, vague and ill-defined, but which, to medieval people, were nuanced and, perhaps, even precise: "*fidedigni*" [the trustworthy], "*plus sufficeauntz*" [the more substantial], "*valiores*" [the more worthy], "*boni et graves*" [good and serious men or people].[61] Clearly, it was those men of "good fame" rather than those of "ill fame" who were to share in offices; gradations of wealth and status determined where in the official hierarchy men were to serve. The phrasing of the warrant issued to aldermen to call their ward moot inquests reminds us that subtle distinctions determined the roles men were to play in the ward: the representatives chosen for the city's Common Council—the highest political post below alderman—were to be the most "sufficiant men of good & wysest discrecion"; the ward moot jury was to be staffed by "þe worthiest men of all your Ward"; and constables, scavengers and beadles, important if lower-status ward officials, were to be "honest persones."[62] Those filling the higher offices at least, from alderman through the ward moot inquest jury, often served year after year.[63]

A London man's participation in civic politics, at whatever level was suitable to his status, was one aspect of his patriarchal duty and privilege of governance. At the same time, such public service helped to define and reflect his identity as a respectable and worthy man.[64] Through formal and informal means, senior men sought to oversee the relationships of those for whom they held responsibility, including their children, their servants and sometimes their neighbors. But patriarchal duty was not only directed outwards: London men also had the responsibility to govern themselves.

GOVERNANCE AND SEXUAL MORALITY

In 1476 Alice Hobbys sued her husband, Master William Hobbys, doctor of medicine and surgery and principal physician to the king,[65] for divorce on the grounds of adultery.[66] On being questioned by the official, William admitted that, despite twenty years of marriage and five children, he had committed adultery from at least 1462, sleeping with many different women in Calais, Saint-Omer, Southwark, the City of London and other places. Alice, however, had been unaware of his infidelities, he said, until she came to hear of it around Christmas 1475, first from their neighbors and then from his own confession. Since then, Alice had refused to fulfill the marital debt, he complained, contemptuously rejecting his embraces. Several other witnesses came forward to testify in the case. Two surgeons, Richard Chambyr and John Staveley, who had joined Hobbys as part of the king's military expedition to France in the summer of 1475,[67] testified that Hobbys had misbehaved while overseas. Chambyr deposed that while both he and William Hobbys were in the town of Péronne (in Picardy), he saw William lying on a bed with a prostitute, both of them naked. He told William at the time, he testified, that he marvelled [*mirando*] that William would want to commit adultery with a prostitute. John Staveley testified that he had seen William Hobbys entering brothels on many occasions in Calais, Saint-Omer and Péronne, and that William used to stay there suspiciously, committing adultery, as Staveley believed, with the said prostitutes. William also resorted to prostitutes while at home, according to other witnesses. Thomas Rolf and Robert Halyday,[68] likewise barber-surgeons, both told the official that a year ago the previous June, they had been called to a brothel in Southwark to minister to the brothelkeeper. While there, Rolf and Halyday happened to look into another room, where they saw William Hobbys lying on a bed with a prostitute, described as a "young girl" [*juvencula*]. Like Richard Chambyr, they too "marvelled" at William's illicit deed [*facto illicito*]. Soon after, the older of the two, Robert Halyday, confronted William Hobbys and upbraided him for his nefarious deed, with the intention, he claimed, of persuading William to eschew such behavior in future. After hearing these witnesses and considering the motions put forward by the lawyers for each of the parties to the case, the official granted a decree of divorce, noting that William had rashly violated the matrimonial bed by committing adultery. Henceforth, William and Alice would not be required to consort or cohabit, nor to render the conjugal debt.[69]

Some recent scholarship has argued that adultery like Hobbys's would have been seen as normal by his wife and largely irrelevant to his coworkers and neighbors—several historians have asserted that while women's sexual behavior was central to their reputation and their identity, men's sexual conduct inside or outside marriage was largely immaterial.[70] Yet, at least according to their depositions, two men, marvelling at his unusual behavior, felt it necessary to chide William Hobbys, perhaps the most prominent man in their profession in the land, for his adultery.[71] In their testimony, the witnesses portrayed themselves as honest, upright men who found Hobbys's behavior to be both unusual and reprehensible. The similarity of some aspects of their depositions may indicate some coaching and coordination of the witnesses by Alice Hobbys's proctor or lawyer (a common aspect of marital litigation), but the sentiments they expressed would have had to be credible to be effective.[72] In other cases, it is clear that disapproval of irregular sexual unions was more than rhetoric designed for the ears of ecclesiastical officials: Thomas Wulley's father and mother, for instance, took considerable pains to end his fornication with Margaret Isot, a relationship that they clearly felt was dishonorable to him and to them. Moreover, when parental dissuasions were shown to be ineffective, Thomas's father could rely on the local constable and a posse of neighbors to arrest the misbehaving couple, a group that apparently did not find his objections to his son's fornication offensive or foolish.

These pieces of evidence do not make sense if we accept that men's reputations were not based in any way on their sexual behavior. While I, too, would argue for a gendered notion of reputation in late medieval London, I would argue against a full-blown double standard—in other words, men's sexual behavior *was* relevant to their reputations and sexual impropriety, such as that evinced in the cases of William Hobbys and Thomas Wulley, could potentially be as damaging to men's good names as to the good names of women.[73] Late medieval patriarchy brought with it the concept of governance: not just the rule of men over women, but also the responsibility of men to use that rule wisely. In addition, each man was expected to rule himself and contain his own lustful will. The limits of respectable behavior were placed differently for men and for women, but by no means was a man's sexual life irrelevant to his good name. Indeed, throughout England, the later decades of the fifteenth century witnessed increasing anxiety about sexual misbehavior, part of a larger concern with disorder and misgovernance.[74]

For both sexes, sexual misbehavior was public, open and notorious, and it symbolized lack of good governance and proper rule. These notions of publicity and governance, however, were gendered and, thus, were constituted very differently for men and for women. Men were the public actors in medieval society; it was they who participated formally in government, served on juries, operated in the most visible roles in the world of commerce. Public activity of the right kind in many ways defined the respectable male. Not so for the respectable female: late medieval London women's lives were much less circumscribed than those of their sisters in the Mediterranean world,[75] but a "public"[76] life for a woman was connected with disreputability. Similarly, the ideal of good governance was gendered. For a woman, to be governed wisely usually implied obedience to properly constituted authorities; for a man, governance could imply his submission to a father or an employer (especially as a youth), but also his rule over his dependents and his own self-rule. Women were, of course, still responsible for their own actions, but to a lesser extent than were men; women who acted in an unruly way were often described as having been "enticed and steered" into such actions by an evil and unscrupulous person.[77]

A crucial aspect of sexual misbehavior was its publicity or notoriousness; indeed, it was one's *reputation* rather than one's actions that was important in a society that placed huge importance on rumor and fame—knowledge which embraced, in other words, both what other people knew about a person and what they thought they knew. For women, acting in the public realm was frequently associated in such rumors with sexual misbehavior. This was particularly true, of course, for the most public of women, the prostitute.[78] Conversely, a man's ability to perform a public role relied on his reputation as a sober and honest man. In 1494, for instance, William Huntyngfeld defamed a woman named Cecily Clerk by calling her a "strong hor of her tong," and suggested, moreover, that Cecily's husband, John, should cede his place at the ward moot inquest to his wife. This both challenged John Clerk's right as a man of a certain status to act publicly and at the same time impugned Cecily's reputation as a respectable woman, since women normally appeared at the ward moot inquest only when charged with a sexual offence. As a result of Huntyngfeld's words, Cecily was forced to purge herself of adultery before the Lord Commissary.[79] As this case shows, a woman's reputation for chastity and respectability depended not only on her physical integrity but also on her representation in public by a man; a man's reputation for honesty, good fame and status conversely depended on his ability to protect and control his dependants and to act for them in the political arena.

Governance was a crucial concept in fifteenth-century notions of appropriate comportment. All were to be properly governed, but there were significant gender differences regarding who was responsible for the governance. For women, absence of proper rule rendered them wild and uncontrollable. A twelve-year-old servant girl, Joan, who constantly ran away from her employers and was known to spend the afternoon in a bawd's house with a "yong felowe," was described as "of right wanton disposicion."[80] While such lack of restraint reflected partly on a woman's own internal self-control, it also implied, explicitly or implicitly, absence of male control or, at least, absence of proper, reputable and righteous male control. Sometimes sexual misbehavior in women meant a turning upside-down of true governance. Herman Ryng, a Hanseatic merchant living in London, complained to the chancellor in the 1490s that he was busy about his work in the Steelyard when he was approached by a certain Joan White, singlewoman, about whom it was reliably known that she was "wont to daunce and make revell in hir maisters hous, some tyme in mannys clothing and somtyme naked." Just as her master failed to govern her properly, so also did she offer Herman a form of perverted rule: Ryng said that she presented herself to him sexually, "to be at his commaundement."[81] Although Ryng himself was perhaps not well-governed (he was summoned before the Commissary Court several times in 1490 and 1491 to answer to charges of fornication and adultery),[82] he used conventionally gendered notions of governance and rule to frame his Chancery petition. In a similar way, a husband petitioned the chancellor because Thomas Hervy, a canon of St. Mary Overie, allegedly enticed his wife away; as a result, complained the husband, she was "oonly at his [Hervy's] rewle and comandement."[83] This adulterous relationship, the husband implied, made a mockery of true governance, where a wife was under the rule and commandment of her husband, her natural ruler.

The strictures placed on women's behavior were different from those placed on men: women's good name was constructed largely[84] through others' knowledge about their sexual behavior, which in turn was related to their governance by a properly constituted male authority. But men also had to guard against public sexual misbehavior if they wanted to retain good reputations. Their governance, like that of women, could also be related to their submission to proper authority, but men's rule was much more frequently self-governance. Sexual misbehavior that showed their lack of control of themselves, their misgoverned state, could result in disreputability and ill fame. Men accused of misdeeds or bad behavior commonly pledged significant sums of money to the chamberlain of the City that they would henceforth be "of good rule and honest conversation."[85] Respectable people shunned men charged with sexual misconduct: when Anastasia Reygate accused Thomas Hay of committing adultery in the home of a local bawd, witnesses reported that many people, including his wife, avoided his company and there was a good deal of murmuring against him.[86] Similarly, when William Boteler told people that John Stampe had carnally known Joan Folke, the "status and good fame of both Joan Folke and John Stampe were greatly injured."[87] Indeed, a man's sexual misbehavior might provide his wife with justification to withdraw herself from his governance: a Cornish woman, told by three men that her husband, away serving his master, was enjoying the embraces of other women, refused to obey her husband any longer.[88] Male adultery could apparently occasion a man's loss of his rights to govern and, indeed, it could even serve (if infrequently) as the grounds for a divorce *a mensa et thoro,* as we have seen already in the case of Hobbys c. Hobbys.[89]

Were allegations of sexual misbehavior more damaging for women than for men? Quite possibly: while sexual reputation was significant for men, the impugning of a woman's chastity potentially had more serious repercussions. Witnesses in several cases where women claimed defamation swore that these women lost value on the marriage market because of allegations of sexual misbehavior.[90] In the later fifteenth century, when women had few economic options apart from marriage,[91] such attacks were potentially very damaging. For men, marriageability was not at issue, or at least not in the same way; the sources do not indicate the same direct relationship between a man's marriage prospects and his sexual reputation that applied to women. But while virginity per se may have been less important to men on the marriage market than to women, a reputation for misrule rather than serious and sober behavior certainly harmed their overall good names.

Witnesses regarded both men and women accused of inappropriate sexual behavior as generally disreputable; male adulterers and fornicators were mentioned in the same breath as thieves, the indigent, the idle and even actors. John Waldron, who described himself as a sawyer living in the precinct of the hospital of St. Katherine by the Tower, testified in the London Commissary Court case of Gilis c. Broun in October 1491.[92] In December of the same year, a number of witnesses were brought forward to impugn Waldron's testimony. In attempting to convince the court that Waldron's testimony was unreliable, the deponents focused on a number of different kinds of misconduct that included poverty, dishonesty and sexual irregularity, calling him a perjurer, a vagabond, a bawd and an adulterer. They testified that he had been the landlord of Stewside brothels in Southwark and that he lived there adulterously with a woman named Joan, who had another husband. After the Bishop's Official of the diocese of Winchester had summoned them for their adultery and enjoined penance on them, Waldron and Joan fled Southwark and went to live together in the precinct of the hospital of St. Katherine by the Tower. There, the witnesses reported, Waldron continued his bawdry, took up with another woman and consorted with prostitutes, vagabonds and thieves, gaining a reputation as an adulterer and a thief himself. He also associated himself with a band of infamous and perjurious men in Westminster called "le Knyghtis of the post." Waldron's fellow witness, William Alston, was also discredited as a man of ill fame, a vagabond and an adulterer; he had abandoned his wife to go to live in St. Katherine's precinct, leaving her to make her living by shameful means. There he committed adultery with many women, as he himself had admitted before the honest men of the neighborhood.[93] As with women, sexual impropriety in men was seen as part of a complex of generally bad behavior; for men, it was related especially to the sorts of faults associated with men who refused their responsibilities to their families and to their communities and threatened other men's rule over their dependents.[94] The public humiliation of an indictment for adultery or fornication—often accompanied by several mortifying hours in the stocks—could not have improved a man's (or a woman's) position in a town. Witnesses, discrediting the testimony of Thomas Carpenter of Enfield, disdainfully reported not only that he was poor and out of work, but that he was widely known to have been put in the stocks in Stratford Langthorne for his adultery with two women.[95]

Unquestionably both men and women were liable to prosecution for sexual misbehavior, although the focus of official interest might shift from men to women at different times. In fifteenth-century London, secular and ecclesiastical officials charged both men and women with adultery and fornication through a process of presentment by local juries and other such bodies.[96] Civic juries were not consistent throughout the fifteenth century in their presentments; as Marjorie McIntosh has shown, concern about misbehavior of various kinds tended to ebb and flow over the decades.[97] At some points, London civic officials were apparently more interested in men's sexual misconduct than in women's; at other times the focus reversed.[98]

Even at times when civic officials targeted men, were all men equally liable to indictments for sexual misbehavior? Was all extramarital sexual activity in men seen as disreputable? Were lower-status men, for instance, more or less likely to find rumors and accusations about sexual misbehavior damaging to their fame? It is certainly plausible that men with little influence were more vulnerable than men of higher status: disreputability was frequently connected with poverty, honesty with substance.[99] Wealthier men were certainly not immune, however, from accusations of sexual misbehavior, as Master William Hobbys found out. Other wealthier, high-status men also found themselves subject to prosecutions of various kinds. In a 1445 case, the ward moot inquest of Farringdon Without indicted George Fynse, "esquire," for "open fornication and adultery" and he was imprisoned for some time.[100] Alexander Marchall, son of a rich merchant and father-in-law of a "gentleman," was, despite his status, also arrested and imprisoned for adultery in 1471. Witnesses to the case testified before the mayor's court that the beadle of Candlewick Street ward

> abought xj of the Clok afore mydnyght founde a woman in the Chambre of the said Alexander sittyng by his beddes sidd and no moo persones beyng with theym, wherupon the same Symon [the beadle] brought the same Alexander and þe said woman into the Countre.[101]

This behavior was not appropriate to his station, and Alexander's father, Robert Marchall, a man of considerable wealth, had, in fact, made Alexander's good and virtuous governance a condition of inheritance. But, as the executors of Robert's will said, "the governaunce of þe said Alexandre after the decesse of his said Fader was neiþer good nor vertuous but yave hym to Riotte and vices," including adultery "with divers women," so they argued in the mayor's court that he should not have been able to inherit his father's estate.[102] Nor were the strictures placed on Alexander Marchall by his father unprecedented; at least one other young man, when sent by his father at a "tender age" to study law at Thavie's Inn, was bound by his father to govern himself properly or forfeit £20, a very considerable sum.[103]

At what point did sexual activity outside the marriage bed become "misbehavior"? Was occasional and discreet fornication more acceptable than notorious or excessive sexual adventures (as in the cases of Alexander Marchall, George Fynse or William Hobbys)? Letters from the late fifteenth-century merchant family, the Celys, reveal that it was common for young unmarried merchants of the Staple to keep mistresses in

Calais, where they often spent several years in their twenties learning the trade. The Cely letters seem to indicate (although by no means conclusively) that such philandering ceased upon return to England and marriage.[104] Perhaps what was tolerable at one stage of life ceased to be suitable after crossing over into the next. Or perhaps it was the fact that this activity was away from home, out of the sight of London society, that made it acceptable. Marchall's and Fynse's misbehavior, on the other hand, was local and, apparently, very public and notorious. As the mayor and sheriffs of the City of London argued in 1446, the City had jurisdiction over various disturbances of the peace, including *public* adultery, perhaps making a distinction between the sin (a matter for ecclesiastical correction) and the threat to order constituted by open and notorious sexual misbehavior.[105]

It is also possible that there was a conflict between "bourgeois" and "aristocratic" moral values in relation to extramarital sexual behavior for men; objections to noblemen or gentlemen who used London as a sexual playground may have lain behind presentments of men like Marchall and Fynse or, indeed, accusations against the women with whom they allegedly had relations. In 1483, two women were accused of committing adultery with a Master William Paston, likely either William II or William III Paston of Paston letters fame.[106] In the second case, a woman and her husband successfully claimed that she had been defamed when neighbors spread the following story about her:

> Mawde Nesche is a stronge hore and a stronge strumpet for Master William Pastone schuld leue in a voutry with hyr and had a do with her in her howse and sent hys meny down to kepe the dore and he kepyt her in a howse in seynt Georgys fyld as a stronge hore and harlot as sche ys.[107]

While the defamatory story was told about Maude Nesche rather than William Paston and the venom directed primarily at her, nonetheless, there is also an air of resentment against such men and their ability to call upon a "meny" (retinue) to guard the door when they engaged in their adulterous activities.

No doubt Londoners of whatever station disagreed about the appropriateness of extramarital sexual activity for men: the limits seem to have been contested territory, some seeing sex outside marriage as a blameless natural tendency in men, others viewing it as a venial sin, and yet others regarding it as a very serious fault. On the one hand, London and environs abounded with prostitutes and brothels, designed to service male needs and, as Ruth Karras has argued, effectively tolerated by the authorities.[108] Moreover, as Lyndal Roper has reminded us, the uncivilized, wild, out-of-control male behavior that civic ordinances sought to suppress was, nonetheless, integral to constructions of masculinity, and, indeed, of governance.[109] A case appearing before the Court of Aldermen in 1515 shows the importance of virility and sexual prowess in male reputation: Robert Harding testified that he had bedded the "whore" Katherine Worsley simply to prove that he could, because otherwise Katherine might tell women in the parish that he was impotent and scuttle his courtship of a wealthy widow.[110] On the other hand, male fornicators and adulterers were presented by local juries and churchwardens to ecclesiastical and secular authorities, just as female misbehavers were, indicating that at least some men thought that male sexual misbehavior was a problem to be corrected. Our sources do not easily allow us to measure these differences of opinion.

Some historians have argued, however, that the late fifteenth century witnessed a shift in attitudes toward adultery and fornication. While concern with sexual misbehavior was by no means novel in 1450, there are suggestions that such concern became more acute from midcentury, perhaps related to a tightening of the English economy.[111] We may see, in the later fifteenth century, an attempt by men of the civic elites to redefine their roles to include proper sexual behavior as integral to the conduct of the respectable patriarch. Civic ordinances of 1492 from the city of Coventry, for instance, connected good governance, appropriate sexual behavior and enjoyment of the fruits of wealth and power. Officials were concerned not only about women "of evell name" who corrupted the honor of a town or about the behavior of apprentices, but also about the moral lives of the city's governing class as well: mayors, past mayors and members of the ruling Common Council were enjoined to maintain a flawless personal life or to face removal from office. Indeed, higher standards of behavior were applied to those of more elevated political position, indicating that the Coventry civic leaders felt that their status behooved them to lead an exemplary life.[112] Londoners may have practiced the same ideas even if they did not codify them: in the 1440s, a London sheriff's clerk was removed from his office in perpetuity because of fornication.[113]

For both men and women, then, perceptions of sexual behavior were an aspect of reputation. Inappropriate heterosexual behavior in men did not necessarily transgress gender norms in the way that sodomy or cross-dressing might have, as the fascinating case of John Rykener, a tranvestite prostitute, shows.[114] But in the sense that gender was performative, as Judith Butler argues,[115] sexual misbehavior was an important element in the construction of the disorderly and misgoverned man. Reputation, like gender identity, was continually forged, both by the individual and by others, through their reaction to their knowledge about the individual's actions; in a sense, reputation was a story that assigned meanings to actions, written and rewritten by those who told and heard it. The same actions might be interpreted differently depending on the actor, on the interpreter, on the circumstances. The construction of reputation and the meaning assigned to sexual activities (rendering them proper or improper, reputable or disreputable) were shaped particularly by the gender of the actor; but this double standard did not create a completely asymmetrical moral code where men's sexual activities were irrelevant to their reputations. For women and for men, the gendered notions of publicity, and especially of governance, shaped the concept of sexual impropriety. Women who notoriously transgressed sexual codes were out of any man's real control, disrupting the proper social order where women should be governed by the male head of their household. Public male adulterers, fornicators and patrons of prostitutes contributed to this misrule and were also themselves "misgoverned" and disreputable, or at least some men who acted this way were considered to have gone over the line.

Crucial to understanding the nature of respectable masculinity in late medieval London civic culture are the relationships between patriarchy, governance and sexual reputation. It was the duty of the respectable man to supervise the relationships of those in his sphere of influence, a sphere that included both his household and others who lived around him in his neighborhood, parish and ward. Just as he might act as a mediator between a courting couple and a presider at the exchange of marriage vows, so also he might intervene, either informally or officially, when a couple engaged in a relationship he regarded as inappropriate, illicit or sinful. While the extent of responsibility and the power to police relationships depended a good deal on the status of the man, all householders owed this duty at least to some extent. Those who refused it (for instance, men who pimped for their wives or who maintained prostitutes—"bawds" or "strumpetmongers") were challenging the social order as surely as women who refused proper governance. Similarly, in a heterosexual matrix in which it takes one of each sex to create an instance of sexual misconduct, men who fornicated or committed adultery were refusing the responsibility to govern themselves and to respect other men's women.

NOTES

1. I would like to acknowledge Caroline Barron, Marjorie McIntosh, Larry Poos, Eric Reiter and Stephanie Tarbin for their advice and the opportunity to read forthcoming work; graduate research assistants Celeste Chamberland, Nick Kluge and Dominique McCaughey for their help; the efforts of Harriet Jones of the Greater London Record Office in providing missing folios from microfilm; and the Social Science and Humanities Research Council of Canada and Fonds FCAR of the Government of Québec for financial assistance.

2. London, Guildhall Library, MS 9065, Commissary Court of London Deposition Book, 1489–1497 [hereafter GL, MS 9065], fol. 54r. Dates have been converted so that the year begins on January 1.

3. GL, MS 9065, fols. 48v–49v, 53v–55r (Calton's testimony and quotations, fols. 49rv). Note that Margaret Isot denied that she had ever exchanged vows with Thomas (fol. 48v). Thomas's father (there named also as Thomas) and his mother were called before the Commissary Court in early 1472 to answer to the charge of impeding the solemnization of the marriage between their son and Margaret "Isaac," a charge that they denied. London, Guildhall Library, MS 9064/1, fol. 134r.

4. On the contradictions inherent in premodern masculine identity, see Jacqueline Murray, "Hiding Behind the Universal Man: Male Sexuality in the Middle Ages," in *Handbook of Medieval Sexuality,* ed. Vern L. Bullough and James A. Brundage (New York: Garland, 1996), 129–39; and Lyndal Roper, *Oedipus and the Devil: Witchcraft, Sexuality and Religion in Early Modern Europe* (London: Routledge, 1994), 108–09, 119–20.

5. See Shannon McSheffrey, "'I will never have none against my father's will': Consent and the Making of Marriage in the Late Medieval Diocese of London," in *Women, Marriage, and Family in Medieval Christendom: Essays in Memory of Michael M. Sheehan, C.S.B.,* ed. Joel T. Rosenthal and Constance M. Rousseau (Kalamazoo, Mich.: Medieval Institute Press, 1998).

6. William Langland, *Piers the Plowman,* ed. Walter W. Skeat (Oxford: Oxford University Press, 1886), B Text, Passus ix, lines 116–19.

7. For London, two books of depositions, mostly from marital litigation, survive: London, Greater London Record Office, MS DL/C/205, Consistory Court of London Deposition Book, 1467–1476 [hereafter GLRO, MS DL/C/205]; and GL, MS 9065 (see note 2). The workings of the fifteenth-century ecclesiastical courts overseeing marriage are discussed most fully in Richard

Helmholz, *Marriage Litigation in Medieval England* (Cambridge: Cambridge University Press, 1974), 1–25; and also in Richard M. Wunderli, *London Church Courts and Society on the Eve of the Reformation* (Cambridge, Mass.: Medieval Academy of America, 1981). These and similar records have been studied by historians mainly to investigate the application and influence of canon law. See Michael M. Sheehan, "The Formation and Stability of Marriage in Fourteenth-Century England: Evidence of an Ely Register," *Mediaeval Studies* 33 (1971): 228–63; idem, "Choice of Marriage Partner in the Middle Ages: Development and Mode of Application of a Theory of Marriage," *Studies in Medieval and Renaissance History* n.s. 1 (1978): 3–33; Helmholz, *Marriage Litigation;* Charles Donahue Jr., "The Canon Law on the Formation of Marriage and Social Practice in the Later Middle Ages," *Journal of Family History* 8 (1983): 144–58; Martin Ingram, "Spousals Litigation in the English Ecclesiastical Courts, c. 1350–1640," in *Marriage and Society: Studies in the Social History of Marriage,* ed. R.B. Outhwaite (New York: St. Martin's, 1981), 35–47; Ralph Houlbrooke, *Church Courts and the People During the English Reformation* (Oxford: Oxford University Press, 1979), 56–67, 83–85. P.J.P. Goldberg and L.R. Poos have availed themselves of fifteenth-century depositions to study how marriage patterns fit into the economic lives of late medieval women and men. P.J.P. Goldberg, *Women, Work, and Life Cycle in a Medieval Economy: Women in York and Yorkshire, c. 1300–1520* (Oxford: Clarendon Press, 1992); idem, " 'For Better, For Worse': Marriage and Economic Opportunity for Women in Town and Country," in *Woman is a Worthy Wight: Women in English Society, c. 1200–1500,* ed. Goldberg (Gloucester: Alan Sutton 1992), 108–125; L.R. Poos, *A Rural Society after the Black Death: Essex 1350–1525* (Cambridge: Cambridge University Press, 1991). Early modernists have recently employed sixteenth-century deposition books to good effect to investigate the nature of social bonds in the postmedieval period. See Laura Gowing, *Domestic Dangers: Women, Words, and Sex in Early Modern London* (Oxford: Clarendon Press, 1996); Eric Josef Carlson, *Marriage and the English Reformation* (Oxford: Blackwell, 1994); Miranda Chaytor, "Household and Kinship: Ryton in the Late Sixteenth and Early Seventeenth Centuries," *History Workshop Journal* 10 (1980): 25–60; Peter Rushton, "Property, Power and Family Networks: The Problem of Disputed Marriage in Early Modern England," *Journal of Family History* 11 (1986): 205–19; Diana O'Hara, " 'Ruled by my friends': Aspects of Marriage in the Diocese of Canterbury, c. 1540–1570," *Continuity and Change* 6 (1991): 9–41.

   8. See GLRO, MS DL/C/205, fols. 3v, 12r, 34rv, 36v, 138v, 231r; GL, MS 9065, fols. 36r, 56r–57r; Diana O'Hara, "The Language of Tokens and the Making of Marriage," *Rural History* 3 (1992): 1- 40.

   9. See for instance the efforts of Margaret Hawkyns, widow, on behalf of her female servant, GLRO, MS DL/C/205, fols. 122r–124r.

10. There has been little discussion of the role of intermediaries in the making of marriage. See short discussions in O'Hara, "Ruled by my friends," 15; Poos, *A Rural Society,* 137; John Bossy, "Blood and Baptism: Kinship, Community and Christianity in Western Europe from the Fourteenth to the Seventeenth Centuries," *Studies in Church History* 10 (1973): 131–32. P.P.A. Biller notes the assumption of the existence of mediators in Italian *pastoralia* but not in English: "Marriage Patterns and Women's Lives: A Sketch of a Pastoral Geography," in *Woman is a Worthy Wight,* ed. Goldberg, 66. Alan Macfarlane, in his discussion of courtship, insists that individuals married without any outside help ("courtship was a game that, on the whole, people played for themselves," 295). Alan Macfarlane, *Marriage and Love in England: Modes of Reproduction, 1300–1840* (Oxford: Blackwell, 1986), 292–95.

11. See O'Hara, "Ruled by my friends," 10–11, regarding "friends" functioning as "fictive kin" in the sixteenth century.

12. For example, Stephen Robert claimed that he had refused to make a marriage contract with Angela Harewe before he had gained permission from his "friends." The terms of his father's will (where Stephen and his brother were to be delivered their inheritances only at the discretion of their guardians if they married before the age of twenty-four) make it very likely that he meant these guardians when he spoke to Angela of his friends. GLRO, MS DL/C/205, fols. 37r–38r, 39r–41r; London, Public Record Office [hereafter PRO], Prerogative Court of Canterbury 11/4, fol. 169r, Will of John Roberd of Cranbrook, January 1461 (probated February 1461).

13. "Dicit quod fuit mediator inter eosdem et laborauit ad inducendum eos ut contraherent matrimonium adinuicem, rogatus ad huc per utramque partem." GLRO, MS DL/C/205, fol. 34v, cf. fols. 63v, 66v, 108v–110v, 123r–124r.

14. He had only known them for four and two years respectively. GLRO, MS DL/C/205, fol. 33r.

15. GLRO, MS DL/C/205, fols. 34rv, cf. fol. 36v.

16. "Dixit eidem si potuit inuenire in corde suo ad diligendum eum tanquam maritum suum, ipse Johannes esset sibi et suus pro futuris." GL, MS 9065, fol. 22r. Some depositions from this case have been translated in Shannon McSheffrey, *Love and Marriage in Late Medieval London* (Kalamazoo, Mich.: Medieval Institute Publications, 1995), 37–40.

17. GL, MS 9065, fol. 22r.

18. This is a contentious issue. Helmholz's suggestion (*Marriage Litigation,* 29–30) that the private vows were a normal, or at least common, prelude to a public church wedding makes the most sense of the evidence of the deposition books. See, for example, GLRO, MS DL/C/205, fols. 221r–223r; GL, MS 9065, fol. 17r. But the apparent typicality of clandestine marriages may be, as many historians have pointed out, simply due to their greater likelihood to present

problems and thus be recorded in court documents (see, for instance, Poos, *A Rural Society,* 138). Nevertheless, the court documents portray such marriages as normal and familiar both to deponents and the court; it is only when they break down that they depart from a conventional pattern. See also for discussions of clandestine marriage James A. Brundage, *Law, Sex and Christian Society in Medieval Europe* (Chicago: University of Chicago Press, 1987), 239, 276, 336, 361–64, 415, 441–43, 500; Sheehan, "Formation and Stability," 249 ff.; Donahue, "Canon Law on the Formation of Marriage," 147–56; Goldberg, "For Better, For Worse," 113–14. Although canonically clandestine marriages were those made outside a church, in the depositions witnesses called marriages clandestine when they were illicitly procured (e.g., when one of the partners was excommunicated or was inhibited from marrying because of a pending suit), whether or not they were performed in a church. See, for example, GLRO, DL/C/205, fols. 21r, 110r.

19.   Cf. Lyndal Roper, " 'Going to Church and Street': Weddings in Reformation Augsburg," *Past and Present* 106 (1985): 65–67.

20.   For example, GL, MS 9065, fols. 10v–11v.

21.   On consent and the canon law of marriage, see John T. Noonan, "Power to Choose," *Viator* 4 (1973): 418–434; Donahue, "Canon Law on the Formation of Marriage," 144–47.

22.   Sheehan, "Formation and Stability," 244–45; Ingram, "Spousals Litigation," 46; Helmholz, *Marriage Litigation,* 34–38.

23.   The question of exact words spoken and whether they constituted present or future consent was tricky. Helmholz found that the focus was usually on the verb used—"I will take" meaning future consent, "I will have" meaning present consent (*Marriage Litigation,* 34–38). I have not yet found another case that differentiated between plighting faith and troth, although cf. GLRO, MS DL/C/205, fols. 81v–82v (see below, note 26).

24.   GL, MS 9065, fols. 23rv.

25.   There are many other examples; see, for example, GLRO, MS DL/C/205, fols. 4v–5v, 10rv; GL, MS 9065, fols. 7r–8r.

26.   See also GLRO, MS DL/C/205, fols. 81v–82v, where witnesses to an exchange of consent also argued about the proper form of words. After Margaret Mylsent and Thomas Alcote had said their vows (in the form "Ego volo habere te in maritum meum/uxorem meam"), "tunc Johannes Clerke [one of the witnesses] dixit eidem Margarete quod deberet contrahere sub hac forma, 'Ego volo habere te *per fidem meam,*' et ipsa dixit hoc non erat necessarie pro eo quod per prius habuit tres maritos et nunquam dedit eis fidem suam in contractibus suis nec unquam erat falsa eisdem maritis."

27.   GLRO, MS DL/C/205, fol. 16v.

28.   GL, MS 9065, fols 4r–5r.

29. A number of Chancery cases relate to fees promised for the procuration of marriages. See PRO, C1/20/137; C1/26/286; C1/43/65; C1/46/212; C1/64/271; C1/66/387; C1/66/402; C1/67/166.

30. GL, MS 9065, fols. 10r–12r.

31. GLRO, MS DL/C/205, fols. 19r–19v, 29r. Chapman claimed the contract was conditional.

32. GLRO, MS DL/C/205, fol. 23r.

33. For example, GLRO, MS DL/C/205, fols. 31rv.

34. "Ubi et quando iste iuratus, pro eo quod in dicta parrochia publice dicebatur quod prefatus Richardus nimis suspiciose frequentabat domum eiusdem Agnetis, iste iuratus dixit eidem quod non haberet tales frequentes secursus ad eam nisi sciret utrum vellet habere eam in uxorem vel non." GL, MS 9065, fol. 12v.

35. "Et ultra dicit quod iste iuratus fecit instancias diuersas Willelmo Hathewey ut acciperet dictam Petronillam in uxorem et dimitteret dictam Margaretam Spyndeler quam tenuit in adulterio ut dixit." GLRO, MS DL/C/205, fols. 9rv, quotation at 9v.

36. See Helmholz, *Marriage Litigation,* 70–71, for office cases, noting they usually arose from consanguinity problems; and L.R. Poos, "Sex, Lies, and the Church Courts of Pre-Reformation England," *Journal of Interdisciplinary History* 25 (1995): 585–607.

37. "Maior pars vicinie ibidem opinatur et sentit premissa fuisse et esse vera et male loquitur de eisdem ut dicit." GLRO, MS DL/C/205, fol. 21r.

38. GL, MS 9065, fols. 49rv.

39. See Barbara A. Hanawalt, "Patriarchal Provision for Widows and Orphans in Medieval London," in *Gender, Kinship, Power: A Comparative and Interdisciplinary History,* ed. Mary Jo Maynes et al. (New York: Routledge, 1996), 201–13.

40. "Ulterius interrogatus, dicit se tantum scire quod quodam die profesto contingente infra duodecim dies immediate contingentes post festum natalis domini ultimum preteritum, quem diem aliter specificare nescit, dictus Johannes Palmer venit ad quemdam locum vulgariter nuncupatum Hewlyns Place, ubi et quando post meridiem eiusdem diei idem Johannes Palmer presentauit se coram xiii personis nominatis, assumptis, et electis per dominum Georgium Irlond, Aldermannum Warde vocate Cordewere Strete, ad inquirendum <et> inuestigandum de et super criminibus in dicta Warda perpetratis et de et super personis criminosis de dicta Warda expellendis propter suum malum regiminem et crimina perpetrata per eosdem et usitata." GLRO, MS DL/C/205, fols. 146v–147r.

41. *Munimenta Gildhallae Londoniensis,* pt. 1, *Liber Albus,* ed. Henry Thomas Riley, Rolls Series 12/1 (London: 1859), 275, 283, 332, 337–38, 456–60.

42. London, Corporation of London Record Office [hereafter CLRO], Journals of the Court of Common Council, Journal 8, fol. 49v. In using the Journals, I was greatly aided by Caroline Barron's card index to Journals 1–6, situated at the CLRO.

43. *Liber Albus,* 457–60; CLRO, Letter Book [hereafter LB] K, fol. 179r; *Calendar of Letter Books Preserved among the Archives of the Corporation of the City of London* [hereafter *CLB*], *Letter Books A-L,* ed. Reginald R. Sharpe (London: Corporation of London, 1899–1912), *CLBK,* 230–31.

44. See the Commissary Court Act Books for 1470–1501 (GL, MSS 9064/1–8), which record many prosecutions for fornication, adultery, bawdry and sexual defamation. The relationship between the two jurisdictions, ecclesiastical and secular, is not entirely clear, but it does not appear to have been unfriendly. Civic officials routinely turned over clerical offenders to the ecclesiastical ordinary in the late fourteenth and fifteenth centuries (e.g., CLRO, LB H, fol. 238r; [*CLBH,* 339]; LB I, fols. 287r–290r [*CLBI,* 277–87]; CLRO, Journal 6, photo 360 [fol. 217v]; Journal 8, fol. 92v); similarly, the diocese of London Commissary Court frequently noted that accused wrongdoers had been arrested by civic officials when it prosecuted adulterers, bawds and prostitutes, suggesting that the arrest itself prompted the citation before the ecclesiastical court (e.g., GL, MS 9064/1, fols. 3v, 6r, 7v, 8v, 13v, 15v, 16r, 18v, etc.). Cf. Wunderli, *London Church Courts,* 35.

45. Examples of such presentments, ranging from the 1440s to the 1490s: CLRO, Journal 4, fols. 60r, 135r, 137r–138v, 141v, 221r; Journal 5, fols. 214r, 234r; Journal 6, photo 110 (fol. 122v); Journal 8, fols. 92r, 230v; Journal 10, fols. 78v, 109r.

46. CLRO, Journal 9, fol.129r (1486).

47. *Liber Albus,* 275, 283, 332, 337–38, 456–60; *CLBG,* 149; CLRO, LB H, fol. 238r (*CLBH,* 339); LB I, fols. 286r–290r (*CLBI,* 273–87); LB K, fols. 11rv, 168r, 179r (*CLBK,* 17, 215, 230–31); LB L, fols. 83r, 275v–276r, 282rv (*CLBL,* 103, 269, 276). See also evidence cited below from GLRO, MS DL/C/205 and GL, MS 9065.

48. One set of fifteenth-century ward presentments survives in original written form: CLRO, Portsoken Ward Presentments, 1465–1482 and 1507. Other wards probably also recorded their presentments, at least according to a reference to "rotulo Wardemote" of Billingsgate Ward in 1456 (CLRO, Journal 6, photo 6 [fol. 30v]; see also references to "indentures and veredictis" of the inquests, Journal 9, fol. 129r). Other evidence from the civic records for ward moot presentments and activities of ward officials can be found in: CLRO, Journal 4, 13r, 16v; Journal 5, 54r, 214v–215r, 216v; Journal 6, photos 512–13, 519 (fols. 20rv, 7v); Journal 8, 47r–50v, 87v–88r; Journal 10, fols. 10v, 39v; *Calendar of Early Mayor's Court Rolls Preserved among the Archives of the Corpora-*

tion of the City of London at the Guildhall, AD 1298–1307, ed. A.H. Thomas (Cambridge: Cambridge University Press, 1924), 23–24, 211, 218–19; *Calendar of Plea and Memoranda Rolls Preserved among the Archives of the Corporation of the City of London at the Guildhall, 1323–1482,* ed. A.H. Thomas and Philip E. Jones (Cambridge: Cambridge University Press, 1926–1961) [hereafter *CPMR*], 1:108–09, 116, 124–26, 156, 167, 173, 187–89, 212; 2:7, 139, 151, 156–57, 244; 3:148; CLRO, Plea and Memoranda Rolls [hereafter P&MR], Roll A50, mm. 5a–7b; Roll A51, mm. 2a–4b; Roll A71, m. 4b; Roll A72, m. 3b (*CPMR,* 4:115–41, 150–59; 5:72, 88).

49. See Ruth Mazo Karras, *Common Women: Prostitution and Sexuality in Medieval England* (New York: Oxford University Press, 1996), passim, esp. 16–17, 27–28, 131.

50. CLRO, Portsoken Ward presentments, mm. 12, 14, dated 1480 and 1482. On male prostitution and accusations of sodomy, see Ruth Mazo Karras and David Lorenzo Boyd, "'Ut cum muliere': A Male Transvestite Prostitute in Fourteenth-Century London," in *Premodern Sexualities,* ed. Louise Fradenburg and Carla Freccero (New York: Routledge, 1996), 99–116, esp. 102, 105.

51. The Journals, for instance, frequently record that a couple was caught ("capti fuerunt") by the beadles or constables of the ward, but nothing more. See CLRO, Journal 4, fols. 75v, 92v, 211v; Journal 5, fols. 52v, 61v, 116v, 161r, 195v, 217v, 251r, 268v; Journal 6, photo 98 (fol. 116v), photo 360 (fol. 217v); Journal 7, fols. 59v, 102r.

52. Nicole Castan, "The Public and the Private," in *A History of Private Life,* vol. 3, *Passions of the Renaissance,* ed. Roger Chartier, trans. Arthur Gold-hammer (Cambridge, Mass.: Belknap Press, 1989), 402–45, has an interesting discussion of privacy, publicity and domestic space, although the interpretation offered here views the division between private and public spaces differently.

53. For example, CLRO, LB I, fols. 288r–289r (*CLBI,* 282–85).

54. GL, MS 9065, fol. 197v.

55. GLRO, MS DL/C/205, fols. 263r–264r.

56. In other examples the constables were also assisted by neighbors: CLRO, Journal 5, fol. 268v; Journal 6, photo 360 (fol. 217v).

57. See note 3 above.

58. As a result of his loss of reputation, William Stevenes sued John Palmer for defamation (GLRO, MS DL/C/205, fols. 146v–148r; see also McSheffrey, *Love and Marriage,* 87–88). In 1377, Matilda Bakere had also sued for defamation in a church court after ward moot jurors presented her as a "woman of bad character." *CPMR,* 2:244.

59. GLRO, MS DL/C/205, fols. 191r–192v; see also McSheffrey, *Love and Marriage,* 84–85. Ecclesiastical courts also sometimes directed fornicating couples to exchange marriage vows in court. See L.R. Poos, "The Heavy-Handed

Marriage Counsellor: Regulating Marriage in Some Later-Medieval English Local Ecclesiastical-Court Jurisdictions," *American Journal of Legal History* 39 (1995): 297; and Helmholz, *Marriage Litigation,* 172–81.

60. "Tam timore corporis sui <quam> pudore comparacionis coram maiore et Aldermannis iste iuratus contraxit ibidem matrimonium cum prefata Agnete." GLRO, MS DL/C/205, fols. 266r–266v; the rest of the case appears on fols. 252v–256r, 258v, 265v, 275r–276v. See also McSheffrey, *Love and Marriage,* 81–82.

61. For example, GLRO, MS DL/C/205, fols. 86r, 147v–148r, 158v, 244r–246r, 248v, 249r, 268v; Sylvia Thrupp, *The Merchant Class of Medieval London* (1948; reprint, Ann Arbor: University of Michigan Press, 1976), 15–16.

62. *CLBK,* 215. This is the wording used in 1437 and still followed in 1461. See also Gwyn Williams, *Medieval London: From Commune to Capital* (London: Athlone Press, 1963), 42–43, 80.

63. See Thrupp, *Merchant Class,* 80–81; Wunderli, *London Church Courts,* 34; and CLRO, Portsoken Ward Presentments.

64. See Shannon McSheffrey, "Jurors, Respectable Masculinity, and Christian Morality," *Journal of British Studies* 37 (1998): 269–78.

65. On Hobbes, see C.H. Talbot and E.A. Hammond, *Medical Practitioners in Medieval England* (London: Wellcome Historical Medical Library, 1965), 401–02.

66. GLRO, MS DL/C/205, fols. 315r–320r.

67. Talbot and Hammond, *Medical Practitioners,* 187, 276, 401–02. Staveley is called Stanley in Talbot and Hammond, but it seems likely that it is the same man.

68. Halyday appears in Talbot and Hammond, *Medical Practitioners,* 296. He would become warden of the Surgeons' Company of London in 1489.

69. The recording of the sentence (and a number of other administrative matters related to the case) in the deposition book is very unusual, perhaps because of the exceptional nature of the case.

70. Posited, for instance, in Karras, *Common Women,* 31, 42–43, 52–53, 76, 134; Keith Thomas, "The Double Standard," *Journal of the History of Ideas* 20 (1959): 195–216; Susan Dwyer Amussen, *An Ordered Society: Gender and Class in Early Modern England* (Oxford: Blackwell, 1988), 102–104; Laura Gowing, "Gender and the Language of Insult in Early Modern London," *History Workshop Journal* 35 (1993): 1–21 (Thomas's, Amussen's and Gowing's arguments relate to a period a century or more after the material considered here). On gender and sexual reputation generally, see also Poos, "Sex, Lies." For the Continent, see Margaret King, *Women of the Renaissance* (Chicago: University of Chicago Press, 1991), 29–30; Guido Ruggiero, " 'Più che la vita caro': Onore,

matrimonio e reputazione femminile nel tardo rinascimento," *Quaderni Storici* n.s. 66 (1987): 753–75; Roper, *Oedipus and the Devil,* 40–41, 46, 65, 107, 119–20; Roper, " 'The Common Man,' 'The Common Good,' 'Common Women': Gender and Meaning in the German Reformation Commune," *Social History* 12 (1987): 1–21.

71. It should be noted that Hobbys's divorce does not seem to have affected his career as surgeon to the king (he continued in this role through the reign of Richard III). Talbot and Hammond, *Medical Practitioners,* 401–02.

72. A similar point regarding legal sources is made in Karras and Boyd, "Ut cum muliere," 101.

73. For other challenges to the idea of the double standard, see Marjorie Keniston McIntosh, *Controlling Misbehavior in England, 1370–1600* (Cambridge: Cambridge University Press, 1998), 73–74, arguing (as here) that sexual reputation was important for both men and women; Goldberg, *Women, Work, and Life Cycle,* 153–57, 232, 330; and Barbara A. Hanawalt, *Growing Up in Medieval London: The Experience of Childhood in History* (New York: Oxford University Press, 1993), 121, 186–88, who contend that chastity was *not* particularly important for late medieval women (or men) below the elite, Goldberg referring particularly to the early fifteenth century.

74. See especially Marjorie K. McIntosh, *Controlling Misbehavior,* 11–14, 70–71, 127–28, 131–32, 162–64, 175; McIntosh, "Finding Language for Misconduct: Jurors in Fifteenth-Century Local Courts," in *Bodies and Disciplines: Intersections of Literature and History in Fifteenth-Century England,* ed. Barbara A. Hanawalt and David Wallace (Minneapolis: University of Minnesota Press, 1996), 87–122, esp. 90–97, 112–13; Ben R. McRee, "Religious Gilds and Regulation of Behavior in Late Medieval Towns," in *People, Politics and Community in the Later Middle Ages,* ed. Joel Rosenthal and Colin Richmond (Gloucester, Eng.: Alan Sutton, 1987), 108–22.

75. See Ruggiero, "Più che la vita caro."

76. I am using the word "public" here not so much in a geographical or topographical sense but as it relates to activity; the dichotomy that I describe here (public/private) can also be understood by the dyads official/unofficial, formal/informal. See my discussion of these issues respecting late medieval English sectarian life in *Gender and Heresy: Women and Men in Lollard Communities, 1420–1530* (Philadelphia: University of Pennsylvania Press, 1995), 48–49, 65–69, 108, 118–25. In relation to women's sexual behavior, the notion of public as "common" is also important: whores were women who belonged to no one particular man but to all. See note 78 below.

77. See, for instance, PRO, C1/61/382; C1/61/574; C1/63/176; C1/66/259; C1/150/54; C1/158/35; C1/214/91; C1/229/18; C1/234/71; CLRO, Journal 4,

fol. 113v. The placing of primary responsibility for a wife's or daughter's misbehavior on another, especially a man, is partly due to the structure of the English law (wives and daughters could not be sued by husbands or fathers, but their seducers could be). Nonetheless, assumptions about women's culpability in the Chancery petitions reflect widespread notions of women's lack of agency.

78. See Roper, "The Common Man"; Karras, *Common Women,* 10–11, 86, 138; Jacques Rossiaud, *Medieval Prostitution,* trans. Lydia G. Cochrane (Oxford: Blackwell, 1988), 32–37.

79. GL, MS 9065, fols. 182r–183v.

80. PRO, C1/64/1158.

81. PRO, C1/158/47.

82. GL, MS 9064/4, fols. 38r, 83r, 227v, 239v, 263v.

83. PRO, C1/29/400.

84. I would, however, argue that it was not constructed *entirely* of their sexual reputation as some historians have alleged (see e.g., Karras, *Common Women,* 31); it was possible for a woman to be defamed or slandered for misdeeds regarding her property or her occupation. See, for instance, PRO, C1/31/493; GLRO, MS DL/C/205, fols. 162r–164v.

85. CLRO, Journals 5–8 and 10, passim (e.g., Journal 5, fols. 39v, 71r, 72r, 107r, 244r; Journal 6, Photo 136 [fol. 174r], Photo 297 [fol. 169v], Photo 445 [fol. 3v]; Journal 7, fols. 12r, 25v, 29r, 34v, 50r, 51r, 153v, 177r, 200r; Journal 8, fols. 20r, 89r, 120r, 178v; Journal 10, fols. 3v–4v, 12r, 16v, 25v, 43v, 47r, 60v, 70r, 97v, 98v, 101v, 104r, 147v).

86. GLRO, MS DL/C/205, fols. 283v–290v.

87. "Prefatus Willelmus Boteler dixit huic iurato circiter idem tempus quod quidam Johannes Stampe carnaliter cognouit quamdam Johannam Folke, quorum pretextu status et bona fama prefate Johanne Folke quam prefati Johannis Stampe multum ledebantur et grauabantur." GLRO, MS DL/C/205, fol. 305r.

88. PRO, C1/45/46. See also PRO, C1/32/34.

89. GLRO, MS DL/C/205, fols. 315v–319v.

90. GL, MS 9065, fols. 70rv, 85r, 86v, 184r, 267r; PRO, C1/45/24, C1/70/126.

91. See especially Goldberg, *Women, Work, and Life Cycle,* 7, 155–57, 261–63, 276–78.

92. GL, MS 9065, fols. 2rv.

93. GL, MS 9065, fols. 1r–2v, 90r–93r.

94. For other examples, see GLRO, MS DL/C/205, fols. 79v–80v, 83v–84r, 221r–225v, 234v–240v, 257v–258v, 262v, 263r, 304v–306r; PRO, C1/27/417; CLRO, P&MR, Roll A50, m. 6 (*CPMR,* 4:124), Roll A51, m. 2b (*CPMR,* 4:152), Roll A51, m. 3 (*CPMR,* 4:154).

95. GLRO, MS DL/C/205, fols. 304v–305v (his original testimony at fols. 270rv). For such punishments, see *Liber Albus,* 456–60; CLRO, LB I, fol. 290r (*CLBI,* 286–87); LB K, fol. 11rv (*CLBK,* 16–17); LB L, fols. 275v, 282rv (*CLBL,* 269, 276).

96. See the London Commissary Court Act Books for 1470–1501 (GL, MSS 9064/1–8), which record many prosecutions before this ecclesiastical court for fornication, adultery, bawdry and defamation for sexual offences, men and women being cited in roughly equal numbers (see Wunderli, *London Church Courts,* 86). For examples of prosecutions of men for sexual misbehavior by London civic officials, see CLRO, LB H, 238r (*CLBH,* 339); LB I, fols. 286r–290r (*CLBI,* 273–87); LB L, fols. 83r, 106rv, 123r, 275v (*CLBL,* 103, 125–26, 145, 269); CLRO, Portsoken Ward Presentments, mm. 12, 14; CLRO, Journal 2, fol. 107v; Journal 4, fols. 37v, 52r, 62rv, 65v, 75v, 82r, 84v, 92v, 106v–107v, 122r, 134v, 141v, 149v, 208v; Journal 5, fols. 52v, 53r, 54r, 60v, 61v, 116v, 135v, 161r, 173r, 182rv, 188v–189r, 195v, 214r, 214v, 217rv, 248v, 251r, 252r; Journal 6, Photo 184 (fol. 241v), Photo 360 (fol. 217v), Photo 512 (fol. 20r), Photo 519 (fol. 7v); Journal 7, fols.18r, 57v, 59v, 92v, 148v, 167rv, 173r, 188v–189r, 193r, 206r; Journal 8, fol. 14r, 15v, 18r, 47r–48r, 49r, 87v–88r, 92r, 92v, 142r, 153v, 177r; Journal 9, fols. 230v, 264rv, 294r, 295rv, 296v, 297r; Journal 10, fols. 1v, 3v, 31v, 78v; CLRO, P&MR, Roll A50, mm. 5ab, 6ab (*CPMR,* 4:122, 124, 127, 131, 134); Roll A51, m. 3a (*CPMR,* 4:154); Roll A71, mm. 4b (*CPMR,* 5:72); Roll A72, m. 3v (*CPMR,* 5:88); Roll A90, mm. 1a–2b (*CPMR,* 6:57–64). Marjorie McIntosh has similarly found that juries in local courts outside London presented both men and women for sexual offences. *Controlling Misbehavior,* 71–74.

97. McIntosh, *Controlling Misbehavior,* 167–68.

98. Stephanie Tarbin, "Tropes of Behaviour: The Prosecution of Sexual Misconduct in Fifteenth-Century London" (paper presented at the Medieval Congress, Leeds, Eng., July 1996).

99. For example, GLRO, MS DL/C/205, fols. 86r, 147v–148r, 158v, 244r–246r, 248v, 249r, 268v; Thrupp, *The Merchant Class,* 15–16. McIntosh has found that those marginal to the local community were more likely to be presented by juries than those who were at the center. *Controlling Misbehavior,* 12–13, 96–97, 191.

100. CLRO, P&MR, Roll A71, m. 4b (*CPMR,* 5:72). Margaret Kirby, formerly one of Fynse's servants, claimed in 1446 that Fynse's wife "lette the said Marget to ferme" to a friar, for the price of a piece of cloth and forty shillings in money. CLRO, Journal 4, fol. 66v.

101. CLRO, P&MR, Roll A90, mm. 1–2b (*CPMR,* 6:57–64).

102. CLRO, P&MR, Roll A90, mm. 1–2b (*CPMR,* 6:57–64).

103. PRO, C1/94/14.

104. *The Cely Letters, 1472–1488,* ed. Alison Hanham, Early English Text Society, Original Series 273 (1975), 50, 81–82, 92–94, 107, 128–30, 156, 167, 173.

105. CLRO, P&MR, Roll A72, m. 3b (*CPMR,* 5:88).

106. William II (1436–96) lived in London from 1474, while William III (1459-after 1503) is known to have visited London in the early 1480s. *The Paston Letters and Papers of the Fifteenth Century,* ed. Norman Davis, 2 vols. (Oxford: Clarendon Press, 1971), 1:lvii, lxiii.

107. GL, MS 9064/3, fol. 179v. The other case mentioning "Master Paston" is at GL 9064/2, fol. 1v.

108. See Karras, *Common Women.*

109. Roper, *Oedipus and the Devil,* 108–109, 119–20.

110. Cited in Karras, *Common Women,* 96; Larry Poos first brought the case to my attention.

111. See McIntosh, *Controlling Misbehavior,* 13–14, 128, 158–64, 175–77; eadem, "Finding Language for Misconduct"; Goldberg, *Women, Work, and Life Cycle,* 7, 155–57, 261–63, 276–78. Margaret Spufford ("Puritanism and Social Control?" in *Order and Disorder in Early Modern England,* ed. Anthony Fletcher and John Stevenson [Cambridge: Cambridge University Press, 1985], 41–57) suggests that the so-called "Puritan" attempts to control behavior from the 1580s onward were paralleled by similar efforts in the early fourteenth century; she connects in both cases anxiety about misbehavior to difficult economic conditions.

112. See *Coventry Leet Book, 1420–1555,* 4 parts, ed. M.D. Harris, Early English Text Society, Original Series 134–35, 138, 146 (1907–1913): 544–45, 568.

113. CLRO, Journal 4, fol. 82r.

114. See Karras and Boyd, "Ut cum muliere," esp. 106–109.

115. Judith Butler, *Gender Trouble: Feminism and the Subversion of Identity* (New York: Routledge, 1990), 24–25, 139–40.

"Loved Him—Hated Her"
Honor and Shame at the Medieval Court

JOHN CARMI PARSONS

> *Forsaking the example of the great emperor*
> *and the king of France—who do not allow their*
> *honor to be trampled by their wives or their*
> *wives' kin and countrymen—the king, lacking*
> *money and nearly bankrupt, depleted his realm*
> *and everywhere let it be lacerated. Become*
> *uxorious, he allowed his land on all sides and*
> *any occasion to be chewed up and the goods of*
> *the land throughout the realm to be sucked up*
> *by aliens—Poitevins, Germans, Provençals,*
> *Romans.*
>
> MATTHEW PARIS[1]

Thus, in the middle years of a troubled reign, the English Benedictine
chronicler Matthew Paris (d. 1259) described his sovereign lord, King
Henry III (r. 1216–1272). While Matthew is evidently careful to avoid
naming the woman he clearly blames for Henry's shortcomings, his criticism of his susceptibility to his wife's influence—and, by extension, of
her use of that influence to induce the king to forget his duty to his subjects—underpins a crushingly negative portrait of a weak male ruler,
dominated by foreigners. Matthew could (and did, as we will see) pen far
more audacious condemnations of Henry's vulnerability to Eleanor of
Provence (1223–1291).[2] But for introductory purposes, the quoted passage neatly illustrates this chapter's point of departure: medieval writers'
tendency to depict male rulers and their wives as moral packages—
queens or empresses tied to their husbands as paired examples of regal
propriety or deficiency, or even blamed outright for male rulers' perceived failures.[3]

We are accustomed to think in terms of constant recourse to binary
opposites in medieval thinking about male and female,[4] but such pairings
as that cited above elicit consideration, as well, of the ways in which
medieval ideas of masculinity and femininity might have constructed or

279

reinforced each other. It is a commonplace today that medieval society identified women primarily through their relationships with men, either by birth or marriage; likewise, if a woman's qualities were deemed to merit praise, her attributes would be lauded with the masculinizing term "virago," but any lack of virtue was as readily ascribed to the moral weakness that was inescapably hers as a female. The passage quoted above, however—and a host of similar comments on kings and their wives—suggests the opposite was in a sense true as well: the writers of medieval narratives could manipulate female figures to construct or identify males. Given women's peripheral importance to narrative writers, who dealt chiefly with male activities and concerns, any references to women such writers chose to make are likely to have some particular meanings. The reasons *why* they said *what* they said about women—and *how* they said it—therefore deserve some scrutiny.

This was certainly so in literature and in art. Female characters in eleventh- and twelfth-century *chansons de geste* were created to contrast with the male counterparts they nursed and heartened in their comfortable castles, before urging them to return to battle and uphold family honor. The twelfth-century chronicler Orderic Vitalis likely had this image in mind when he portrayed an historical countess, Adela of Blois, successfully exhorting her husband, amid their conjugal embraces, to return to the Holy Land after he had abandoned the First Crusade.[5] Perhaps the most visible example was the Virgin Mary's husband Joseph, whom medieval artists gradually transformed from decrepit old man to virile paterfamilias, while Mary herself changed from hieratic goddess to loving human mother. The change was easily rationalized on the grounds that a young, vigorous Joseph gave greater point to a chaste marriage and could better protect and provide for Mary and her Son.[6] In either case, chivalric epic or religious effigy, the female image exerted a decisive influence on the male.

Of course, epics and saints alike represented idealized scenarios. The historical rulers whose deeds appear in chronicle, eulogy or history were "real people" observed amid their contemporary political dramas. Orderic's Adela anecdote, however, reminds us that even as chroniclers observed their world in all its beauty and chaos, and afforded it what order they could, they too created images of their contemporaries subject to as much manipulation as the figures in epic or legend. Bearing in mind that medieval women rarely speak for themselves, but are known chiefly through literary or narrative male writings, a suggestive pattern has been noted in twelfth-century romance poetry. The Lady in troubadour lyric represents what the poet or lover wishes to become but can never be—an idealization of the moral perfection he seeks. That is, twelfth- and thirteenth-century male poets used woman's image to define their own maleness, and romance authors similarly modeled female figures on male heroes.[7] A number of studies on both secular and ecclesiastical aspects of medieval society expound, explicitly or implicitly, the ways in which masculine and feminine interacted to construct or reinforce each other.[8] I suggest, then, that male writers of chronicles and narratives also manipulated the images of particular women to color their portrayals of the men with whom those women were intimately associated, the men who were the authors' main interest. In other words, while women are often marginal figures in medieval narrative, the way in which authors portrayed them might still tell us something about the central male characters. Medieval chroniclers' tendency to praise kings and queens lavishly—or liberally vilify them—offers a trove of sources to survey for ways in which ideas of masculine virtue, or the lack thereof, could be shaped by reference to corresponding feminine virtue or vice. This chapter accordingly examines narratives, sermon *exempla* and record evidence for portrayals of medieval male rulers in tandem with their wives.

The focus here on queens—the medieval women most visible to contemporaries and modern scholars alike—requires comment. Until recently, queens were understood to have functioned only as passive diplomatic brides, dynastic mothers, patrons of writers and artists or monastic founders. Political, administrative, diplomatic or military historians dismissed queens' share in such matters as negligible save in a few cases, swiftly if not apologetically excused by the absence of a male ruler. As women who enjoyed eminence, wealth, leisure or education as mere accidents of birth and marriage, medieval consorts were so far removed from most medieval women's experiences that feminist medieval historians saw no reason to study their lives. But medieval queens were, in fact, the women closest in proximity, indeed intimacy, to male centers of power. As most were consorts, not queens-regnant, queenship in the Middle Ages cannot escape a male referent; nor could kingship really avoid a female referent. Queens thus functioned in pivotal ways to shape the kingly image. The western tradition of rulership, for example, gave a male ruler's wife a role as the Esther-like counselor who elicited his mercy; her fertility, moreover, assured the realm's survival and proved the king's vital powers were intact.[9] Few medieval kings thus failed to wed, but no queen unambiguously benefited from marriage. A unique social prominence exposed her to constant scrutiny;

her behavior was minutely observed and, as chroniclers' criticism implies, she was expected to conform unhesitatingly and publicly to the narratives that governed women's behavior. Queens were, then, the women who had to contend most immediately and urgently with their society's views on women's relationship to power. As they thus inevitably emerged as exemplary figures for women, modern studies of their careers—and their critics—can examine the ways in which their images modeled portrayals of their husbands.

Two sermon *exempla w*ill illustrate what is meant here. In a familiar biblical story widely used by medieval preachers, the image of Ahasuerus is constructed by those of two women. Vashti defies and humiliates him before his men so he must disown her; Esther's submissive plea then allows him to manifest wisdom and magnanimity by annulling an unjust decree, implicitly restoring his stature.[10] Esther's acquiescence to her husband's authority modeled one aspect of queenly behavior, but there were other, more serious matters to be addressed. When Jacques de Vitry, in the thirteenth century, retold the well-worn tale of Phyllis and Aristotle as an *exemplum,* he transformed Phyllis from Alexander's mistress into his queen (deleting her name in the process). As ever, beauty humbles wisdom; Aristotle escapes Alexander's death sentence by noting that if a woman can humble the wisest in the realm, she could do the same to the king.[11] Much is implied in Phyllis's promotion. The troubling inversion of "the woman on top" is somewhat negated by her marriage, which implies her subjection to Alexander's authority; so are the egalitarian overtones of a noble man's illicit sexual involvement with, and possible lust for, a woman of lesser birth.[12] But even this could not wipe out the humiliation of age and wisdom by youth and beauty. Rather, a safety valve of sorts was afforded by Phyllis's mutation into a nameless queen. She thereby became a prominent, familiar and seemly figure. In the medieval Christian context, she also became the king's legitimate sexual partner and the mother of his heirs. Ironically this increased her latent threat to a male order now epitomized by a royal husband whose lineage must not be tainted by adultery.[13] Marriage, therefore, also intensified her need to guard her chastity. Faced with Aristotle's lechery, she kept her purity, and with it the king's honor. Her prudence and cunning enhanced the image of the king with whom she was now, as a wife, intimately identified. Aristotle's advice against man's domination by woman remained as but one among the multivalent meanings in medieval queenship.

These cases suggest how female figures could be manipulated to reveal something about a man and how female behavior reflects positively or negatively on a man. Recent studies have discussed historical royal couples in terms anticipating such analysis.[14] By comparing the empress Judith to Jezebel, for example, ninth-century writers implicitly likened her husband, Louis the Pious (r. 814–40), to Ahab, whom Jezebel easily duped into killing a man to get his vineyard. Adultery charges not only impugned Judith's virtue; they threatened a bastard birth into Louis's family and insinuated his inability to defend his exclusive sexual rights to his wife's body.[15] The eleventh-century English queens, Emma (d. 1052) and Edith (d. 1075), sponsored written accounts of their respective careers as the wives of Æthelred II (r. 978–1016) and Cnut (r. 1016–1035) and Edward the Confessor (r. 1042–1066). Penned by male authors under each queen's œgis, the works present both as complementary pendants to their husbands. Emma's marriage to the beleaguered Æthelred is almost ignored by the *Encomium Emmæ Reginæ*'s author; she is, rather, the conquering Cnut's worthily resolute consort and determined widow, who works to preserve the English realm's unity in her sons' reigns. The *Vita Edwardi Regis* offers a serious, courtly Edith as a sympathetic consort to holy Edward, in contrast to what was rather more likely a peevish and distrustful political marriage.[16]

These were not the last such texts created for a queen of England. Matilda II (1078?-1118), wife of Henry I (r. 1110–1135), sponsored a *vita* of her mother, the holy Margaret, queen of Scotland (d. 1093), probably by Margaret's confessor Turgot. The *Vita Margaretae* authorized a spectrum of queenly activities, in many of which Matilda actively engaged. But at a time when such fields of action were being closed to queens by the growth of royal bureaucracies, evolution of learned jurisprudence and the stiffening of gender boundaries, Matilda's correspondence with Archbishop Anselm of Canterbury also approved the Esther-like queenly intercessor, who complemented the king as male powerholder. Matilda exploited this role to create an image of herself as an informal if influential royal counselor, and English writers praised her in consequence.[17] But, while she may not have intended, thereby, to make any particular comment on Henry, appeal to Esther's image—and praise of a queen who took it as her model—might also easily hint that the king in question was thought to stand in some need of such compassionate counsel.

Remembered for centuries as devoted, pious and widely loved, Edward I (1239–1307) of England's first queen, Eleanor of Castile (1241–1290), was distrusted by the English as a greedy foreign landgatherer.

Linked to Edward's vigorous policies and blamed for urging him to rule harshly, she was rarely approached as a mediator with him. Ultimately, perceptions of this queen fostered a king's image as a severe ruler.[18] Edward's second wife, Margaret of France (1279–1318), was never politically influential but he let her intercede often with him, in a sense exploiting the intercessory role himself, just as queens did—perhaps to improve his own reputation for mercy at a troubled period in his reign. One chronicler reassuringly noted that at sixty, Edward promptly impregnated his twenty-year-old bride; even a later story that he used Margaret to dupe Philip IV, deliberately leaving false information for her to find and send Philip, creates a canny Edward in full control of both wife and enemy.[19] In the often violent politics of Edward II's reign (1307–27), Queen Isabella of France (d. 1358) was active enough to attract much contemporary comment. The chroniclers' rhetorical device, in her case, was not criticism but praise, notably of her fertility, throwing into negative contrast an indolent and fickle king dominated by male favorites: his noble, beautiful and loving queen worked to help the English people, and bore the king's children despite his neglect.[20]

Others who might figure in a wider survey are Richard II of England and Anne of Bohemia, or Henry VI and Margaret of Anjou.[21] Obviously, however, queens' behavior was observed and linked to their husbands' reputations; and that queens stood, in this respect, as exemplary figures to medieval society is shown by the fourteenth-century text known as the *Ménagier de Paris*. The elderly husband, who ostensibly wrote this text for his young wife, cited Valois queens' behavior as examples for a bourgeois wife whose behavior must not compromise her husband's good name: from her wedding day, no queen of France kissed any man but her husband—not even her father—and the only letters she opened in private were from the king. To avoid all suspicion she opened any other letters only before witnesses, specially summoned if need be. The author advised his teenaged bride to imitate such courtly customs lest she dishonor him, or any other man she might marry if she outlived him.[22]

Matthew Paris's reference to a queen's ruinous effect on her husband's honor, thus, suggests further nuances in light of an extensive anthropological literature linking male honor to female shame or modesty. In social systems based on idealized agnatic bonds, and in economic systems in which men control resources and provide for dependents including women, masculinity/superiority is associated with autonomy and femaleness/inferiority with dependence, connections that conform to and strengthen prevailing social structures. For societies that express female inferiority in intrinsically moral terms, moreover, women's devalorization is tied to their dependent status through perceived links to their maligned sexuality and reproductive behavior. Women in such societies, therefore, are not understood to have their own honor, but if properly modest they can, like Alexander's wife, safeguard and increase the honor of male kin or affines. Immodest or shameful female behavior, in contrast, weakens male claims to virtue, control or status. The man dominated by a wife or besotted with a woman invites ridicule; he has lost his autonomy and may be the less able to protect his dependents. Invested with moral worth, willing submissiveness and modesty thus become a woman's path to renown, apart from the social standing she may claim through her male kin. She must guard herself carefully lest she ruin that status—to her children's loss as well as her own.[23] Medieval society, thus, faced the task of balancing woman's moral inferiority with a queen's approved roles as counselor to the king, his legitimate sexual partner and the mother of his children.

Of necessity, given a manifest plethora of evidence, the selection of exemplary cases for further discussion has been complex. I have chosen the images of Louis IX of France (r. 1226–1270) and his wife Margaret of Provence (d. 1295), and Henry III of England and Eleanor of Provence, partly because of the amount and nature of the extant sources and partly because the two sisters were wed to such very different husbands. As most commentators dwell on Louis IX's relationship with his mother, Blanche of Castile, his union with Margaret is rarely discussed in detail, especially as portrayed by that intimate and informed witness, John, lord of Joinville.[24] His memoir of Louis apart, few chroniclers noted Margaret or her relationship with Louis. Even when an anonymous Reims chronicler recorded their eldest son's death, early in 1260, he only briefly noted Margaret's grief and (wrongly) her advanced pregnancy, before he went on to detail the archbishop of Rouen's counsel to the king, who was so heartened thereby that he soon put aside his sorrow. (The chronicler's decision to exaggerate Margaret's pregnancy does serve to color his picture of the king, however, by implying a more emotional, even physical, quality to her grief, in contrast to Louis's calmer "male" temperament, so amenable to the prelate's reasoned arguments.)[25]

Joinville's Margaret is good-humored and aware of her dignity, but by no means a helplessly ethereal aristocrat[26] and, on one occasion, able to show frustration with Louis. In a storm at sea returning from Palestine, Margaret feared they would sink and asked Joinville's advice; he suggested she vow a pilgrimage to St. Nicholas at Varangéville. She

agreed, but "The king is so contrary that if he knew I had promised without him, he would never let me go." Joinville told her to make the vow;
he would take her offering to Varangéville. The storm subsided.[27] The
incident implies that Joinville, Louis's companion in arms, saw nothing
wrong in conspiring behind his back to help Margaret—with whom he
clearly sympathized—while outwardly preserving Louis's control over
her. Joinville is, indeed, often sympathetic to Margaret at Louis's
expense; his account of her arrival at Sidon has been called his harshest
criticism of Louis. Joinville was at mass with Louis when Margaret's
ship docked. Joinville left to see her to her quarters and, when he
returned, Louis said he knew Joinville had gone to meet the queen and
asked if she and the children were well. Joinville was unimpressed: this
was the first time in the five years he had been with the king that Louis
had mentioned his family, and "It did not seem right to me that he was so
distant with his wife and children."[28] To this we may compare Joinville's
remark upon his own departure for the crusade: "I dared not look back
lest my heart be saddened for the fair castle I was leaving, and my sweet
children."[29] Louis did, in fact, attentively give his children moral instruction, but few sources imply his warm intimacy with Margaret after the
first years of their marriage.[30]

Comparison with what other evidence can be brought to bear here
tends to confirm Joinville's implication. Margaret evidently recounted
much about life with Louis to her Franciscan confessor, William de St-
Pathus, one of whose stories shows how differently various sources treat
one couple. Louis, as is well known, abstained from conjugal relations to
honor many holy days, and as he disciplined the flesh, so he did his eyes:

> My good lady, the Lady Queen Margaret his wife, told me that on such
> days as he was accustomed to be continent, at times when he was free
> of business he rested for recreation where the said queen and their chil-
> dren were. As the holy and chaste king spoke to the queen while they
> sat together, he kept his eyes fixed on the ground. Seeing this the lady,
> fearful lest she had done something to offend him, said to him, "Lord,
> what is this? You do not wish to look upon me? Have I done anything
> that you should be offended with me?" He answered, "No, lady."
> "Why, then, do you not look at me?" said she. He responded, "It is not
> good for a man to look upon what he cannot possess."[31]

When she told St-Pathus this, Margaret might well have been expressing
some frustration at life with such a man; she might even have expected a

little sympathy. The possibility that she might have displeased the king was, moreover, a troubling prospect for any queen, and the concern she described to St-Pathus was doubtless real. But when the friar wrote out the story, the centerpiece became Louis's moralizing comment: Margaret's anxiety merely served to manifest an aspect of Louis's piety.

St-Pathus tells other, similar stories: Margaret putting a robe over Louis when, oblivious to the cold, he rose in the night to pray, or her vexation with his plain clothing, which she felt unsuited to his dignity (Louis said he would dress as *she* wished if she dressed as *he* thought she should).[32] Simple tales, at first glance—a wife mindful of her husband's health, a vainglorious female rebuked by a sensible male. But in the first case, St-Pathus appropriated Margaret's solicitude and subverted it to stress the piety of a king intent on his orisons. Her views on Louis's attire need to be understood in the context of medieval queens' established role as curators of the splendors of the palace and the royal households—especially the king's raiment—so he could make a proper show.[33] Seen in this light, Margaret's comment was perfectly understandable; but in a work devoted to Louis's virtues, the friar manipulated it to suggest her vanity and to invite Louis's unanswerable retort.[34]

Margaret's recorded role in government and administration offers a third element to consider. She was devoted to her sister, Queen Eleanor of England, and did everything in her power to help Eleanor and Henry III when civil war threatened England in the 1260s. As the crisis between Henry and his barons sharpened early in 1263, Margaret met her brother-in-law's envoys at St-Germain-en-Laye; Louis was in Paris. A January 1263 letter from one English envoy to Henry's chancellor says bluntly that he found Margaret "tedious in word and deed."[35] This could mean that her enthusiasm surpassed her ability, but more light is cast on the situation by another letter sent home two weeks later by English envoys lately arrived in France: at St-Germain, Margaret urged them not to see Louis until she could return to court and induce him to hear them favorably.[36] She might also, then, have put off that first, disgruntled envoy until her return to Paris.

At first glance, it is unlikely Margaret would suggest inclining Louis to favor Henry had she not had reason to think he would listen; otherwise Henry's envoys would have had no reason to consult her. By promising to speak with Louis, however, she was perhaps only hoping to create a role for herself in his counsels or make herself appear more important than she was. By this time—long after the period Joinville's memoir most directly addresses—strains were developing in her relationship with Louis. After her eldest son's death, Margaret had tried to secure her influence over her son Philip, the new heir to the throne, inducing him to swear that whenever he succeeded to the throne, he would remain in her tutelage until the age of thirty. Louis learned of this, and in July 1263 papal letters absolved Philip from his oath. Urban IV put it all down to the youth's pliability and filial reverence, not to Margaret's ambition, but the defeat must have resonated in her relationship with Louis.[37] It is unclear if Louis knew of Philip's oath by January 1263, but certainly Margaret's influence was already waning; Louis never decisively upheld Henry against the English barons.[38]

Record evidence thus suggests that, despite Margaret's zeal for politics and diplomacy, Louis was right not to trust her, any more than he unduly indulged his physical desires with her.[39] The historian's problem is to reconcile Joinville's jolly, decisive Margaret with the friar's attentive, apprehensive wife and the records' devious, ambitious queen. Like the friar's account of Louis's virtues, record evidence is chiefly the work of clerics, and as such may be expected to represent a woman unfavorably. It has been said, indeed, that holy kings can wreak havoc on their wives' reputations;[40] but in the contexts argued here, it might well be suggested that the image of a restless, ambitious wife offered opportunities for such a king (or rather, his clerical eulogists) to manifest his patience or forbearance. Joinville's memoir, in contrast, is that of a knight who respected Margaret as any knight might honor a lady of rank. On the whole, his picture of her implies encoded criticism of Louis and raises questions about a king (let alone a saint) who behaved in such fashion. Joinville often makes himself a voice of reason in his dealings with Louis—a sensible man whose judgment Louis respects and whose advice he often (not always) follows, almost gratefully. Joinville seems to imply Margaret, too, in some situations, had more sense than Louis, most obviously when she and the lords present (including Joinville) insisted the royal party should land at Hyères, not Aigues-Mortes.[41] Did Joinville, like the poets and authors of romances he probably knew, idealize Margaret in the advisory role in which he saw himself? As a ranking noble, he knew well the king's crucial duty to accept counsel and his nobles' right to advise him and, by all indications, he also understood Margaret's role as a wifely counselor and appreciated the qualities that would have allowed her to function effectively as such. Her right to speak in that capacity, and Louis's duty to hear her, would have been strong.[42] Joinville may well have had such ideas in mind when he decried Louis's distance from Margaret and when he chose to repeat her remark on Louis's contrariness. What does seem inescapable is that both he and St-Pathus really had Louis in the front of their thinking when they wrote about Margaret, and so portrayed her to extend or complement their depictions of him.

Let us return to Matthew Paris's portrait of Henry III of England and Eleanor of Provence. In 1237, the year in which Matthew included the passage quoted earlier, Eleanor was at most fourteen years old. Henry's undoubted indulgence of her at this time apart, the extent to which the young girl really was able to sway him may be doubted. Here, then, her mere presence—insignificant as she likely still was in 1237—was a launch pad to criticize a profligate, pliable husband. In the early 1240s, Paris's criticism of the maturing queen increased sharply, though one incident he recounts implies Henry could, on occasion, overrule her. After he gave her the ward of a baron's lands, she tried to present a clerk to a parish church on those estates, though Henry had kept that right for himself. Matters grew so heated that, Matthew says, Henry barked at Eleanor, "How high does woman's arrogance rise if not restrained?"[43] In the English civil strife of 1258–1265, Eleanor was a convenient foil for those assigning blame for various crises. She reputedly alienated Henry from their son Edward in 1260, and in 1261 reconciled them; but then Edward, "flattered by his mother, held to his father's party and favored foreigners as his kin." Her foreign birth was blamed again when Edward installed alien mercenaries at Windsor in 1263.[44]

Perhaps the most vituperative of Matthew's famously venomous passages on this pair was penned well before the crises of 1258–1265, in a stingingly masterful paragraph on a 1242 dispute Henry had with the Church. He had worked for a favored clerk's election as bishop of Chichester, but the man was found deficient in learning; the archbishop of Canterbury (Eleanor's uncle, Boniface of Savoy) quashed the election and named another in his place. Henry at first resisted what Matthew saw as an outrage against the English church, but:

> when it was whispered to him that he should not be angry at the archbishop over Robert's dismissal . . . because it was useful and lucrative to the king as [Robert] daily cared diligently for royal revenue, the king was (as it was said) odiously softened [*turpiter emollitus*], made as if a woman [*muliebriter*] in his proposed resistance by womanly intercession [*muliebri intercessione*]; for the word "woman" [*mulier*] is rightly etymologized as "softening the master" [*molliens herum*], or "enervating" [*enervans*]. Nor, alas! did the king manfully stand and expedite

matters as was proper for the Church's redress . . . nor for the care of
his realm nor the honor of the holy bishops . . . but abandoned England
to that archbishop.[45]

Matthew, again, avoided naming Eleanor in this passage, but her role, as
he saw it, is clear. To help her uncle, she whispers in Henry's ear; he is
softened, made womanly, enervated. Even the notice of "woman's intercession" is revelatory. Intercession was a primary means by which a
queen could convincingly manifest her compliant subordination to royal
authority. Here Matthew inverts its meanings to imply that Eleanor was
meddlesome, Henry unable to withstand her or meet his duties to realm
and Church. It is hard to imagine more insulting words about a king.
Every term applied to Henry implies unmanliness (*molle* and *enervans*
can connote effeminacy); dominated by a woman, he could neither
uphold the Church's honor nor care for his realm, and so was without
honor himself—just as a woman would be.

Neither Joinville's nor St-Pathus's Margaret, nor Matthew Paris's
Eleanor, comes before us on their own terms. They are presented to us by
male writers who had their own agendas, to which these women were
marginal. The tales Joinville and St-Pathus tell us are probably true; Paris
at least honestly reported what we may accept was common fame. All
three, however, exercised some discretion in selecting and shaping their
material. Some purpose must have underlain that process, and it would
have been less germane to the female than to the male figures, who were
clearly front and center in male writers' thinking. Indeed, the contrast
here is less between Eleanor and Margaret than between their husbands.
Margaret was more intrusive than Joinville or St-Pathus imply, but they
describe her in ways that reflect on Louis IX's virtues; both used her to
say things about a husband who resisted her craving for political action
and, as implied by Matthew Paris's comment quoted at the outset of this
essay, preserved his honor. Ironically, Eleanor was the more competent
sister, but wed to a more inept husband; it was convenient to associate his
failures with her. Matthew used her to say things about Henry III, who
dishonorably let her divert his resources to those who had no right to
them, impoverishing his subjects and leaving him unable to provide for
or defend them as he should have done. However unfavorable her fame
in Henry's lifetime, however, Eleanor's long widowhood let her become
the preferred intercessor with her son Edward I. In effect, she filled a vacuum created by distrust of her daughter-in-law, Eleanor of Castile,
becoming a "good" queen-mother analogous to Blanche of Castile, as

Margaret of Provence became a "bad" queen-consort like Eleanor of Castile.[46] Vashti and Esther were not mother and wife, but there is a telling parallel here with the influence those two queens exerted on one king's reputation.

I earlier linked Vashti and Esther with Phyllis, and do so, again, here. Phyllis was transformed from the antihierarchical role of mistress into that of wife and queen; signifying hierarchy's restoration, she incurred an obligation to support that male-defined order. Such duties were multi-faceted in a society centered on agnatic inheritance. Any threat to lawful succession undermined that social order, as did any sign that a king was under a woman's influence. Medieval queens' images were thus used in narrative, art and literature to approve wifely submissiveness and chastity; such modesty—crown of the disempowered—sustained the male honor that was the basis of all hierarchy. In narrative writers' pages, as in their behavior in life and their representations in death, queens were made to function significantly in creating and upholding a male-centered order to which they were, themselves, outsiders.[47]

To what extent those images disseminated such ideas to women in medieval society at large is hard to determine. Few signposts exist apart from the *Ménagier de Paris* or similar male-authored works destined for women, like the *Book of the Knight of the Tower,* which—meant as it was for a nobleman's daughters—often draws on queenly images of vice or virtue. Sermon *exempla* and the familiar stories of Esther or (in a cautionary vein) Jezebel effectively broadcast such images; individual queens' bad or good reputations could also implant such points in popular thinking. But the highest of queens surely had the most prominent role in guiding medieval women to accept normative heterosexuality and male superiority: the many medieval associations between the Queen of Heaven and her earthly counterparts made them, in effect, her deputies in disseminating such standards of feminine conduct.[48] Thus prepared, women's ideal modesty and acquiescence to male authority could help construct the male image. To judge from chroniclers' comments on women of rank, the extent to which any woman was seen to do so had an impact on what was thought of her husband, or the degree to which he could assert these norms.

That medieval women, indeed, internalized such precepts can be fairly readily judged. Even so learned a woman as Abbess Heloise of the Paraclete might find her authenticity as she embodied the feminine *exempla* available to her, but only "vis-à-vis the one man whom she had constituted as her sole living authority."[49] Heloise was admittedly an exceptional case; but what glimpses we do have of "real" medieval women in their daily lives imply they, too, understood, or at least accepted, the need to sustain their menfolks' honor by their own behavior. This is one very obvious explanation, for example, for the Pastons's battles over one strong-willed daughter's clandestine marriage to a family retainer and another, equally unbending, woman's refusal to accept the man the family insisted she marry: recalcitrant or headstrong women suggested opposition to male authority, even a man's inability to control his womenfolk at all. (We must account, too, for the Paston daughters' resistance; what could have modeled such defiance? Ironically, they could well have absorbed the idea of personal marriage choices from the examples of royal women who ignored paternal or political orders and, with a self-confidence often ascribed to medieval noblewomen, chose second or third husbands for themselves after illustrious first husbands died.[50])

I began with a humorous cliché often used to express one couple's reaction to friends of friends whom they perhaps met briefly, at a cocktail party. I end with another. I hope I have not protested too much (all right—*two* clichés) that we may find out a great deal about medieval men by observing women. (After all, authors and artists manipulated male figures too.) But I do think we can uncover a good many helpful bits and pieces if we remember to *chercher la femme.*

NOTES

1.   Matthew Paris, *Chronica Majora,* ed. H.R. Luard, 7 vols., Rolls series 57 (London: Eyre and Spottiswoode, 1872–1884), 3:388. Emperor Frederick II had married Henry's sister Isabella in 1235; Henry's wife Eleanor of Provence and Louis's wife Margaret were sisters.

2.   On Eleanor, see now Margaret Howell, *Eleanor of Provence: Queenship in Thirteenth-Century England* (Oxford: Blackwell, 1997).

3.   That such tendencies still obtain is shown by the "Hillary factor" associated with the Clinton presidential administration. Contrasted images of the late Diana, Princess of Wales, and Prince Charles, shaped perceptions of him as dull, bitter or remote; British writers today suggest that her tragic death will let the prince's real character reemerge. Likewise, Marie-Antoinette's grace and beauty intensified perceptions of Louis XVI as a stumbling hulk (Lynn Hunt, "The Many Bodies of Marie Antoinette: Political Pornography and the Problem of the Feminine in the French Revolution," in *Eroticism and the Body Politic,* ed. L. Hunt [Baltimore, Md.: The Johns Hopkins University Press, 1991], 108–30, a reference I owe to Andrew Taylor).

4. Susan M. Stuard, "The Dominion of Gender: Women's Fortunes in the High Middle Ages," in *Becoming Visible: Women in European History,* ed. Renate Bridenthal, Claudia Koonz and Susan Mosher Stuard, 2nd ed. (Boston: Houghton Mifflin, 1987), 153–74.

5. Penny Schine Gold, *The Lady and The Virgin: Image, Attitude and Experience in Twelfth-Century France* (Chicago: University of Chicago Press, 1985), 4–18. On Adela, Orderic Vitalis, *Historia Ecclesiastica,* ed. and trans. Marjorie Chibnall, 6 vols. (Oxford: Clarendon Press, 1969–1978), 5:324 (bk. 10, ch. 20); the story is clearly invented (Kimberley A. LoPrete, "Adela of Blois as Mother and Countess," in *Medieval Mothering,* eds. John Carmi Parsons and Bonnie Wheeler [New York: Garland, 1996], 313–33, esp. 316–17).

6. Rosemary Drage Hale, "Joseph as Mother: Adaptation and Appropriation in the Construction of Male Virtue," in *Medieval Mothering,* Parsons and Wheeler, 101–16.

7. E. Jane Burns, "The Man Behind the Lady in Troubadour Lyric," *Romance Notes* 25 (1985): 254-70, esp. 258–59; Joan M. Ferrante, *The Conflict of Love and Honor: The Medieval Tristan Legend in France, Germany and Italy* (Paris: Mouton, 1973), 81.

8. Of very numerous examples, Caroline Walker Bynum, "Jesus as Mother and Abbot as Mother: Some Themes in Twelfth-Century Cistercian Writing," chap. 4 in eadem, *Jesus as Mother: Studies in the Spirituality of the High Middle Ages* (Berkeley: University of California Press, 1982), 110–69, discusses male clerics' use of maternal imagery to explicate abbatial duties. Nearly all articles in *Medieval Masculinities: Regarding Men in the Middle Ages,* ed. Clare E. Lees (Minneapolis: University of Minnesota Press, 1994), assume implicitly that the male is definable largely through reference to the female.

9. John C. Parsons, *Eleanor of Castile: Queen and Society in Thirteenth-Century England* (New York: St Martin's, 1995), 249; idem, "The Queen's Intercession in Thirteenth-Century England," in *Power of the Weak. Studies on Medieval Women,* ed. Jennifer Carpenter and Sally-Beth MacLean (Champaign-Urbana: University of Illinois Press, 1995), 147–77; and idem "The Pregnant Queen as Counsellor and the Medieval Construction of Motherhood," in *Medieval Mothering,* ed. Parsons and Wheeler, 39–61, esp. 44.

10. On medieval preachers' use of this story, Lois L. Huneycutt, "Intercession and the High- Medieval Queen," in *Power of the Weak,* Carpenter and MacLean, 126–46; for an example, Phyllis B. Roberts, "Stephen Langton's *Sermo de Virginibus,*" in *Women of the Medieval World. Essays in Honor of John H. Mundy,* eds. Julius Kirshner and Suzanne F. Wemple (Oxford: Blackwell, 1985), 103–18.

11. Goswin Frenken, ed. *Die Exempla des Jacob von Vitry. Ein Beitrag zur Geschichte der Erzählungsliteratur des Mittelalters.* Vom Mittelalter u. v. d.

Lateinische Philologie des Mittelalters, gen. ed. Paul Lehmann (Munich: Beck Verlag, 1914), 105–06 (no. 15).

12. Natalie Zemon Davis, "Women on Top: Symbolic Sexual Inversion and Political Disorder in Early Modern Europe," in *The Reversible World. Symbolic Inversion in Art and Society,* ed. B. Babcock (Ithaca, N.Y.: Cornell University Press, 1978), 147–90; Steven M. Parish, *Hierarchy and its Discontents. Culture and the Politics of Consciousness in Caste Society* (Philadelphia: University of Pennsylvania Press, 1996), 190–93.

13. On queenly adultery, especially the adulterous queen as scapegoat, see Peggy McCracken, "The Body Politic and the Queen's Adulterous Body in French Romance," in *Feminist Approaches to the Body in Medieval Literature,* ed. Linda Lomperis and Sarah Stanbury (Philadelphia: University of Pennsylvania Press, 1993), 38–64; and *The Romance of Adultery: Queenship and Sexual Transgression in Medieval French Narrative* (Philadelphia: University of Pennsylvania Press, 1997).

14. A nonroyal couple much discussed in this vein are Abelard and Heloise. See especially Catherine Brown, *"Muliebriter:* Doing Gender in the Letters of Heloise," in *Gender and Text in the Later Middle Ages,* ed. Jane Chance (Gainesville: University of Florida Press, 1996), 25–51; Bonnie Wheeler, "Origenary Fantasies: Abelard's Castration and Confession," 107–28, and Martin Irvine, "Abelard and (Re)writing the Male Body: Castration, Identity, and Remasculinization," 87–106, both in *Becoming Male in the Middle Ages,* ed. Jeffrey Jerome Cohen and Bonnie Wheeler (New York: Garland, 1997).

15. Elizabeth Ward, "Caesar's Wife: The Career of the Empress Judith, 819–829," in *Charlemagne's Heir: New Perspectives on the Reign of Louis the Pious (814–840),* ed. P. Goldman and R. Collins (Oxford: Clarendon, 1990), 205–27; and "Agobard of Lyons and Paschasius Radbertus as Critics of the Empress Judith," in *Women in the Church,* Studies in Church History 27, ed. W.J. Sheils and D. Wood (Oxford: Blackwell, 1990), 15–25, esp. 19, 22, 24.

16. Pauline Stafford, *Queen Emma and Queen Edith. Queenship and Women's Power in Eleventh-Century England* (Oxford: Blackwell, 1997); for Edith, cf. Frank Barlow, *Edward the Confessor* (London: Eyre and Spottiswoode, 1970). See also Stafford, "The Portrayal of Royal Women in England, Mid-Tenth to Mid-Twelfth Centuries," in *Medieval Queenship,* ed. John Carmi Parsons (New York: St. Martin's, 1993), 143–68.

17. Matilda II is better known as Edith-Matilda, but I follow her modern biographer, who accepts the intitulation on Matilda's seal and calls her Matilda II: Huneycutt, "Intercession and the High-Medieval Queen"; eadem, "Images of Queenship in the High Middle Ages," *The Haskins Society Journal* 1 (1989): 61–71; and eadem, "The Idea of the Perfect Princess: The *Life of St. Margaret* in

the Reign of Matilda II (1100–1118)," *Anglo-Norman Studies* 12 (1990): 81–97. See also Parsons, "The Queen's Intercession," and idem, "Ritual and Symbol in the English Queenship to 1500," in *Women and Sovereignty,* ed. Louise O. Fradenburg, *Cosmos* 7 [for 1991] (Edinburgh: University of Edinburgh Press, 1992), 60–78.

18. Parsons, *Eleanor of Castile,* 65–67, 112–13, 153–55; and idem, "Pregnant Queen as Counsellor," 52.

19. *The Chronicle of William de Rishanger of the Barons' Wars,* ed. J.O. Halliwell (London: Camden Society, 1840), 193, 397; John C. Parsons, "The Intercessionary Patronage of Queens Margaret and Isabella of France," in *Thirteenth-Century England 6. Papers from the Durham Conference, 1995,* ed. M.C. Prestwich, R.H. Britnell and R. Frame (Woodbridge, Eng.: Boydell, 1997), 145–56; Michael C. Prestwich, *Edward I* (Berkeley: University of California Press, 1988), 129–31.

20. Parsons, "Intercessionary Patronage"; and Sophia Menache, "Isabella of France, Queen of England—a Reconsideration," *Journal of Medieval History* 10 (1984): 107–24.

21. Paul Strohm, "Queens as Intercessors," in idem, *Hochon's Arrow. The Social Imagination of Fourteenth-Century Texts* (Princeton: Princeton University Press, 1992), 95–120; Andrew Taylor, "Anne of Bohemia and the Making of Chaucer," *Studies in the Age of Chaucer* 19 (1977): 95–119; Patricia-Ann Lee, "Reflections of Power: Margaret of Anjou and the Dark Side of Queenship," *Renaissance Quarterly* 29 (1986): 183–217, esp. 197–200.

22. *Le Ménagier de Paris,* ed. G.E. Brereton and J.M. Ferrier (Oxford: Clarendon, 1981), 56 (pars. 24–27). The text's author admits ignorance of the truth of these stories and, if they are true, why queens do so. But see par. 24: "Et puis que si haultes dames et si honnorees le font, les petites qui ont aussi grant besoing de l'amour de leurs maris et de bonne renommee le doivent bien faire."

23. Literature on these themes is rich but problematic. For orientation to the complexities, Michael Herzfeld, "Honour and Shame: Problems in the Comparative Analysis of Moral Systems," *Man* 15 (1980): 339–51; and Unni Wikan, "Shame and Honour: A Contestable Pair," *Man* 19 (1984): 635–52. I have found helpful Lila Abu-Lughod, *Veiled Sentiments: Honor and Poetry in a Bedouin Society* (Berkeley: University of California Press, 1986); Carol Delaney, *The Seed and The Soil: Gender and Cosmology in Turkish Village Society* (Berkeley: University of California Press, 1991); and Anne Meneley, *Tournaments of Value: Sociability and Hierarchy in a Yemeni Town* (Toronto: University of Toronto Press, 1996).

24. Maureen Slattery (*Myth, Man and Sovereign Saint: King Louis IX in Jean de Joinville's Sources* [New York: Peter Lang, 1985]), mentions Joinville's

Margaret only at page 118. Cogently discussing Louis's personality, William C. Jordan refers to the queen not by name, nor with reference to Joinville's work ("The Case of Saint Louis," Persona et Gesta: The Image and Deeds of the Thirteenth-Century Capetians—2, *Viator* 19 [1988]: 209–17); cf. Jordan's remarks in William C. Jordon, *Louis IX and the Challenge of the Crusade: A Study in Rulership* (Princeton: Princeton University Press, 1979), 4–6.

25. *Chronique anonyme de Reims* in Martin Bouquet, *Recueil des historiens des Gaules et de la France, nouvelle édition* (Paris, 1869–1904), 22:325–26 [hereafter cited as *RHF*]. Margaret's son died in January 1260; her next child was born the following August (Parsons, "Pregnant Queen as Counsellor," 45).

26. Jean de Joinville, *Histoire de Saint Louis,* ed. Natalis de Wailly, 9th ed. (Paris: Hachette, 1921), 166–67, 253, 271–73; in general, Gérard Sivéry, *Marguerite de Provence: une reine du temps des cathédrales* (Paris: Fayard, 1987). Cf. Margaret as "able but frustrated" by Louis's control (Jordan, *Louis IX,* 12), but "not . . . up to" a regency (Howell, *Eleanor of Provence,* 112). Her letter to Henry III of 5 October 1265 playfully notes her worry lest he, given her sister Eleanor's long absence from England, contemplate life with the wealthy dowager countess of Gloucester (Howell, *Eleanor of Provence,* 231–32).

27. Joinville, *Histoire,* 265–66.

28. Joinville, *Histoire,* 250; comment in Slattery, *Myth, Man and Sovereign Saint,* 117–18.

29. Joinville, *Histoire,* 53. In fairness, Joinville does not mention his own wife, Alix de Grandpré, in this passage—only his children. Translators differ on whether Joinville's "dous enfans" should be taken as "two" or "sweet" (two sons had been born by 1248); one English version unjustifiably opts for an all-inclusive "two sweet children."

30. On Louis's instruction to his children, see Joinville, *Histoire,* 306; cf. Godefridi de Bello Loco, *Vita et sancta conversatione piae memoriae Ludovici quondam regis francorum, RHF,* 20:7–8. On the apparently happy relationship between husband and wife early in the marriage, see Jordan, *Louis IX,* 5, and note 13.

31. Henri-François Delaborde, "Une nouvelle oeuvre de Guillaume de St-Pathus," *Bibliothèque de l'Écôle des Chartes* 63 (1902): 263–88, esp. 285. Geoffrey de Beaulieu says that if Louis shared Margaret's bed but wished to abstain, and her proximity aroused him, he would walk about the chamber until desire was subdued (de Bello Loco, *Vita et sancta conversatione piae memoriae Ludovici, RHF,* 20:6–7).

32. Guillaume de St-Pathus, *La Vie de St. Louis par le confesseur de la reine Marguerite,* in *RHF,* 20:106; Delaborde, "Nouvelle oeuvre," 286.

33. Parsons, *Eleanor of Castile,* 53, and note 164; Stafford, *Queen Emma and Queen Edith,* 107, 115–17.

34. Jordan ("Case of Saint Louis," 215–16), gives a somewhat different interpretation of the conversation on Louis's clothes.

35. W.W. Shirley, ed., *Royal and Other Historical Letters of the Reign of Henry III,* 3 vols, Rolls series 27 (London: Eyre and Spottiswoode, 1862–66), 3:235 (Peter of Limoges to Walter de Merton, 28 January 1263).

36. Shirley, *Royal and Other Historical Letters,* ed. Shirley, 3:242–43 (John de Chishull and Imbert de Montferrand to Henry III, 16 February 1263).

37. J.B. Teulet, ed., *Layettes du Trésor des Chartes,* 6 vols (Paris: Plon, 1863–1909), 4, no. 4859 (6 July 1263). Presumably Margaret induced Philip, born in April 1245, to take this oath soon after the elder son died in January 1260.

38. Margaret Wade Labarge, *Saint Louis* (Boston: Little, Brown, 1968), 198, 210–11.

39. Jordan, *Louis IX,* 4.

40. Stafford, *Queen Emma and Queen Edith,* 9.

41. Joinville, *Histoire,* 10–11, 14–15 (for Louis's esteem of Joinville's "subtle understanding"), 288 (on Margaret's support for the Hyères landing).

42. Sharon Farmer, "Persuasive Voices: Clerical Images of Medieval Wives," *Speculum* 61 (1986): 517–43.

43. Paris, *Chronica Majora,* 5:298. The quarrel was exacerbated when Bishop Grosseteste upheld Eleanor's man and excommunicated the clerk Henry presented (Howell, *Eleanor of Provence,* 65- 66).

44. *Annales Prioratus de Dunstaplia,* ed. H.R. Luard in *Annales Monastici,* 5 vols, Rolls series 36 (London: Eyre and Spottiswoode, 1864–1869), 3:215; *Annales Londonienses,* in *Chronicles of the Reigns of Edward I and Edward II,* ed. W. Stubbs, 2 vols, Rolls series 76 (London: Eyre and Spottiswoode, 1882–83), 1:57, 59.

45. Paris, *Chronica Majora,* 4:510; on the dispute and Eleanor's role in it (not necessarily as Matthew presents it), Howell, *Eleanor of Provence,* 41–43.

46. Parsons, "Intercessionary Patronage," 149–50.

47. Abu-Lughod, *Veiled Sentiments,* 118–19; Parsons, "The Queen's Intercession"; and " 'Never was A Body Buried in England with Such Solemnity and Splendour': The Burials and Posthumous Commemorations of English Queens to 1500," in *Queens and Queenship in Medieval Europe,* ed. A. Duggan (Woodbridge: Boydell and Brewer, 1997), 317–37.

48. Pamela Sheingorn, "The Maternal Behavior of God: Divine Father as Fantasy Husband," in *Medieval Mothering,* Parsons and Wheeler, 77–99; Parsons, "Queen's Intercession," passim; and idem, "Pregnant Queen as Counsellor," 55.

49. Barbara Newman, "Authority, Authenticity, and the Repression of Heloise," *Journal of Medieval and Renaissance Studies* 22 (1992): 121–57, esp. 152; reprinted in Newman, *From Virile Woman to WomanChrist. Studies in*

Medieval Religion and Literature (Philadelphia: University of Pennsylvania Press, 1995), 46–75, esp. 71. Newman's position is contested by Brown, *"Muliebriter,"* 28–29. On Julian of Norwich's internalization of her female inferiority to a male deity, see Laura Rose, "The Voice of a Saintly Woman: The Feminine Style of Julian of Norwich's Showings," *Women and Language* 216 (1993): 14–17.

    50. John C. Parsons, "Mothers, Daughters, Marriage, Power: Some Plantagenet Evidence, 1150-1500," in idem, *Medieval Queenship,* 63–78; Penelope D. Johnson, *"Mulier et Monialis:* The Medieval Nun's Self-Image," *Thought* 64 (1989): 242–53, esp. 243; Anne Haskell, "The Paston Women on Marriage in Fifteenth-Century England," *Viator* 4 (1973): 459–71; Jacqueline Murray, "Individualism and Consensual Marriage: Some Evidence from Medieval England," in *Women, Marriage, and the Family in Medieval Christendom. Essays in Memory of Michael M. Sheehan,* ed. Joel T. Rosenthal and Constance M. Rousseau (Kalamazoo, Mich.: Medieval Institute, 1998), 121–51.

Contributors

Vern L. Bullough's research spans several different fields. He began as a historian of science and medicine in the medieval and early modern periods. He has also written extensively on medical and nursing history, and on gender and related issues. In addition to a PhD, he received a degree in nursing. He was SUNY Distinguished Professor of History and Sociology and currently is a visiting professor at the University of Southern California, in the Department of Nursing. He has written, edited, or co-authored some fifty books, contributed seventy-five chapters and is the author of over 150 articles in refereed journals.

Rachel Dressler is Assistant Professor of Art at the University of Albany-State University of New York, where she teaches medieval and islamic art. Her publications include "*Deus Hoc Vult:* Visual Rhetoric at the Time of the Crusades," *Medieval Encounters. A Journal of Jewish, Christian and Muslim Culture in Confluence and Dialogue* 1 (1995); a study of the sculpture on the Royal Portal at Chartres Cathedral; and entries in *French Romanesque Sculpture. An Annotated Bibliography* (1987). Her current research focuses on corporeal representation and gender construction in English medieval tomb sculpture. She is writing a book on armored effigies of the later thirteenth and fourteenth centuries. She is also the founder of the Capital Region Art Historians.

Jenny Jochens is the author of *Women in Old Norse Society* (Cornell University Press, 1995) and *Old Norse Images of Women* (University of Pennsylvania Press, 1996), as well as numerous articles on social history in the Norse world. For many years she taught medieval history at Towson University in Maryland. She is now professor emerita, free to devote all her time to research.

Ruth Mazo Karras is Professor of History at Temple University. She is the author of *Common Women. Prostitution and Sexuality in Medieval England* (Oxford, 1996) and numerous articles on the history of gender and sexuality. She is currently working on a book entitled *Making Men. The Formation of Masculinity in the Later Middle Ages.* She is General Editor of the University of Pennsylvania Press Middle Ages Series.

Brian Patrick McGuire is Professor of Medieval History at Roskilde University, Denmark. He received a DPhil from Oxford, working on Saint Anselm under Sir Richard Southern. He emigrated to Denmark in 1971, where he now lives and teaches. His books include studies on the Cistercians in Denmark and friendship in monastic life. His most recent book is an introduction and translation for the Classics of Western Spirituality series: *Jean Gerson. Early Writings* (Paulist Press, 1998).

Megan McLaughlin is Associate Professor of History and Women's Studies at the University of Illinois at Urbana-Champaign. She has written on the social and cultural significance of rituals for the dead in the Middle Ages, as well as on the history of women and gender. Her recent publications include "Abominable Mingling: Father-Daughter Incest and the Law," *Medieval Feminist Newsletter* 24 (1997); and "The Bishop as Bridegroom: Marital Imagery and Clerical Celibacy in the Eleventh and Twelfth Centuries," in *Medieval Purity and Piety. Essays on Medieval Clerical Celibacy and Religious Reform* (Garland, 1998). She is currently working on a book-length study of the role of gender and sexuality in the Investiture Conflict.

Jo Ann McNamara lives in New York City and is professor emerita of Hunter College and the Graduate Center of the City University of New York. She has worked on various issues of women's history since 1970. After the publication of *Sisters in Arms. Catholic Nuns through Two Millennia* (Harvard, 1996), she has gradually shifted her attention to men's history and the broader issues of gender that help to decode it. She hopes that one day no history will be written without consideration of gender issues.

Shannon McSheffrey is Associate Professor of History at Concordia University in Montreal. She has published *Gender and Heresy: Women, Men, and Lollard Communities, 1420–1530* (Pennsylvania, 1995), and a collection of primary source translations entitled *Love and Marriage in Late Medieval London* (Kalamazoo, 1995). She is currently working on a book on courtship, marriage and gender in fifteenth-century England.

Jacqueline Murray is Associate Professor of History and Director of the Humanities Research Group at the University of Windsor. She has edited *Desire and Discipline. Sex and Sexuality in the Premodern West* (University of Toronto Press, 1996) and translated Agnolo Firenzuola's *On the Beauty of Women* (University of Pennsylvania Press, 1992), both with Konrad Eisenbichler. She has published articles on various aspects of marriage and family, gender and sexuality in medieval society. Her current project is a study entitled *Men's Bodies, Men's Minds. Male Sexuality in the Medieval West.*

John Carmi Parsons holds a PhD in Medieval Studies from the University of Toronto and a Licenciate in Mediaeval Studies from the Pontifical Institute (Toronto). He has taught history and diplomatics at both institutions. His published works include *Eleanor of Castile. Queen and Society in Thirteenth-Century England* (St. Martin's, 1995), and two edited anthologies: *Medieval Queenship* (St. Martin's, 1993) and, with Bonnie Wheeler, *Medieval Mothering* (Garland, 1996). His interest in medieval gender-power relations is also reflected in a series of articles on medieval English queenship.

Susan Mosher Stuard is a medieval historian concerned with social and economic questions. She received her PhD from Yale University and is Professor of History at Haverford College. She is editor of *Women in Medieval Society* and *Women in Medieval History and Historiography,* and the author of *State of Deference. Ragusa/Dubrovnik in the Medieval Centuries.* She won the Berkshire Prize in 1996 for "Ancillary Evidence on the Decline of Medieval Slavery," *Past and Present* 149 (1995).

Andrew Taylor is an Assistant Professor of English at the University of Saskatchewan. He is co-editor with David Townsend of *The Tongue of the Fathers: Gender and Ideology in Twelfth-Century Latin* (University of Pennsylvania Press, 1998), and one of the co-editors of *The Idea of the Vernacular: An Anthology of Middle English Literary Theory, 1280–1520.* His current research focuses on medieval reading practice.

Index